THE REFORMER'S DILEMMA

THE REFORMER'S DILEMMA

AND THE NEED FOR A RADICAL MIDDLE

RICARDO ROSSELLÓ NEVARES

MANUSCRIPTS
PRESS

THE REFORMER'S DILEMMA
And the need for a Radical Middle

ISBN   979-8-88926-029-5   *Paperback*
       979-8-88926-030-1   *Hardcover*
       979-8-88926-028-8   *Digital Ebook*

To Claudia, Pedro, and Beatriz

Contents

The unexamined life is not worth living.

—SOCRATES

Introduction

Life comes at you fast. Javier Danes's illustration interposes the whirlwind of the hurricane with that of social unrest and serves as a good visual to prepare the reader for this book.

It was the summer of 2019, and I was the governor of Puerto Rico. In a tenure filled with challenges, I was about to face the steepest—a personal political crisis covered around the world. Just two months earlier, I was leading all polls for reelection by at least twenty points (Jardim 2019). A month after those polls came out, I presented my budget, which included the lowest unemployment rates in the history of Puerto Rico (Bernal 2018), the first year of economic growth in fifteen years (World Bank 2023), and the successful largest municipal bond restructuring in the history of the United States (Slavin 2018).

However, I was now considering resigning my position as governor.

I pondered alone in the executive mansion's office—a pompous and beautiful relic of the sixteenth century. In the span of two days, two former top executives in my administration had been arrested for corruption charges. A few days after that, an unvalidated chat[1] communication I was part of came out. The chat was insult-laden and contained poor judgment. These two things sparked a firestorm that essentially froze my government, provoked massive protests, and became an international news story.

Those two weeks were hard. I had to reconfigure the way *I viewed* things and how *others viewed me*. I went from being a slam dunk for reelection (the youngest in history) to becoming portrayed as the worst kind of villain. In that process, they threatened my family's life, and I clearly realized I would not be able to reform or govern effectively anymore.

One day, I had a group of people in my executive room, a small and modern space that was ultra-secure where I would hold daily briefings with my top officials. There, an arsenal of lawyers assembled to explain to me why I should *not* resign.

"Governor, there is no substantive reason for you to resign," said one of the lawyers. They went on to present all the legal and procedural arguments to show if I chose to stay, no one could do anything to "get you out of power."

I remember saying, "That's convincing… but answer this question: What's the point? *What's the purpose?*"

Purpose is an important theme in my life. It drives me and energizes me. At that point, I remembered why I took the oath of office. It was not to have power. It was to use that power to change the conditions for the people of Puerto Rico for the better. *That was my purpose.* Sure, I was also in it for the glory part of the job, but what drove me was being the leader who could solve problems. For as long as I can remember, problem-solving has always sparked my curiosity. Whether figuring out puzzles, math problems at a later age, how to play tennis and win with a lower skill set, or engaging in public discourse… the search for a solution always lit a fire in my belly.

But the moment that truly got me enthralled with the idea of politics happened when I was nineteen years old.

I attended a small town hall in a poor municipality on the mountainous regions of our island. A gentlemen named Tatito stood up and said, "I want you to thank your father… because without his *tarjetita* (healthcare card), I would not be alive today." He proceeded to unbutton his shirt and show everyone a scar in the middle of his chest from his heart surgery.

Eureka! Though I hated politics—the fights, deceit, bickering, and lies—at that moment I realized reform *can* help people in meaningful ways, even save their lives. A reform that had started only five years before gave *all* Puerto Ricans access to health care (Rosselló 2012). If this had happened five years later, Tatito would not be alive.

I believe many people have great intentions and see politics as a way to help. But it is also imperative they know the risk, the process, and possible lessons learned that could prevent things I experienced from happening to them.

---

1   After a lengthy investigation that extended almost two years on the 889 pages of the chat, an independent prosecutor found the chat was "unvalidated," and further, it was "*not original and modified*" (Panel Sobre el Fiscal Especial Independiente 2020). In addition, it found that even if taken as true, there were no crimes or intent of crimes or corruption.

How do we connect the beautiful aspiration of reform with the real obstacles many will face? What other phenomena will arise as we uncover the path to reform? Can these reform dynamics tell us something about the capacity to reform—and more broadly—the future of democracy?

In this book, we examine three main themes:

1. **The Reformer's Dilemma:** Our society requires a rapid rate of change, yet it is hard to come by. Why? Crisis if you do, crisis if you don't. That is the dilemma. Using my experiences, I attempt to break down what is happening and how to create a viable path to change and reform as well as the tradeoffs within the process.

2. **Framework to Reform**: We must understand the underlying environment that creates obstacles to change and—by consequence—hinders society's progress. Here, we weed out the factors that impact the pace of reform and create the basis for a model to simulate the *capacity to* reform under different circumstances. We will examine several scenarios that may yield insights into the current state of our democracy.

3. **The Radical Middle:** Given the vast majority of us don't identify with the polarized extremes of the political spectrum, we have an opportunity to rethink and reshape the middle into one that directly tackles the challenges to reform in democracies and provides a better path forward (Figure 1).

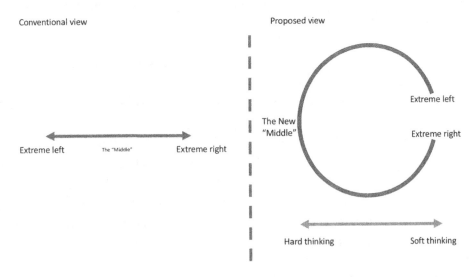

Figure 1. The conventional gradient of the political spectrum assumes political affiliations as a straight-line continuum. In part 6, we will explore a warped alternative to this conventional wisdom.

As such, this book is *not a memoir* nor is it written in chronological order. The book only contains a subset of stories—not all.

Rather, this book is an exploration of a topic I feel compelled to examine through my experiences and observations coupled with the insights of others. I broke it down into six parts.

Part 1 summarizes the biggest stories from which I draw insights and experience to help shape my observations about the current environment and the challenges to reform. In part 2, I take a look at

Figure 2. Newspaper article from the *Daily Sun,* highlighting some of the implications of my scientific work (Santiago 2009).

four drivers of the challenging environment to reform: (1) words over actions, (2) soft thinking, (3) dehumanization, (4) extreme polarization. Part 3 examines the *key variables and parameters* that can affect the proper execution of a reform, and part 4 offers a few strategies aiming to overcome the challenges of reforming.

Based on the examination of the content above, I develop a first draft reform dynamics model in part 5. After examining the outputs of the model, I propose the creation of a radical middle in part 6.

My formation is as a scientist. As a bioengineer to be more precise. My research focused on tissue regeneration (Rossello 2009), stem cell reprogramming, and the vocal learning pathway in the human brain. I was a university professor and researcher, and I was also an entrepreneur working on market applications to some of our findings (Rosselló 2013; Grens 2013) (Figure 2, 3).

I love science.

So, why the hell did I leave that behind to become a politician? For cheers and jeers? For a significant portion of the population to consider me an *enemy* as soon as I set foot into the arena? I did it because I thought I could add value as a scientist to the political realm and, by doing so, provoke meaningful change.

My hope is this book piques the curiosity of the five out of six people who are not into political extremes and the 85 percent of us who feel the system needs to be completely reformed (Pew Research Center 2021a). With such a broad target in mind, an even more compelling number comes up. A recent study showed that while most people overwhelmingly support their democracy, well over half of them think we can't reform the system (Pew Research Center 2021b).

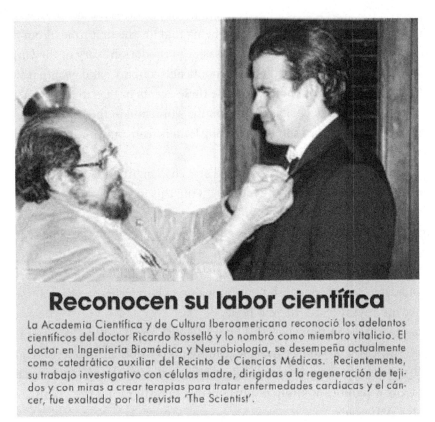

Reconocen su labor científica

La Academia Científica y de Cultura Iberoamericana reconoció los adelantos científicos del doctor Ricardo Rosselló y lo nombró como miembro vitalicio. El doctor en Ingeniería Biomédica y Neurobiología, se desempeña actualmente como catedrático auxiliar del Recinto de Ciencias Médicas. Recientemente, su trabajo investigativo con células madre, dirigidas a la regeneración de tejidos y con miras a crear terapias para tratar enfermedades cardiacas y el cáncer, fue exaltado por la revista 'The Scientist'.

Figure 3. Newspaper note from *El Vocero*, with the heading "Recognizing His Scientific Work" where the Iberoamerican Academy of Science and Culture named me the youngest lifetime member (El Vocero 2012).

But why do so many think change is impossible? Because if a group impedes change—particularly when thoroughly needed—people lose their *trust* and *confidence* in the system and in their leadership and institutions. So, tackling this impasse is paramount to our future.

In my view, reform is the key tool to achieve progress and change. Reform drives how we conceive and implement progress and change, and reform determines what dynamics are involved that make things more likely to happen than not. Without reform, in the best case, we idly stand still while others pass us by. In the worst case, we stand to die by inaction. If we are serious about *change*, we need to be serious about *reform*. We, therefore, need to be cognizant about the *minefield environment* and challenging parameters inherent in it—some of them of our own doing.

The path to depolarization does not happen by bringing the extremes closer together but rather by creating a new political sector based on reason, results, and consensus. That political sector is the vast majority of us. By rallying this sector, we may stand on the precipice of examining the formation of a Democracy 3.0, one that stands true to its *principles* but examines its shortcomings to make it a better, more effective system for the people. The aspiration is that democracies everywhere will be in a stronger position to serve their citizens and to counter the challenges posed by certain autocratic regimes looking to unseat power by the people.

Many of the stories I will use in this book are being told for the first time. From the mental and emotional toll of the most devastating natural disaster in modern history of the United States and my ten hours with President Trump to the fiscal, political, economic, and eventual social crisis that provoked my (temporary) exit from politics—I use these events in Puerto Rico as a cautionary tale for situations that are bound to happen elsewhere in the world and in the United States. Recognizing views can be different, I interviewed some compelling leaders from our time who have faced hardship and solicited their observations on reform.

Being in politics and public life has been a wild and challenging ride for me and my family, as it will likely be for any aspiring leader in the future. I write this in the hopes that leaders and citizens who desire meaningful change can learn from my observations, victories, and mistakes.

I am doing this now after a bit of time has gone by, wherein I took the time required for a self-reflective journey coupled with a deep evaluation of my experiences. I write this now, four years removed from office and two years from being the first person in the history of Puerto Rico elected as a write-in candidate (Bernal 2021). I did not campaign to be a write-in, nor did I raise money, but the people elected me anyway. So… there is hope.

As of the closing of this edition, an *Atlas Intel* poll with the headline "A Strong Preference for Rosselló for Resident Commissioner" had me leading all possible primary contenders by at least twenty points (NotiCel 2023). I am honored and grateful that, even though I have stated I would not seek office this term, a significant group of my constituents still values the vision and work we put into reforming the status quo.

As famed Latin American leader José Marti wrote to his friend José Dolores Poyo in 1893: "¿Qué importa que, cómo albañil, nos caigan encima de la ropa de trabajo unas cuantas manchas de cal o de lodo? Nosotros, cómo el albañil, al quitarnos la ropa de trabajar, podremos decir: ¡Hemos construido!'" (Guevara 2020).

Translation: "What does it matter that, like the construction worker, a few spots of lime or mud fall on our clothes? We, like the construction worker, when we take off our work clothes, can say: 'We have built.'"

My work was not in vain. People do want results—even if the path is treacherous.

PART I

INFLUENTIAL STORIES

CHAPTER 1:

A Geopolitical Blackhole

Many in the states and globally overlook Puerto Rico's colonial status for the past five hundred years. This image captures my attempt to discuss decolonization and statehood with President Trump, his expression reflecting confusion (Bayon 2016).

"We're going to give you some ways to finally understand what the heck black holes really are. We'll take a mind-bending journey into a black hole to a place where the laws of physics break down past the point of no return. Buckle up. It's going to be awesome."

—EMILY KWONG, NPR, "WHAT WOULD IT BE LIKE TO FALL INTO A BLACK HOLE" (2020).

I promise… this quote will make sense.

In May 2018, merely eight months after the most devastating hurricane in modern US history ravaged our island, we were on the brink of a long recovery and poised to begin reconstruction. This process demanded collaboration from numerous stakeholders. So I embarked on a quest to find them.

As *Time* magazine described, it was "just one stop on a whirlwind tour Rosselló is making to some of the most prominent companies in Silicon Valley, as he tries to take advantage of the bittersweet limelight that the category 4 storm has put on the US territory. Devastation also means a chance to reimagine things as the island rebuilds, and the thirty-nine-year-old is casting Puerto Rico as a 'blank canvas' for innovators to come and experiment" (Steinmetz 2018).

By *blank canvas*, I envisioned a chance for Puerto Ricans to establish an innovation hub, building upon the island's inherent strengths and attributes. Amid a flurry of questions from reporters about the island's recovery and the visitor economy, one question stood out.

Q: "Does it surprise you that such low numbers of Americans were aware that Puerto Ricans are US citizens?"

I responded, "Puerto Rico is a very delicate issue. It is sort of a geopolitical black hole. In the past, because there were so many issues—the United States has to deal with Russia, Iran—you could sort of put it into a second or third tier. Not a lot of people would fight about it, and we didn't have the political structure—because we don't have senators or congressmen—to put that idea out there. Now, after the storm, there is this awareness about Puerto Rico."

When later asked to elaborate on why I termed Puerto Rico a geopolitical black hole, I referred to physicist Kip Thorne's description of a black hole's singularity as a point where all laws of physics cease to apply. Similarly, in Puerto Rico, the rules seem markedly different. These disparities have precipitated numerous crises, necessitating substantial reform and change.

The Environment Requires Change

On a sunny day in 2011, I can't quite recall the exact date, possibly in the summer, I had just finished playing tennis with my father. This was—and still is—our special bonding time. We exercise, take a brief intermission of about fifteen minutes to talk about life, and then conclude our session. On this particular day, our intermission lasted longer.

I had been writing biweekly columns on the issue of statehood for *El Vocero*, a local newspaper. My focus was to pragmatically examine the connection between Puerto Rico's colonial status and the well-being of its citizens. I aimed to delve into the data and demonstrate this link. I like to think I achieved that goal, at least to some degree. It was like peeling an onion, uncovering many layers after the first.

"Now what?" I asked my father, reflecting on how the political system was hindering our growth.

"Son, the social and political environments require change… and change is not easy. It demands blood, sweat, and tears," he replied.

At that moment I started to understand change—however evident and necessary—comes with a heavy cost and is not without significant difficulty (Figure 1).

Figure 1. A recent picture of me and my father playing tennis.

Much to his dismay (my father never wanted me to enter politics), I took these words to heart and began a project called Plan for Puerto Rico. The objective was to "understand the root cause problems of the island and tackle those in a scientific manner to achieve meaningful results and progress." The understanding that the social and political environments required change drove this project, which took five years to complete. To achieve this, we needed to (1) identify the root cause problems, (2) study best practices, (3) present an initial draft of proposals, (4) involve people in a public civic engagement setting, and (5) prepare the actual bills we wanted to implement, all before becoming an elected official.

People in general were longing for something different. As Galston and Kamarck state, "It is not surprising that public support is very high for fundamental change in our political system to make the system work better. There is no party of the status quo in contemporary America: both sides want changes, but they disagree about the direction of change. Unfortunately, about six in ten Americans do not think the system can change" (2022).

Merely saying we wanted change was not enough. We had to dig deep into the fundamentals to create reform. We needed enough support to make it through politically and pragmatically.

You can apply these concepts of reform to many other areas where change is necessary. Whether addressing climate change or certain social justice issues, a thoughtful and structured set of objectives and actions is necessary. A dialogue must open the possibility of change. On paper, it may seem easy, even trivial, but in practice, overwhelming obstacles often prevent change from happening. This has significant implications for the future of society.

This premise compelled me to write this book—a conversation that stands at the juncture of science and policy and one that has profound consequences.

But could what happened in Puerto Rico possibly provide meaningful insight for reform in other states or countries?

Absolutely. Puerto Rico might just be a foreshadowing of things to come elsewhere, where certain actions catalyzed the onset of diverse and distinct crises.

For example, Germanwatch's global climate risk index has Puerto Rico at number one in the world (Eckstein et al. 2020). The effects of hurricanes, coastal erosion, and droughts have been notable. When I was in office, there was a small island in the northeast part of Puerto Rico called Palominito. By the time I left office, it was no longer there. The same conditions that accelerated on the island will eventually manifest in a similar fashion in Florida, Louisiana, and other states.

Another example is the fiscal nature of Puerto Rico. Being a territory and not a state of the union, we are domestic for federal law but foreign for tax purposes. The unequal footing and "fiscal tricks" used for survival led to a rapid accumulation of debt. Specifically, Puerto Rico's triple-exempt bonds were attractive in the municipal markets for their tax-free status and favorable interest rates. However, eventually, with the compounding effect of unpaid bonds and creating new issuances to pay old ones, the financial structure collapsed quickly. Other states like Connecticut, Illinois, and even independent nations are on a similar path (Phaneuf 2023).

So while these conditions might be unique to the island, the outcomes are a cautionary tale for other jurisdictions. The good news? We still have time to learn and change outcomes.

To understand the background of many of the stories in this book, a high-level understanding of the history of Puerto Rico is imperative.

A Brief History of Puerto Rico

After more than five hundred years as a colonial territory, first under Spanish rule for four hundred years and then under US control for more than 120 years, Puerto Ricans have never been treated as equal citizens. About fifty years into US territorial status, Puerto Rico was rebranded as a "Free Associated State" locally, known in the US as a *commonwealth*. This status is distinct from that of commonwealth *states* like Massachusetts or Virginia (Rosselló 2005) (Figure 2).

Initially, the commonwealth status brought tangible improvements to Puerto Rico, primarily through the shift from agriculture to industrialization. The commonwealth's promise was to reduce inequality and poverty relative to the states. However, these benefits soon began to wane. Throughout this period, Puerto Ricans grappled with defining their political identity, torn between becoming an integral part of the US or seeking independence.

An ideological struggle has marked the past fifty years trying to resolve this status issue. As our socioeconomic position deteriorated, people rallied against the existing colonial regime.

Governmental irresponsibility further exacerbated the situation. "Since Puerto Rico gained self-rule in the late 1940s, improvident governments have lavished additional pension benefits on public employees, from holiday bonuses to loans for international travel. These measures have rarely been accompanied by moves to pay for them, and occasional efforts to fill the funding gap have fallen short" (Brown 2016).

This situation underscores the island's geopolitical black hole nature with unique and exotic rules yet lacking real political power. Misuse of these exotic advantages was rampant. The triple-exempt nature of Puerto Rico's municipal bonds is one example. Their tax benefits made them highly attractive to investors, but lack of accountability led to a financial disaster.

Another issue was the "Government Development Bank" (GDB), unique to Puerto Rico (Kaske 2016). This institution controlled both fiscal policy and bond emissions. The GDB often financed politically motivated, fiscally unviable projects through bond emissions, leading to exponential debt growth and unsustainable financial practices.

The mismanagement of the retirement pension fund is a third critical issue. The government repeatedly failed to make payments to the fund and, under Governor Acevedo Vilá, even speculated with retirees' futures. As more people retired, the fund was practically depleted (Figure 3).

The economy has largely been rent-seeking rather than value-adding (Collins, Bosworth, and Soto-Class 2016). The limitations of being a colonial territory have restricted the resources and actions available to counter these negative trends (Rosselló 2012).

The closer to the geopolitical black hole, the stronger the gravity of the situation pulls you toward collapse.

This has widened the gap between Puerto Rico and the states in terms of poverty, inequality, and economic disparity, which are now greater than they were in the 1960s.

Characteristics of theses government practices during this period are (1) generating debt without repayment sources, (2) using funds to create a welfare state and government gigantism (not for capital improvements), (3) mismanaging the retirement system, (4) economic decline, (5) increased tax burdens, and (6) rampant corruption. The rise in debt and government spending,

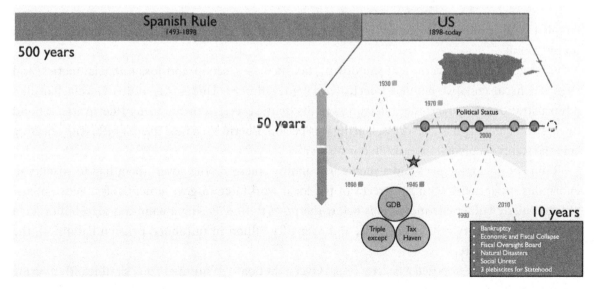

Figure 2. A scaled timeline showing Puerto Rico's five-hundred-plus years of colonial rule: first four hundred under Spain and then more than 120 under the US. The last fifty years have seen a rapid collapse of the foundational basis.

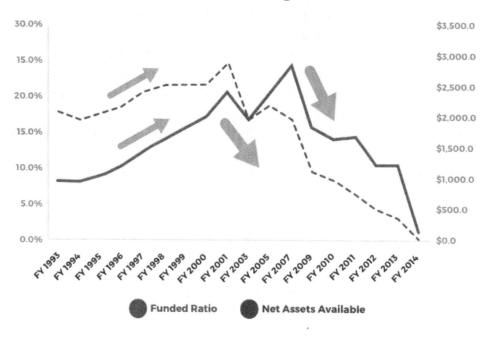

Decapitalization of the Retirement System

30.0%	$3,500.0
15.0%	$3,000.0
20.0%	$2,500.0
15.0%	$2,000.0
15.0%	$1,500.0
10.0%	$1,000.0
5.0%	$500.0
0.0%	$0.0

FY 1993 FY 1994 FY 1995 FY 1996 FY 1997 FY 1998 FY 1999 FY 2000 FY 2001 FY 2003 FY 2005 FY 2007 FY 2009 FY 2010 FY 2011 FY 2012 FY 2013 FY 2014

● Funded Ratio   ● Net Assets Available

Figure 3. This graph shows the historic decapitalization rate of the pension fund, which was virtually empty by 2014.

coupled with economic downturn and infrastructure deterioration, brought Puerto Rico to a boiling point.

From 2006–2016, government shutdowns, tax increases, scoop-and-toss financial tactics, and eventual fiscal collapse defined Puerto Rico's government. Under Alejandro García Padilla's administration, the government defaulted on its debt, severely downgrading Puerto Rico's bond ratings and blocking market access. During this period, Puerto Rico held its first plebiscite rejecting colonial status—a pivotal moment in our history.

Rampant unemployment and a stagnant economy emerged. The government had to sustain an enormous 135 agencies with 25 percent of the local workforce in government roles. Pension cuts plunged many vulnerable individuals below the poverty line. Facing a daunting $120 billion debt liability (over seventy billion in bonds, and over fifty billion in unfunded pension liabilities), the situation seemed dire.

In response, they imposed a Federal Fiscal Oversight Board in summer 2016, significantly altering governance (Guadalupe 2016).

I ran for governor in this context.

Kickstarting My Tenure

"As a politician, Rosselló, thirty-nine, is as un-Trump-like as they come. He trained as a scientist (he has a PhD in biomedical engineering from the University of Michigan) and speaks in a way that suggests logic and rationality are the highest virtues. He understands cellular reproduction much better than he understands the media: On TV, he is often stiff and overeager, looking like an A student called upon to recite his homework. But he is also a person who has kept his head in the face of extreme weather, both natural and political. And when it comes to science-related subjects like climate change, he's strikingly articulate and well-informed"

—*ROLLING STONE MAGAZINE* (GOODELL 2018)

In 2016, I entered the political race with the Plan for Puerto Rico as my platform. This plan, which I will delve into later, was a strategic policy blueprint encompassing scientific support and civic engagement. The primary was challenging, against the highly regarded two-time Congressmember Pedro Pierluisi. Defying most predictions and after nine debates, I narrowly won (51 to 49 percent). Spoiler alert: I later appointed Pedro Pierluisi to succeed me in 2019. However, political games within his own party derailed his appointment. Nonetheless, Pierluisi was subsequently elected governor in his own right (Figure 4).

On November 7, 2016, I won the general elections. I took the oath of office on January 2, 2017, and resigned on August 2, 2019. The next chapters will highlight key events of my administration and the stories behind them, serving as cornerstones for the rest of the book.

A Cautionary Tale

My story, and that of Puerto Rico, is a cautionary tale, a catalyzed process that could soon unfold elsewhere. While some of Puerto Rico's political challenges are extreme, similar outcomes are foreseeable in other places.

Fiscal collapse, exacerbated by our situation as a colonial territory, is not unique to Puerto Rico, but it did accelerate here. Many states and countries are on a similar trajectory, as seen in the fiscal crises of Greece (Council on Foreign Relations, n.d.) and Argentina (Independent Evaluation Office 2023) and in cities like Detroit (Bomey and Gallagher 2013) and New York (Gramlich 1976). The question is: Can others recognize the signs and act before it's too late?

Nobody needs to convince me of the climate crisis. I've witnessed its effects firsthand in Puerto Rico. I've felt the fury of a hurricane at its peak and seen beachfronts eroded and land swallowed by the sea.

And the data supports this.

"The Climate Risk Index may serve as a red flag for already existing vulnerabilities that may further increase as extreme events will become more frequent or more severe due to climate change," the report reads (Eckstein 2020). Puerto Rico is number one on this list. An EPA report in 2016, a year before Hurricanes Irma and Maria, stated, "Puerto Rico's climate is changing. The commonwealth has warmed by more than one degree (F) since the mid-twentieth century, and the surrounding waters have warmed by nearly two degrees since 1901. The sea is rising about an inch every fifteen years, and heavy rainstorms are becoming more severe" (Eckstein 2020). The signs were there, but the previous administrations did little about it.

But we are not alone. Other countries and states will soon start seeing similar effects. Louisiana is losing a football field worth of land every day (Schipani 2017). Florida, like Puerto Rico, faces hurricane threats and beachfront erosion (Staletovich 2023). The devastating wildfires in Canada and California (Czachor 2023) are further evidence. A recent headline stated, "July 2023 is the hottest month in 120,000 years" (Awasthi 2023). Are we prepared to mitigate this impact? (Figure 5)

Social unrest is bubbling up worldwide. The signals are there. Understanding the root causes is crucial to addressing them before it's too late. Public sentiment needs respect and constructive channeling, avoiding obstruction for obstruction's sake, which hinders reform.

You can liken the powerlessness of being a colonial territory to the feelings of marginalized or silenced groups everywhere around the globe. This occurs across the political spectrum.

And as if enduring centuries of political powerlessness wasn't enough, we were about to face the wrath of nature in the form of a catastrophic thousand-year storm named Maria.

GOBERNADOR

RESULTADOS ISLA

Ricardo Rosselló Nevares

205,108   51.29%

Pedro R. Pierluisi

194,811   48.71%

TOTAL: 399,919

*OTROS VOTOS		PARTICIPACIÓN	
EN BLANCO	3,249	INSCRITOS UNIDADES REPORTADAS	2,494,782
NOMINACIÓN DIRECTA	314	TOTAL DE PAPELETAS	403,713
		PARTICIPACIÓN	16.18%
TOTAL DE PAPELETAS	403,713	TOTAL DE INSCRITOS	2,857,901
AÑADIDOS A MANO		**OTROS DATOS**	
TOTAL DE SOBRES DE ELECTORES QUE VOTARON AÑADIDOS A MANO	811	MAL VOTADO	231
		NO VOTADO	0

Figure 4. Final results of my tightly contested primary with Pedro Pierluisi (Source: Comisión Estatal de Elecciones 2016).

CRI 1999-2018 (1998-2017)	Country	CRI score	Death toll	Deaths per 100 000 inhabitants	Total losses in million US$ PPP	Losses per unit GDP in %	Number of events (total 1999–2018)
1 (1)	Puerto Rico	6.67	149.90	4.09	4 567.06	3.76	25
2 (3)	Myanmar	10.33	7 052.40	14.29	1 630.06	0.83	55
3 (4)	Haiti	13.83	274.15	2.81	388.93	2.38	78
4 (5)	Philippines	17.67	869.80	0.96	3 118.68	0.57	317
5 (8)	Pakistan	28.83	499.45	0.30	3 792.52	0.53	152
6 (9)	Vietnam	29.83	285.80	0.33	2 018.77	0.47	226
7 (7)	Bangladesh	30.00	577.45	0.39	1 686.33	0.41	191
8 (13)	Thailand	31.00	140.00	0.21	7 764.06	0.87	147
9 (11)	Nepal	31.50	228.00	0.87	225.86	0.40	180
10 (10)	Dominica	32.33	3.35	4.72	133.02	20.80	8

Figure 5. Long-term climate risk index from Germanwatch (Eckstein 2020)

CHAPTER 2:

One Hundred Hours Post-Hurricane Maria

Battling Hurricane Maria was like playing against a chess master. Even with diligent effort and strategic moves, they always surprise you with unexpected tactics. (Bayon 2017).

"There are no lights. It is dark. Entirely dark, and apparently it could take months to get the power back on. Just think about that for a second in the modern world. Months with no power. This is part of the United States of America."

—ERIN BURNET, CNN NEWS, SEPTEMBER 20, 2017

Close your eyes and envision this: You're navigating a corridor of shattered infrastructure. Trees and debris litter the roads. Everything is in ruins. Water floods the landscape, turning green to brown. Travel from one town to another is impossible. Communication has ceased; without electricity, cell phone and radio towers are inoperative. The full extent of the devastation remains unknown.

This scene isn't from a postapocalyptic movie. It was my reality, hours after the storm, as my team and I assessed the damage. But don't just take my word for it. Listen to the experiences of others:

"Everything has damage. We had no place to sleep. We had nothing."

—JANET GONZALEZ CRUZ, PRESIDENT OF PUNTA SANTIAGO, HUMACAO.

"It lasted so long, so many hours, I thought it would never end."

—AMARILYS RIVERA, STRANDED ON THE ROOFTOP OF HER LEVITTOWN HOME.

"Those terrible gusts, where we started seeing the roofs falling and houses collapsing."

—JOEL *RODRÍGUEZ DÍAZ*, COMMUNITY LEADER, BARRIO QUEBRADA GRANDE, LAS PIEDRAS (Figure 1).

No matter your perspective outside Puerto Rico, the reality was far worse. Hurricane Maria transformed the landscape—both physically and psychologically.

I told my wife and a few close advisors, "There will be a Puerto Rico before Maria and a very different one after." I was right, but even I underestimated the profoundness of that statement.

Figure 1. Two images from NOAA depicting the size and magnitude of the hurricane covering the entirety of the island (National Environmental Satellite, Data, and Information Service 2017).

Figure 2. A depiction of the damaged roads, hindering passage between municipalities and complicating communication and supply delivery (Photo Credit: Magdiel Lugo).

"From having it all—communications and basic services—we suddenly regressed to the early nineteenth century. No electricity, no internet. Just informing the people of Puerto Rico about what happened was an extremely difficult task," recalled my secretary of public affairs, Ramon Rosario (Figure 2).

A natural disaster strips society to its core.

It creates a scenario thrusting people into extremes under unforeseen circumstances. It tests our humanity. You witness fight or flight, the level of preparedness, who continues to play politics, and who adapts. In chaos, uncertainty reigns. Amplification meets confusion. During this time the darker aspects of our nature emerge, but the better angels of our society also shine through.

The Un-Calm Before the Storm

"You have to evacuate. Otherwise, you will die." (Figure 3)

This grave warning came from Secretary of Public Safety Hector Pesquera on September 18, two days before the storm. When asked about this prescient statement, he explained, "I had spoken to the weather service. There was nothing to alter its trajectory. We were in its path. No one in PR had experienced a hurricane of this magnitude, and many underestimated its potential devastation." He mentioned the prevalent belief of past hurricanes sparing them and felt compelled to send a strong message. "I think the message got through, and it worked. I wouldn't have forgiven myself if I hadn't said it."

The day before, I convened my cabinet to discuss the impending second storm in two weeks. At that time, Maria was still a small storm, but preparation was crucial. Weakened by Hurricane Irma, we rallied to prepare as best we could.

"What are our most vulnerable areas?" I asked. My team provided a map. "Let's move those people to shelters ASAP. Open them up as soon as possible. I will announce it today." (Figure 4)

Figure 3. Safety briefing, hours before Hurricane Maria's landfall, with Hector Pesquera, William Villafañe, and other team members (Photo Credit: Magdiel Lugo).

Figure 4. Evacuating residents from their homes due to Hurricane Irma's impact in Loiza (Photo Credit: Magdiel Lugo).

I announced the evacuation, but some accused me of alarmism. The belief in divine protection and past sparing experiences created a false sense of security. Overcoming this perception was vital.

"If you are in a floodable area, your life is in jeopardy. If you live in a wooden home, your life is in danger," I warned in a press conference. We had 450 shelters ready, with food for 240,000 people for twenty days.

Truthfully, my team had prepared for months. We knew our vulnerabilities, as demonstrated during Hurricane Irma, a category 3 hurricane. Even the opposition openly received our response to Irma. A headline on September 9 read: "Rosselló passes his first hurricane with outstanding grades: The governor's opponents recognize his performance" (Caban 2017).

We responded swiftly to Irma, restoring power and providing basic support. We even served as a rescue platform for more than five thousand people stranded in the Lower Antilles, later called Operation Safe Haven.

I remember the images of societal collapse in the Lower Antilles, sparking our urgency to act. St. Martin and other islands were in chaos. Anarchy prevailed, and we needed to intervene.

A Puerto Rican medical student in St. Maarten, José Sebastian, described the hurricane's ferocity. "The hurricane pulled poles and statues, slamming them against buildings. A time share in front of us was partially torn apart."

Figure 5. Rosselló passes with good grades his first hurricane. Read the headline, denoting that even "adversaries of the governor recognize his performance"

Figure 6. Makeshift emergency center in La Fortaleza with key staff and FEMA (Photo Credit: Magdiel Lugo).

Senator Iris Martinez (Chicago), vacationing there, recalled it as a nightmare. "There were moments when I thought it was the last day of my life. I prayed, bracing for the worst."

Alex Woolfall tweeted about the terrifying noise, likening it to "standing behind a jet engine! Constant booms & bangs" (Hartley-Parkinson 2017).

Our National Guard rescued them, and upon arrival in Puerto Rico, Secretary of State Luis Gerardo Rivera Marin ensured their safety and provided necessities. (Figure 5)

One of them was quite famous and someone I had profound admiration for.

"Sir Richard Branson—one of the world's most recognizable business magnates, investors and philanthropists—has also now become the face and force behind the reconstruction of the British Virgin Islands, which were virtually erased from the map last week after Hurricane Irma struck."

An article by Michelle Kantrow-Vázquez titled "Sir Richard Branson: P.R., Rosselló have been 'fantastic'" tells part of the story (2017).

We were able to support him and others to mobilize help quickly.

Branson stated, "Your governor here has been really helpful. I've spoken to him two or three times today. If we need the National Guard from here to help over there, he's willing to supply them. If we need food, he's willing to supply it. It's been fantastic," (Kantrow-Vázquez 2017).

From Irma, we recovered quickly… but another storm was brewing. This storm felt different. With a narrow margin for error and still vulnerable, every passing minute eerily approached the sum of all fears. (Figure 6)

I told our team, setting a precedent for our administration, "We will work in three phases. First, the emergency phase, focusing on saving lives. Second, the recovery phase, aiming to restore normalcy. Finally, the rebuild phase, an opportunity to reengineer our infrastructure for a better quality of life."

It was crucial to balance urgency with hope. Our goal shifted from reform to survival and eventual rebuilding. In this dire situation, I needed my team to see hope, despite the long journey ahead.

"Looks Like a Bomb Hit"

"I'm telling you, it was shocking for me. I've never seen such a thing at my age"

— DORIS SERRANO, COMMUNITY LEADER IN BARRIO EL CERRO, NARANJITO (FIGURE 7, 8).

Figure 7. Aerial and on-ground images a few days after the storm (Photo Credit: Magdiel Lugo and Ricardo Rosselló).

Figure 8. Transmission lines devastated. Towers collapsed across the island's main arteries (Source: Ricardo Rosselló).

On the night of the storm, we huddled in a secured room. My priority was the safety of my wife, seven and a half months pregnant, and my three-year-old daughter.

"Daddy, is Maria going to kill everyone?" my daughter asked amid the tumultuous winds battering our shelter. In San Juan, the impact was relatively less severe, though it had the highest death toll. My heart ached for those in the southeast, feeling a mix of powerlessness, despair, and anxiety (Figure 9.

In an interview, I recounted, "I remember being here (in my office) and, in one of those fleeting moments of communication, I spoke with the president. While the hurricane was still over Arecibo (northern part of the island), we verbally declared Puerto Rico a disaster zone."

This was a pivotal moment.

"The truth is, despite anticipating devastation, nothing prepared me for the sights I encountered later that day on the streets."

The devastation was postapocalyptic.

Figure 9. A personal photo with my daughter during the hurricane (Photo Credit: Beatriz Areizaga).

But how intense was Maria? Dr. Jeff Masters' article, "Climate Change Made Hurricane Maria's Heavy Rains Nearly 5 Times More Likely to Occur," provides insight. This is relevant to later discussions in the book.

"At the beginning of the observational record in the 1950s, a storm like Maria was likely to drop the peak observed rain of 40.51 inches once every three hundred years. But in 2017, that recurrence interval dropped to about once every one hundred years," according to the study (Masters 2019). Others classified it as a five-hundred-year storm (Boteler 2017). Regardless of the range, it was a multigenerational event.

Maria struck Puerto Rico on September 20, 2017, as a category 4 hurricane with 155 mile per hour winds. The damage from its winds, rains, and storm surge are estimated at more than $120 billion (COR3 and Rosselló 2018), making it America's deadliest disaster in fifty years. Normalcy in essential services like energy and education took nearly a year to restore. This severely disrupted medical care, including emergency respiratory equipment, dialysis, and insulin delivery. The official death toll, encompassing direct and indirect effects, was 2,975 (Milken Institute 2018).

Figure 10. Helicopter images surveying the damage (Image: Magdiel Lugo).

Four days post-storm, we surveyed the damage from the air. The sights were as heart-wrenching as they were a testament to nature's fury. My island was unrecognizable from above. A National Guard official remarked, "It doesn't look like a storm passed through. It looks like a bomb exploded." (Figure 10)

When It Rains, It Pours

It was 2 a.m. on September 21, 2017. I had not slept since the day before the hurricane. I was about to shut my eyes on a broken-down couch in our makeshift operations center when my satellite phone rang.

"Governor, the levee broke down in Toa Baja. People are swimming to their rooftops," Carlos Mercader reported from Washington, DC, having received a message of despair from a citizen. Because of the immense damage, dire situation, and almost absolute lack of communications—we had to get notice from Washington, DC, about what was happening just ten miles away from our operations center.

"Get all the National Guard headed that way," I told him. "You are closer to them over there at the center."

He responded, "I'm on it."

Without phones, radio waves, or roads, our primitive communication method was to send runners to different parts of Puerto Rico. We did this prior to the hurricane's landfall. We gave the runners limited satellite phones, hoping the clouds would not interfere. In many cases, they did not work. Runners then had to return and sketch out the landscape. We were getting some information by foot.

Flight was not available until a few days after because of the storm's coattails. With limited resources, we had to make sure we safeguarded the most vulnerable areas. Toa Baja, Levittown, was one of them (Figure 11).

I got into one of the trucks and led a caravan of amphibious vehicles into Toa Baja. I remember telling a local news reporter, "It was a feeling of deep sadness, surreal… Puerto Rico looked like a war zone. There was no road access. There was no air access. There was no communication."

Figure 11. Aftermath of the overflow of water into Levittown, Toa Baja (Source:BBC 2017) and an aerial look at Levittown, Toa Baja (Photo Credit: Magdiel Lugo).

"Where is the mayor?" I asked once I got to town.

"Nobody knows," someone in the command center replied. At the moment, we feared for his safety, but it turned out that Betito Marquez had disappeared for a few days, overwhelmed by the situation. This happened to quite a few leaders (Figure 12).

Luis Orengo, a member of the National Guard, creates an impacting visualization of the events. "Once the winds subsided, at about 5 p.m. on the twentieth, the neighbors of my urbanization came out, started moving trees, and cleaning, with the purpose of opening the way to see how things were after the storm. Later the next night, I started seeing the water begin to rise. In a matter of fifteen minutes, a small stream of water turned into a lake." (Figure 13)

Amarilys Rivera was one of the more than two thousand folks we picked up that night. "Areas were filling quickly with water. At one point, I told my husband... this is not good. We could not even identify where the water was coming from. When we decided to leave for safety, we couldn't because the whole park was full of water," she said.

"There was nowhere to go. I desperately sent a message to PRFAA," Puerto Rico's federal office in Washington, DC.

"It was about 1 a.m. and I received a text message. They had tried to communicate with the authorities but weren't able to get anyone," Mercader recalls. "The first thing that occurred to me was to directly call the governor and tell him the situation. At that point, he called upon all the National Guard resources to go to Levittown. He went directly with the National Guard and helped rescue people, which started what is today known as the 'rescue of the two thousand in Levittown.'"

Amarilys recalls, "It was an enormous relief. My daughters called me when they heard the rescue vehicles, which was super gratifying."

Figure 12: Together with the National Guard in our efforts to aid people struck by the high levels of water and devastation, by transporting them away from their homes and into shelters (Photo Credit: Magdiel Lugo).

Figure 13. Flooded houses in Levittown, Toa Baja (Photo Credit: Magdiel Lugo).

That day changed my life. I remember one of the first homes we reached. The water was barely three inches from the ceiling. In the pouring rain, I could see a family, what I presumed was a grandmother and her three grandchildren, all girls, standing on the roof. The three girls were more or less my daughter Claudia's age.

Later in an interview she said, "I was with my girls, explaining to them what was going on, and it was only after a while I realized the governor was there in the car, helping to rescue us. He made zero gestures to have me identify him. I think the need to help was his only purpose" (Rosselló 2018).

Close call… Crisis averted… but more challenges awaited.

Drinking from a Firehose

As we were getting the citizens of Toa Baja to their refuge and began assessing the situation, we gave our typical update to the press. The press core was growing by leaps and bounds. It was standing room only.

The context of communication is paramount to this book, and it was fundamental to our effort pre- and post-Hurricane Maria. We made it a priority to communicate the information we had in hand and to provide the most accurate picture possible to those on the island and in the world. Information, mistakes, challenges—we discussed it all. By doing so, we figured we could identify problems early on.

Soon thereafter, we received the first airborne help from New York's Governor Andrew Cuomo (Figure 14, 15).

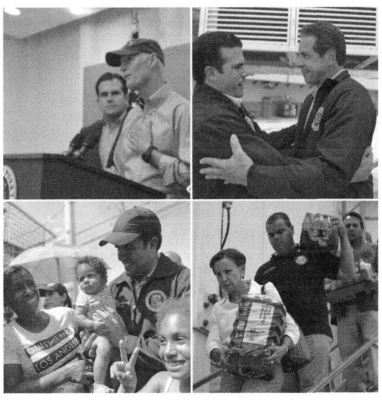

Figure 14, 15.

Make no mistake about it, Governor Cuomo was a hero to the people of Puerto Rico. He was continuously supportive throughout the emergency, recovery, and rebuild process. His counterpart from Florida was also a beacon of light, Rick Scott. My relationship with Scott soured for political reasons, but I give credit where credit is due.

Without Cuomo and Scott—a Democrat and a Republican—things would have definitely been bleaker.

Cuomo came several times. This one was a brief passthrough where he connected with people, brought much-needed supplies, and pledged his commitment to help. He delivered. Once Cuomo left, I was on my fourth day without a minute of sleep. I went to the convention center to see if I could take a nap, and all of a sudden, I receive this message: "At 2:10 p.m., dam operators reported the Guajataca Dam is failing causing flash flooding downstream on the Rio Guajataca."

"Do we have communication with Isabela and Quebradillas?" I asked.

"None."

This tweet was the only way we could get that information from our sources.

We had to do something. I told the resident commissioner to come with me as we tried to go to the other side of the island. We were still not clear to take off, so we had to travel by land. She was hesitant on going, but I convinced her.

The excursion also became an impromptu assessment of the roads. We identified trouble spots and mapped them. We only managed to plow through because of the strength of the National Guard's vehicles and the experience and skill of the people driving them.

What typically was a one-hour ride took us four and a half hours (Figure 16).

Figure 16. The Twitter message sent by the NWS San Juan on September 22, 2017.

Figure 17. After hours of searching, we found the mayor of Isabela in a shelter to inform him the dam was at risk of breaking. I was four days without sleep at this point (Photo credit: Magdiel Lugo).

"Does anyone know where the mayor is?" I asked when we arrived at Isabela's police station.

They all appeared stunned. Maybe it was because the governor came in out of nowhere. Maybe some were shellshocked from the wrath of the storm. "We don't know where the mayor is," said one of the officers. After further digging, someone told us he might be in one of the shelters.

I asked the supervisor, "Did you hear about the Guajataca dam potential failure?"

He responded, "We have not received a message from anyone. We have a disconnect in communication."

The National Weather Service warned Friday the failure of Guajataca Dam in northwest Puerto Rico was *imminent* and could lead to flash flooding affecting some seventy thousand if it collapsed.

I left them a satellite phone and told them to start evacuating the people in the vicinity of the dam (Talmazan and Helsel 2017). We drove up the mountaintop, where we found the mayor in a shelter. We left him a satellite phone and asked him to work with the Quebradillas mayor to move people to safety (Figure 17).

The mayor of Quebradillas decided *not* to do anything. He claimed I was creating a chaos, and it will not flood. I believe this stems from the embedded notion we had in Puerto Rico that things would solve themselves, and we did not have to worry. The truth of the matter is the dam did not fail as anticipated. Though severely damaged, they averted complete collapse with intervention. But what if it had?

Figure 18. This is the aerial look of the dam. (Photo Credit: Ricardo Rosselló)

Would you risk blindsiding seventy thousand people by the breaking of the dam, a large portion of which would die? Or would you let them stay in their house and *hope*—like many hoped Maria would not pass as it did—that nothing happened (Figure 18).

Those are the types of decisions where you have to proceed with extreme caution in the most delicate times of the emergency. I would much rather err on the side of caution with a devastating once-in-five-hundred-year storm than to neglect a clear message sent by outside sources. If the scenario repeated itself, I would very much proceed in the same way.

With shattered communications, the outlook was bleak. But in the toughest times, people came through in a big way for the people of Puerto Rico.

SOS Heard around the World

"At 4 a.m., the sea came in. Thank God for houses with second stories; neighbors helped others… Our people were literally drowning," recounted Janet *Díaz*.

Janet was the leader in Punta Santiago, Humacao, one of the communities most devastated by Hurricane Maria in Puerto Rico (Figure 19).

Hurricane Maria's landfall was particularly catastrophic in Punta Santiago, Humacao. Many lost their homes, and the community was left without power or running water for months. In the aftermath, residents united to clean up and rebuild.

"Here, our people suffered immensely. Nothing arrived. We didn't even have a place to sleep. People walked two hours to the town center," Díaz recalls, her voice tinged with pain.

Kim Kardashian ✔
@KimKardashian

This picture breaks my heart! I will be donating to
Puerto Rico and help them get the food & water they
desperately need. Please donate!

1:01 AM · Sep 26, 2017   ⓘ

♡ 72.8K   ◯ Reply   🔗 Copy link

Figure 19. Messages from celebrities, like Kim Kardashian, highlighted our plight. This particular image helped us locate and assist a stranded community (2017).

Figure 20. Our first moments in Punta Santiago, delivering essential items.

We were completely unaware of their plight due to the severe communication breakdown.

Then, a pivotal moment occurred. An online image from Punta Santiago showed an intersection with the message: SOS we need water and food!

"We wrote an SOS on the ground for helicopters to see, to spread the word we needed help," Janet explained.

Celebrities and influencers, including Kim Kardashian, amplified this plea by sharing the image on their platforms. This global exposure helped us identify the location and respond to their needs. Social media became a crucial tool for visibility.

Once cleared for flight, we headed straight to Punta Santiago. On arrival with supplies and assistance, we found their only access point completely blocked (Figure 20).

This situation highlighted the novel and challenging nature of our circumstances. We gathered information from any available source—runners, social media, anything—and had to validate and act quickly, as every minute was crucial for saving lives. That day, I was accompanied by Beatriz. It seemed like she never left Punta Santiago thereafter. "I feel very happy because the First Lady Beatriz Areizaga came as if she were part of our family," Janet expressed. "She visited our home as if she had known us all our lives."

Our Better Angels

"I felt proud to have them next to me and to see how they treated my people. It wasn't just one or two visits; she came many times over," Janet Díaz said, referring to the efforts my wife Beatriz made during the emergency. Notably, she provided food to people before FEMA even arrived. I believe her leadership and resolve spurred federal entities to act more swiftly (Figure 21).

Beatriz not only delivered food and set up camps but also established community areas for basic needs. She spearheaded *Unidos por Puerto Rico*, channeling aid to those in need, which regrettably, would later be used against her. Remarkably, she did all this while seven and a half months pregnant.

I recall telling her a few days after the storm, "Beatriz, you've done a fabulous job over these past three weeks. You're nearly eight months pregnant. It's time for you to take a break."

She smiled. I thought she had agreed. But she could not. "I could not just sit there. I had to help."

The next morning, I saw her on TV at a press conference, highlighting efforts to deliver food where FEMA couldn't yet reach. She established forty-six centers across the island for food distribution, formed alliances for phone charging, and created spaces for families to momentarily escape the tragedy.

Cynthia Santiago, Beatriz's right hand during this time, was instrumental in coordinating these efforts. "The first lady's office focused on social initiatives and connecting people with nonprofits. During the hurricane, our role shifted to immediate aid distribution as FEMA's response was not immediate," she explained.

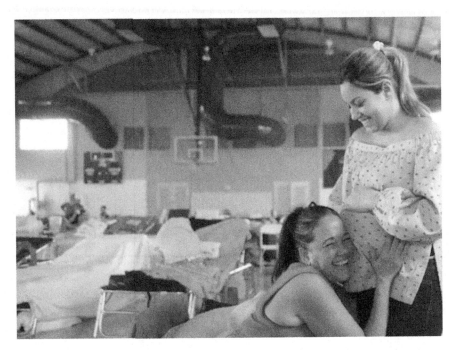

Figure 21. Seven and a half months pregnant, Beatriz led efforts to provide food, resources, and medicine, often before FEMAs arrival (Photo Credit: Magdiel Lugo).

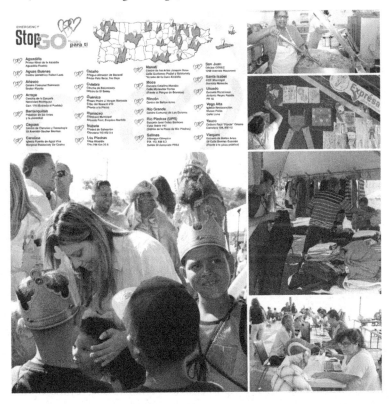

Figure 22. A collection of images from Beatriz's initiatives during and after the hurricane (Photo Credit: Mariela Falero).

The achievements were remarkable, especially considering the limited resources and Beatriz's pregnancy:

- Unidos por Puerto Rico supported 192 nonprofits, executed 220 projects, and aided more than 1.5 million people.
- The emergency stop-and-go reached more than a quarter of a million people before federal aid.
- Over six hundred nursing homes received food, personal care, and essential items.
- The organization created resting spaces for external first responders.
- They delivered hundreds of tons of food and supplies immediately post-storm (Figure 22).

Despite later attacks on Beatriz, her impact was undeniable. Cynthia recalls, "Just yesterday, Doña Lola from Toa Baja, inspired by our initiatives, appeared in the newspaper for improving her community's quality of life."

"We have built," she exclaimed. Amen.

Like Beatriz, many gave their all during this challenging time. National Guardsman Luis Oquendo noted, "We had officers who lost everything, yet they showed extraordinary strength of character."

It was inspiring to see my team and others, regardless of rank, contribute tirelessly. "The will of the Puerto Rican people to overcome this disaster is unbreakable," Secretary Pesquera reflected.

Pam Patenaude, Undersecretary of HUD, saw "the resilience and faith of the people" during her visit.

The hurricane's aftermath indeed brought out the best in many though it was not without challenges, pain, or mistakes.

Post One Hundred Hours

This was just a short window into the first one hundred hours after the hurricane. However, to this day, residents still feel the aftermath. The evolving challenge had constantly emerging and unprecedented problems. I personally made mistakes—the death toll count being the most notable one. We wanted the most transparent process backed by experts to address this. So we hired a university as an independent third party to assess and give recommendations. You will find more about this in other chapters in the book. I also fell into the trap of agreeing to rebuild the energy grid with the corps of engineers. Their initial estimate of forty-five days was not only wrong, but they did not even start by that time. This was costly.

The challenges, successes, and failures working with the federal government and President Trump were always MAGA-sized. It was a roller coaster—the lack of logistic preparation to deliver items to our island, the immediate help after the storm passed from his office, the lack of players to connect on his administration that actually were able to help, which dwindled as time passed, the excellent work done by the US Army as we worked the recovery, his invitations to the White House, rarely extended to a Democratic governor, and the misconstrued and factually wrong claim that President Trump had given "ninety-one billion dollars to Puerto Rico" (Levin 2019).

I discuss my first interactions with Trump in the next chapter and follow-up encounters scattered throughout the book.

Figure 23. After the storm (Source: Magdiel Lugo).

The direct and indirect conflict we had in our situation of powerlessness surfaced as the press cameras left the island for the "next disaster." At that point, we were able to see which of the leaders who came to the island and "pledged their full support" would actually do it. Spoiler alert: Not many did (Figure 23).

As a consequence of our "geopolitical blackhole," most American citizens did not know Puerto Rico was part of the US. Before the storm, polls showed that *under* 40 percent of US citizens in the mainland knew Puerto Ricans were citizens as well. Right after the storm, it was just more than 50 percent (Hansen 2017). After several months of coverage due to the impact of Maria, now more than 94 percent know Puerto Ricans are also Americans (Wilson 2018). We made a point of mentioning it as a team every time we had an opportunity. Every sentence to the press would start with "*as American Citizens…*" (Dropp and Nyhan 2017).

Mistakes abounded, conflicts were present everywhere, and the whole aftermath tested the nature of our humanity in many different ways. I spread these themes throughout the book. In my view, they are very valuable insights—as they showcase a raw scenario that supports some of the lessons and observations we pose throughout the book.

In the end, validation is internal. I know we gave it our all for the people of Puerto Rico in one of the most challenging disasters in the modern history of the United States. Whether it was enough or not, I leave that for others to contemplate. I was proud to lead during a chaotic time. I could see how our people rebounded from the absolute depths of despair. I saw how my wife continued a mission to feed and help anyone and everyone on the island. I saw how the very worst of circumstances can bring out the very best in people—a great lesson to behold.

CHAPTER 3:

Ten Hours with Trump

Image depicts President Trump shooting tweets and ignoring mine (Bayon 2017).

"You are a hardworking governor… I'll tell you what. This man well represents the people of Puerto Rico because we like him and respect him."

—TRUMP ON ROSSELLÓ (NOTIUNO 2017)

"A terrible governor"

—TRUMP ON ROSSELLÓ (REUTERS 2019)

If you expect me to just crucify Trump, you are mistaken. If you expect me to "praise him bigly" you will be disappointed. This chapter might draw the ire of extreme elements from both the right and the left. My aim is to understand this important figure in the world, his characteristics, and what his persona tells us about the state of the globe's environment.

Not unlike many of his relationships, ours did not end particularly well. It was not for lack of trying. In fact, trying gained me plenty of enemies. But I had a clear understanding of a few things.

First, he was the president of the United States. Second, because Puerto Rico is not a state, we were under his direct—almost unchecked—influence. Puerto Rico has no voting representation in Congress, so we had to do most of the work on the executive side. Items relating to disasters and declarations thereof were his call. The president can issue a disaster declaration through the Federal Emergency Management Agency, activating federal assistance and resources for affected areas (FEMA 2023). Without having any political leverage, I had to be very effective convincing him to make those decisions. Sometimes I was. Others I was not. Lastly, Trump knew no in-betweens. Either you were with him, or you were against him.

This last point was apparent the first time I met him in person. My wife Beatriz, daughter, and I waited on the tarmac of the military base on October 3, 2017, as Air Force One arrived on the island. This was the first time a sitting president had come to Puerto Rico after a major storm. I was anxious. I was excited for the possibility of aid. I was concerned. There was a strong tug and pull with this larger-than-life man; more so now that he was president. Connecting with him could mean the difference between getting aid or having it stopped—a life or death decision for many of my people (Figure 1).

Although the sleepless nights after Hurricane Maria and the titanic task ahead were daunting, I could not help but feel the magnitude of the moment.

I recall telling my wife I was looking forward to having the opportunity of explaining the situation in Puerto Rico and the ways we could help the island take a giant leap forward if we worked together on a few simple items. These included healthcare disparities, Puerto Rico's unique tax situation, and the potential to transform this crisis into a model of development, innovation, and growth. This collaboration would transcend politics, displaying cooperation between a Democratic governor and a Republican president for the common good.

Figure 1. Beatriz (eight months pregnant with Pedro), Claudia and I receiving the president and first lady on the tarmac (Photo Credit: Magdiel Lugo).

One critical issue was the healthcare disparity in Puerto Rico, long-standing and in need of urgent attention. Medicaid funding for US territories like Puerto Rico is markedly lower than for the states (Government Accountability Office 2019). This stems from a capped block grant that falls short given the territories' lower per capita income. Consequently, Puerto Rico's Federal Medical Assistance Percentage (FMAP) is only 55 percent, compared to 83 percent for poorer states (Rapfogel 2022). This funding gap significantly impacts the quality of healthcare available to local residents.

Another pressing matter was the potential impact of the proposed federal tax reform on Puerto Rico. Puerto Rico would benefit if treated as part of the US. However, the US considering Puerto Rico *foreign* for tax purposes would be detrimental to the island. The reform aimed to penalize foreign entities operating in the states, presenting an opportunity for Puerto Rico to shed the nonsensical label of "foreign for tax purposes" and receive full integration into the US tax system. I will delve deeper into this complex issue later, but for now, it suffices to say it was a complicated and pressing matter.

Finally, I wanted to let him know about the unique opportunity for statehood, and what that meant for his *legacy*. He wanted to make America greater? What better way than to add states—diverse ones at that.

"All I need is five minutes," I said to Beatriz. "I will make him see the opportunity and the low hanging fruit to help Puerto Rico, particularly after this disaster that has achieved global recognition."

He will see it clearly. He can even benefit from it greatly politically, I thought. I was sure I would get through…

I was *wrong*.

We saluted the president and the first lady and quickly went to his car. This is where I started to make my case, but the president had none of it. You see, the president seemed not to care about policy at all. That much was clear. I don't mean it as a dig. He does not care to let you know he does not care. So, as one might imagine, I was having quite a hard time getting through to the man in the onset of our conversation. He would interrupt continuously to make random, superficial statements.

"I hear baseball is big here in Puerto Rico. I love baseball."

"This is a beautiful island… beautiful."

"I used to own a golf course here. It was great."

"This was such a massive hit. It's going to cost us a lot, you know?"

A particular revelation was his connection to his wife. As an outsider, I thought they had some sort of estranged relationship from what the media disseminated. However, my experience was different.

"Melania, what do you think about writing off the debt? I think they should write off the debt." She nodded.

He would later go on to restate this publicly in the press conference and in other interviews (Bomey 2017).

"They owe a lot of money to your friends on Wall Street and we're going to have to wipe that out," Trump told Fox News (Bomey 2017). "You can say goodbye to that." Once he uttered those words, the markets moved dramatically. This instance highlights the far-reaching impact presidential speeches can have. Narrative moves the world.

"How are you doing? Do you need anything?" he would ask her as he was holding her hands.

At one point, my wife said to the first lady, "Thank you for coming. You are so beautiful." She went on to ask Melania about a reading program for kids that Beatriz wanted to implement on the island. Melania responded in Spanish that she would love to help. A month later, she did just that.

Trump jumped in. "Are you kidding—she is the best and most beautiful first lady ever. She is wonderful. If she were a Democrat, the magazines would be all over her all the time."

My wife and I were pleasantly surprised to see he was very caring and conscience of the first lady. Not the portrayed image at all.

As all this was unfolding, I was having a hard time engaging with Trump. "Mr. President—I think we have a great opportunity to fix Medicaid for Puerto Rico." Because we were not a state, Puerto Rico's inequality on healthcare had increased over the past couple of decades, relative to the states. "A simple change to the…"

President Trump interrupted. "People love Trump? Look at that!" said the president as he pointed outside to some people holding signs welcoming him. "That's wonderful. Wonderful people."

I tried to talk about healthcare about four times and got nowhere.

In my final attempt, my wife stepped in and said, "I am half Cuban, and most of them are fans." Carmen, Beatriz's mother was born in Cuba and had to escape in November 1968.

He immediately connected and started a conversation. No more interruptions. Laser focused. He moved away from the chitchat and shifted to engage on topics he truly had an interest in and was intuitively gifted: media and politics. He mentioned, "I love the Cubans, they voted for me in Florida, you know. I love them." She opened the door for me. My wife's emotional IQ (and regular one, for that matter) is evidently much, much higher than mine.

In this instance, it was clear. *You are either with him or you are against him.* My goal was to engage and work with him. Why did I have to strike down the president of the United States without giving a real shot to collaborate? Just because we were from opposing parties? Was I supposed to choose theatrics over substance? Why enrage the president when my people were in large part at his mercy?

Irshad Manji, author and founder of the Moral Courage Project points out that "If all we are doing is barking past each other and the side in power at the moment imposing its solution on the others, there is no triumph. There is no solution" (2020). I needed a solution, both for the immediate aftermath of the storm, and for the long-term political prospects of the island.

As it turns out, that was one of many interactions with the president. Some were positive. Others were baffling. It just highlighted the instability and unpredictability of the current, unstable environment.

Time with Trump

I was with President Trump directly for about ten hours.

My interactions with him by phone, in the field after the storm, and at the White House gave me insights into the characteristics of the leader of the free world and his unorthodox ways.

"You couldn't imagine anyone more unfiltered than [Trump]. He came from the outside; the elites didn't like him; but he was different—different from anyone else who ever might have been president," Gautam Mukunda, renowned Harvard Kennedy Center for Public Leadership Research fellow and author of *Picking Presidents: How to Make the Most Consequential Decision in the World* mentioned in a forum I participated (Mukunda 2023)

Like everyone, he had both good and bad qualities, just amplified. Some revered Trump as a savior. Others reviled him as an absolute pariah. In my view this is more a reflection of the times we are living in. In other words, while some people suggest Trump is the *cause* for the current environment, I believe he is just a symptom.

One particularly telling moment was his press conference in Puerto Rico. The president asked me for several data points. Particularly the death toll. "I hear it is low number for deaths…"

I replied, "It's low right now. It's likely going to get much higher. We have not been able to get in contact with many towns. Hospitals are still running things manually. Information is not arriving. In addition to the lack of electricity, water, and access to roads, we expect the numbers to go up as people don't have access to services like dialysis and other life-sustaining treatments."

I hoped this would make sense to him and establish that the death toll at that time was really just a rudimentary tally of what we could get our hands on. We followed CDC protocol, but communication lines broke. I hoped he would see this was not an actual projection of the potential numbers.

His response? "Yeah, but it's low. If somebody dies afterward, they are going to blame me for it, even if the hurricane did not do it!"

I don't think he understood what was happening. Perhaps he didn't want to.

At that moment, I started explaining the *harvest effect,* a condition that epidemiologists say happens after many disasters. The harvest effect is a mortality deficit in a particular time period causing deaths displaced to an earlier time. This was the reality in Puerto Rico. We had conditions likely to produce further excess deaths if not corrected urgently.

And of course, they did.

Researchers at the esteemed George Washington University Milken Institute School of Public Health released an independent research report that assessed the number of excess deaths in Puerto Rico following Hurricane Maria. Their findings suggested that between September 2017 and February 2018, a total of 2,975 individuals lost their lives due to the consequences of the hurricane (2018).

"The results of our epidemiological study suggests that, tragically, Hurricane Maria led to a large number of excess deaths throughout the island. Certain groups—those in lower-income areas and the elderly—faced the highest risk," said Carlos Santos-Burgoa, the principal investigator of the project and a professor of global health (GW Today 2018).

I wanted to get through to the president… but it was too late.

These facts and data points were just white noise to him. He was already set in his narrative. A key item that—in my view—made him a formidable politician but eventually was his undoing as a chief executive during the COVID-19 pandemic. Picking and choosing your facts to fit your narrative works well when there are no explicit and large consequences at the other end. He would always double down on narrative. Even if it was wrong, it needed to fit with his broader objectives.

What was his narrative? What underlying objectives was he attempting to achieve? Those all came in full circle in the press conference held after his arrival.

The first objective was to downplay what happened in Puerto Rico compared to Hurricane Katrina. Of course he used the death toll count as his foundation, even as I told him these numbers would grow tremendously. "'Every death is a horror,' Trump said in a meeting with Puerto Rico's Gov. Ricardo Rosselló and other Puerto Rican officials in San Juan, 'but if you look at a real catastrophe like Katrina and you look at the tremendous—hundreds and hundreds and hundreds of people that died—and you look at what happened here with, really, a storm that was just totally overpowering, nobody has ever seen anything like this'" (Levy 2017).

A "real catastrophe." This was as the lights were still out and were going to be out for almost a year. This was as food and support were struggling to make their way to the island. Many felt gaslit by this. But the "certified death count" drew ire. In hindsight, this was a mistake on my part. Even though we knew this number would rise, we still produced the official statistic based on the CDC's protocol.

"Sixteen people certified," Trump said. "Sixteen people versus in the thousands."

I felt a piercing dagger in my heart.

After laying the foundation to minimize the event, he followed through with his next objective— counteracting the media narrative that he was not helpful.

Figure 2, 3.

Trump said, "Right from the beginning, this governor did not play politics," he said. "He didn't play it at all. He was saying it like it was, and he was giving us the highest grades."

By minimizing the event and having it not be a "real catastrophe," Trump then allowed himself to detach from what happened and started focusing on how this projected onto him. He used it to counter punch his political opponents—some of which were on the island—but mostly directed at those in the states. Again, a big mistake (Figure 2, 3).

And then it happened: He turned the hurricane into a money issue. "Now, I hate to tell you, Puerto Rico, but you've thrown our budget a little out of whack because we've spent a lot of money on Puerto Rico. And that's fine. We've saved many lives."

None of these things sat well with the people of Puerto Rico. They could not understand how the president would downplay what happened here. They did not like his engagement with opponents on such a sensitive topic. Lastly, it was clearly apparent that—different to Florida and Texas, where the president stated, "Give all resources to those states"—here, he was counting pennies.

As Chris Cillizza from CNN put it, "President Donald Trump faced a major test on Tuesday as he traveled to storm-ravaged Puerto Rico: Show the American citizens struggling for survival on the island that he understood their plight, sympathized with them and was doing everything in his power to make it better as quickly as he could" (2017).

"He failed. Hugely" (Cillizza 2017).

Things got a little choppier the rest of the day. Some things are public. Others are not. But that's not the point. The point was his *audience*.

His audience were folks who did not want to spend money on issues not stateside related. His audience were folks who didn't feel comfortable with diversity, a bill the people of Puerto Rico certainly fit. To that audience, he was successful. To all others, it was a catastrophe. It appeared he was always thinking of narrative—how to change the direction of the discourse and how to pierce the most basic fears and aspirations of his supporters so they would follow him, no questions asked.

The Paper Towel Incident

After the press conference, we got in the car and went to Guaynabo for a walk around affected areas and an event in a faith-based organization.

We first walked through an affected community with the president. My first impression was he was more engaging and kinder in person than projected on TV. The same went for First Lady Melania Trump. I recall a moment when she stepped away from the group and reached out to a group of kids, stroking their hair and listening to them. For our people, at that time, it meant the world. My wife recalls, "The camaras were rolling until that point. They just stopped recording that special moment for no reason. All of them." The press also controls the narrative (Figure 4).

We then entered this packed faith-based community center. As the president came in, people were shouting, "Mr. President, here!" They took pictures with the president and first lady. There was a dividing line made by tables that had consumables and important materials: clothes, food, water, and yes… paper towels.

Figure 4. Walking with Beatriz, President Trump and First Lady Melania Trump through some of the rubble in Guaynabo Puerto Rico (Source: Magdiel Lugo).

This is when the president made his now-infamous gesture of throwing towels to folks. The true story is a bit different. A barrier in the center of the room separated the people from the president. As President Trump and others started handing out items of first need, someone from the back of the room yelled, "Mr. President, throw it to me!"

"Mr. President, throw it to me!"

Trump was holding a paper towel. He threw it. Then others continued to ask.

The image plastered in history was one that demonstrates disdain and repulsion for the people. The title on the *Washington Post* was "In Puerto Rico, Trump's paper towel toss reveals where his empathy lies." It opens by saying "A century from now, men and women yet to be born will shoulder the complex duty of identifying the precise moments, the public statements and images that captured the complex essence of President Trump and his influence on American life… In those images, the forty-fifth president can be seen at a supply distribution point, dressed in a dark suit sans tie while tossing rolls of paper towels into a crowd" (Ross 2017).

A century from now? Take a look at this picture at that precise moment (Figure 5).

Figure 5. Image of President Trump was throwing paper towels to people in a faith-based community center in Guaynabo, Puerto Rico. (Photo Credit: Magdiel Lugo).

I'll ask the reader to look at everyone's face in the crowd and you determine if you think it offended anyone there (Nakamura and Parker 2018).

Was it dumb and incredibly thoughtless? Yes. The president *should* have known better. But that does not detract from the true story: The media narrative got carried away, which is happening more often than not in our political culture.

I bring this point up because a similar thing—on a smaller scale—happened to me. The press blasted me for taking a "selfie with President Trump." In reality, I was taking a picture of my daughter sitting with the secretary of Homeland Security (image below). Even as I got the picture out there and demonstrated this claim was false, it did not matter. The opposition already had its narrative, and it was more powerful than any evidence.

If this power does not worry you, it should (Figure 6).

Just recently a blogger wrote, "That image, unerasable, unfortunate, even painful, of the governor of Puerto Rico taking a selfie with Donald Trump during his visit to San Juan, at the same time that hundreds died for lack of attention" (*El Nuevo Dia* 2019).

Figure 6. Top picture, widely circulated across media, portrayed me taking a selfie with President Trump. Bottom picture was the actual picture taken of my daughter and secretary Elaine C. Duke (Photo Credit: Magdiel Lugo and Ricardo Rosselló).

This is the sort of politics and actions that—in the long run—will affect our democracy. Shoot first, ask questions later. And even if the questions receive answers, the original narrative sticks with most of the people. This in part has diminished the role and perception of political leaders within the past century. And the media plays a huge role here. There is no accountability for falsifying, so it goes unchecked.

The aftermath? Diminishing trust in our government institutions. In 2019, a Pew Research study showed that two-thirds of adults think other Americans have little or no confidence in the federal government (Rainie, Keeter, and Perrin 2019). How can we actually get things done if leaders are constantly throttled and trust continues to erode? We will definitely dive in deep to this idea later on in the book.

Returning to Trump's paper towel throwing incident, even as it was happening and people in his team pointed it out, his thoughts seemed elsewhere.

Image of Failure

As we left the center, our next stop was a helicopter pick-up to show the president the damage done. In that walk, I detected the first sign of testiness from the president. He shifted the conversation to two topics: George W. Bush and Kim Jong Un.

The first one came when we were discussing our upcoming helicopter flight to oversee the damage. "No, I'm not getting in," the president said. "Bush got into a helicopter, flew over Louisiana, and that was the image of failure."

Luckily, General John Kelly, the president's chief of Staff, was there and could handle him effectively and elegantly. Kelly's main goal as White House chief of staff was to restore discipline and efficiency to the West Wing. I saw firsthand how he could manage some of the erratic behavior of the president and steer him out of trouble. No surprise, however, they ended up having a tumultuous relationship. Trump has publicly mocked and criticized Kelly on several occasions (Miller and Jaffe 2020).

Here however, before their falling out, he convinced the president he should, indeed, get on the helicopter.

"I will not take the picture of failure," said the president.

"This is different, Mr. President," Kelly responded.

"How so?"

"President Bush was not on the ground, sir. You were. You will also fly to the aircraft carrier to meet with Governor Mapp." He referred to the governor of the Virgin Islands at that point in time.

"Is he Republican?"

"I believe so, sir."

Somewhat dejected, President Trump continued his walk. Without stating it, he followed General Kelly's advice. We got into the chopper. You should not understate the power that Kelly had. In a way, he carefully balanced the desires of the president that were reasonable and those that seemed erratic.

If it was just one event, I'd probably ascribe it to something random. But, to my surprise, it happened again.

We all crammed together in Marine One, the president's helicopter. FEMA head Brock Long, the president, General Kelly, and the first lady were among the people inside.

The general said, "Mr. President, we are going to fly over the damaged areas now."

"No, let's just go to the aircraft carrier, no flyover," the president replied.

One of the Navy officials looked at Kelly, a bit startled. He calmly nodded to her. This time, Kelly allowed the helicopter to fly a little bit over the beach, started pointing out some observations about the terrain. President Trump started talking to me about his uncle and how he studied in MIT. Kelly pointed out the damage through the window.

"Look at that," he said.

"Nature has a way of coming back," said the president. "Well, it does until it does not. Who knows with nuclear warfare what will happen..."

And then, he said the one thing that made me more concerned than anything else in the entire visit.

Figure 7. Landing in the aircraft carrier with Governor Mapp and President Trump (Photo Credit: Magdiel Lugo).

"But I tell you what…" He paused for effect. "If nuclear war happens, we won't be second in line pressing the button."

This statement floored me. I could not believe what I was hearing. It was surreal. Was he really talking about total annihilation as we flew over the ravaged sights of the island? The previous months' worth of emergency response exhausted me. I stared natural destruction right in the eye. Now, with a simple comment, all of that paled in comparison to man-made global nuclear annihilation.

I took a deep breath. I told myself to focus on the task at hand. I could not help but look over at some of the others in the helicopter. They seemed to have been numb to the idea of hearing these things fly out of the president's mouth.

"How about we see a bit more," said Kelly, changing the subject and waiting for the appropriate opportunity.

Once again, Trump did not say yes or no. He just started looking out the window.

Kelly pointed at the officer and said in a very low tone, "Proceed with original plan." (Figure 7)

My view is Kelly provided much-needed support to Trump. He was not a crony. He was not a yes-man. He recognized the president's hierarchy above him and demonstrated great respect toward him. However, he was there to help him and the nation in the best way he could. Evidently, he was a successful executive with his military background. But his biggest skill at this juncture was being able to manage the president and save him from himself.

As time passed, Trump lost people who could help him maximize his strengths and avoid catastrophe in his flaws. I can't help but wonder if the handling of COVID-19 pandemic would have been different if Trump had this type of support next to him.

Snapshot

Looking back, Beatriz recalls after seeing me a bit tired, "I asked you, 'How do you feel?' You took a deep breath and responded, 'I am very concerned.' I was surprised, and said, 'But you got some of the things you wanted to—to move things for Puerto Rico.' After a few seconds, you looked at me and said, 'Yes... but my concern now is for the world.'"

This is just a sample of my ten hours with Trump—a man I consider underestimated dramatically by the opposition. And to this day he continues to be so. I could see the strength and weaknesses firsthand. I could see what those who supported him liked and those who opposed him loathed. This dichotomy, I believe, is a root source of the challenges we have now and ones that *will* get bigger as time passes.

I saw him at his best, responding quickly to our request for emergency support right after the storm. I saw him at his worst, flummoxed by the perception he could narrate away any problems, like Hurricane Maria and the COVID-19 pandemic.

In my view, Trump had the best political instincts of anyone I've ever come in contact with. He was not afraid to play with fire, particularly if he could light an even bigger one at a moment's notice. Trump's use of words would move markets, opinions, and emotions. And he knew it. He would move the entire news cycle with a single tweet.

The spectrum of his supporters and opponents will view anything he does—good or bad, ill intent or otherwise—in completely different ways. If this pattern of behavior is to sustain, we are on the cusp of a society where the ends don't meet. Where collaboration and consensus are evermore impossible to achieve. Where anyone who governs won't get even the benefit of the doubt because they are "the others." Is this really what we want? Or can we identify a path to reengage with opponents even if we disagree. The conditions are against it. Political victory seems to favor the extreme although it severely limits what we can accomplish.

In my opinion, the current predicament calls upon the worst nature of our humanity. Can we overcome this?

CHAPTER 4:

The Summer of 2019

The summer of 2019 was a high-pressure, intense moment. Going from general approval to rejection. This illustration captures a bit of the pain, darkness, and anxiety generated during those days (Bayon 2019).

July 10, 2019, was a rainy, muggy day. I was just into the third day of my first vacation in two and a half years. I scheduled a five-day Disney Cruise in the Mediterranean to take my kids and spend some time with them and my wife. Suddenly, I receive a barrage of texts.

One from my press secretary read: "*The news is reporting the arrest of Angie Avila,*" a former head of the health insurance entity in Puerto Rico. I was in disbelief. This was not the Angie I knew. Could it be possible? What were they charging her with? Before I could concretely get my thoughts together… another hit.

Not an hour passed, when she writes: "Governor, they also arrested Keleher," my former secretary of education. My head was spinning. How could this happen? Once, Mike Tyson said, "Everyone has a plan until they get punched in the mouth" (Nag 2021). At that moment, I understood what he meant… and how it felt.

As the news broke, I found myself sitting on a small bench overlooking the water in Monte Carlo. Families strolled happily around me, their sounds fading into a distant murmur. Time seemed to slow, and the serene scenery felt like the calm before an impending storm.

That very day, Chairman Grijalva of the Natural Resources Committee called for my resignation. This demand seemed excessive and premature. After all, Grijalva, a known ally of former Puerto Rican Governor Aníbal Acevedo Vilá—who federal authorities arrested (CNN 2008)—had never sought Acevedo Vilá's resignation. It appeared to be a politically motivated move from an established opponent with whom I had had several clashes. I suspected this was an early move in a larger strategy about to unfold. The situation was escalating rapidly.

Feeling the pressure, I realized I had to cut my trip short and respond in person.

On a turbulent ride back to the airport, I drafted a statement: "As I said last week, I have been planning this family trip for months, which is my first vacation in two and a half years. Recognizing the importance and impact of today's arrests on government activities, I have decided to return immediately. It is time to be present on the island and personally reaffirm that the government's agenda will continue, despite the efforts of those undermining public trust."

Thus, we disembarked in Pisa. I left my family on the cruise and embarked on a journey involving three flights. Thirty-two hours later, I was back in Puerto Rico (Coto 2019).

This moment marked a pivotal turning point, leading to events that culminated in my resignation just two weeks later. From a seemingly assured reelection to casting me as a villain—how did this dramatic shift occur? (Figure 1)

Sixty Days Prior: Winning by a Landslide

On May 3, 2019, I awoke early, as was my habit, to a striking headline in *El Nuevo Día*, a leading daily newspaper on the island: "Rosselló Has Little Electoral Competition" (2019).

The newspaper had released its traditional preelection poll eighteen months before the election. The poll presented various potential candidate matchups, and in each scenario, I was leading. Against declared candidates, my lead was at least fourteen points, reaching twenty in some instances (Figure 2).

In Puerto Rico, an incumbent leading in the polls is not the norm. "A sitting governor being ahead was an anomaly. In the past twenty years, the projections for every incumbent were to be losing by more than fifteen points at this stage of their administration," William Villafañe, former chief of staff and current state senator, explained during a conversation for this book.

For the past two decades, Puerto Rico's fraught political landscape brought a lack of the populace's faith in their government by the third year. The prevailing sentiment was in favor of "anyone but" the incumbent. This anti-incumbent trend, a staple of Puerto Rican politics for twenty years, seems to be gaining global traction.

This shift is becoming increasingly evident in Latin America. Patricio Navia observes, "A closer look at recent election results—especially those that have occurred since the pandemic began to ravage the region—tells a much simpler story: People are consistently voting against incumbents" (Navia 2021).

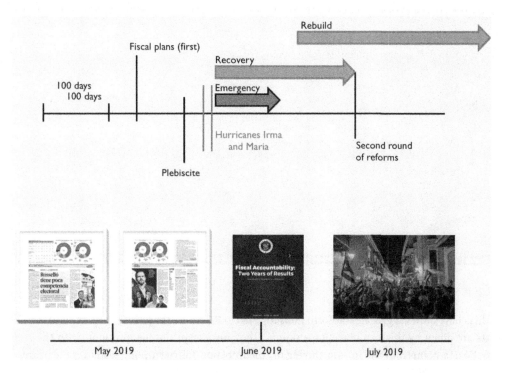

Figure 1. A high-level timeline depicting my first two years in office (top) and the last ninety days.

This is Puerto Rico's evident pattern for the last twenty years. For instance, my predecessor, before opting not to run, was trailing by more than twenty points against me (and Pierluisi) around this time in 2015. His predecessor, Luis Fortuño, was down by twenty-two points. Fortuño had once led by as much as thirty-five points over the previous incumbent, Aníbal Acevedo Vilá.

Figure 2 . Midterm poll published by *El Nuevo Día*. The headline reads "Rosselló Has Little Electoral Competition" (2019).

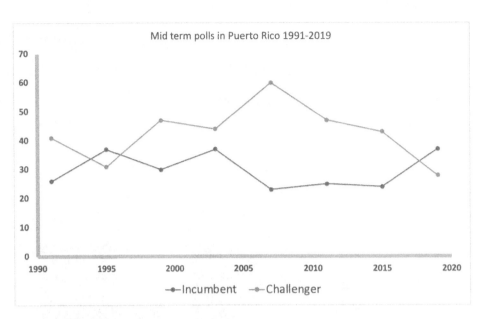

Figure 3. This chart shows aggregate midterm polls for Puerto Rico over the past twenty-eight years. On average, incumbents are down by thirteen percentage points. The only exceptions were in 1995, with the reelection of Pedro Rosselló (six-point lead) and in 2019, during my incumbency (fourteen-point lead over the nearest declared challenger). (Source: *El Nuevo Día* 2019)

The common factors contributing to this trend are stagnant economic growth, corruption, and a growing preference for change over continuity.

For a moment, it appeared I might break this two-decade-long anti-incumbency cycle, despite my anticipation of serving only one term (Figure 3).

Make Your Time Count

A few years prior to my election, I recall some of my closest advisors cringing when I went to fundraisers. I would grab the microphone and say, "I am here to do my job for the next four years. I am very likely to be a one-term government, so whatever we need to do, we need to accomplish in four years."

"Why are you telling them that you will only be there for four years? This scares them away," a member of the campaign fundraising staff told me.

I thought about this strictly scientifically. And perhaps this was shortsighted of me. Perhaps it is just a reflection of my professional formation. While it is important for anyone running for office to have irrational confidence (I certainly had my fair share), I returned to my scientific upbringing. What does the evidence say?

The evidence was pretty clear. You only get four years in office. Getting any more time would be an outlier in statistical terms, an exception to the rule. Therefore, whatever you were going to do, you had to plan to do quickly, always prepare yourself and make your *time count*.

They failed to see the trends. I did not. Well, I did miss one part.

Little did I know, it would be *even less* than the time I expected.

So you could probably imagine my surprise when I saw the polls in the newspaper giving me a clear advantage. Not only the fact of being ahead, but mainly not to convert into a de facto lame duck as some of my predecessors were.

Being ahead in a time when we had to make drastic changes with a Fiscal Oversight Board—the largest budget cuts ever while facing two debilitating natural disasters in the span of two weeks—was close to impossible. But here we were, and our internal polls confirmed what the public ones stated: *Quantitatively*, things were looking good, and we would soon give more evidence to support this general trend and feeling.

Thirty Days Prior: Fundamentals Were Strong

I began my budget address in June of 2019 by stating, "The exercise of governing effectively lies in leading and managing the state by listening to the will of the people. Such will require channeling in a budget that fulfills our island's objective of investing in initiatives that improve theobernay of life of our citizens and stimulate the highest level of economic development possible."

Figure 4. A few images from the budget presentation. Moving the message allowed for more people to come in and see it in person (Photo Credit: Magdiel Lugo).

For the first time in history, the delivery of the budget message occurred outside the halls of our legislature. Ponce Convention Center is on the south of the island and is in one of the biggest cities outside of San Juan. The objective was simple: To start moving these important messages outside of the traditional centers of power and make them more accessible to the people.

The budget message is similar in nature to a State of the Union address. In it, a governor can outline the actions he took during the prior fiscal year, the results that came out of that, and unveil the new budget priorities (Figure 4).

I was proud to show that even under terrible and challenging circumstances, we were able to come out on top.

We produced the lowest unemployment rates in the history of Puerto Rico at that point (Agencia EFE 2019). We had the biggest economic turnaround in thirteen years. We were able to downsize government and employee payroll by 20 percent (Cortes Chico 2018). We had enhanced the coffers of government from 350 million when I came in to 6.4 billion at that point. We had reduced crime rates to their lowest levels in history. We had positioned the pensions system in a place where we did not have to enact cuts after plenty of battles with the oversight board. For the first time in history, we reduced the debt. We had restructured and reduced it by six billion dollars (Bradford 2019). All while doing energy, education, healthcare, government, procurement, and labor reforms. Not to mention while facing two devastating hurricanes (Figure 5).

Not too shabby.

The fundamentals were not only good. They were actually *very* good. So, if I was ahead in the polls by a landslide a month prior to this announcement, surely this would only improve my stock. Or so

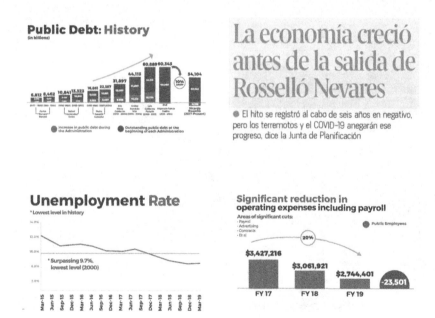

Figure 5. Highlights of some of the trends and actions, along with a headline stating the economy grew prior to my exit (*El Nuevo Día* 2019).

I thought. Yet, that same hubris blinded me to some signals of tension and uneasiness brewing below the surface. My takeaway: Even when things seem okay in the fundamentals, other things might be ready to blow up if you don't pay attention to them.

"Don't let your monkeys turn into gorillas," former congressman and author of *The Partisan Divide: Congress in Crisis* Tom Davis always reminds me. I have the privilege of working with him teaching a course at George Mason University. "It is better to tackle head on your problems when they are small than to let them get unmanageable."

In my case, a storm was brewing—one that would get out of hand. I was oblivious to it.

Arriving to a Two-Week Storm

After leaving my family on the Disney Cruise and flying for more than a day, I came in exhausted to meet the press. It was a huge deal with international press flying in as well. In one of the planes, someone took a picture with me and then published it to let people know when and where I was arriving. Of course, he did so with a few choice words.

This is when I started seeing things escalate. This is when I felt an anger that went beyond what I had experienced before. I have to admit, it shook me. For better or worse, just a few weeks back I was arguably in the best position I had been. The opposition was having a hard time articulating a message against our reforms, results, and vision.

Two competing issues were at hand provoking the political crisis. First, the aforementioned arrests. Second, an apparent chat communication I was part of. These conversations contained inappropriate language and poor taste that were later determined to be fabrications and manipulations (*more on this later*). However, at that point I was not aware of it. I recognized I had used language like that in the past, and so, I presumed them to be authentic. A local paper wrote on July 9, 2019: "Excerpts from the messages in which Rosselló Nevares and his trusted team appear to make fun of PPD President Aníbal José Torres, and the president of the Senate, Thomas Rivera Schatz, as well as the former secretary of justice, Wanda Vázquez Garced" (*Primera Hora* 2019).

At that point, it was only a few messages. One advisor told me, "If you don't know if this conversation is real, I recommend you don't accept it." Wise advice, but at that point two things were pulling me against it. First, I felt it to be disingenuous. I knew I probably had written some unflattering things. Saying otherwise felt like a copout. I could not do it. Second, and perhaps more predominantly, my hubris—again—would not allow it. I thought this was a minor setback, a mistake like many others. I presumed this was an unmodified and valid chat. I thought I should just admit it, take a hit, learn from it, and move forward.

I clearly underestimated the environment. Notwithstanding, I arrived, took a shower, and spoke to my press secretary.

"They are out for blood," said an advisor. "You can always cancel until tomorrow."

Hubris again, I said, "Let's go."

It was a marathon, one in which a shift occurred. The press went from being opponents of my administration to being activists against my persona. Even so, I was able to fend off questions for about two hours.

"I apologize for what I wrote in a private chat… I am the governor of Puerto Rico, but I am also a human being with my faults and virtues" (Figueroa 2019). Probably not the best way of stating my case.

The papers next day read, "Downcast and notably tired, Governor Ricardo Rosselló Nevares went to the country to give the first accountability after a skein of scandals emerged that lacerated the credibility of his administration and his moral image as governor and candidate for the next elections" (Figueroa 2019).

And although I took a big hit, the press conference seemed to have at least mitigated some of the escalation. And then it happened.

Pages and Pages of Texts

One day later, on the morning of July 13 at around 2 a.m., I receive a text: "Governor, 889 pages of the supposed chat have been released." Floodgates. I mean… wrath of Thanos type floodgates.

The next day it was all about the 889 pages. And the following… and then thereafter.

The storyline escalated quickly. Since everyone assumed everything that came out prior was authentic, so was this. The storm was about to swallow me whole and destroy my reputation in the process. I went from having the most open administration to women and the LGBTQ+ community to being misogynistic and homophobic in the span of a few seconds.

Death threats started to pour in by the hundreds. *Primera Hora's* headline on June 22 read "Another Death Threat for Rosselló." Bullets and rifles where stolen and someone left a message on a wall reminiscent of the Pablo Escobar sayings: Plata o Plomo (money or bullets).

I was okay with it, but it went beyond me. The threats now extended to my family, which still baffles me to this day. I mean, I made mistakes. They were mine—not theirs. This both angered and scared me. Yet I had to focus. My first course of action was to make sure my kids were safe. We took them off the island immediately along with my parents.

The next couple of days were tumultuous to say the least. Social uprising started. The beautiful streets of Old San Juan where vandalized. The mayor of San Juan, from the opposition party, said it was okay to do so. A few protesters engaged with the police. It was not a pretty sight. It ranged from spitting to throwing stones and other objects at them. It is important to state that these were the few. Some of these people had been protesting and destroying private property for years. The vast majority did not engage violently.

As commander in chief of the Police, I asked the force not to engage unless it was life threatening. On July 16, I had another long press conference. Emotions were flying high. Media members were pushing me and throwing things at me at my own house. One of them flipped the bird to my wife once she arrived.

"No point in doing any more press conferences," my press secretary told me. "They are just not listening."

Not listening was an understatement. They smelled blood and were on the hunt. They didn't fact check any story. Anything negative went forward—from interviews of alleged former friends I had little to no relationship with to allegations I had killed someone when I was thirteen years of age. Everything and anything they could say was amplified and used against the big bad villain.

All the while, I did see some of the texts—not all of them. And a few of them caught my attention.

To the Mountains for a Genuine Apology and Epiphany

On that same day the texts were released, I went to Lares, a town in the middle of the island known for agriculture, great folks, and the epicenter of an independence cry called "El Grito de Lares." People there are humble and hard-working. I went there because I received a text from a friend and legislator that read: "I can't believe you made fun of one of our beloved members of the youth."

The text showed I was joking around with his weight. I recognized it.

"He is one of your greatest supporters."

I felt like shit.

I managed to go to his house, which was a humbling experience. They received me in their home with a group of their family members. Their house was in a hardworking community dedicated to agriculture. They all had dejected looks when I came in. I felt the burn.

He told me how he had been struggling to lose weight. "It's always been an issue, even when I tried," he said. "It was very hurtful to see what you wrote."

I started crying. So did they.

I listened to their pain and thought, *I never want to make anyone feel this way ever again*. Not at the expense of a joke. Not anything. I knew I had to do some soul-searching. Suddenly, everything I faced seemed distant and unimportant. Getting him in a better state of mind was the only thing.

After an hour of catharsis, we engaged in other talk. I recall his dad saying, "This is bad. We all make mistakes." And then, he dropped the bomb on me. "But please, don't resign. You have been doing a wonderful job."

This is when it dawned on me. Resignation is a *real consideration*. Perhaps hubris was again steering me away from this understanding. Perhaps it was the fact that I'd had to battle many protests in my two and a half years. At that moment, I realized if others felt *half* as bad as the good people in Lares felt, emotions could run over and inhibit any chance at being an *effective* governor.

Meanwhile, the president of the House of Representatives was plotting a takedown. Johnny Méndez and Thomas Rivera Schatz (president of the Senate), members of my own party, had been a thorn in the administration's side from the get-go. Most recently, they'd attempted to pass a bill to limit reproductive rights of women, and I vetoed it. They only needed one vote to get over the veto, which left them with a sour taste in their mouth. But their continuous scheming and undercutting ways were nothing new, just something I had grown accustomed to. Méndez was a crony of the resident commissioner (Jenniffer Gonzalez). Rivera Schatz always felt he lost his opportunity to be governor when I decided to run. Both were integral parts of the status quo and heavily resistant to change.

Ivan Rivera, a well-respected lawyer and political commentator adds, "Thomas Rivera Schatz became accustomed in the four-year period from 2009 to 2013 to practically governing from the presidency of the Senate. During the time of Governor Fortuño, they took the position to avoid confrontation with him, so he granted all his requests and demands. During the governorship of Ricardo Rosselló he encountered plenty of resistance. That much is clear from the public record. On top of that, the PNP [New Progressive Party] base showed a strong inclination to support Ricardo Rosselló's positions on occasions when there were differences between him and Rivera Schatz. The numbers from polls demonstrated greater favor if the voter identified as a member of the PNP for Ricardo Rosselló than that shown for Rivera Schatz. Clearly this angered him, and he felt his own political survival, and therefore power, was at risk of disappearing."

"But why attack?" I asked Ivan.

"He reacted and acted like the wounded animal in the middle of the jungle."

The narrative elevated from a chat with foul-mouth language to one of corruption and crimes. Méndez decided to get a committee of *so-called renowned lawyers* to give him advice on the possible *crimes* committed in the chat. The issue being that all lawyers were from the opposition party. Not surprisingly, the lawyers determined there "was plenty of supporting evidence that I committed crimes." Nobody was in a mindset to counter that. They did not even have to show what that evidence was. At that point, they had established I was a criminal too.

Ramon Rosario, a member of my administration and implicated in the chat conversation remembers that "They went so far as to choose excerpts from it to say Rosselló was threatening Mayor Carmen Yulín and Police Monitor Arnaldo Claudio. The mercenary jurists appointed by the House Speaker Carlos 'Johnny' Méndez Núñez, concluded there was a possible commission of crimes, and the impeachment process for the governor should begin. A considerable amount of misinformation, lies, and demagogy occurred even by lawyers who know the law and gave their opinion knowing they were not telling the truth."

Ramon concludes, "For instance, I faced accusations from the police monitor claiming I harbored a political agenda. However, these statements had been part of my public discourse with the media for years. The question then arises: How could they construct expressing such views, already shared openly for an extended period as a crime?"

But it did not matter. This grew exponentially. Internationally, the story had begun to escalate, and by that point, my reputation shattered. For all intents and purposes, I was a corrupt, misogynistic, homophobic, dictator.

Within the overflow of commentary and innuendos, a group of lawyers came and said to me: "If you resign now, you will lose your leverage with these corruption allegations." This is something I presume other politicians who have stuck to their positions have feared.

I told them, "They are all *false*. I have no need to stay in a seat in power to demonstrate that."

Spoiler alert—a year and a half after I resigned, I received complete exoneration of any crime or intent of crime. It was all a power play on their part. It was all a sham. Period. (PR Newswire 2020). In fact, the investigation showed the 889 pages were *"not original and was modified"* (In Re, Ricardo Rosselló et al. 2020). In addition, the federal prosecutor's office dismissed one of the two arrests related to corruption that shocked my administration and initiated the summer of 2019 firestorm four years after the arrest (Kumneger Media 2023).

By mid-July, I could barely go back to La Fortaleza (the executive mansion) to sleep. Most days I would do so in the car. Well, sleep is an overstatement. I was taking fifteen-minute naps here and there. I was mentally and physically exhausted. I was emotionally drained. Protests outside were plentiful. On July 20, I started moving the pieces for my possible resignation.

To start laying the foundation, I announced on July 21, I would not seek reelection, the idea being the reduction of friction. It worked in quite the opposite way, sparking bigger protests. It became evident no rational process would tame things. I would either weather the storm and hold our government hostage in the meantime or resign and allow it to move on.

Having chosen the latter, internally, I had to start establishing a transition plan. Constitutionally, succession of power in Puerto Rico when the governor is not in office goes first to the secretary of state and then to the secretary of justice if there is no secretary of state. But because I had no secretary of state at that time. The succession plan was not evident. I also wanted to allow the government to move as effectively as possible. In October 2019, a poll showed that while I had an approval of barely double digits (11 percent), close to 60 percent of those polled supported my reforms and actions (Figure 6).

Apoyo a las reformas gubernamentales que está realizado el Gobernador Ricardo Rosselló

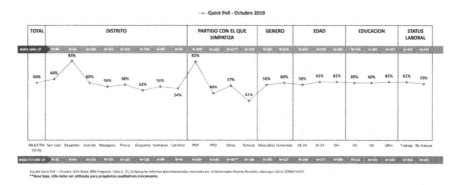

Evaluación del gobernador Ricardo Rosselló

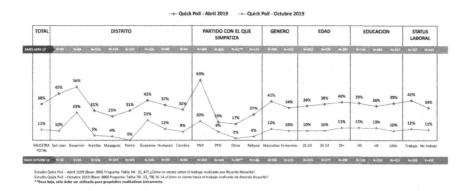

Figure 6. Internal poll numbers a few months after my resignation, showing low approval ratings but high support for my reforms.

This was intuitive to me. I knew people supported what I was doing, even though I had lost their support and trust. I did not, however, think the disparity would be as large. Almost *half* the population supported my reforms but did not support me. But still, qualitatively it was on my mind. So how was I to make a decision on this?

The solution was as evident as it was painful to me: I had to *remove myself from the equation.*

Solving this problem allowed me to somehow keep my emotions at bay. Feeling shattered, I would have time in the future to reminisce. But my internal programming to solve problems by design focuses on the big issue at hand. I could not allow instability and chaos to rule, creating a state of anarchy. However painful it could be—and it was—I needed to stay a bit longer to make sure the transition was effective. And that's what I did.

This was not easy, as the attacks were now filtering into my family. For example, when my wife and kids came back home the media published the flight and time of arrival in an effort to harass her.

On July 23, I announced I was "pondering and reflecting." On July 24, I announced my resignation. I made it effective August 2, so as to have time to reconcile with my team, establish a transition to the successor and allow the government to move forward.

A Few Days to Transition

Philippe Mesa remembers the final days. "Turmoil reigned in La Fortaleza. It was a very tough couple of weeks that drained everybody thoroughly. To me the worst was the internal enemies, who seemed to validate the politically motivated reasons for the protests."

Even with that, we kept on working.

"The last three weeks of July we worked nonstop," Philippe recalls. We had plenty of your reforms still shuffling over from the legislature — from procurement reform and the Freedom of Information Act, among others. Philippe paints a picture of what it was like those days: "It was hard to get to La Fortaleza and hard to leave because of the protests. I remember entering La Fortaleza through the governor's personal entrance, which protesters discovered and blocked that entrance and exit as well. I remember a Sunday in July, when protesters trapped us in La Fortaleza for more than eight hours by blocking all the exits. The only way we were able to exit the premises was closely following the police superintendent's convoy. This dangerous and complicated operation threatened the police officers who assisted us in exiting. Even though I was driving my own unmarked vehicle, protesters were throwing orange barrels at my car just because I was exiting La Fortaleza without knowing who I was. It was a very stressful time indeed."

Philippe continues, "For me it was surreal to be part of the team you tasked to brainstorm to see who they would appoint secretary of state, and therefore, the next governor. Even with that stress, the destruction of your reputation, and the threats to you and your family, you kept your cool and focus. I will never forget this."

So who did I pick? Remember Pedro Pierluisi? I made the decision to appoint him as secretary of state, thereby successor to the governorship. Although he was once a political opponent, I felt he had the qualities and qualifications to lead during this turbulent time. Unfortunately, the same folks who wanted me out avoided his confirmation. A year and a half of uninspiring and dysfunctional government ensued. This was the expectation. Interestingly, the people sided with my choice, as in November 2020, and they elected Pedro Pierluisi as governor on his own right. Full circle.

When I announced my resignation, I said, "I hope this decision serves as a much-needed call for citizen reconciliation to move forward with the well-being of Puerto Rico as our goal. My mandate is over, and the most I wish for is peace and progress for our people.

"Transformation and progress do not link to a single person. It is the product of the united work of a people. That was my goal with the Plan for Puerto Rico, which was my goal as governor, which will continue to be my slogan for the future.

"May the unified strength of the people channel into constructive energy. May law, order, and progress be an essential part of that recipe, that we choose to create and build institutions that respond to the people, and do not produce chaos and misgovernment.

"Thank you for the privilege of allowing me to serve you. It has been the greatest honor for me and my family.

"God protect Puerto Rico!"

And so, with that warning, I focused on the transition. As Philippe mentioned, it was surreal. Let's just say it made *House of Cards* look like a children's book. But… that's a story for another time.

Aftermath

I was the main target of the summer of 2019. I was not the only one. It affected the lives of others implicated in the chat as well. Secretary of Public Affairs Ramon Rosario was one of them. I asked him to reflect on that time:

"The summer of 2019 was a complicated stage for those involved. The number of falsehoods told is incalculable. Personally, I was at the crossroads of whether to go to the media to explain the falsehoods or wait for the investigative procedures to conclude and the truth to come out. So I decided to let the process run because the atmosphere was such that demagogues would have said I wanted to interfere with the investigation. In the end, the truth came out. The person who published the chat admitted he altered it. And no crime was committed contrary to what they tried to sell for more than two years." The issue of how things can escalate out of control will be one we dive into in this book. Otherism becomes such a strong force that the truth seldom matters, and narrative dictates where things go.

The effects are long lasting, if not permanent. "The lies and falsehoods have lasted for too long." Ramon continues, "Attacking many of us is their norm. Meanwhile, after all of the turmoil and smoke, Ricardo Rosselló was elected a congressional delegate, making him the only candidate elected in the history of Puerto Rico by direct nomination (write-in). Today everyone assumes that if he returns to politics, the members of his party would comfortably elect him."

The Vulnerability of a Mandate

I went from the very top to rock bottom in a matter of weeks. I went from being a sure thing to be reelected governor to scavenging my way from apartments to apartments in the first three months after my administration ended with no job, few savings, and figuring out a way to keep my family safe and at peace. I had the blessing of a strong family core. My wife was my rock. My parents, my uncles, and my in-laws (Carmen and Tito) were a bedrock of support. My kids were an ever-present motivation. Notwithstanding, it was a rough time.

Understanding that a democratic mandate can end very quickly and violently is a fundamental takeaway here. Mandates are vulnerable, especially to social uprising and traps set by political opponents. When used adequately, social uprisings can be a powerful tool of democracy, allowing people to express themselves and embody a petition to their leadership. Abused, social uprising can hinder progress completely and allow fringe minority groups to rule, therefore destroying democracy. It can allow rogue players to rally an aggregated opposition.

This was just a high-level description of the last ten weeks of my administration. Scattered throughout this book, I will share stories about this fateful process, where I recognize my mistakes and have hoped to learn from them. However, it is more than just that. It is also about the parts, which were *not* mistakes but were portrayed as such and utilized against me and others. They branded me as corrupt, an assassin, and someone who did not care for the people of Puerto Rico. All of these I vehemently reject, and later, all were proven false.

But it did not matter. The ends justify the means. With so much polarization, low tolerance, and vilification of public authorities… can democratic governments survive?

CHAPTER 5:

#DecolonizeThisPlace

This illustration depicts my hands (as identified by my logo) attempting to extract the "DNA" from Tennessee, which pioneered the famed Tennessee Plan, pressuring Congress to change their status from a territory to a full state (Bayon 2017).

"Whether we like it or not, it is gut check time for America. It is the time for us to define what we want to be in the future. Do we want to be the standard bearer of democracy in the world, nor do we want to have hiccups in our backyard, where 3.5 million US citizens chose not once, but twice that we want to become a state... and nothing has happened."

—RICARDO ROSSELLÓ AT THE 109TH ANNUAL NAACP CONVENTION (ANTHONY 2018).

And still... not much has changed (Figure 1).

In the library study of La Fortaleza, a quaint corner of the executive mansion overlooking the bay, the light danced through a mosaic of colored crystals in the window. The stunning contrast of the beautiful ocean view against the path of devastation left by Hurricane Maria was striking. That day,

Figure 1. Delivering a speech at the National Association for the Advancement of Colored People on the unequal treatment of the people of Puerto Rico. This event bolstered our claim (Photo Credit: Magdiel Lugo).

two senators from Connecticut, Chris Murphy and Richard Blumenthal accompanied me (Stacom 2018). They were among more than a dozen congressional delegates visiting the island in the weeks following the hurricane, each pledging their support for Puerto Rico.

In a sudden shift, Murphy's tone changed from empathetic concern to urgent necessity. He addressed the energy crisis on the island. "It's been more than a month, and the vast majority of people still don't have power."

I nodded in agreement.

"In my state, a week without power would cause an uproar. I commend your people for their resilience," he said.

This observation was telling. In any other part of the nation, a crisis like Maria would demand swift resolution. Implicit in this was a stark disparity, highlighting Puerto Rico's unequal status.

After a brief pause, I responded, "Yes, Senator, our people are resilient. But why should this be the norm? The bottom line is we receive different treatment. We are second-class citizens without a representative in Congress to advocate for us and prompt urgent action."

"Absolutely, we want to do everything we can to help," Congressman Murphy replied.

"Then I ask you to commit to ending colonialism and support a path to statehood."

Both senators responded similarly: "We will support whatever Puerto Rico decides."

The irony here is Puerto Rico had already decided. In the last decade, our people have voted for statehood three times, yet significant action remains elusive (Congressional Research Service 2022).

It's crucial to acknowledge the collaborative efforts and citizen engagement, such as the extended delegates (delegates.us), which led to the passage of a bill in the federal House of Representatives (HR. 8393) at the end of 2022. However, in a familiar pattern, after considerable effort, the bill was reviewed at the eleventh hour of Congress and lacked sufficient time for Senate consideration. Thus, the process begins anew...

The pressing question for anyone reading this is: How are we still here? How does the largest democracy in the world continue to govern the oldest and most populous colonial territory?

Powerlessness

We all feel powerless at some point, wanting to do something and simply having no ultimate say on a matter. It's no different in policy making. There is always a trump card. In my case, I had to face several. One was systemic. Puerto Rico is a colonial territory and therefore lacks political participation on equal footing with other US citizens. It is like starting a race while tied to a five-hundred-pound boulder.

The others were manifestations of this reality. On the one hand, Puerto Rico was under the guise of a Fiscal Oversight Board—a complete contradiction of democratic principles. And while, yes, oversight boards have happened in places within the US, like New York City, they have had the power of the vote to change their fortunes and the direction of government. We don't have that luxury. The US government imposed a Fiscal Oversight Board on Puerto Rico, and we have *no* input on the matter. Period.

On the other hand, when Hurricane Maria blasted through the island, shuttles of congressmembers came by the island. One of those was Senator Marco Rubio.

He made a direct appeal to the White House, seven days after the storm. "The challenges are extraordinary and they will take a much more aggressive federal reaction than we would traditionally see to turn the corner" (King 2017).

A few weeks later, he would go on to state that "Congress isn't doing enough to help Puerto Rico" (Daugherty 2017). Although he was talking about the hurricane, it would become painfully obvious it went beyond that.

Late December 2017, three months after the hurricane had devastated the island, there was an opportunity to help Puerto Rico within the context of the Tax Cuts and Jobs Act. The objective of the law, as per the president's own message was to "create American jobs." To achieve this, impose higher thresholds on companies in foreign soil. Guess who's foreign for tax purposes? You got it. Puerto Rico.

Several news outlets caught wind of this and started publishing articles. *The Washington Post* ran an editorial subscribed by their editorial board, which said in part, "The supposed goal is to protect and create American jobs, but, as Puerto Rico Gov. Ricardo Rosselló told us, it would actually kill American jobs in Puerto Rico, devastating an already struggling economy. "Unconscionable," he said of the proposals, pointing out how members of Congress have traveled to Puerto Rico, seen the catastrophic damage, and promised help. "True hypocrisy" (*Editorial Board* 2017)

The title of the editorial was "Congress Should Help Puerto Rico—Not Hurt It" (2017). It is a recurring theme.

THE TASK FORCE MAKES THE FOLLOWING RECOMMENDATIONS:

The Task Force believes that Puerto Rico is too often relegated to an afterthought in congressional deliberations over federal business tax reform legislation. The Task Force recommends that Congress make Puerto Rico integral to any future deliberations over tax reform legislation.

The Task Force recommends that Congress continue to be mindful of the fact that Puerto Rico and the other territories are U.S. jurisdictions, home to U.S. citizens or nationals, and that jobs in Puerto Rico and the other territories are American jobs.

The Task Force is open to the prospect of Congress providing U.S. companies that invest in Puerto Rico with more competitive tax treatment as long as appropriate guardrails are designed to ensure the company is creating real economic activity and employment on the island.

Figure 2. Slide from a presentation I made to the local legislature on the task force recommendations as they pertained to the tax reform that would pass Congress.

This bill went against everything most congressmembers were saying, claiming in the greatest time of need they would support the island. The bill also went against the Whitehouse's task force on Puerto Rico. The president's task force on Puerto Rico's status was a body of advisors created in 2000 to provide options for Puerto Rico's future political status, economics, and relationship with the United States. A summary of the findings of the 2017 Task Force is below (Figure 2).

If this bill passed and kept Puerto Rico as foreign for tax purposes, it would impact 20–25 percent of our budget, and precipitate job loss. The vote tally was tight. One of the key members who was undecided or had expressed objection to the Republican-backed tax bill was Senator Marco Rubio.

Luckily, I surmised, there was a solution to this problem. Add a sentence that says, "For the purposes of corporate tax, treat Puerto Rico as domestic." That's all that needed adding. No other changes, no exceptions, no complicated formulas.

I sat down with Senator Rubio in his office to discuss this issue. He was very clear.

"I will not support the bill unless it has the provision for Puerto Rico." This prospect excited us. Carlos Mercader was with me in those encounters. It was a late afternoon meeting. We sat down and he told the governor directly "I am going to make sure this language for Puerto Rico is there." Referring to the disposition to treat Puerto Rico as domestic. He did not stop there. He told the governor, "I am going to let you know how it's going." Rubio and the governor had already exchanged texts. Not many, but some. Senator Rubio said at the end of the meeting, "You have my word."

Leaving the office, I felt optimistic. I sent the senator messages throughout the night as things started moving in the Senate.

Mercader remembers the next morning the governor said, "Carlos, can you call Marco. He has not responded." I called. All of a sudden, bills come out. The language was not there. The senator never called us (Figure 3).

Figure 3. Speaking to Senator Rubio on the days before the vote for the federal tax reform (Photo Credit: Magdiel Lugo).

His colleagues went to negotiate with him. He held possibly one of the key votes to pass the bill. The negotiation occurred late at night, and he ended up negotiating for child tax credit—but not for Puerto Rico.

"The governor was irate. He lambasted Rubio after that," Mercader recalls.

I told the Miami Herald I was "very disappointed with the fact the Senator Rubio is going to be voting for this tax bill particularly when we had the opportunity to address the potentially devastating effects on Puerto Rico."

Rubio told *Politico* magazine my remarks surprised him because he helped Puerto Rico defeat a "truly devastating" measure in the bill (Caputo 2017).

For Senator Rubio, losing what could amount anywhere from 25–30 percent of our budget, after a devastating once in a half-millennium hurricane, with a Fiscal Oversight Board… was not "truly devastating." Ask yourselves if this had happened in Florida, would his response have been the same?

He also fired back at me: "I find it disappointing. He knows better than anyone how much we have done before, during, and after the storm."

What he had done? Stand in on press conferences and write letters. When it came to taking actions—absolutely nothing. "*A paper champion*" one of my staffers called him. Worst of all was his "*about-face*" on the whole issue.

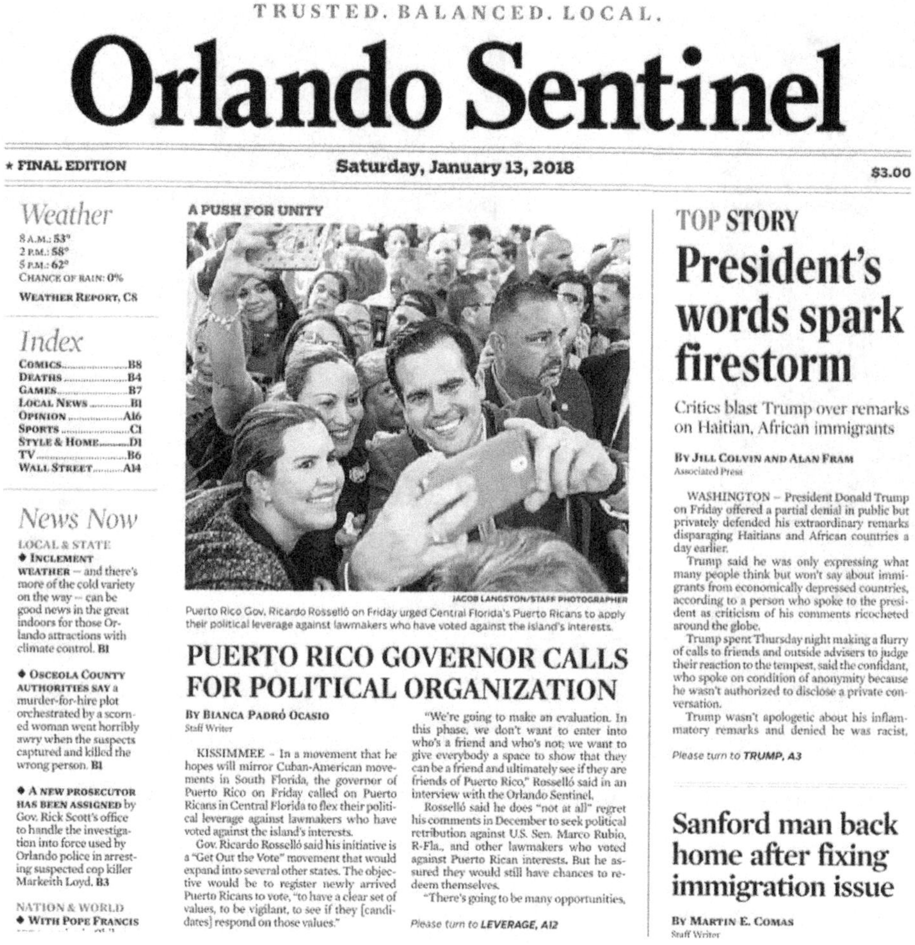

TRUSTED. BALANCED. LOCAL.

Orlando Sentinel

★ FINAL EDITION | Saturday, January 13, 2018 | $3.00

Weather

8 A.M.: 53°
2 P.M.: 58°
5 P.M.: 62°
CHANCE OF RAIN: 0%

WEATHER REPORT, C8

Index

COMICS B8
DEATHS B4
GAMES B7
LOCAL NEWS B1
OPINION A16
SPORTS C1
STYLE & HOME D1
TV B6
WALL STREET A14

News Now

LOCAL & STATE

◆ **INCLEMENT WEATHER** — and there's more of the cold variety on the way — can be good news in the great indoors for those Orlando attractions with climate control. **B1**

◆ **OSCEOLA COUNTY AUTHORITIES SAY** a murder-for-hire plot orchestrated by a scorned woman went horribly awry when the suspects captured and killed the wrong person. **B1**

◆ **A NEW PROSECUTOR HAS BEEN ASSIGNED** by Gov. Rick Scott's office to handle the investigation into force used by Orlando police in arresting suspected cop killer Markeith Loyd. **B3**

NATION & WORLD

◆ **WITH POPE FRANCIS**

A PUSH FOR UNITY

JACOB LANGSTON/STAFF PHOTOGRAPHER

Puerto Rico Gov. Ricardo Rosselló on Friday urged Central Florida's Puerto Ricans to apply their political leverage against lawmakers who have voted against the island's interests.

PUERTO RICO GOVERNOR CALLS FOR POLITICAL ORGANIZATION

BY BIANCA PADRÓ OCASIO
Staff Writer

KISSIMMEE – In a movement that he hopes will mirror Cuban-American movements in South Florida, the governor of Puerto Rico on Friday called on Puerto Ricans in Central Florida to flex their political leverage against lawmakers who have voted against the island's interests.

Gov. Ricardo Rosselló said his initiative is a "Get Out the Vote" movement that would expand into several other states. The objective would be to register newly arrived Puerto Ricans to vote, "to have a clear set of values, to be vigilant, to see if they [candidates] respond on those values."

"We're going to make an evaluation. In this phase, we don't want to enter into who's a friend and who's not; we want to give everybody a space to show that they can be a friend and ultimately see if they are friends of Puerto Rico," Rosselló said in an interview with the Orlando Sentinel.

Rosselló said he does "not at all" regret his comments in December to seek political retribution against U.S. Sen. Marco Rubio, R-Fla., and other lawmakers who voted against Puerto Rican interests. But he assured they would still have chances to redeem themselves.

"There's going to be many opportunities,

Please turn to **LEVERAGE, A12**

TOP STORY

President's words spark firestorm

Critics blast Trump over remarks on Haitian, African immigrants

BY JILL COLVIN AND ALAN FRAM
Associated Press

WASHINGTON – President Donald Trump on Friday offered a partial denial in public but privately defended his extraordinary remarks disparaging Haitians and African countries a day earlier.

Trump said he was only expressing what many people think but won't say about immigrants from economically depressed countries, according to a person who spoke to the president as criticism of his comments ricocheted around the globe.

Trump spent Thursday night making a flurry of calls to friends and outside advisers to judge their reaction to the tempest, said the confidant, who spoke on condition of anonymity because he wasn't authorized to disclose a private conversation.

Trump wasn't apologetic about his inflammatory remarks and denied he was racist,

Please turn to **TRUMP, A3**

Sanford man back home after fixing immigration issue

BY MARTIN E. COMAS
Staff Writer

Figure 4. Cover of the *Orlando Sentinel*, in which I call for the political organization of Puerto Ricans in the states (Padro Ocasio 2018).

In a press event, I said, "My message was not directed at Rubio. He has opened his doors for us in the past. My disappointment was at that vote. In the larger picture there's going to be an aftermath… We will evaluate those who gave the good fight for people of Puerto Rico and those that didn't, who in our greatest time of need either didn't do anything or actually took decisions that hurt Puerto Rico" (Caputo 2017).

It was a bit of an angry response, but it opened the door to a key idea: Create pressure on Congress with the 5.6 million Puerto Ricans who live in the states. They do, in fact, have the right to vote. It was a half-baked idea at the time with my administration. I did some work, but the well-being of the people of Puerto Rico, the pensions, the hurricane, social unrest, reform, oversight board, bondholders… all drew attention away from it (Figure 4).

But now, I am fully employing it as Puerto Rico's elected shadow congressman. And this has allowed us to gain some traction in Congress. Without knowing it, these seeds started turning powerlessness into power later… stay tuned (Figure 5).

Figure 5. Congressmembers on the island visiting after the devastation of Maria.

The take-home message, however, is clear.

- Even at the moment of greatest need for the island, when everyone's eyes were on Puerto Rico because of the storm and it's devastating toll.
- Even after dozens upon dozens of congressmembers came and paraded down to Puerto Rico to take pictures among the people.
- Even after they all pledged they would support us after the debacle…

That *still* was not enough to get a simple provision into a bill that would avoid a catastrophe for the economy of the island, which was one vote away from securing it.

My friends, this is the definition of *powerlessness*.

Invisibility

Ask yourself: Did you know Puerto Rico was part of the United States before Hurricane Maria in 2017? Surprisingly, as late as 2015, only about 30–40 percent of mainland US residents were aware that Puerto Ricans were US citizens.

And we have been part of the United States for more than a century...

How can we amplify this issue's visibility? Is it even feasible?

At the time of writing this book, the US was grappling with the protection of voting rights. Yet, the bill in question had a significant limitation. This is a classic example of legislation that appears to have a clear objective but, upon closer inspection, fails to meet it and, in many cases, contradicts it. The devil is in the details.

A few days after the anniversary of the Capitol Hill insurrection, Vice President Kamala Harris spoke about her priorities. She emphasized the need for a voting rights bill to "guarantee the freedom and right of every American, to have access to the ballot, to be able to vote" (Harris 2022). This came in the wake of several groups being denied voting rights in various states, casting doubt on the integrity of the democratic process.

When the vice president uses the term "all Americans" (as many voting rights advocates do), it begs the question: Does this include Americans in Puerto Rico and the District of Columbia? We have no reason to believe it doesn't. Otherwise, it would be a completely different discussion.

Assuming it does, why then are Puerto Rico and Washington, DC, not included in a broader plan to protect voting rights for all Americans?

The reason is they render Puerto Rico invisible in terms of national agenda issues.

Both Puerto Rico and DC suffer from geographic discrimination. Their residents are US citizens, yet they lack the right to vote for congressional representation with voice and vote. In Puerto Rico's case, the US deprives us of the right to vote for the president.

What greater violation of voting rights can there be than completely denying the right to vote to an American residing in the District of Columbia or Puerto Rico? The disenfranchisement faced by groups in states is equally applicable to *all citizens* in these two jurisdictions.

House Majority Leader Steny Hoyer stated his intention to find a consensus bill. In November 2021, I wrote to the leader discussing this possibility (NotiCel 2021), specifically, allowing the people of Puerto Rico to choose between viable alternatives. The extended delegation for Puerto Rico worked tirelessly. Against all odds, we finally reached a consensus.

Yet it was an arduous journey to even bring the bill to the House floor. I believe our success was due to a confluence of factors, including Puerto Ricans in the states organizing to advocate for a resolution to the status issue. Once congressmembers realized this issue was resonating with their constituents, perspectives shifted. Ideally, the threat of losing voter support shouldn't influence policy, but this is the harsh reality. We must leverage this approach moving forward.

In this endeavor, I remembered what I told Senator Rubio years ago. I organized extended delegates from all fifty states, united by a common mission. We have grown to more than twelve thousand members (Perez 2023). Our primary goal is to exert political pressure on Congress to initiate a federally mandated process to eliminate colonialism.

Taking it a step further, given the current historical context, why not strengthen the voting rights issue by including these two marginalized jurisdictions, where minorities are the majority (Puerto Rico >98 percent Latino, DC> 44 percent African American) (World Population Review 2023)?

If a bill passes Congress defending the rights of minority groups within states, it would still be incomplete, excluding more than four million US citizens in these two jurisdictions. How can we celebrate a voting rights initiative that, by design, perpetuates legal discrimination against a population larger than 1 percent of the total US population?

There is an opportunity to build a more compelling case for voting rights while advocating for equality for two communities seeking statehood. Otherwise, when we talk about voting rights for all Americans, we are blatantly discriminating against Latinos and African Americans, perpetuating the worst possible treatment for these populations: invisibility and powerlessness.

And as if that weren't enough, powerlessness and invisibility have allies with powerful interests...

Status Quo Interests

Opening scene:

Picture a young girl in her school outfit.

That girl can be anyone's daughter.

She's singing the Puerto Rican national anthem with a small flag.

As she concludes, someone shuts her off with a tag on her mouth that says, *"English only."*

The ad ends by saying, "Bear the consequences."

As with all colonial regimes, a status quo element stands to benefit from the antiquated system. Those are the established families—much like in oligarchies—who retain control. These, along with deep economically rooted interests have hindered the path forward out of the colonial territory.

They use fear tactics to control the narrative and the votes. This ad was telling Puerto Ricans if they voted for statehood... they would not be able to speak Spanish.

This might seem like a ridiculous claim—and it is. Consider that today the US is the second-largest Spanish speaking nation in the world (only behind Mexico) (Thompson 2021). And if you happen to go to South Beach Florida, you will be hard-pressed to find anything in English—*¡Se habla español!*

But back in the 1990s, that fear carried a lot of weight. Many people bought it. So the colonial regime survived.

Today, a similar fearmongering campaign is rising. This time, they know they can't propagate the same lies within the island as before. The internet had a lot to do with giving visibility to these arguments. But they *still* do so within Congress. Here are some of the false narratives.

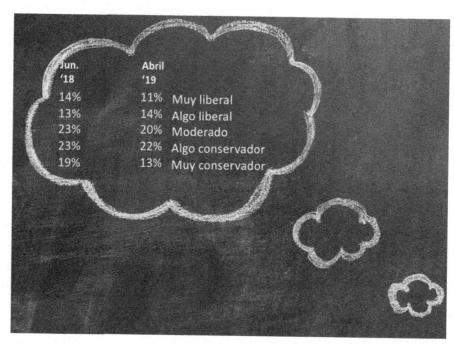

Jun. '18	Abril '19	
14%	11%	Muy liberal
13%	14%	Algo liberal
23%	20%	Moderado
23%	22%	Algo conservador
19%	13%	Muy conservador

Figure 6. Internal poll showcasing the distribution of liberal versus conservatives in Puerto Rico. Numbers denote a notable majority as conservative, defeating the conventional wisdom (Internal Poll 2019).

False narrative #1: Puerto Ricans want independence.

The truth of the matter is Puerto Rico has never had an independence movement that reaches the double digits. Yet for some reason, the national narrative is that too many Puerto Ricans *want* independence. Some influential people at the national level along with key members of the press have *generated* this story. Yet just by comparing polls, there is a larger independence movement in Texas, and other states for that matter, than in Puerto Rico (Failla 2021). Puerto Ricans who support independence have *always* been in single digits.

False narrative #2: Puerto Rico will be a Democratic state.

This is highly speculative. In my view, Puerto Rico would be a battle ground state. In the political spectrum, the island's residents seem to have a slightly more conservative view. Here is the breakdown from one of the final polls I commissioned in 2019. Conservative incline outpaced liberal by ten points. As I was revising this book, a new poll came out (October 19, 2023) by NotiCel that had 35.7 percent identifying as right and 10.1 percent as left. The gap has grown. In places like Florida, Puerto Ricans voted for the Republican candidates 55 to 45 percent (Sesin 2022) Figure 6.

False narrative #3: Puerto Rico will take away congressmembers from your state.

This is, of course, one of the most potent arguments toward keeping things as they are. The fear of losing a congressional seat. The argument goes: "If you give Puerto Rico statehood, they will get five

DC statehood

	Strongly support	Somewhat support	Somewhat oppose	Strongly oppose	Not sure
Pennsylvania	28	11	26	7	27
North Carolina	25	14	25	9	27
Michigan	25	13	27	7	27
Maine	26	16	26	11	22
Iowa	27	10	28	8	27
Florida	26	17	22	8	27

Puerto Rico statehood

	Strongly support	Somewhat support	Somewhat oppose	Strongly oppose	Not sure
Pennsylvania	37	19	20	7	17
North Carolina	32	20	19	10	18
Michigan	32	17	23	11	18
Maine	33	23	19	10	16
Iowa	33	19	21	9	17
Florida	34	22	17	7	19

YouGov Blue

Strongly support · Somewhat support · Not sure · Somewhat oppose · Strongly oppose

DATA FOR **PROGRESS**

Figure 7. One of many polls showcasing support of US citizens in the mainland for statehood for Puerto Rico (McElwee and Ray 2020).

congressional members, that will come out of other states." This is also false. Others established the way to work this out in the past. As Puerto Rico transitions into a state, they will get one delegate with a vote (for some years), and then the total number of congressmembers will augment. So if it is 435 today, it would augment to 440.

False narrative #4: US citizens don't want statehood for Puerto Rico.
Another completely unsubstantiated claim. As a matter-of-fact, most polls show almost two to one in favor of Puerto Rican statehood (McElwee and Ray 2020) Figure 7.

Migration Is Killing the Island:
Opening scene: Picture a young woman. She is sad. She is packing her bags and heading to the airport with her parents and daughter.

The sadness and pain filter through the TV screen.

Families separate because she is leaving Puerto Rico in search of opportunities in the states.

It was my most powerful ad in the campaign. It connected because it is a real and deep-rooted problem in Puerto Rico—the separation of families, the abandonment of talent, and the pain that goes along with that.

While it was an ad, this was happening to thousands of families across the island daily.

Andrew Van Dam of the *Washington Post* started his compelling article from September 2022 with this comment: "For much of the postwar era, America's territories thrived. Remnants of the age of

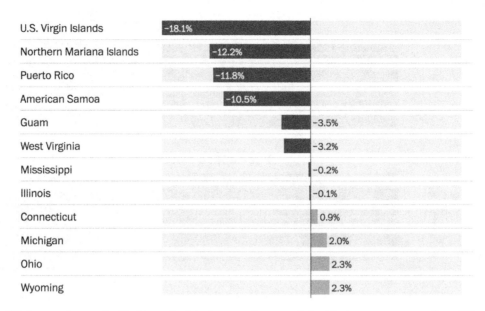

U.S. Virgin Islands	−18.1%
Northern Mariana Islands	−12.2%
Puerto Rico	−11.8%
American Samoa	−10.5%
Guam	−3.5%
West Virginia	−3.2%
Mississippi	−0.2%
Illinois	−0.1%
Connecticut	0.9%
Michigan	2.0%
Ohio	2.3%
Wyoming	2.3%

Figure 8. US Census data embedded into the *Washington Post* article highlighting migration from US territories (Van Dam 2022).

imperialism, the five far-flung Caribbean and Pacific outposts added residents faster than most states. But the 2020 Census revealed a troubling turn: Every territory is now shrinking, losing population faster than any state" (2022).

It is staggering (Figure 8).

"The largest US territory, Puerto Rico, has 3.3 million people and Spanish and West Indian traditions tracing back to Columbus. The nearby US Virgin Islands (population 87,000) were previously settled by Denmark. Over in the Pacific between Japan and Australia, Guam (population 154,000) and the Northern Mariana Islands (pop. 47,000) share Chamorro heritage and tourist economies oriented toward East Asia. And American Samoa (population 50,000), in the heart of Polynesia, still employs a communal system of land ownership and lies closer to New Zealand than Hawaii. One big thing unites them: US rule" (Van Dam 2022).

US *colonial* rule, I would add.

In addition, the migration patterns from Puerto Rico are *not* to other countries but rather to other states. More than 98 percent of these are going to the states. In the past it was highly focused on the Northeast. Now it's scattered, with Florida leading the way.

Why are they doing it?

Research we aggregated found the quality-of-life parameters were staggeringly different for those living on the island than those living in the states (Rosselló 2012). In short order, they earned more than twice as much, their surroundings were five times more secure, their kids' educational outcomes improved several fold, and the access to healthcare was superior. Not to mention the workforce participation rate increased a whopping 30 percent when compared to the island.

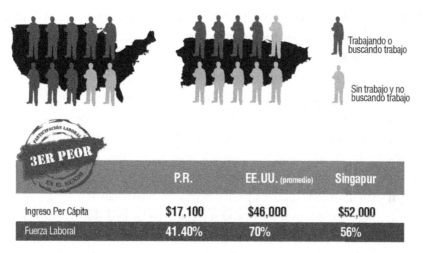

¿Cuántos trabajamos?

	P.R.	EE.UU. (promedio)	Singapur
Ingreso Per Cápita	$17,100	$46,000	$52,000
Fuerza Laboral	41.40%	70%	56%

Trabajando o buscando trabajo

Sin trabajo y no buscando trabajo

3ER PEOR

Figure 9. Data showing some of the most troublesome facts about the labor participation rate on the island. In 2012, Puerto Rico had the third worst labor participation rate in the world (Rosselló 2012).

Maver Rivas, one of our founding extended delegate members, recalls the painful moment she had to decide to leave the island she loved. "We decided to leave in search of better job opportunities, quality of life, and a good educational system for our son. Paying for private school and the high cost of electricity consumed almost half of my salary. Even though we are young professionals and educated, the pay on the island is not substantial. I tried to get a better salary, and I only got offers with better titles but without a salary increase. In the end we took a chance, not knowing the area, and made Pennsylvania our new home. In one month, we had a job doubling the salary we received on the island."

This could be any one of thousands of Puerto Ricans who have left their homes. And like them, there is the clash of logic versus heart. "We have prospered in Pennsylvania, but I don't deny our hearts are still 1,706 miles away."

Recall the ad a few paragraphs above? That was Maver.

Goes to show that colonialism has its root cause problems, such as powerlessness, invisibility, and oppression. But that quickly turns into pragmatic realities, such as poverty, lack of opportunities, crime, and massive migration. How do we add visibility to this unfortunate reality? (Figure 9)

Decolonize This Place Movements

Museums play a pivotal role in storytelling, using objects to connect visitors with unfolding narratives. The decolonize the museum movement aims to identify biased, overlooked, or erased stories due to a singular perspective, often that of the victor.

Over the past seventy years, the world has witnessed the rejection and formal eradication of colonialism. Yet a gap remains between formal decolonization and the persistence of neocolonialism. Addressing this gap, a global movement to decolonize museums has emerged, defined as "a process that institutions undergo to expand the perspectives they portray beyond those of the dominant cultural group, particularly white colonizers" (Hatzipanagos 2018).

Culturally, this shift involves moving away from the traditional focus on "dead white men" in school curricula and advocating for the recognition and inclusion of cultural artifacts and expressions from previously oppressed, invisible, and "primitive" groups.

"Can you decolonize a museum within a colonial territory? Puerto Rico is a black hole in decolonization efforts. The island presents a unique case for examining the limits of the current decolonization movement for several reasons," states Beatriz Areizaga, former first lady and a museum and curatorial graduate from Georgetown University. "The colonial situation in Puerto Rico offers a distinctive opportunity. It acts as a concrete example of modern-day colonialism that has remained largely invisible and continues to have detrimental effects on its residents. Bringing Puerto Rico's situation into international discourse could pave the way for meaningful action."

If our goal is to decolonize the mind, spirit, and soul, can the United States justify holding a colonial possession? The answer is unequivocally no.

This is where the newly established congressional delegation in Puerto Rico becomes relevant…

A Shadow Delegation

Don't call the Rev. *Jesse Jackson* a *"shadow senator."* *"That's not the title,"* he protests. *"It's United States senator from Washington"* (Berke 1991).

Bravo, Mr. Senator.

The concept of shadow delegation comes from the British implementation of a "Shadow Cabinet" (UK Parliament 2023). The idea behind it is quite simple: The shadow cabinet is the team of senior spokespeople chosen by the leader of the opposition to mirror the cabinet in government.

In 1796, the territory of Tennessee had petitioned on several occasions for admittance as a state of the nation. Congress was ignoring the petition—something I fully comprehend as a Puerto Rican. So, what did they do? They took action. Tennessee self-organized, selected their congressional delegation— and sent them to the capital as a means of highlighting their cause and provoking the crisis that would allow for a resolution.

Ballsy.

And it worked.

Following the tradition established by Tennessee in 1796, Puerto Rico embarked on an effort to send a shadow delegation to Congress. Seven states utilized this strategy that had petitioned statehood, but action had not been forthcoming. These were Michigan, Iowa, California, Oregon, Kansas, and most recently, Alaska. Currently, Washington, DC, has a shadow delegation as well. Jesse Jackson being the first senator.

In 2017, as a programmatic commitment of the Plan for Puerto Rico, I put forth the legislation to create our shadow delegation (Puerto Rico Statehood Commission, Act 30-2017). That delegation was composed of two senators and five representatives. Among them, I appointed three former governors to serve as shadow delegates.

Figure 10. Picture of organically generated art that inspired the write-in movement for my candidacy as a congressional delegate (Photo Credit: Marybell Rivera).

That was only a first step. To give more power to the commission, we needed an election. We had prescribed this while I was in office, effectuating a year and a half after I resigned. Little did I know, this cause and the mechanism I created would suddenly, and unexpectedly, come back squarely into my life.

Write-In and the Birth of a Congressional Delegation

"If you accept the nomination, they will bury you forever. You need to say no or say nothing about it. Write-ins never win, and you'll go down with it" one political operative who works in the media told me.

"The party will never have it. Think about it, should you win, that means their candidacies are *never* going to be safe. It means someone can come last second on a write-in candidacy and displace them or take votes away from them," another friend told me.

They were talking about a mounting wave of support for a movement that proposed my candidacy for congressional delegate of Puerto Rico. They had websites. They passed handouts. They made murals. (Figure 10)

I sat and watched, inspired and grateful, but I never really considered the actual possibility of this panning out. I had to say it was quite a turn from what had happened just under two years prior.

"Ricardo, what are you going to do?" Beatriz asked me a week before the special election. She had gone to the island a few weeks before and met with people pushing the write-in movement. Beatriz kept visiting Puerto Rico to meet with family, key statehood leaders, and communities she passionately worked to help.

el Vocero
de Puerto Rico

> LUNES, 17 DE MAYO DE 2021 >NUM 14342 >SAN JUAN, PUERTO RICO • WWW.ELVOCERO.COM

La verdad no tiene precio

RICARDO ROSSELLÓ EL MÁS VOTADO

➤ El exgobernador recibe miles de votos en la elección especial para seleccionar a los delegados que abogarán por la estadidad en Washington. >P3/6

Figure 11. Cover from *El Vocero*, a local newspaper, denoting voters elected me by receiving thousands of votes by way of write-in (2021).

"Write-in votes have never materialized. It's great to see the support, but to expect people to go out and do it is a little too much," I said. Mind you, I had not gone back to the island since I resigned on August 2, 2019. My focus was elsewhere, namely making sure I could support my family and grow professionally.

"Well, one way or another, you need to tell your supporters something. They deserve that, even if some are not expecting it," she responded.

As usual, she was right. A few days before the special election I received an invitation to go on a radio program (NotiUno 2021). The host asked me: "Would you accept a direct nomination."

I replied, "I will not reject it. If that is the will of the people, I will go forward."

That set in motion a series of events in the final days before the election. People did not know how to vote for me; whether they had to mark the ballot for me on the Senate side or the House side. Others were telling people they could not reelect me because I was no longer a resident of Puerto Rico though the law stated otherwise.

Why did I do it?

Because it is a *passion*. Because it is a *cause* I feel I highly identified with. Because no matter what had happened, there was an opening to inch closer to solving the five-hundred-year colonial dilemma.

Once I accepted on radio, people wanted me to campaign. I did not.

I did not campaign. I did not raise funds. In that same radio interview, I said I would decline the salary for the position.

On May 17, 2021, the elections took place. Around midnight it was clear; I was the first person ever elected on the island through the write-in mechanism. Roxana Soto Aguilu, one of the few people who was with me on the day I resigned, remembers that night. "What an epic moment. The first time anyone won the election by write-in. It was around 6:30 p.m. when the results were coming in. The atmosphere was electric. I went out to the streets to participate in a celebrate rally for Hato Rey with a live broadcast where more than one hundred thousand people were streaming watching our rally celebrating his election. The ironic thing was our winner was not physically in the rally. He was in Washington, DC."

Nor had I been there since I left office. The Hill reported: "Former Governor Ricardo Rosselló's speedy return to politics has been met with everything from disdain to disbelief, but he remains one of the most recognizable Puerto Rican faces in national politics." The article goes on to say "Rosselló's election by write-in ballot was an unexpected show of strength for a politician whose public career was widely perceived to be at an end" (Bernal 2021).

"A week before the election I still saw a write-in candidacy as practically impossible," I told *The Hill* in an exclusive interview. "It had never been done in Puerto Rico" (Bernal 2021).

Without a doubt it was an emotional moment for me. I'd been through the highest of highs, and the lowest of lows. It is easy to get lost after a period of darkness (Figure 11).

"You are proof it can happen. You are on the other side of the mountain, my friend," Governor Cuomo told me in our interview.

Although roadblocks were waiting for me soon after the election, my objective was clear: How do I help to #DecolonizeThisPlace?

CHAPTER 6:

To Reform or Not to Reform

This illustration, published in the early days of my administration, denotes my eagerness to enact reform. It also adds the speaker of the House and president of the Senate, who became nodes of resistance to reform, as they supported the status quo in many of these. While the intent was to display the labor reform as drowning (it did not), it was a foreshadow to the battles I had to wager and the static mentality from leadership in my own party (Bayon 2017).

"The phenomenon of [Ricardo] Rosselló, is not about one chat or any of the sorts. It is about a constant fight that is sustained in Puerto Rico between the reformers of the system like him and those that don't want reform."

—IVAN RIVERA, ESQ., *EL VOCERO* (RIVERA 2021).

June 14, 1998 was a hot summer day in Puerto Rico (El Tiempo 1998). I had just flown in from MIT, fresh from gaining my freshman fifteen [pounds]. Back at the executive mansion—the oldest in the western hemisphere—my father was about to receive a visit from one of the most impacting figures of the twentieth century. *Mikhail Gorbachev.*

Figure 1. Personal picture of me with Mikhail Gorbachev in 1998 at La Fortaleza.

I remember coming into the room and seeing Gorbachev and his wife RaiSa with their interpreter. It was an awe-inspiring moment. Here was one of the key figures who defeated the Cold War, in the flesh. This man had literally given his life and the capacity to stay at his home, just for the *chance* to make it—and the world—a better place (Figure 1).

The conversation was kind of clumsy because of the pause for Interpretation in between. He seemed to be comfortable and used to it. My father, a reformist himself, asked him about his mindset.

"I knew I everyone would hate me." He paused. "But I did it for the next generation. It will take time. Perhaps, I won't be alive to see it." The interpreter stopped. Gorbachev said in English, "It's better future. Not now. Better for people."

I know the exact quote because I wrote it down and embedded in my consciousness.

Reforming was the spark that ignited my interest in science and politics. For better or worse, I believe it is an intrinsic part of who I am at this point. Something likely triggered me that one hot June afternoon.

To think, observe, and act for a better outcome; to engage creatively and produce results; to be curious about how things are and how they can change—these things captivate me. I believe that was my main differentiator from some of my predecessors and other candidates. It prompted me to create a Plan for Puerto Rico, which embarked on an enormous number of reforms.

Free Access to University

In November 2018, I called upon some of my closest team members to present to them one of our next reforms.

"Here is the foundation for a model to create free access to university," I told them.

Some were skeptical. All were worried.

Ramon Rosario, secretary of public policy, recalled, "Was he just going to put something in as a promise he could not achieve? This was very uncharacteristic of him. But then he started explaining the details. It was a different type of model—one that could be achievable. He used curated Massive Open Online Courses (MOOCs) and a collaboration with the University of Puerto Rico to establish an online platform. The idea was to reach people who could not afford it and give them a pathway to do it. This was not only a high aspiration. He found thoughtful ways to get it started."

They asked many questions that day. Some questions had answers. Others needed work. But we had a path. I assembled a team and told them, "Nobody has done this. This is precisely why it will work."

I presented the concept in my State of the Union address, which was met with attacks... mostly by people who'd wanted free access to university in the past (Figure 2).

Figure 2. Cover of the newspapers outlining our proposals for free access to a university education and a new healthcare model.

The president of the Association of Puerto Rican Professors said I was a cynic for proposing this (NotiUno 2019). He went on to suggest I was doing this to "give private interests contracts." Student leaders said it was an *unreal proposal.*

Ricardo Llerandi, my chief of staff and head of the committee to provide universal access to a university education recalls, "This was met with resistance from a variety of stakeholders. Why? It meant increasing access to Education to a disadvantaged population." And the resistance came to the meetings. "The status quo voiced skepticism but were really just concerned of losing potential clients. As such, a media campaign started to diminish the value of the university degree as an *invented certificate.* The people wanted it—and we were going to do it—but they slowed things down enough."

I was never able to get this reform through. I did not have enough time, and many of the obstacles to reform manifested themselves.

A central theme throughout my tenure was therefore reform. Reform also drives the basis for this book. Most of the experiences or clashes engaged are based on one fundamental struggle: To reform or not to reform. I chose the former, but many of my predecessors chose the latter.

Stagnation and Status Quo: A Case Study from Puerto Rico

Paul Pierson's work, *Politics in Time: History, Institutions, and Social Analysis,* offers crucial insights into the difficulties of policy reform. He emphasizes the role of institutional inertia and path dependency, highlighting how historical and institutional contexts often resist change (Pierson 2004).

Reflecting on my predecessors, I perceive a tendency to uphold the status quo. Many, it seems, were either intentionally or inadvertently maintaining existing systems, primarily focusing on preserving existing conditions. While there were exceptions, a general lack of foresight and initiative for reform was evident.

Take the case of Sila Maria Calderon, who assumed office in 2001. The economy was flourishing, and the previous administration had implemented numerous reforms. However, Calderon's tenure marked a shift in focus: (1) political persecution of opponents and (2) dismantling previous reforms.

This approach, which I term "un-reforming opportunism," prioritized political strategy over public welfare. By attempting to discredit the opposition and reverse their reforms, Calderon focused more on eliminating political adversaries than on building upon a successful foundation.

Nancy MacLean, author of *Democracy in Chains* and a professor at Duke University, discusses how some leaders, often swayed by influential groups or ideologies, seek to negate the achievements of their predecessors.

A significant issue during Calderon's term was the misallocation of resources. For instance, the proceeds from the sale of the government-owned telephone company, rather than addressing the unfunded pension liability, diverted to a fund for "special communities"—a decision that yielded negligible results (*El Nuevo Día* 2010).

Rather than streamlining the government, Calderon expanded it, often to accommodate political allies. They financed this expansion by increasing borrowing relative to GDP (Rosselló 2018), leading to disastrous outcomes. Each new government position represented a long-term financial burden without sustainable funding. Faced with poor results, Calderon chose not to seek reelection.

Negligent Decision-Making for Short-Term Gain

In her place stepped in her resident commissioner, Aníbal Acevedo Vilá. Significant collapses and self-inflicted wounds marked his administration: There was the first government shutdown, hikes in taxes, negligent speculating on pensions fund and he was prosecuted (but not convicted) at the federal level as a sitting governor.

In October 2004, a month before his election, Acevedo Vilá made a debate promise: "I will be governor and I won't sign a law that will have a new tax on consumption [Sales Tax]" (NotiUno 2016). However, he later reversed this stance. Such political shifts are not uncommon, but his response to a legislative error offers insight into his approach. The original bill was to levy a tax of 5.5 percent.

In July 2006, former House Representative Hector Ferrer highlighted a discrepancy in a tax bill, noting the tax levied was higher than initially discussed (NotiUno 2016).

"Governor, here we have the 5.5 percent plus the 1.5 percent," Ferrer pointing out the mistake.

Acevedo Vilá's response was dismissive. "Well then shut your mouth," he said, laughing.

This incident reflects a broader issue of nonreformist governance under Acevedo Vilá, particularly in the context of Puerto Rico's pension crisis. Nick Brown, in a Reuters article, outlined the bond and pension crisis, emphasizing a problematic bond issue during Acevedo Vilá's tenure: "BOND BUST: Former Governor Aníbal Acevedo Vilá oversaw a bond issue meant to stabilize one of the island's major pensions, but it ended up only worsening the problem" (2016).

Brown further details how Acevedo Vilá's attempt to boost pension funding backfired. To avoid legislative approval, his administration arranged for the Employees Retirement System (ERS) to issue its own bonds, using employer contributions as collateral. The intention of this unconventional approach was to raise seven billion, but they only sold $2.9 billion in 2008 (2016).

MacKenzie's 2010 report criticized the bond deal, calling some elements "obviously flawed and not logical," suggesting a possible misunderstanding by island officials (2016).

Brown also noted they hired UBS to place the bonds locally after Merrill Lynch failed to do so internationally, indicating a lack of market interest. The report criticized Alfredo Salazar and then GDB chairman for not realizing raising less than seven billion would be insufficient to cover the pension's liabilities, exacerbating the fiscal situation (Brown 2016).

Acevedo Vilá wanted a shortcut for his short-term political survival, which would undo the long-term prospects of the island's retirees—a negligent step that precipitated a fiscal debacle. Not surprisingly, he lost in the biggest landslide in modern history to Luis Fortuño.

Scoop and Toss

Fortuño originally made some strides—some popular, others utterly unpopular—but most of them were sidetracked. His Law 7, whose intent was to reduce government payroll by laying off public-sector employees, impacted less people than originally stipulated. In addition to being a moral precipice, the mismanagement was evident, and many of those laid off returned to work (Internews Service 2013).

But my focus here is on the infamous scoop-and-toss technique employed by the Fortuño administration. It is a microcosm of the *kicking the can down the road* leadership. This strategy exemplifies this behavior. The *Wall Street Journal* wrote: "The maneuver, called scoop and toss, involves selling new long-term debt to raise funds to pay off maturing bonds, effectively extending the timetable for retiring municipal borrowings. Refinancing that aims to reduce interest rates typically keep the same maturity schedule" (Cherney 2013).

In 2011, Puerto Rico issued $356 million in bonds maturing in 2024, using some of the proceeds to pay off a bond from 1989 due in 2011. This action essentially transformed a twenty-two-year bond into a fifty-seven-year obligation, akin to using one credit card to pay off another and deferring the burden to future generations.

Lyle Fitterer, head of Tax-Exempt at Wells Capital Management, commented on this strategy: "The scoop-and-toss strategy might be a good strategy for a short-term solution, if you have a temporary economic recession. But obviously, the longer it goes on, the more difficult it is to argue that it's a good long-term solution" (Cherney 2013).

Puerto Rico's situation was far from a temporary recession, making this short-term fix inadequate for addressing the underlying issues. Such approaches, while offering immediate relief, often neglect the need for substantial structural changes, ultimately leaving future administrations to grapple with the consequences.

Oblivious to Collapse

This left us with the administration that preceded mine. The people elected Alejandro García Padilla under the promise of job creation and safeguarding the civil servant. This could have been his true intent. But one thing's for sure: He demonstrated himself to be oblivious and outmatched.

A defining moment occurred on April 1, 2013, during a press conference about the pension system. When questioned about negative credit agency projections for Puerto Rico Bonds, García Padilla, less than one hundred days into his office, responded dismissively, "Whatever they think of me, like Maná says, 'me vale'"—a phrase from a Mexican rock band, the meaning of which is "I couldn't care less" or "I don't give a damn" (*Primera Hora* 2013).

This approach, treating the situation as a personal battle with credit agencies like Moody's and Standard and Poor's, was ill-advised. It suggested a failure to transition from campaign rhetoric to the nuanced understanding required for effective governance. The consequences were immediate: Puerto Rico's bond values plummeted. By the following year, "Two of the three biggest credit-rating agencies in the world have downgraded the credit rating of Puerto Rico. Standard and Poor's has downgraded the Caribbean state to 'BB' status" (Meyer 2014).

On November 3, 2013, Governor García Padilla claimed he had "saved the finances" of Puerto Rico, despite indicators suggesting the contrary. The article read, "He [García Padilla] keeps talking as if he was still on the campaign trail, discussing his wins and laying most of the blame on his predecessor" (Cortes Chico 2013) Figure 3.

By February of the following year, they downgraded the debt, and by June 2015, García Padilla admitted "the debt was unpayable" (Meyer 2014). In July 2016, Puerto Rico defaulted on two billion in bond payments, a historic default on its constitutionally guaranteed debt.

"Salvamos las finanzas"

García Padilla repasa sus gestiones en La Fortaleza a un año de ser electo como gobernador

Figure 3. Governor García Padilla claims he "saved the finances" of Puerto Rico. A year later, Puerto Rico defaulted on its debt under his leadership, leading to an economic and fiscal collapse (Cortes Chico 2013).

García Padilla, a proponent of the colonial regime, ironically told the *Wall Street Journal* that Puerto Rico had become "a colony of Wall Street" over the years (*Primera Hora* 2013).

His inability to enact reforms or grasp the gravity of the situation became increasingly evident. By the end of 2015, he realized he could not seek another term.

In the end, crisis will emerge for nonreformers. They come in all shapes and forms. But in an environment that requires change, aiming to "sustain the ship" with a steady hand alone won't cut it. The tendency to tackle today's issue at tomorrow's cost, the frightful lack of foresight, and the continuous intervention of day-to-day politics is akin to quicksand. Issues are becoming more complex, and without the capacity to adjust, things will collapse. The nonreformer cannot lead in challenging and changing times.

So, what about reformers?

To Reform

"Great spirits have always encountered violent opposition from mediocre minds."

—ALBERT EINSTEIN

This quote reminds me of two outstanding reforming governors, whom I had the privilege to observe and learn from. One was my father. He is bold, bright, and brave with reforming embedded in his DNA. Leaving things as they were was not an option. Even if they cost him dearly.

Figure 4. Governor Cuomo was a potent ally and supporter of Puerto Rico. His intervention saved lives. Nobody has to tell me. I witnessed it firsthand (Photo Credit: Magdiel Lugo).

Another is a contemporary governor who was Puerto Rico's greatest source of support after the devastation suffered by Hurricane Maria. Andrew Cuomo, the three-term governor of New York was strong, decisive, and effective. This, of course, garnered him some enemies (Figure 4).

I picked their brains on a variety of topics for this book. Perhaps their best introduction is as an example of reform.

When I asked Governor Cuomo to reflect on a challenging reform and issue, he said, "Well, we got an issue. We passed an assault weapon ban; no more than ten bullets in a gun. And this is New York, which is a progressive state. It was the most controversial bill to pass."

He then remembers how he could make it move. "Change can come when you seize the moment." Timing and time are critical variables in the successful execution of reforms. Knowing when to strike is essential, which is a theme we'll come back to again and again.

"What ended the rhetoric was when, much like in Sandy Hook, children were killed." Cuomo continued, "I proposed the gun bill that day after it happened… and I called for the vote that week. Why? Because we used the crisis, channeled the focus of the energy, and the side of the majority rose up in the immediate aftermath. And in that moment, I put the gun bill on the floor and pushed to get it voted on immediately, knowing the politicians don't know how to deal with this enraged citizenry."

Surely, this must have helped him politically. Right?

"The politicians did it because it was good for them. The weekend the bill passed, my popularity *dropped fifteen to twenty* points. I had demonstrations with more than ten thousand people … and it was constant. I still get death threats from people who say I trampled their Second Amendment rights."

Even in the face of a significant political hit, the governor went with the reform he had proposed because he thought it was the right thing to do. Polls can easily change the minds of politicians who aim to reform. And those polls are fickle as a function of time. The question is: Do you want to get things done? Do you have the wherewithal to do it? And if so, at what cost? After this battle, he clearly had a group of Second Amendment activists who would oppose him—not only on gun laws—but on everything.

Does it take a toll? *Yes, it does.*

"Let me tell you a story," he said. "The single most disruptive vote for me, however, was marriage equality. The Catholic Church was very unhappy. I went to mass that Sunday with my daughters to hear the priest and his homily condemn me for passing it. As a boy who is a Catholic, to hear that kind of condemnation in your own church… That was personally difficult."

As a reformer, sometimes you have to go against groups where you have personal ties to achieve those goals. This includes your own supporters and legislators.

"We were the first big state to pass marriage equality. It had just lost the year before. Why? Because it was a difficult issue. The Catholic Church was against it and the legislators just didn't want to have to deal with the opposition that was inevitable. The only way to get it done was to equalize and surpass that pressure by organizing the LGBTQ community and their supporters to pressure those legislators. So, yes, it wound up passing. We created a new civil rights paradigm, a great achievement for the state of New York. But the legislators now are unhappy, feel pressured, and are resentful you created that pressure for them," Cuomo concluded.

Many new opponents. Second Amendment rights, the Catholic Church, legislators… it starts to aggregate. Yet what is the alternative? Governor Cuomo said, "Don't take a position on a controversial issue. Don't alienate anyone if you don't have to. The cost? You make no changes."

And if you choose change? "The more changes you make, the more scar tissue builds up," he said, but here is the kicker. "The beneficiaries of change will be less invested than opponents."

Armed with this knowledge… which path would you choose?

Reform… For What?

Reform is the heartbeat of progress, the bold stroke that paints a brighter future on the canvas of the present. Imagine a child in a remote village, her potential stifled by the lack of basic amenities. One policy shift could electrify her world, literally and metaphorically. It's about turning the lights on in a doctor's clinic where healthcare workers store life-saving vaccines, ensuring they don't spoil in the tropical heat. It's about building roads that connect the fisherman's catch to far-off markets, transforming a subsistence livelihood into a thriving business.

Consider the story of "The Man in the Fortress." Known for his wisdom and empathy, he spent years in his stronghold, studying the histories and cultures of the surrounding lands. As he journeyed from one village to another, he listened intently to the villagers' stories of hardship and injustice. He observed their daily lives, learning about their challenges in agriculture, trade, and governance, and he began to see the interconnectedness of their struggles with broader societal issues. Armed with this knowledge, he used his influence to advocate for reforms. He organized meetings with local leaders, proposing culturally sensitive and sustainable solutions. His approach was not to impose change but to empower communities to enact reforms themselves, guided by his insights and support. His legacy was not just in the reforms he helped to implement but in the mindset he fostered among the people.

This is the crux of reform. It's personal, it's real, and it's transformative.

For example, my personal connection to the police force, developed during my formative years, gave me a deep appreciation for their sacrifices and dedication. I vividly recall the positive impact of the salary raise they received in the late 1990s.

However, over the subsequent two decades, support for the police force waned. Issues like delayed overtime payments, reduced healthcare benefits, and declining public perception plagued the force. Senator at Large and former police officer Gregorio Matias reflects on this period: "The lack of action and neglect under the opposition party led to a police reform. During that time, my colleagues saw no light of hope. The situation worsened with unpaid retroactive salaries amounting to around $360 million and a devastated retirement system, especially after Alejandro García Padilla enacted the disastrous pension cuts law."

Recognizing the urgent need for change, my administration embarked on a mission to improve conditions for our police officers. Our efforts included securing their pensions, increasing salaries, clearing overdue overtime from previous administrations, inaugurating a new police academy, and enabling their participation in social security. These steps were part of a comprehensive structural reform that integrated all public safety agencies, aiming to streamline costs and enhance operational efficiency.

Senator Matias noted the significant changes during our tenure: "During Governor Ricardo Rosselló, things changed dramatically. The police officers' salary increased by 30 percent, which for many meant an additional $1,500 a month. We also integrated the police into social security and addressed the $360 million debt to the police, resulting in payments of up to $64,000 in some cases. It took four governors to finally feel overwhelming support for the men and women who risk their lives for Puerto Rico. The change was palpable. The police officers felt supported by the government and hopeful for a dignified retirement."

These initiatives not only empowered the police officers but also demonstrated the government's commitment to public safety. The revitalized police force, feeling supported and valued, delivered tangible results for the people of Puerto Rico. Here are some of them (Figure 5):

- Crime reduced to the lowest levels in modern history.
- Type 1 crimes reached a historic low, down 20 percent to 28,517.
- Violent crimes dropped to the lowest in Puerto Rico's history, totaling 6,365.
- For two consecutive years, murders decreased by 7 percent, marking the third-lowest figure in modern Puerto Rican history (660 in 2018 and 606 in 2019).
- The theft and burglary rates were the lowest in three decades.
- The crime rate per hundred thousand residents was the lowest in three decades, at 233.

Everyone in society benefited from this sequence.

Precisely this type of tangible, personal reality drove me passionately to create reform. I could see the thousands of levers in my head, moving them and seeing what the outcome would be. I

Figure 5. Newspapers displaying salary hikes and a new public safety department.

likened the pursuit of reform as that of the role of a conductor orchestrating a grand symphony with a diverse orchestra. Each section of the orchestra—strings, brass, woodwinds, and percussion—represents different facets of society, such as the economy, culture, politics, and social welfare. Just as a conductor skillfully integrates these distinct sections to create a harmonious and cohesive musical piece, a reformer should aim to harmonize various societal elements through his reforms. This requires a deep understanding of every decision. When executed in proper sequence, it is magical. One misstep, and the beauty can quickly turn into damaging noise.

Well-executed reform also compounds. Consider the ripple effect of change. The impact of reform is much like a stone thrown into a still pond; the ripples touch shores far and wide. A single policy change can set off a cascade of improvements. Better education leads to informed citizens, who then drive a more robust democracy. Improved healthcare results in a healthier workforce, boosting economic productivity. Each reform is a thread in the fabric of societal advancement, weaving a tapestry of collective progress.

Without reform? That tapestry would degrade; the orchestra would be aimless. So here is another key point. Reform is not a luxury. It is *absolutely* necessary. It's the lifeblood of progress, the oxygen that breathes life into the aspirations of millions. As we stand at the crossroads of history, the choice is clear—to reform is to thrive; to resist is to wither. The path of reform is rugged, but my belief is it's the only road to a future that promises hope, prosperity, and an enduring legacy of positive change. Those who understand this see no other alternative than pursuing reform. Even at the ultimate price.

Many Examples of Reformers

History has plenty of examples of reformers. The most famous come to mind: MLK, Gandhi, Aung San Suu Kyi, Lyndon Johnson, Ronald Reagan. Many of them had to pay high prices for their success. Many others perished within the process.

Nelson Mandela, the former president of South Africa, is a prominent example of a leader who pursued significant reforms at great personal and political cost. Mandela fought against apartheid, a system of racial segregation and discrimination, and dedicated his life to dismantling it. His efforts led to his imprisonment for twenty-seven years. However, he continued to advocate for justice and equality, eventually becoming a symbol of reconciliation and playing a key role in the peaceful transition to democracy in South Africa.

Referencing the challenges after achieving reform, he said, "I have walked that long road to freedom. I have tried not to falter. I have made missteps along the way. But I have discovered the secret that after climbing a great hill, one only finds that there are many more hills to climb" (Mandela 2013).

The key concept: Change is always going to be a constant, so achieving a reform is not the end result. Reforming is the continuous capacity to do, reflect, and see what needs to happen again in the future. The solution that was brilliant yesterday might be archaic today. A reformer needs to understand this.

In addition to facing enormous challenges and personal cost is the element of actual execution. How do you actually get it done? Once again, we can gain some insights from the former leader of the Soviet Union.

Humanity and Demonization...

Tony Robbins is a highly regarded American author, motivational speaker, and life coach. He is renowned for his dynamic seminars, self-help books, and motivational content, aimed at inspiring personal growth, success, and transformation in individuals. I had the opportunity to listen to him during a YPO event in collaboration with A360.

Tony was on an airplane with Mikhail Gorbachev and asked him: "What ended the Cold War?" Gorbachev replied: "The end of demonization."

Mikhail Gorbachev is widely known for his reform policies, including the introduction of perestroika (restructuring) and glasnost (openness), which aimed to bring political and economic changes to the Soviet Union and promote greater transparency and cooperation with the West, ultimately leading to the end of the Cold War and the dissolution of the Soviet Union (Gorbachev 2007).

Robbins didn't find satisfaction with the answer. "He looked at me and then started talking in a singsong tone like when someone told many people the same thing over again. What he said was, it was the end of demonization. Mr. Reagan was saying we're the evil empire."

Robbins was not satisfied, so he pressed. "I want to know the moment," he interrupted.

He recalls Gorbachev replied laughing, "No one has ever asked me that question before. I will tell you. Reagan and I were together. We were having an argument, and he was lecturing me on the evils of communism. I said to him, you are not my teacher, and I am not your student, and you will not speak to me this way. I was so mad I felt my face burning."

This did not look to be going anywhere. Then something incredible happened.

"All of a sudden Mr. Reagan stood up and said, 'This is not working.' He took two steps away and went back and said, "Let's start fresh. Shall we? My name is Ron. Are you Mikhail?"

Gorbachev said, "You have to love the guy. This is a man I could do business with."

"Doing business with…" Translation: I could actually sit down beyond the differences, and we could put our heads together to get things done for the betterment of the people.

This is a fast-fading art, my friends.

As it turns out, Robbins recalls that President Reagan told him something similar. They were in Reykjavik, and they were negotiating over the first destruction of long-range nuclear weapons. Reagan said he was talking to Gorbachev, and it was getting more and more heated. Reagan suddenly said, "Why don't we go on a walk?" And I guess Gorbachev's response was, "Is he crazy?"

Robbins reflects on the action of taking a walk: "Think of the genius of this action. They're sitting across… fighting. All sudden, they get to put on their coats and leave. It changes their whole state of mind. They are walking outside in the freezing cold and side by side they made the first agreements toobernaoy long-range nuclear weapons in the history of the world."

The reformers mindset changed the world. But more importantly, the capacity to work together—not against each other—changed *everything*.

Crisis If You Do, Crisis If You Don't, A Reformer's Dilemma

Seeing the experiences of some reformers and nonreformers, you can't escape the notion of a catch-22. If you don't reform, the social and political environment will eventually absorb you. It used to be the case, that you could hold on to what was working, and carry through. My observation is things are changing quite rapidly, and the nonresponse from governments to those changes will provoke crisis. In addition, complexity is arising in several fronts. Whether fiscal and economic challenges, climate change, or pandemics—these will drag you down if you don't act.

Paradoxically, the same outcome is true if you do reform—but for a different reason. If you do reform, you will have the vehement opposition of those that stand to benefit from the status quo. These entities will do whatever it takes to make you fail. And if you do succeed, it will likely be at great personal and political cost.

"There is nothing more difficult to take in hand, more perilous to conduct, or more uncertain in its success, than to take the lead in the introduction of a new order of things."

—NICCOLO MACHIAVELLI, *THE PRINCE*

I discussed this quote with Governor Eric Greitens from Missouri. He had to face blowback from some of the big reforms he pushed. Like Cuomo and me, he had to resign his position after public outcry over personal issues and allegations of corruption. And like Cuomo and me, he got a full exoneration with absolutely "no evidence of wrongdoing" from the allegations (Beck 2020).

He said, "It is hard because everyone's who's already invested in the system as it is will be there to fight you. Those who would benefit do not have the same level of commitment." His point is reform is an incredibly dangerous thing for a leader for exactly this reason.

What factors control this reality? Can we do anything about it?

The rest of this book will tackle this global question and some of its implications.

But first, we need to understand the social scenarios we are facing before we can tackle some of the factors that can control reforms. In the next part of our book, we will dive into a series of observations that are causing major disruption in the reforming space, explore how narratives are dominating actions, and consider the challenge of growing complexity with a need for simpler explanations. We will do a bit of introspective work on the dehumanization of leaders and the future consequences that entails, unveiling in the process the unsatisfying truth that extreme factions are gaining the upper hand.

PART II

EVALUATING THE CURRENT ENVIRONMENT

CHAPTER 7:

Words Speak Louder than Actions

This illustration shows my wife Beatriz asking me why I wrote something in social media. While the context was another one, it seemed to foreshadow what I would face a year later (Bayon 2018).

"No matter what you do—what matters is your narrative." An old advisor told me this in October, 2018 as a group of us was finishing an internal meeting.

"I will let my actions speak for me," I said, quite confidently.

Well, I was wrong.

You are not reading the chapter title incorrectly. It's not a typo. It is a play on the old adage. To support it, evidence abounds.

As a mathlete, tennis player ,and a scientist, admittedly, I originally did not give words the power to outdo actions. I was in an arena where actions mattered more than words. In tennis, you play. You win. You lose. You own it, no one else. Can't argue your way out of an ace. In math, there is a solution. It can be elegant or not, but there is a solution. No amount of words will get you away from that (well,

Figure 1. Personal picture of Puerto Rico's first International Mathematical Olympiad representation in 1997 (Photo Credit: Ricardo Rosselló).

maybe partial credit by some). In science, words did matter, but it was mostly in crafting the way to describe your results (actions).

As Herbert Meyer describes it, "The fundamental difference between science and politics is that in science results count and being right matters" (1993).

Eric Greitens agrees: "I believe if you really care about people, if you really love them, if you really are there to serve them, you must care about the results. You must care about whether or not your policies are, in fact, working. If not, you just care about the media, your next race, or some other special interest."

The concepts of solving problems and getting results are embedded in my professional and personal development. This is why I thought I could thrive more on my actions than my words. Fate, it would seem, had another plan.

It is no accident I am starting this part of the book with the exploration on words. For using the wrong words is an item that defines me to this day and shattered my reputation.

Massive protests erupted during my tenure because of some of the words I used to describe political opponents and media members in a private chat, later shown to be manipulation. Big mistake on my part. I regret doing so. Interestingly, words also categorized and framed me in an exaggerated way or they were flat-out untrue. Those words ran rampant and grew in intensity exponentially.

Those words, not the ones on the actual chat, precipitated persecution of my family and shattered my reputation. Words like criminal, corrupt, misogynistic… those words unlocked a bogus criminal investigation, and some news outlets already declared I had committed felonies before any process whatsoever (Univision 2019). After that, the dominoes kept falling uncontrollably and the narratives got more exotic and entangled.

How did this whirlwind unfold?

Opponents who had aggregated and had plenty to lose due to the changes to the status quo used the mistake I made against me. The starkest opponents? Officials from my own party feared change. I became their enemy. It was the straw that broke the camel's back.

I am not unique to this onslaught. As it turns out, this tactic is becoming very common. So why are people being so harsh to political opposites?

In a study conducted in 2020, "othering" happens when "a group conceives of its rivals as wholly alien in every way. This toxic form of polarization has fundamentally altered political discourse, public civility and even the way politicians govern" (Finkel et al. 2020). And the way to convey this message is to brand and define those we disagree with by using stories and the appropriate trigger words.

It happens everywhere. It even happens in academia. I was recently at a Triple Nine conference, where I gave a talk on reform in longevity. One of the members, Rain Simons, was presenting on intelligence research. At one point she said, "We had a very powerful speaker at a conference that was talking about intelligence research in general being under threat." Why would any research be under threat? The purpose is to find evidence. Why would someone censor it? This means that legitimate researchers will have work interference with and possibly their careers derailed if they tackle controversial topics.

While you can see these behaviors in the interactions between citizens, they magnify a thousand-fold on their leaders, athletes, and politicians. The charged environment is full of people who don't need too much to spark them. They built headlines upon headlines to achieve the desired perceptive outcome. In many instances, this is done purposely to destroy or *cancel* your target.

Irshad Manji, *New York Times* best-selling author, professor, and lecturer at Oxford University notes, "Cancel culture personalizes the criticism. It seeks to humiliate and punish rather than to counter and argue with" (Manji 2020).

For instance, here is a headline used to define me: "Misogyny, corruption, and leaked messages: The story of the demise of Puerto Rico's governor" (Serrano 2019a)

The opposition branded me with several scarlet letters that are hard to combat, given the strong emotional response they elicit. So, I was a homophobic, corrupt, misogynistic dictator. I had no chance to argue it. However, I will use this space to make my case. I'm not compelled to convince you one way or another, but I do feel compelled to express it.

Case #1 Homophobic

Although my party was mostly socially conservative, I tended to be more socially liberal, albeit very fiscally conservative. What united our party, the New Progressive Party (Partido Nuevo Progresista, or PNP), was not the traditional left and right divide but our shared pursuit of statehood, and therefore, equality. The PNP's roots are in the old Republican party, and many of those conservative values persisted. As such, I made several proposals that did not align with the base of the PNP.

Puerto Rico recibe el premio Destino del Año LGBTQ +

Puerto Rico es el destino del año para la comunidad LGBTQ+, de acuerdo con la guía de viajes GayCities.com. Dicha guía tiene un programa anual de premios de viaje en el que los miembros votan en 15 categorías diferentes para seleccionar sus lugares favoritos de viaje. Este año, Best of GayCities presentará dos premios especiales que fueron seleccionados por los editores: Premio al Innovador (Fred Dixon de NYC & Company) y Destino del Año (Puerto Rico). **SUMINISTRADA**

Figure 2. Newspaper blurb indicating that *GayCities* selected Puerto Rico as the "destination of the year" by *GayCities* (Metro 2018).

Among these were my proposals within the "Plan for Puerto Rico," which included thirteen main goals for the LGBTT community. Impressively, we accomplished eleven of those. Our achievements included launching an antibullying campaign, establishing a coeducational schools pilot program, enabling changes in birth certificates for transgender individuals, setting guidelines for civil service treatment, providing training for police on civil rights and respect for the community, offering mental health support, enacting an HIV bill of rights, promoting tourism campaigns welcoming the LGBTQ community, and establishing the first council on LGBTQ policy (Consejo Asesor del Gobernador en Asuntos LGBTT 2019). Objectively, by 2018, Puerto Rico ranked second among countries in the Americas in the global barometer for gay rights (F&M Global Barometers n.d.). In the same year, the island was honored as the Destination of the Year by GayCities.com (2018) Figure 2.

By the end of 2018, Puerto Rico ranked as the twenty-fifth country (out of 203) in terms of tolerance, with a GBGR score of 89/100. This placed us ahead of the US as a whole, which was ranked forty-eighth (Dicklitch-Nelson et al. 2021).

Cecilia La Luz, an icon of the LGBTQ movement, was instrumental in helping this shift happen.

Figure 3. Highlights media recognition of my executive order banning conversion therapy (Human Rights Campaign 2019).

"It seems to me that when the Human Rights Campaign put us on the map, it was when they introduced the bill banning conversion therapy. After a critical debate the Senate approved it but not the House. Then Governor Rosselló issued an executive order prohibiting it, which is still in effect. After that, we became one of the prominent jurisdictions in the Americas," Cecilia said. Despite her global respect and decades of advocacy, she faced backlash for supporting my administration.

"The attacks actually occurred when the chat incident happened. Although I publicly criticized the writings in the chat, I defended and will continue to defend you for being the governor who has achieved the most for the LGBTQ community," Cecilia recalled.

Yet her support led to accusations of betrayal within her community. "Different people from the LGBTT community contacted me to ask if I still supported you. Some community leaders threatened to publicly label me a traitor. They did, launching a Facebook campaign against me," she said.

Politics can be brutal.

The community branded a pioneering advocate for the LGBTQ community a traitor for standing by her beliefs.

Naysayers claimed my support for LGBTQ initiatives was to "expand my base," but in reality, it cost me politically. I lost part of my base, particularly among strict social conservatives. My focus was not on vote-getting but on necessary reforms for both the LGBTQ and faith-based communities.

"The goal in politics is to sustain your base," former Virginia Congressman Tom Davis once told me. "Without it, you're vulnerable to attacks."

I lost some party leaders and part of my base because I supported actions I believed were in Puerto Rico's best interest.

Yet I called a member of my own party (who internally was an opponent) a "mamabicho" (cock sucker) in a private chat. This is typically a slang word. This was used to label me as homophobic and antigay. To this day, some of the key figures who protested against me use it liberally and without repercussion.

Pedro Julio Serrano, an activist and consistent opponent, said, "This is how Ricardo Rosselló will be remembered—a legacy of homophobia, misogyny, discrimination, corruption..." (2019b)

I expected such comments from Serrano. But the overall sentiment caused me great pain. I have always aimed to alleviate the struggles of the LGBTQ community. I was a late supporter of legal marriage for gay couples but an early advocate for equal rights for couples.

In the end, you could call me many things, but homophobic should not be one of them. Yet it seems words often speak louder than actions (Figure 3).

Case 2 Misogyny

When asked if I was a feminist in 2018. Here is what I answered, "I believe in equal opportunity for women. I believe women are equally or more qualified than men to exercise many of the functions or trades of the modern world. Evidence of this is that in my administration the largest budgets, the last time I calculated it, women managed 80 percent. I do believe in a world where my daughter, who is the light of my eyes, can have the same opportunity to develop, to win, to be happy and given the respect she deserves... If that makes me a feminist, then, yes, I am a feminist" (Rivera 2018) Figure 4.

Of course, these are just words. Everyone understandably questioned these words when the chat came out.

Particularly because the most controversial words I used in the private chat were when I used the pejorative *puta* (bitch) referring to a former speaker of the council in New York City, who had lost several other elections afterward and is a staunch opponent of statehood.

She seized the opportunity to define me, "Unveiling the machismo of Governor Rosselló. When a misogynistic man wants to devalue a woman, he uses words like puta to dehumanize and degrade her" (Thompson 2019).

This became a rallying cry. People made signs, made shirts, evoked artistic expressions, and those words resonated. There was even a clever merger of the words to the claim I was corrupt.

My choice of words was unacceptable, as I have now come to understand. Words matter and the last thing I would want to do is minimize and diminish women. I do, however, believe I showed with my actions, that I believe in women, value them, and support them. And it started with actions in my own cabinet.

Rosselló se proclama feminista

Maricarmen Rivera Sánchez, EL VOCERO   26/11/2018

Figure 4. Newspaper clipping showcasing me as a feminist (Rivera 2018)

The headline of a local newspaper article read: "Women Assume Leadership of the Country." No small claim. Would a misogynistic leader allow this to happen? (Figure 5)

Our administration had the highest number of woman executives by a landslide (44 percent). In addition, we became the fourth jurisdiction to enact equal pay for equal work laws (SinComillas 2017). We created an online school for women to get their certificates while working from home (Maletin Empresarial para la Mujer). We established procurement protocols requiring women to be in executive positions so the government could hire their services. We invested a historic amount in preventing domestic violence (Concilio de Mujeres 2019). We created a law for special leave for victims of domestic violence and provided the first women's government council to establish public policy for the equality of women.

I also saw the results. For example, In the toughest times, my wife Beatriz spearheaded efforts to get food to people, providing access to mental healthcare and other items of necessity. Without her leadership, those efforts wouldn't have been nearly as effective. Women led the way to enact permits reform, education reform, innovation reform, tax reform, infrastructure, and energy. Leadership matters, and most of the women in my administration delivered.

Maria Palou was part of that initial cohort and an integral part of the recovery process. She reflects on the first months of breaking the traditional barriers of gender in government administration. "I must confess that in the first months I occupied the position occasionally people would meet with me and highlight the fact I am a woman. But we broke through. It comes from the top and leadership. Many professional women were part of the team. They were able to do an excellent job thanks in large part to the unconditional support of the governor."

**MUJERES ALCANZAN EL 40%
EN EL PODER GUBERNAMENTAL**

De las 63 designaciones que ha
hecho el gobernador
Ricardo Rosselló, 25 son mujeres

Administran el 33% del presupuesto
con cargo al Fondo General,
que alcanza los $8,987 millones

PUERTO RICO HOY PÁGINAS 4-6

Figure 5. Cover of a local the newspaper denoting women achieved 40 percent of the power in government (Caro Gonzalez 2017).

Do I regret calling someone a bitch? Of course, I do. I processed it, self-evaluated, and committed myself to being mindful of the usage of words and the damage they can cause. I don't want to cause that harm. My awareness has grown, and I aim for continuous improvement. But… does that make me *antiwoman*? Does a low point, a spur of the moment expression, define who you should be forever? I know there are likely a variation of answers. However, what we can definitely conclude is words do carry power that can overshadow actions.

Case #3 Corrupt Dictator

"If you are committed to finding and battling corruption, you will find it."

I always started with these *words* when I was addressing the issue of corruption. We had a goal to eradicate it. My point was a simple one: if you will battle corruption and search for it everywhere, you will find it. That seems straightforward enough, but the implications are a catch-22.

If you do nothing about corruption, you won't find it. Therefore, people won't associate your administration with corruption. At least not explicitly. On the other hand, if you *do* something about corruption, you *will* find it, and people will associate *you* with corruption. Again, politics can be brutal.

We opted to do the second strategy, understanding the consequences. And we did so with all the might of the executive. The stakes were high since the opposition was salivating to tag me and my team as corrupt.

December 2016, a few weeks before taking office. I sat on the porch of my house with a group of friends next to a spectacular mango tree on a breezy day. Our home was a colonial two-bedroom house. Just big enough for the three of us. Beatriz fell in love with it on the spot. The garden was mesmerizing and the kind of place to sit down and have meaningful conversations. The previous weeks were intense with transition hearings. In between the bickering, we actually had to identify data. This would prove to be a challenge as—in many instances—there were no formal systems to collect it. Parallel to that, I was in the identification process of talent to become members of my cabinet.

A close friend of mine took a deep breath and said, "This is going to be a challenge."

Some of the others agreed and started discussing the challenges: fiscal, economic, social, and otherwise.

"Those are all important… but that's not what I mean." He paused. "Battling corruption is going to be a challenge," he continued. "You can survive any other drawback. This one you can't. I know you won't do anything, but the people surrounding you can't either."

I responded, "We'll need to break the system and add good people. Otherwise, it will break us."

Fast forward, on July 10, 2019, two of my former executives were arrested for corruption (Blad 2019)—secretary of education and executive director of health insurance.

A few days later, texts came out.

Then, the news coverage tagged me for corruption—even when this was clearly not the case. An article in CNN by Brian Stetler read "These Journalists Exposed the Corruption That Led to Puerto Rico's Mass Protests" (2019). And just like that, journalist branded me as *corrupt*.

This was a very hard personal blow—one that still remains in some circles today, even as all evidence shows my exoneration from any crimes or intent of crimes (Soto 2020). On top of that, we had worked tirelessly to create an environment that could identify, capture, and dissuade corruption.

Our anticorruption reform agenda included establishing greater transparency parameters on the financial front—ones we did not find in the transition hearing, for example. There was no clarity, and we made them public. We also created the office of the inspector general as a mechanism to tackle corruption in real time (Hernandez 2018). Some elected officials were *not* happy. We created an anticorruption code (Ruiz Kuilan 2018). We established historic agreements of collaboration with the federal government. Narcos were *not* happy. Death threats increased.

As one of my last efforts, we established a registry of lobbyists. There was a dark cloud of trust surrounding the lobbying efforts on the island. One key driver was nobody knew who was lobbying and for what. This created the environment for lobbyists to be on radio shows as talking heads without knowing what they were explicitly lobbying for. So, I signed an executive order to create a registry for transparency. Lobbyists were *not* happy (Agencia EFE 2019)

The new entity created to manage the billions of dollars' worth of reconstruction funds post-hurricane had the highest guidelines of compliance and transparency. The federal government approved. This required more centralized visibility and less dispersed control at the local levels of government.

Procurement has been a disaster in Puerto Rico and one of the primary sources of corruption. There was little visibility as to the decision-making process. We aimed to change that. We established a *procurement reform* that would not only give transparency and efficacy, but it would also save more than one hundred million dollars within the first five years of its implementation. Now mayors and other executives wouldn't have a hand-picked team to procure for their contractors. Mayors *were* not happy.

We created a freedom of information act. There was none before. As such, information was hard to identify and access. Now, there would be a clear path and a request process for all citizens. The media was *not* happy. Some in the press did not like it because they no longer had the edge over ordinary citizens. Now it was equal footing for all.

We externalized management of severely mismanaged education funds ($1.5 billion a year). Education contractors were *not* happy. No more easy contracts through friends with zero accountability and zero results. Now, it would have a robust merit structure. Any contractor would have to deliver. Stark change from the status quo.

We created a tax reform that would identify theft and loopholes at the highest levels. Achieved record high revenues for Puerto Rico (Hacienda 2019). Some people were hiding their wealth and not paying their taxes or were paying significantly lower rates than people who earned less because of accounting tricks. That was over. The status quo was *not* happy.

Even with all these efforts, they branded me as corrupt. Why? Because it is fairly easy to do. This is why my friend cautioned me this would be a challenge. As an opposition strategy, it has a very powerful bang for its buck—the sort of branding that leaves a mark for decades.

Corruption Has a First and Last Name

"The first thing I would say is corruption is an individual act. It has always been an individual act." This is the first thing that former Ethics Director of Puerto Rico Zulma Rosario told me when we sat down to talk about the ills of corruption.

"There could be schemes, and people doing it together… but in the end, it is an individual decision. This needs understanding at our core." She quickly recalls a tipping point on the island when this changed. "Back in the late 1990s, there was a watershed moment when this perception crumbled. We have been aiming to fix this since then."

"I recall turning on the TV and seeing the Federal Prosecutor, a supposedly unbiased man say 'Corruption has a first and last name… and it is the PNP'" (Delgado 2019). In reference to the New Progressive Party—my party. These words were a powerful game changer. They were also a complete mischaracterization. But like a tattoo, they permanently imprinted.

The PNP (New Progressive Party) is the party for statehood in Puerto Rico driven by a core cause to provide equality for the people of Puerto Rico as US citizens. This stunning statement aim was not at identifying one person who had done harm—or even a group of people. This was tailor-made to throw dirt over the statehood movement in Puerto Rico. Unfortunately, they achieved their objective.

What might bring a person or a group to knowingly stain the perception of a whole movement, even knowing they are wrong? "*Power*… all they want is power," Rosario said. "They [the status quo] get more and more creative every day in finding words that strike the heart and soul to gain power."

When asked, Leo Díaz Urbina, a former president of the New Progressive Party took the reins under these circumstances. "Nobody was from the PNP," he recalls. "Everyone was afraid to say so. If they did, they would be immediately implicated with corruption."

Once again we see the powerful impact of *words*. There was nothing to merit this overall perception, but the words built upon themselves. First it started with one individual. Then a group of people. Quickly it became a whole movement. I see this strategic move for a short-term power grab is enticing. But is this type of orchestrated polarization helpful for society? Think about it. If a hardworking citizen, say a teacher, said they were associated with the PNP at that point, the *narrative* dictated they were corrupt.

About a decade later, Rosario became executive director of the ethics commission—a position that spans ten years. Her goal was clear. "I need to start working at the root cause of these trust issues—through civility."

Your Values Count

"We needed to start with the kids from the ground up. It is the fundamental basis. Kids with bad examples in their communities—drugs, crime—need another chance in life."

She emphasized the six major values of the "Tus Valores Cuentan" (Your Values Count) program: respect, responsibility, justice, civics, kindness, and trust. These core values were immutable. "These are not my ideas," she clarified. "This is grounded in the work many others have done before me, which has yielded results."

One might assume such a program would have universal support. Yet as we've seen with reforms and reformers, it is never that simple. Be prepared for opposition and criticism.

"[Governor] García Padilla and [Education Secretary] Roman dismantled what we had started. It was only beginning, but the results were already showing." Their sole reason? "Because it originated from a different administration."

They gave no consideration to the impact of discontinuing this program. It's tragic that children miss out on crucial lessons because adults fail to collaborate. In 2017, when I became governor, we revived the "Your Values Count" program. I faced intense criticism, this time from extreme factions on the left. "When Keleher initiated the program, the media frenzy began. They spread falsehoods, transforming a program about respect and morality for kids into a controversy over corruption."

Corruption—that ever-present political trump card.

How could they associate corruption with a values program? Zulma recalled an encounter with Anna Irma Rivera Lassen before she became a senator for the MVC party. "She criticized my proposal, dismissing it as 'a religious program that has no place in education.'"

The program became a battleground between left and right, secular and religious, driven by extreme viewpoints. This polarized debate overshadowed the program's actual merits and its potential benefit to the majority.

Rosario responded to the criticism: "I couldn't stay silent. I asked her, 'Which of these values is exclusively religious?'"

Rivera Lassen's response was silence.

Yet the narrative was set. They twisted a program designed to foster values and combat corruption into—ironically—a supposedly corrupt scheme.

This demonstrates a critical lesson in politics: Someone can manipulate your strongest attribute into your biggest liability. This tactic is devastatingly effective. Why attack an opponent's weaknesses, which are often obvious and yield only marginal gains? Instead, use narrative and words to turn their strengths into weaknesses. The impact is far greater. The higher they are, the harder they fall.

Building a Culture Against Corruption

Figure 6. Illustration depicting my thumb provoking the exit of the mayor of Guaynabo (Bayon 2017).

"Your anticorruption code was a significant step toward ensuring people understood the rules," Rosario commented on the bill I introduced that codified and simplified all acts of corruption. "This, along with the MOU with the federal government, were game changers in building an understanding of what corruption is, its penalties, and helping people comprehend their responsibilities."

Based on this framework, she recalls, we were able to identify corrupt officials. "You were catching all of the O'Neills," referring to a former influential mayor of Guaynabo who styled himself as an old-school political boss. Due to sexual misconduct, they pushed him out, and he later pleaded guilty to these charges (Ibarra-Vázquez 2021). They removed anyone engaged in corruption.

But there's always a caveat. "You were stepping on too many toes [estabas pisando muchos callos]... and that's why they didn't want you there," Zulma concluded.

Amen.

In the end, they twisted something I had worked hard for—a framework against corruption, which was a strength—and turned it into a perceived weakness. By the summer of 2019, many who demanded my resignation labeled me as corrupt. They claimed I stole public funds, which was absolutely false (and later proven so), but narratives took hold. Some believed where there's smoke, there's fire.

This persisted even as I struggled for months without a job and any financial resources. Not even a year-long investigation that found no criminal activity or intent, exonerating me of any wrongdoing, could remove this label (Panel Sobre el Fiscal Especial Independiente 2020). With doubt sown, they branded my name. And to this day, opponents still hope for criminal charges against me, even without justification.

Othering, moralizing, and aversion have such effects.

We see what we choose to see. We overlook actions that contradict our beliefs and cling to any label or descriptor that validates our stance.

Words are indeed powerful. But be warned, they are often wielded as weapons.

The Power of Language and Social Media

"When we use language that is intentional and clear, we create a different world for ourselves."

—JOHN SANEI, *FORESIGHT*

This principle guided my approach to portray my vision for Puerto Rico and communicating our commitment to progress, embedding values like growth, empowerment, innovation, and a bright future into our narrative.

And it was effective.

In debates, I may not have been the most skilled orator (perhaps even the least adept) nor a polemicist known for creating catchy zingers and conflicts for attention. However, I consistently communicated our forward-looking vision, giving me an edge over my opponents who lacked a crystallized vision.

Regardless of the policy at hand, I could always link it back to our vision of moving forward. I created and shared visual maps, like the one below, to help people connect the dots. "Your vision was powerful, and it shone through your hand-drawn maps. I had never seen anything like it. It was distinctive. It was inspiring," remarked a participant at the Aspen Ideas Festival where I presented. (Figure 7)

Polls consistently indicated that "Rosselló has a strong vision for the future" was my most positively viewed attribute. Even after my resignation, when my personal approval ratings plummeted to single digits, the approval rating for my vision remained above 50 percent.

Here, words also had a positive impact.

Generally, negative words tend to dominate attention. There's a growing sense our discourse is becoming increasingly vitriolic and destructive. Irshad Manji observes that arguments are deteriorating, with social media being a significant contributor.

At the Aspen Ideas Festival, presenting our new vision for Puerto Rico post-recovery. I used my handwritten map to illustrate the interconnected aspirations and actions (Photo Credit: Magdiel Lugo).

Rage has become a business. Media entities have realized negative content engages us more effectively. "Technologies are intentionally manipulating us," Manji asserts, "to keep us addicted, turning us into either paying customers or the products themselves."

Quite a reality… quite a challenge.

Takeaways

"I think we have an opportunity to be more purposeful about the types of words we are using to get to a certain outcome. Most people don't think of it like that. We're not purposeful about it. You're just using whatever words you happen to think about in the moment, but if you're purposeful about it, certain words lead to certain outcomes in real life," LaQuita Cleare—author, sought-after speaker, and former actress with expertise in psychology—told me as we were discussing the topic of storytelling.

Good insight. I'll take it to heart. If I am going to postulate the power of words, I should start by using them to express the following.

Several years removed from office and having time to ponder and self-evaluate, I want to make three critical statements.

First, I could see how my words hurt people. More so, I internalized ingrained sexism in some of the words I used. It arises from a culture of sexism we have all experienced. I don't know what the overall solution is, but I will start from a place of being more thoughtful in my own way of communicating and having my kids understand the power of words. They can be beautiful and empowering. They can be devastating and discriminating. We have a choice. In this instance, I chose poorly.

Second, their branding of me as corrupt is unacceptable. I worked throughout my administration to precisely battle corruption and turned friends into enemies because I tackled it. Here too we have a choice. We can choose to either believe everything we hear because it marries to a desired narrative or to dive in deeper and question some of the exotic allegations that will come out. As discussed, this also happened with other claims on my persona. This is a powerful tool polarized extreme elements use. Statements become dogma, and seldomly does anyone question them. It is a real dangerous predicament in our society.

A third relates to the power of context and manipulation. Be very careful. While I do recognize the use of sexist language and hurtful comments, they found the texts "manipulated, edited, and incomplete." To this end, one of the most powerful statements used against me was an edited and purposely manipulated sentence that claims I stated (loosely translated) "We screw over even our own people" (*Cogemos de pendejo hasta los nuestro*). It became a rallying cry, and it remains to this day. A careful look shows the sentence structure and context don't even make sense. My opposition and the media used it as evidence that all I wanted to do was screw over people. This was just one of a myriad of examples. Ironically, in fact, the drivers of this narrative ended up fooling and screwing people over.

On this last point, Ramon Rosario puts it plainly: "The agendas of certain actors in the media, the political opposition and the enemies of Ricardo Rosselló within the PNP caused an avalanche of accusations to eliminate an elected governor. They did this because polls were clear he would have been comfortably re-elected. They needed to get him out in a way that did not include the vote of the people."

I am hopeful that my mistakes and my experiences will help others.

Taken together, you can say something about the way our society can dismiss a lifetime of actions on the back of a few words. This, of course, has a profound effect on our capacity to reform. If we are weaponizing words and stories, less people will participate in governance, and those who do… will likely be hampered from being effective.

In the *post-fact* age especially, it feels more and more like someone's actions aren't even a part of the conversation. They disregard them if they don't fit the narrative of the listener.

So be mindful, for good or for bad "… what we say, becomes our reality."

—JOHN SANEI, FORESIGHT.

Too often words speak louder than actions.

CHAPTER 8:

Oversimplifying Complexity

"Everything Under Control," read the heading on this caricature, illustrating the complex issues I navigated and the delicate, Jenga-like balancing act required. Part of the challenge was to prevent demagogues from oversimplifying our challenges (Bayon 2017).

"The dogmas of the quiet past are inadequate to the stormy present. The occasion is piled high with difficulty, and we must rise with the occasion. As our case is new, so we must think anew and act anew."

—ABRAHAM LINCOLN, ANNUAL MESSAGE TO CONGRESS, DECEMBER 1, 1862

My second State of the Union address (SOTU) felt different. It was the first since Hurricane Maria and a significant shift in energy and education policy. It occurred midway through the island's recovery phase.

In the US, the SOTU, mandated by the Constitution (Article II, Section 3, clause 1), requires the president to inform Congress about the nation's status and recommend necessary measures. Our tradition mirrors this.

But does it matter? A Gallup poll indicates that SOTUs rarely impact public perception or approval, with Clinton's 1998 address as an exception (Jones 2010). Viewership is typically partisan. Democrats tune in for a Democratic president, and vice versa, turning the address into a quasi-political rally. Supporters enthusiastically applaud while opponents express disdain.

However, this SOTU—set against the backdrop of fiscal and economic challenges as well as a major natural disaster—garnered significant interest. Everyone was eager to hear my address.

It began typically, highlighting the past year's actions and achievements. But midway, I declared, "This speech is about accountability. Alongside our successes, I will also discuss challenges, frustrations, and mistakes."

The gallery fell silent. The usual cues for applause were absent, leaving both opposition and media as well as my supporters visibly perplexed. Few had used such a platform to acknowledge errors. Despite a nervous flutter, I felt an imperative to speak candidly, eschewing demagoguery at this critical juncture. It was essential to focus on tangible results and actions—both positive and negative.

William Villafañe, who witnessed the atmosphere, observed, "In that moment, Rosselló was more scientist than politician. His approach to identify results and support them with evidence was novel. The audience misconstrued the absence of applause as a lack of support, leaving them was unsure how to react."

If something was failing, clarity was crucial. Intellectual integrity demanded acknowledging unsuccessful actions and implementing changes. Hard thinking took precedence over soft thinking.

Hard and Soft Thinking

"Hard thinking is thinking about particulars or in terms or language that can convey a clear and precise meaning to other people; putting testable ideas forward, which can be tested, which can be the subject of critical examination; statements that make an intellectual appeal as opposed to a visceral appeal," writes Peter Medwar in *My Life in Science* (1977).

Medwar's definition is incisive. In essence, hard thinking is grounded in science and reason, open to critical examination, and fosters the development of new paradigms. It's a relentless, curious quest for improvement without claiming to offer final solutions.

Conversely, Medwar describes soft thinking as "thinking that makes an appeal to or through emotions; which gives one a nice cozy feeling inside; which attempts to persuade one of what ought to be intellectual truths by nonintellectual means" (1977).

Ahhhh. A lot of that is going on these days.

Soft thinking, inherently ideological, requires no evidence and resists critical evaluation. It's often dogmatic and deliberately vague, relying heavily on emotional appeal.

Sound familiar?

It should.

This trend is evident in our current political climate. Ideological polarization has reached a point where people not only ignore opposing views but actively shut them out, a practice termed *otherism* in its extreme form. Leadership suffers in this environment with many leaders either withdrawing or becoming adept at promoting dogmatic truths. This is a global issue with some regions exhibiting it more starkly than others, and the trend is toward increasing polarization.

Emotions are undeniably important; they are part of our humanity and crucial for storytelling and understanding. However, when manipulative tactics use emotions to instill fear, rejection, and immobility, we encounter a significant problem.

Herbert E. Meyer, a special assistant to the director of the CIA during Ronald Reagan's administration, observed in *Hard Thinking: The Fusion of Politics and Science*, "We have lost our national talent for solving problems." He noted the overwhelming presence of "nonsense, boloney ideological posturing, and outright lies," leading to a national confusion that obscures clear problem-solving (1993) Figure 1.

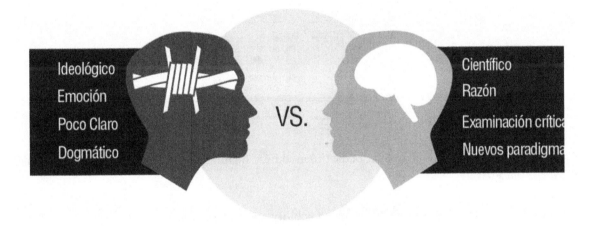

Figure 1. Slide from "Un Mejor Puerto Rico es Posible" demonstrating the clash between dogmatic soft thinking and scientific hard thinking (Rosselló 2012).

Recognizing a problem should, logically, enable us to avoid further mistakes. However, admitting mistakes is often costly.

Reflecting on my 2018 State of the Union (SOTU) speech, the press was initially surprised by my admission of mistakes. An article in *El Nuevo Dia* (2018) dedicated a section to this, titled "mea culpa": "In the midst of plans for the future, Rosselló Nevares took liability for mistakes committed in the process." (Figure 2)

Of course, the element of surprise did not last long.

The opposition quickly used my admissions against me, with the opposition resorting to fear tactics rather than facts. Eduardo Bhatia, a former president of the Senate and gubernatorial candidate, criticized

Figure 2. Mea Culpa: A review of my State of the Union address, highlighting my acknowledgment of mistakes (*El Nuevo Día* 2018).

my speech as "shallow," adding to "the irresponsibility and lack of credibility of Puerto Rico." When pressed for specifics, the response was vague, a typical outcome in such scenarios (*El Nuevo Día* 2018).

Would anyone dare to admit faults in such an address again? Well… like, Britney Spears, *I did it again*. In 2019, *El Nuevo Día* reported: "At the beginning of his speech, the governor recalled some of his mistakes and errors in policy since he arrived at La Fortaleza." These included issues like maritime transportation, management of the forensics laboratory, and the slow recovery of the energy grid post-Hurricane Maria.

Admitting failures and mistakes is crucial in governance. It allows for the abandonment of ineffective strategies and the exploration of new solutions. Thomas Edison famously said, "I have not failed. I've just found ten thousand ways that won't work." During my tenure, this approach enabled us to implement changes, though the stigma of failure was a significant obstacle.

In science and entrepreneurship, we see failures as learning opportunities. I advocated for a culture of accountability and learning from failed projects. The SOTU seemed an ideal platform to share not just victories but also defeats. Would this tradition endure? (Figure 3)

LO DIJO

"Otro de los obstáculos que hemos encontrado en el camino ha sido una actitud hostil de parte de algunos componentes del gobierno federal hacia Puerto Rico"

"En la próxima campaña presidencial, el tratamiento que ha recibido Puerto Rico del gobierno federal y nuestra relación desigual con los Estados Unidos será un asunto importante de derechos humanos a nivel nacional"

teresa.canino@gfrmedia.com

ADMITE ERRORES

Al inicio de su discurso ante la Asamblea Legislativa, el gobernador reconoció algunos de sus errores desde que llegó a La Fortaleza. Aquí, algunos de los que mencionó:

● Transporte marítimo entre la isla grande, Vieques y Culebra: dijo que es inaceptable que estuvieran días sin una embarcación de carga en funciones.

● Negociado de Ciencias Forenses: indicó que le "duele" ver cómo familiares tienen que esperar por los cuerpos de sus seres queridos.

● Reducción de fondos al Centro Médico: dijo que fue un error la merma en el presupuesto que recomendó mientras se aumentaban los gastos de La Fortaleza.

● Muertes tras el huracán María: admitió que el proceso de contabilidad "no fue adecuado".

● Recuperación lenta: dice que la gestión del Cuerpo de Ingenieros para restablecer la energía fue lenta y sin urgencia.

PROCLAMA ACIERTOS

En su mensaje ante la Legislatura, el gobernador enumeró una serie de acciones que, a su entender, constituyen aciertos de su gestión administrando el aparato público.

● Transformación energética: aseguró que este cambio mejorará el servicio y el costo de la electricidad en Puerto Rico. Los principales cambios de esta iniciativa, sin embargo, no se han ejecutado todavía.

● Reforma educativa: resaltó el impacto que tendrá el establecimiento de las escuelas chárter o "alianza" en la educación pública de Puerto Rico. Esta iniciativa se supone que empiece a implantarse durante el próximo año escolar.

● Organización de Mercadeo de Destino o DMO: comenzó a operar en julio de 2018 y la expectativa es que saque la intervención partidista de la promoción turística de la isla.

● Cesco Digital: aplicación que les permite a los conductores hacer gestiones sobre sus licencias y vehículos.

Figure 3. Admits mistakes. Continuing the commitment to acknowledging errors, I did so again in my 2019 State of the Union address (*El Nuevo Día* 2019).

Regrettably, the focus returned to superficial metrics like applause and standing ovations...

How can we foster meaningful change if imperfections lead to the vilification of policies and policymakers? This response discourages officials from admitting mistakes or being accountable. The incentives favor soft thinking and extremism, leading to more dogmatic, manipulative, and vague leaders. Is this what we want from our leaders?

Here's the kicker: Soft thinking infiltrates even more when issues become complex.

Complexity versus Complicated

"Not the same thing," Governor Eric Greitens tells me. "People often confuse them."

And differentiating between the two is key in accurately tackling problems.

"Thinking about the nature of problems is a very important question." Greitens postulates, "What kind of a problem is this? Some people confuse complicated and complex problems. There are *many* complicated problems. I'm looking out my window. There's a skyscraper going up. How to build a skyscraper is a very complicated problem. How you actually put plumbing in a skyscraper and electric is a very complicated problem. Yet once you know how to do it, you don't have to come every day to work and ask the question: How do we build a skyscraper? Complex problems are never fully solved because they *change* as you solve them."

Think of baseball as an analogy. No one simple pitch will help a pitcher solve every batter. Rather he has to consider many things every time he pitches: Who's the batter? Is anyone on base? What was the last pitch I threw? How does my arm feel right now?

You can say the same about treating complex issues like solving poverty, reducing bureaucracy, and working with climate change. They are always changing. The context matters. The initial conditions matter.

If you don't act upon it, you are stuck with people treating complex issues as complicated matter. This is where ideologs are born. They might have experienced a way of solving a complex issue at a specific moment. Now they think the solution to the problem is nonchanging and fixed. This is where those ideologs become demagogues driven by dogma.

Yet this is not as easy to explain as perhaps the baseball analogy.

Explaining Complexity

"Governor Ricardo Rosselló was on a mission to carry out several complex reforms creating natural tensions among elected officials who were under pressure from constituents who were upset by the changes or did not understand their need. Furthermore, the governor wanted to make these drastic changes as soon as possible due to the urgency of the multiple crises he inherited."

—RAMON ROSARIO ON NAVIGATING COMPLEXITY.

Understanding and communicating complexity was central to my leadership. As a professor and aspiring candidate, I relished tackling complex issues, aiming to connect with people in an educational and informative manner. However, this approach was not always effective.

Candidates often resorted to simplistic promises like "I will improve education" or "I will boost our economy." While these are noble goals, they often translated into vague proposals. This redundancy in political discourse led me to question: How could we offer something different?

This curiosity propelled me into formal politics, giving birth to the Plan for Puerto Rico. This comprehensive initiative, developed over five years with numerous collaborators, aimed to address root problems with innovative solutions.

Upon finalizing the plan, my advisors urged me to simplify my message, labeling me "too professorial" and overly detailed. Acknowledging their point, I began employing analogies, a technique that had served me well in science and life. This approach provided a relatable comparison, allowing for deeper exploration if desired.

For instance, explaining Puerto Rico's fiscal crisis was challenging. In an NPR interview, I described it as "a big Ponzi scheme" (Sullivan 2018), a comparison that resonated with listeners and provided a foundation for further discussion.

Yet communication experts continued to push for brevity and simplicity, which to me sounded like a call for vagueness and demagoguery. That's where I drew the line. I recall telling them "This is the very reason I ran for office. To *avoid* being simplistic and vague. To address the situation and to explain how we would govern."

Many advisors viewed this approach as a political misstep. In hindsight, it probably was… I just got lucky.

A Simple Prediction

While identifying Puerto Rico's root problems, I gained insights that led me to accurately predict the island's fiscal collapse years in advance. This foresight, though based on simple calculations, surprised many.

Peter Miller, a lawyer and radio host, recounted, "In 2011, I met this young man for lunch. He explained the exponential factors leading to a grave fiscal collapse, sketching it on a napkin. I didn't pay much attention then, but I distinctly remember him predicting it would happen in 2015."

And, indeed, it did collapse.

Another factor in my favor was my unique policy "language." My novel ideas stood out, gaining traction and dominating debates. My opponents, skilled orators and politicians, inadvertently focused the discussion on my proposals, allowing me to set the agenda.

For instance, I suggested the government become a single employer. This proposal, though not initially sexy, gained attention due to its controversy. *Caribbean Business* described it "the Plan for Puerto Rico proposes to reevaluate the 118 agencies and 340 services to consolidate, eliminate, or make them more efficient without the dismissal of public employees, who we will reorganize under the single employer system. This system seeks to convert public employees into servants of the government and not of their individual entities, so they can move from one agency to another, according to need, without violating their collective agreements" (*Caribbean* Business 2016).

My closest competitor, David Bernier, labeled me "the executioner of the civil servant," a catchy phrase that brought more attention to the idea. This controversy helped embed the concept in public consciousness.

In the debates, my rivals stuck to traditional tactics, attacking my proposals. This strategy backfired, drawing more interest to my ideas. This climaxed in one of the last debates when David Bernier asked me a question. The TV channel hosting the debate *randomly* selected a candidate to ask a question to another… and randomly—Bernier had a golden chance to attack me directly.

He asked, "You propose to cut sixteen billion from the budget. Who will you lay off?" (Anthony 2016).

This gave me a minute to explain my plan in detail, an opportunity I hadn't had before. I clarified my strategy involved no layoffs, seizing this crucial moment to articulate my vision.

Even Jay Fonseca, a critical media figure, acknowledged the potential of my single employer concept (Fonseca 2016).

Defining a Fiscal Oversight Board

In the summer before my tenure as governor, the federal government established a Financial Oversight and Management Board (FOMB) to address Puerto Rico's fiscal crisis. This issue, unusually visible for the island, became a symbol for political extremes. We were, and largely remain, overlooked.

Picture this: a debt exceeding 120 billion dollars (Associated Press 2020), a lending freeze post-default under the García Padilla administration, a shrinking economy at 2.9 percent (World Bank 2023), unemployment nearing 12 percent (Denis 2015), and rampant transparency issues.

And this was just the tip of the iceberg.

Addressing this required nuanced, deliberate, and creative approaches, understanding that no single solution could resolve it.

In Washington, DC, the extremes dominated the narrative. Hard-right Republicans advocated for a fiscal control board, distinct from an oversight board. A control board would entirely, rather than partially, override Puerto Rico's elected government's powers. This was sensitive, given Puerto Rico's limited political representation at the national level.

Senator Orrin Hatch expressed a part of this complexity: "I voted to invoke cloture on the bill, because, thanks to the stubbornness of the Treasury Department and lack of transparency from the government of Puerto Rico, it is the only option on the table, and delaying action would only hurt the Americans who reside on the island" (Senate Finance 2016).

The debate intensified, drawing more public attention. "Democrats want the territory to have the ability to reorganize its seventy-two-billion-dollar debt load, but Hatch opposes this. Last week, he proposed a bill to cut Puerto Rican workers' share of the payroll tax and create an oversight authority that could spend up to three billion dollars to help Puerto Rico regain fiscal stability" (Reuters Staff 2015). They clearly drew the lines.

This debate over a control board in a territory inadvertently opened Pandora's box regarding democracy. The imposition of such a board, especially in a territory where US citizens lack voting representation in Congress or a presidential vote, raised significant questions about their liberty. Some on the hard right seemed indifferent to this, despite its clash with the principle of liberty.

The hard left, not to be outdone, pushed for a bankruptcy mechanism that, in its extreme form, could erase the entire debt. This echoed President Trump's off-the-cuff remarks post-storm. They sought this without fiscal controls, which while not democratically problematic, opened another Pandora's box. If Puerto Rico could cancel its debt and declare bankruptcy, why couldn't states like Connecticut or California? Defaulting would also damage Puerto Rico's market credibility and impact the broader municipal bond market, as many funds held Puerto Rican bonds.

Extreme left activists framed this as a rich versus poor issue, aligning with their broader Wall Street versus Main Street narrative.

Bernie Sanders vehemently stated, "Greedy Wall Street vulture funds must not be allowed to reap huge profits off the suffering and misery of the Puerto Rican people for a second longer" (Giel 2018). He later proposed a bill to cancel the debt. One small detail. It was more than seventy-three billion dollars' worth of debt, and this would have systemic repercussions in the rest of the municipal bond market in the USA.

Eureka! Now we know the reason why Congress was attending to this situation and not other urgent matters for Puerto Rico.

It wasn't about fiscal prudence or class struggle. Addressing Puerto Rico's status and providing equal opportunities for its citizens could resolve much of this. The real impetus for congressional action was the potential impact on *their* states and constituents.

The situation was further complicated by the fact that US states don't have bankruptcy courts. Puerto Rico's default posed a significant problem, especially for institutional investors attracted by the triple tax-exempt status of Puerto Rican bonds. Many holders of these bonds, including retirees, were unaware of their investments' precarious state.

This conflict turned into a multifaceted battle involving the government, bondholders, the public, and the federal government.

With differing solutions and a looming crisis affecting both Puerto Rico and the US, Congress responded in its typical fashion by creating a hybrid solution. The PROMESA bill (Puerto Rico Oversight, Management, and Economic Stability Act) was a vague, compromise legislation lacking clarity and foresight. Ironically, PROMESA means "promise."

Amid confusion and urgency, Congress enacted PROMESA, establishing an oversight board with limited control. This board couldn't change policy but could block it, raising questions about its ability to foster economic growth and the elected government's capacity to implement policy. My administration often clashed with the oversight board over governance issues, but we managed to overcome most challenges.

This scenario was ripe for soft thinking, with uncharted waters, multiple stakeholders, competing narratives, and political motivations.

And this was just the setup. Imagine now addressing the complex issues and powerful opposing stakeholders themselves.

The Debt Rabbit Hole

Remember the scene in *The Matrix* where Morpheus offers Neo the choice between the blue pill and the red one?

I took the red pill.

The enormous and ineffective labyrinth that was the government of Puerto Rico deserves several dedicated volumes. While I attempt to give the reader a sense of the complexities, it will inevitably fall short. Just thinking about the *initial conditions* is mind boggling:

- The bond debt burden was seventy-three billion dollars (Heath and Newmyer 2017)
- Add to that fifty-three billion in unpaid pension liabilities (Stojanovic and Wessel 2022).
- And when I took office, we had a little more than five hundred million dollars in the bank. For reference, that was just about a few payrolls.
- No money coming in from bonds.
- An economy in negative growth for more than a decade. This was the product of many years of soft thinking.

How could you tackle a problem of such overwhelming magnitude and multiple streams? Since before the election, I made it clear the strategy for renegotiating Puerto Rico's debt should comply with certain guiding principles:

- Restore credibility by conducting transparent and good-faith negotiations and respecting the rule of law

- Secure liquidity relief and interim financing to have an opportunity to implement the reforms required to achieve long-term solvency and economic growth
- Reduce the total debt burden and limit future debt growth
- Provide a mechanism to mitigate a portion of any losses incurred by local resident creditors
- Provide a roadmap to restore access to the municipal bond market at reasonable rates

Christian Sobrino was the head of the fiscal agency and was a brilliant key player in the effort to unravel this situation. He explained, "We had a two-pronged philosophy. The first was the building blocks approach, complemented by a divide-and-conquer strategy. The building blocks approach is crucial when facing monumental tasks. Focusing solely on the end goal is a recipe for failure due to overwhelming opposition and numerous steps. It's about breaking down the plan and strategy into manageable segments."

This approach required a meticulously crafted strategy, grit, patience, and a considerable amount of luck. Hard thinking was essential; soft thinking alone wouldn't suffice.

Under the PROMESA bill, we received Title III, a bankruptcy court-like mechanism for Puerto Rico. This provision allowed us to pause payments, creating space to thoughtfully renegotiate the debt.

When I invoked this provision, critics simplistically claimed, "Rosselló has led Puerto Rico into bankruptcy." Such demagoguery was the expectation. Without this measure, bondholders could seize government cash and assets, a dire scenario.

This pause in payments opened the door to start renegotiations with creditors, a daunting task, given their varying claims. The simplistic solution of not paying the debt was both foolish and irresponsible. The challenge was to find a solution amid inevitable criticism.

Our consultants suggested assessing each issuance's starting point and creating proposals. But this approach, potentially beneficial for consultants, lacked a clear strategy. It felt like a fishing expedition.

William Villafañe, reflecting on this, said, "The governor demanded a solution and strategy, or we'd find new consultants." Ahh... the power of words. This ultimatum shifted the meeting's dynamic.

By its conclusion, we had a focused strategy: prioritize negotiations with the two major bond categories, General Obligation (GO) Bonds and Sales Tax backed (COFINA) bonds. These were the largest credits with a clear dispute between them.

For context, the territory's full faith and credit back GO bonds while they fund COFINA bonds directly by sales tax revenue. Both groups believed they had the primary claim to available capital. "COFINA creditors are in litigation with GO bondholders, each claiming rights to sales tax revenue" (Brown 2017).

So, we went on the journey. How did our first efforts go? Not too well. Our attempt at a negotiation with both of these credits went a little like this: Pay me everything (close to 100 percent of the value of my bond) and pay nothing to the rest of the credits.

At least these two credits agreed on "*something*."

This complicated posturing game continued for several months, oversimplifying the narrative in the social sphere. Supporters of the bondholders claimed the government was shortchanging them. So, the narrative was... we were giving them *too little*. Opponents of the administration were saying the government was "stealing money" to pay the "vulture funds." So, this narrative was we were giving them *too much.* However contradictory, both narratives existed concurrently. Fascinating.

Where were we? Stuck in between, thinking, working, grinding to get things *done.*

Picture this. Each creditor group had assembled a small army of financial advisors and bankruptcy lawyers, each having legal theories about why we should pay them first. However, potential holes in their theories could lead to an unfavorable outcome in court. Therefore, both groups were eager to achieve a voluntary agreement. Specifically, both main credits had potentially side-stepped and exceeded Puerto Rico's constitutional debt limits and *could be* found invalid.

We held multiple day-long meetings in both New York and Puerto Rico where one group would sit outside the room for a few hours while we met with the other, looking to find a compromise that would satisfy them both. The debate was also happening outside the negotiation table with cross-fire from opponents, the legislature, other bondholders, retirees, media, congressmembers "supported" by those bondholders… congressmembers supported by different credits…

In the end, COFINA was first agreeable to our terms. With half the equation balanced, we continued negotiations with the GO group to the last minute, even past the temporary stay on litigation granted by PROMESA.

Dizzy already? Let's decouple.

Navigating the legislative process for our debt restructuring proposal was challenging, even with majorities in both houses. Internal opposition and external pressures were rampant, and soft thinking influenced many. They were getting pressure from all angles. A lot of money was thrown in all directions.

I seized the opportunity to act when other reforms started showing results. After intense debates and protests, the bill narrowly passed (Childs 2018). I signed it into law on November 15, 2018, stating, "This agreement allows us to restructure debt from previous administrations. The savings will fund government services and protect the vulnerable while avoiding further costly litigation."

The opposition was livid.

You would hear things from top officials like: "The design of the law is to funnel all income to vultures", "We don't acknowledge the debt as our own," and "Our country owes nothing… it is the US government that has looted us for years."

Statements like these are rife with soft thinking and demagoguery. On top of that… the statements above were factually *untrue.* Nonetheless, it was part of the whirlwind discussion that kept on aggravating constituents and building resentment.

Despite these challenges, we achieved the largest municipal restructuring in US history (Giel 2017). Our efforts preserved pensions and reopened a path to the financial markets for Puerto Rico, closed since 2014.

The Heritage Foundation (2017) noted

On January 2, 2017, Governor of Puerto Rico Ricardo Rossello came into office and inherited a government in dire need of fiscal prudence, economic development and government reform. His first 100 days in office have produced a steady wave of executive and legislative orders intent on transforming Puerto Rico for generations to come.

Governor Rossello has signed over 50 bills and executive orders with immediate effect; controlling government expenses, establishing zero-based budgeting, spurring private sector investment and labor reform, promoting bilingual education, and shrinking the number of state agencies from 118 to fewer than 40 over the next four years

Notwithstanding, communicating and managing this complexity was taxing on both my administration… and on me.

Takeaways

Hurricanes, dealing with complicated world leaders, fiscal chaos, reform, climate change, and social uprisings—these themes are inherently complex. Yet instead of addressing their complexity, they often oversimplified them. The aim was not to explain but to create confusion, fear, and despair—the perfect environment for soft thinking.

But the ability to use hard thinking to explain these complex themes in simple terms is a rare gift. When done correctly, it can be extremely effective. Franklin Roosevelt, for instance, was known for his "Fireside Chats," a series of radio broadcasts where he directly addressed the American people. He explained complex policies, decisions, and the challenges facing the nation in a manner that was both relatable and comprehensible. Through these chats, he successfully conveyed the intricacies of the New Deal, the country's response to the Great Depression, and later, the nation's involvement in World War II. On the other end of the spectrum, Ronald Reagan, dubbed "The Great Communicator," had a unique ability to simplify complex ideas. Drawing from his background in entertainment, Reagan used relatable anecdotes, humor, and consistent messaging to make intricate topics accessible to the average American. He distilled policy matters into core principles, often appealing to shared values and optimism.

What are some actions we can all employ to effectively communicate complex issues?

- Use Analogies and Metaphors: Relate the complex topic to something familiar to the audience. Analogies and metaphors can bridge the gap between the known and the unknown, making the unfamiliar topic more relatable. For example, the Ponzi scheme analogy to the running of finances on the island.

- Declutter: Break the complex situation down into more basic components. It can be challenging, but it gives a better chance of illustrating what is happening. By presenting information in a step-by-step or component-based manner, you allow the audience to grasp each part individually, making the overall topic easier to understand. This was our approach in shedding light on the debt process.

- Visual Aids or Maps: Visual representations can often convey information more effectively than words alone. Charts, diagrams, flowcharts, and infographics can simplify complex data or processes. Throughout this book, we will use some real and handwritten graphics to illustrate key concepts and points.

- Storytelling: Arguably the most powerful tool. We will dedicate a full chapter to this subject. Narratives and real-world examples can make abstract or intricate topics more tangible. By presenting a story or example that encapsulates the essence of the topic, you provide context and make the information more memorable.

Herbert Meyer's warning about the dangers of favoring soft thinking over hard thinking in facing challenges is stark: "A vastly more serious problem" that could lead to "losing our national talent for solving problems" (Meyer 1993). This insight is crucial, as problem-solving is inherent to human nature. Whether in math, sports, science, or policy, we grow by confronting and resolving challenges.

The inability to solve problems impedes our capacity for reform. Soft thinking, as Meyer pointed out, fosters a culture detached from problem-solving. He lamented, "now, more than ever before, these facts, ideas, analyses, and insights were buried beneath an avalanche of nonsense, baloney, ideological posturing, and outright lies" (Meyer 1993).

To counter this, we must reclaim our problem-solving abilities and engage in constructive argument and discussion. Embracing hard thinking is essential; without it, our future is grim.

If we can't *begin* to solve problems, how can we expect to find our true north? It starts with our humanity…

CHAPTER 9:

Dehumanization

Snapshot of a banner used during the protests of the summer of 2019. Illustrates me as the devil (El Diablo). (Photo credit: Mariel Falero)

It was a rainy day on the island in mid-July, the apex of the protests that led to my resignation. Tensions were high. My kids were in the car. When suddenly: *Boom Clack.* A horrible noise made way as the car trembled.

Visibly shaken Claudia, my daughter, yelled, "What is that?"

"It's just a pothole."

My daughter replied, "Thank God, I thought it was the men with machine guns coming to get us and kill us."

Claudia was four years old at that point.

This event rattled me to my core. I had already come to grips with the reality I could no longer operate as a chief executive. A *threshold* had passed. Yet the bottled-up emotions exploded.

When your baby daughter—whom you've tried to shield from just about everything that was going on—thinks people are coming for her, things have hit a new level. Who would want to startle and strike fear into a four-year-old girl? Nobody. Unless you had *dehumanized* me and my family.

We were living in this environment on the final days of my administration. The well-built narrative hardwired into people said I was an evil villain who wanted to kill people, I hated women and LGBTQ, and because of my corruption, I deserved a knife to my throat. This was too much to overcome. My demotion from human to something less than human had occurred.

People even wrote songs about it.

Melodies

Calle 13, iLe, and Bad Bunny released a song titled "Afilando los Cuchillos," which translates to "Sharpening the Knives," in the summer of 2019, directed at me and my family. They called me a piece of shit, homophobic, dictator, and liar, to name a few. They accused me of money laundering, theft, and fraud (all not only false but absolutely baseless). They said my father was the most corrupt bastard in history, insulted my wife, and threatened our lives (Residente 2019).

The song is artistic freedom. There was no push back.

Protesters held signs depicting my dead body that read "Here is the cadaver we want to feed the ravens." Other's showed images of my decapitated head. Protesters set up a "ceremonial guillotine" in front of our home. They threatened and yelled insults at my children.

The experience was akin to a car crash. One second you are driving down the road and everything is fine. The next, chaos emerges, things flash before you, and your life changes.

I understand how these words caused harm. But the reaction seemed to be—and in some quarters still is—completely overblown. Was I wrong for saying the word puta? Yes. Did my family deserve all these insults and threats? Was I a criminal? Was cutting off my head, literally, the desired outcome?

I had a hard time coming to the conclusion, but I finally did. By that point, many protesters did not see me as a human being. I was more of a caricature. A villain. An animal (Figure 1).

I felt completely *dehumanized*.

A Human Zoo

I don't want to stand on my soapbox and claim I've never dehumanized others. I have. But after experiencing it at such a high level, I began to ponder its origins. Dehumanization, by definition, is the act of regarding, representing, or treating a person or group as less than human. This is not a new phenomenon.

"Colonial exhibitions, fairs, circuses, zoos, and museums all participated in exhibiting people from across the world that were deemed as *other* and, thus, curious to observe by white masses that deemed themselves superior and more civilized. In some cases, entertainment was elevated through

Figure 1. Commonly used images on the protests of July 2019 with my head decapitated or as a rat or other animal.

the incorporation of thrilling performances and the display of exotic animal, further animalizing and dehumanizing exhibited humans" (Guy 2021).

Less than a century ago, human zoos were a reality. The core ingredient in such exhibitions was dehumanization. Without it, they couldn't have existed. Viewing others as less than human provides a mechanism for reduced empathy, and at its worst, enables abuse and brutality. And it's not that people were unaware of its implications even then.

In 1906, the *New York Times* quoted Reverend Robert Stuart MacArthur: "The person responsible for this exhibition degrades himself as much as he does the African. Instead of making a beast of this little fellow, he should be put in school for the development of such powers as God gave to him. It is too bad there is not some society like that for the Prevention of Cruelty to Children. We send our missionaries to Africa to Christianize the people, and then we bring one here to brutalize him" (1906).

The legacy of human zoos is far from resolved. Today, the phenomenon of dehumanization is still prevalent. "Dehumanizing allows us to exclude people from our moral concern. If we perceive someone as 'not quite human,' we can justify treating them terribly," explains Andrew Luttrell, Professor of Psychological Sciences at Ball State (Luttrell 2021).

Luttrell cites research from 2001 analyzing a broad spectrum of emotions, with some deemed *uniquely human*. For instance, people attributed basic emotions like joy and fear to animals while complex emotions like compassion, nostalgia, embarrassment, and empathy were exclusively human.

The essence is people often view other groups, especially those they see as distinct or in conflict with, as possessing less-than-human qualities. As I write these words on October 7, 2023, the images of the Israel-Palestine conflict are striking. The merciless killings, the mutilation and humiliation of bodies—a stark example of dehumanization.

Recent research by Nour Kteily, Emile Bruneau, and others attempts to quantify this phenomenon. Their findings indicate "that blatantly dehumanizing representations of Arabs can be just as prevalent among individuals exhibiting low levels of explicit dehumanization (e.g., liberals) as among individuals exhibiting high levels of explicit dehumanization (e.g., conservatives)" (Petsko et al. 2020).

This issue is pervasive.

While this research primarily addresses groups demeaning others, such as in cases of racism, refugees, or historical conflicts, the same concept applies in leadership and politics. This is increasingly evident today as different "groups" become more distinct and less inclined to collaborate, especially when extremism takes hold.

In the past, physical human zoos were the manifestation of dehumanizing behavior. Today, technology and media have become a fertile ground for its perpetuation.

Social Media as a Modern Human Zoo

Governor Cuomo, once highly regarded as a leading US figure and chief communicator during the COVID-19 pandemic, faced his own ordeal with social unrest. Accused of sexual harassment and subsequently investigated, he resigned but officials later exonerated of any wrongdoing.

In our discussions, Cuomo identified two main culprits: cancel culture and social media.

"Social media mentality and cancel culture have fostered vulgarity. What garners the most likes and notoriety is saying the most outrageous thing. In this culture, the politician becomes just a piñata," he observed.

Manji defines cancel culture as more than just disagreement or sharp criticism, which are acceptable in a free society. "Cancel culture personalizes criticism. It seeks to humiliate and punish rather than to counter and argue with" (2020). This behavior stems from dehumanization, seeing the other as lesser, and thereby justifying extreme actions. This mindset led some otherwise normal, nonviolent people to symbolically put my head on a stick.

Cuomo added, "There's no respect, no humanity in these conversations. You're reduced to an icon, an emoji. The culture breeds venom because that's what gets attention."

But what drives social media to provoke such reactions? Manji points to a biological basis. "We think emotionally before rationally. Information first hits the primal part of our brain—the ego, which is there to keep us alive. The problem is the ego can't distinguish between mortal danger and mere discomfort. Disagreement can feel like a threat to our very identity" (2020).

Manji suggests social media platforms amplify emotions by design. "Face-to-face, it's harder to dehumanize someone than in the confines of a comment box. These technologies are intentionally manipulating us to keep us addicted" (2020).

Colectiva Feminista Interseccional UPRA •••
Yesterday at 11:40 PM · 🌐

Estas tambien son putas gobernador.

Figure 2: Dehumanizing my family. A post by the Collective Feminist Chapter in Puerto Rico, calling my mother, wife, diseased grandmother, and four-year-old daughter, *putas* (Celeste 2019).

Consider a post by the "Feminist Collective" during my political crisis. I had inappropriately referred to a political opponent as a bitch in a private conversation. I was wrong to do so. But is it then acceptable for the Feminist Collective, a group supporting women, to use that same word against the women in my family? That's exactly what they did (Figure 2).

How is this acceptable? Why is it not seen as a double standard? Astonishingly, how is this an acceptable form of communication for a feminist group? The vitriol and hate were so intense they faced no backlash. So it's acceptable for one group to use a word, but for another, it's a death sentence? This double standard is another form of dehumanization.

Caricature of Oneself: Taking a Strength and Making it a Weakness

"This is why in the face of necessity we articulate so much that it was important to have a plan. I know the plan is a joke in some lines. Apparently, I repeat the word plan a lot, but I want to clarify the importance of that plan. Plan, plan, plan," the country's chief executive said with a laugh (Metro Puerto Rico 2017).

I was presenting to the Industrials Association when I uttered those words. They became viral. *"Why?"* you may ask.

Because what made me a legitimate candidate—the rigorous development of a strategic plan—also became the bud of jokes, ridicule, and attacks from opponents. In the absence of presenting a plan of their own, the other candidates in the elections decided to make light of the plan. Their goal? Paint me as a fool that just repeated the word plan. Another soft thinking but highly effective tactic.

"Many criticize that the governor, Ricardo Rosselló, mentions the word a lot and he did not miss the opportunity to joke about it in the middle of his message at an event of the Industrials Association," the paper read (Metro Puerto Rico 2017).

That day, instead of running away from it, I embraced it. And as people laughed, then I could explain. "The governor went on to explain the measures, he highlighted the eighteen executive orders he issued, and the laws signed, such as the single employer and the labor reform. Regarding the latter, he alleged it will allow the government to be more competitive." People listened (Metro Puerto Rico 2017).

I always told my team to be careful of becoming a caricature of yourself. And in this case, I could turn it around a bit. But I had experienced this tactic in the past. In 2012, well before I was governor or even a candidate, people already attempted to define me. In an article in *Primera Hora*, the title read "Einstein for Governor?" there was an attempt to mock the fact I was a scientist and to downplay any real chance to become governor (Cruz 2012) Figure 3.

The opening line sarcastically read "the great genius of stem cells is among us and wants to be governor" (Cruz 2012). The idea was to somehow turn a general positive (my scientific preparation, MIT, my membership in Mensa and Triple Nine Society) into a negative. "I have an idea for Ricky, in 2016 present a proposal to cancel the elections and to have him be named governor permanently because he is so unique, specialized, and superior," Cruz wrote (2012).

The seeds of dehumanization by characterization began very early on. Luckily, it did not work. Quite the opposite, in fact. It backfired. For many folks, this was the first time they had read about my preparation and skills—even if the tone was sarcastic. Inadvertently, they validated the possibility of my candidacy.

I was not so lucky the second time around as governor. There, they attacked and defined me negatively by two characteristics I believed to be strong points that helped me get elected.

The first one was the tag of the *robot governor.* I worked heavy hours and was laser focused. By 3:30 a.m. I was in my office every day. In addition, my press conferences became marathons, and I would sustain very matter-of-fact. On a personal level, I did not drink, smoke, or party, and I had a very happy family life. They made this seem like a charade as a ploy to get people to think I was like that. The objective? To dehumanize me. I was no longer a "normal human." I was a robot. With this branding, they were targeting my empathy.

The other one was the *"I don't know"* governor. In many marathonic press conferences, I would have to answer a bunch of questions. Of which, some I did not know the answer. I would generally answer something like, "I don't know. That's a good question. We'll find out." But the tag stuck. Shortly thereafter, people were identifying me as someone who would use the copout of "I don't know" as a

Figure 3. Opinion article titled "Einstein for Governor" (Cruz 2012).

way to avoid giving answers or telling the truth. Many a cartoon and meme out there had my face and the words "I don't know." In this instance, they were targeting my authenticity and my logic.

Not surprisingly one of the leading thinkers in the concept of Trust, Francis Frei, identifies these three elements—empathy, authenticity, and logic—as critical to trust (2022). This is where the opposition and media struck: Lack of empathy (robot governor), lack of authenticity (saying I don't know to avoid answering and hiding something) and lack of logic (using the plan as a shield not to dive in deep, and saying I don't know because I was inexpert).

Interestingly, the root of many of them was quite the opposite. I wanted to make sure my logic was sound, so I dedicated years of my life to a thorough Plan for Puerto Rico. I also wanted to stay within my bounds and not make up things on the fly. As a scientist, I learned to just say, "I don't know," if it's beyond your scope. What a novel concept!

The robot governor mantra came as I was working my tail off and avoided other distractions to attend to the matter at hand—a collapsed Puerto Rico when we took office. The authenticity piece was also important. While I admit this is the weakest of my three core trust variables, others used it to portray me as a liar. The stigma was effective.

So be cognizant that to dehumanize you, they might just use your strengths against you.

Speaking of that.

Pile On

"Look, right now I said *One Hundred Years of Solitude*. It's Gabriel García Márquez, not Paulo Coelho. I was wrong there," Beatriz Rosselló, the first lady of Puerto Rico, acknowledged, shortly after mixing up authors in a radio interview. It was a mistake anyone could make, but the fallout was far from ordinary. The mockery that ensued was not only disproportionate but also widespread, spanning the island and beyond (De Llano 2017).

This incident still pains me deeply. In discussing it with her, she vividly recalled, "I was extremely tired, deeply involved in all of the initiatives," as detailed in chapter 2. "I barely remember how I got to the interview. The doctors had warned me I could give birth at any moment." If that happened, it would likely have been on the USS Comfort, one of the few healthcare options at that time. "I decided to go on *Rubén Sánchez's* program because I wanted to promote 'Isla Bendita.'"

"Isla Bendita" was a collaborative song, similar to "We Are the World," created to raise awareness and aid healing in Puerto Rico.

"In the interview, I mentioned the song's global impact and our consideration of an English version," she explained. "To illustrate why an English version was important, I shared a story about Shakira. Before her crossover, she hadn't considered singing in English until she learned that President Bill Clinton had read *One Hundred Years of Solitude* in English. In my exhaustion, I misspoke, mentioning Coelho instead of García Márquez. I corrected myself a few seconds later, but the damage was already done."

The aftermath was swift and harsh.

"The next day, newspapers and thousands of tweets were ridiculing my mistake, trying to portray me as insensitive and unintelligent," she recounted. "The mockery even spread to Mexico, Spain, and other places."

During this time, she gave birth, facing insults both before and after. "I am human… and it led to depression."

It's crucial to remember this interview happened just over a month after the hurricane struck, at a time when my wife was making outstanding efforts to deliver food and essential items across the island, all while being pregnant.

"Just three weeks away from giving birth, she was tirelessly helping the people. Yet, a simple mistake on a radio show was used to attack her, trying to portray her as somewhat of an idiot, when in reality, she was the driving force behind many of the initial aid efforts," said Cynthia Santiago, an executive assistant to the Office of the First Lady.

Beatriz is a brilliant, thoughtful, and compassionate human being. However, due to political motives, they seized upon this minor slip-up, and social media became the main vehicle for promoting this mockery.

"Technologies are intentionally designed to engage and amplify our emotions," says Professor Manji. "Dehumanizing someone is easier online than face-to-face."(Manji 2020).

Would anyone mock someone they knew who was extraordinarily tired, dealing with the stress of a catastrophe, and heavily pregnant? Unlikely. But dehumanization is a powerful force, blinding people to these facts.

This tendency to dehumanize has become a significant deterrent to participation in government.

Immediately, Half Will See You as Corrupt

You could have the greatest plan and vision—but if you don't have the people, you have nothing. It is like any enterprise, if you are stuck in a position that limits your capacity to get A-players, you will likely be unsuccessful. Therefore, an important task in leading is finding aligned people, who will execute, and will amplify your *bandwidth*.

Makes sense. So, what's the problem?

"Theoretically, finding people to go into office and make the changes is a tough task. The prospect of burned at the stake at the end of the process is not alluring. This is not a sustainable model. For society, this has become an existential question," Governor Cuomo told me in our conversation.

That's the problem.

It made me reflect on the time I asked a well-known lawyer in Puerto Rico to become secretary of justice. He had been a friend, had demonstrated capacity to execute, and was a great communicator. He had the trifecta: Top of field mind, capacity to execute, and loved politics.

I thought it was a slam dunk. So when I asked him, I was surprised with the hesitation.

"Let me sleep on it, Governor," he said.

Two days later, he called back. "Governor, with a heavy heart, I will have to refuse this opportunity. It is something I've wanted to do for the past twenty-five years. But quite simply, it is not in the cards for me now."

"What changed?" I asked.

"My wife hit me with some hard truths. When I informed her they tapped me to be secretary of justice, she replied, 'That's great, honey. Congratulations.' I noticed her somewhat uneasy. When I asked what was on her mind, she said, 'Look, just remember that as soon as you accept that position, half of the people will see you as a horrible, corrupt individual immediately. You need to ask yourself—is this what you want?'"

Evidently, the answer was no. And he is not alone

A longitudinal pew research study gives insights into why. Trust in government—an issue we will address in some detail later—has been diminishing for the past fifty years. Today, it is at its lowest point. It is the crystallization of the "*half of the people will immediately think I am corrupt*" concern (Figure 4).

Guess who it's affecting more? Moderates, much more so than extremist.

"Ideologically moderate citizens—people with more centrist views who believe in political pragmatism—are increasingly unlikely to run for political office, and this has a lot to do with why our legislatures have polarized so dramatically," a Stanford University piece showcased (Hall 2019).

I have an issue with the word *moderate*. It implies weakness. I think there should be a rebranding of sorts, but I'm getting ahead of myself here.

The bottom line is dehumanization does have a tangible effect on our society. People become more untrusting. Speech becomes more lacerating. Dehumanization becomes the norm between opposing factions. If you can add value in government—or elsewhere because of the skill sets you possess—you have to ask yourself the question: Why do it? With more hurdles to make an impact and an almost guaranteed hit on your reputation… Why do it?

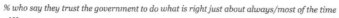

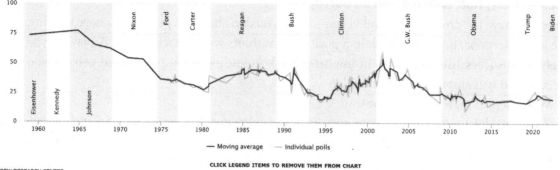

Figure 4. Graphic denoting Pew Research longitudinal assessment of trust in government as a function of time (Pew Research Center 2023).

The follow-up question is then: Who is left?

Two characteristics: (1) More and more extreme folks, that have (2) less translational skills to execute in government. This is very dangerous. More and more people that cling to soft thinking use their words to provoke harm. This is the highway to losing our "national talent for solving problems" (Meyer 1993).

Why is this relevant? Consider these two clashing realities.

- o In 2021, in the US, only 16 percent of the population was progressive liberal or faith and flag conservatives and the "middle" is anywhere from 60 to 84 percent of the population (Pew Research Center 2021).
- o Major network and cable TV news outlets have given the most airtime to members of Congress with the most extreme views (Padget, Dunaway, and Darr 2019), vastly overrepresenting extreme partisans on both sides of the aisle.

These create the environment for extremism to rule, for consensus to be harder to achieve, and for people to keep distancing themselves from the *others* by way of dehumanization.

And this trickles into society. Yes, even to me.

I Also Dehumanized

One of the biggest and most jarring considerations from the published chats was that I dehumanized others. This was a hard pill to swallow and a powerful realization, one I gave careful thought to since the summer of 2019. In my right frame of mind, I would never want to dehumanize another person. So, what can we do to avoid it?

First we need to understand we are under an onslaught of media and messaging that activates our worst angels in the social media platforms. We are susceptible to these messages. Media can be a powerful instrument to brand villains and heroes based on catchy headlines and wordsmithing. But on our daily routine, Manji has a great suggestion when it comes to *label traps*.

"When somebody escalates the conversation based on labels they have of you, don't fall into the trap by escalating further the conversation based on the labels you now have of them. Simply remind them you are more than the label they're assigning to you right now, just as they are more than any label you might put on them. That reminder will actually elevate the conversation. Because you'll be reminding them that you're ready to listen, but that you expect that same ground rule to apply in the reverse" (2020).

I fell into the trap. My wish is others don't have to fall into it and can learn from my experience. It's a costly one.

Takeaways

Dehumanization makes us seem farther apart, to the point we authorize ourselves to treat others in a way that is beneath or inferior to humans. Social media, with all its breakthroughs and advances in the way we communicate with each other, can also bring out the worst in us. We have to stay mindful of this reality.

The evidence is clear. We all lose when *dehumanization* happens. Our government and society lose. Diversity and collaborative efforts lose. It is worrisome that the trend has been increasing in the past twenty years, with no signals that it will stop. The outcomes? Terrible: loss of trust, stalemate, and inaction. Not good when you are attempting to reform.

What can we do to reverse this trend?

1. **Promote Empathy and Active Listening:** Encourage individuals to genuinely listen to and understand the experiences and perspectives of others. By putting oneself in another's shoes, it becomes harder to see them as *other* or to dehumanize them. The challenge is creating the space to do this effectively and at a societal level.

2. **Education and Awareness:** Promote educational programs that emphasize the shared history, values, and experiences of diverse groups. Understanding the contributions and struggles of various communities can foster empathy and counteract stereotypes. We need to challenge the notion of the *us versus them* mentality.

3. **Promote Dialogue and Engagement:** Create platforms for open dialogue between different communities and political groups. Encouraging conversations can help dispel myths, challenge prejudices, and build bridges of understanding. Town hall meetings, community forums, and inter-group dialogues can be instrumental in breaking down barriers and fostering a sense of shared identity and purpose.

Reforms depend on our capacity to overcome these shortcomings. Reducing empathy and solidarity among the populace stunts reforms. When people perceive certain groups as less than human or undeserving, they often dismiss or overlook their struggles and rights. Furthermore, dehumanization can create an environment that normalizes injustices, making it difficult for reform advocates to gain traction or for policymakers to recognize the urgency of change. Polarized extremes will seldomly—if ever—connect for the benefit of society. Make no mistake about it, dehumanization acts as a barrier, preventing collective action and the acknowledgment of systemic issues that require reform.

An effect on the capacity to reform is happening because every day, people are less willing to take the plunge into politics. This limits the ceiling and bandwidth a government has. Sure, politics has always been a rough sport. But now, it has become an almost certainty that a significant segment of the population will see you as a social pariah or worse.

The worst part is what plays out in politics also plays out in society. This virus continues to spread.

In the long run, dehumanization is a force that will provoke the foundations of our society and democracy to crack. The question is, do we wait until it is inevitable, or do we do something about it now?

CHAPTER 10:

Extremes Are Controlling

Illustration of President Trump scraping away from the sole of his shoe a splattered gum in the shape of Puerto Rico. Trump catered to his base. He used a more extreme form of engagement. Anything that was not appealing to his base was garbage beneath is shoe. And it worked for him (Bayon 2017).

Governor Cuomo summed it up quite well in our interview: "The extreme, what they are... they are zealots. They are not reasonable. They're not rational and defy common sense on most issues. They want to argue the point just to argue the point. They want the rhetorical power of the issue rather than the substantive resolution of the issue. That's where they are. So you're not going to win them over. I don't believe it's possible long term and hold the extreme and deal with the mainstream because they resent your domain."

A recent Pew Research Center study says 65 percent of Americans "feel exhausted when thinking about politics." When asked what a one-word descriptor of US politics is these days the most common answer was divisive (Pew Research Center 2023).

People say a lot about polarization. I don't claim to be an expert. I just claim to have lived through it. In every experience, the outcomes seem to be at best unfulfilling and at worst completely catastrophic. When extremes win… it brings out the worst in us.

Our Worst Angels

"We understand you needed to work with Trump, but it's time to take the kiddie gloves off," said a member from the DNC who came to visit the island after the hurricane. We were at the convention center, where we put together a center of operations. This was just a couple of days after the storm. At that point, because of the devastating nature of the storm, we barely heard back from several parts of the island. More than 95 percent of folks did not have electricity. We were still losing people.

Yet… this group of folks decided to question me on my actions regarding my pursuit to collaborate with the president of the United States. Point-blank, they just wanted me to attack Trump and create theater above the possibility of helping the island. And boy, did they have their pitch ready.

"You know, if you do this for us, you will be a star; a young Latino governor, facing Trump. You are a scientist. The contrasts could not be sharper. You'll be on all the covers." They essentially tried to persuade me not by what would help the people in need… but by addressing my ego.

My response took a microsecond.

"No," I replied. "I have a responsibility to 3.2 million people. And you want me to attack *the person* who could provide support to them?"

By this time, you have read some of the stories with Trump. Some are not flattering. The truth is, at this point, we were working together. His team was—for the most part—helping. And some Democrats wanted me to burn that just to get some political fodder points?

How did we get to this point where political opposites are so far apart that otherwise rational people would ask a chief executive to make a call that would severely hurt their people?

Silence met my response—a sort of uneasy pause. They touched upon some other small talk topics and then took the offensive one last time.

"Okay. We wish you and the people of Puerto Rico the very best."

"We'll look for someone else to do this."

And look for someone else they did.

After that, I never quite had the same relationship with the Democratic party. Others always looked at me as an outsider, someone who sided with Republicans on certain issues—mostly fiscal ones. But this was the turning point.

Why is there such unease when someone from a party breaks ranks on an issue? Why are we to assume these parties or groups have to be identical monoliths?

"Any classification according to a singular identity polarizes people in a particular way, but if we take note that we have many different identities… we can see the polarization of one can be resisted by a fuller picture. So, knowledge and understanding are extremely important to fight against singular polarization" (Sen 2007)

Amartya Sen's book *Identity and Violence* explores the complex interplay between individual identity and group identities (2007). One of the central themes in the book is how identity-based conflicts can lead to the alienation of individuals within a group who hold differing viewpoints.

Sen argues that while identity is an important aspect of human existence, it's problematic when we reduce people to a single identity and portray group identities as monolithic and homogeneous. This can lead to exclusion and violence against individuals who do not conform to the dominant narrative of the group (Sen 2007).

This is a root cause of extremism.

Extremism is not only a position at the edges of the political spectrum but also a *behavioral trait*. It provokes people to focus on rhetoric and the demagoguery associated with it. It side steps even the most compelling, rational—and empathetic—actions, to achieve a goal.

This behavioral trait seems to be growing. A recent publication outlines how out-of-party hate has become a stronger driver than in-party love (Finkel et al. 2020). "Out-party hate has also become more powerful than in-party love as a predictor of voting behavior and by some metrics, it exceeds long-standing antipathies around race and religion. This aversion to opposing partisans might make strategic sense if partisan identity served as a strong proxy for political ideas. But given that sectarianism is not driven primarily by such ideas (SM), holding opposing partisans in contempt on the basis of their identity alone precludes innovative cross-party solutions and mutually beneficial compromises."

This short term strategy for political gain craters our long-term prospects for growth. In it, the truth is often secondary—if important at all.

I Gave Them Ninety-One Billion Dollars

"President Donald Trump claims that 'Puerto Rico got ninety-one billion dollars for the hurricane' and that it received 'more money than has ever been gotten for a hurricane before.' Neither of those statements is true." (Farley 2019).

Confronted in a press conference about the alleged ninety-one billion sent to Puerto Rico, I retorted, "If we did get the ninety-one billion, please show me the check."

Naturally, there was no such check. The Federal Emergency Management Agency reported that Puerto Rico had received approximately $11.2 billion in disaster relief payments at that time, barely over 10 percent of what President Trump had claimed.

President Trump's concern wasn't the accuracy of his statement. His objective was to counter criticism that he wasn't doing enough for the island and to craft a narrative for his supporters.

How is such a discrepancy processed? The data could explain and provide context. One group believed Puerto Rico received ninety-one billion and deemed it more than sufficient. Another argued Puerto Rico got only eleven billion though withheld from those who needed it. Yet no one seemed to bridge the gap between these two extremes to clarify the actual situation.

A more thorough analysis would reveal that eleven billion, out of the forty-two billion allocated, went to Puerto Rico. However, this nuanced reality didn't fit the narrative preferred by either side or the media.

Some perceived Trump as neglecting Puerto Rico while others, including himself, saw him as its savior:

"I've taken better care of Puerto Rico than any man ever," he boasted (Galioto 2019). Two years later, an audit revealed that "Funding was 'unnecessarily delayed' by bureaucratic obstacles, after the hurricane killed thousands in 2017" (Murphy Marcos 2021).

This became a battle of words, with the truth getting lost in the shuffle. Why do such disputes attract so much attention, diverting focus from the real issues?

Polarization Makes a Profit

"If the bully gets close, I'll punch the bully in the mouth," I declared on CNN Newsroom (Acosta and Liptak 2019). Those words, I realized immediately, would change everything. Not because of the statement itself but due to its potential for others to take it out of context.

The full exchange went like this:

Acosta: What happens if someone comes to bully you or your island?

Rosselló: "If the bully gets close, I'll punch the bully in the mouth."

Acosta: Just like that?

Rosselló: Just like that. (pause) It would be a mistake to confuse courtesy with courage. (2019)

CNN's piece set the context: "Despite attacks, insults, and threats from President Trump, the governor of Puerto Rico has been relatively diplomatic and careful about hitting back. Today though, that all changed. He has apparently had enough" (2019).

I did seek a good relationship with Trump, despite our differences. Initially, his administration had responsive figures like Tom Bossert, Doug Hoelscher, Pam Patenaude, and General Kelly. But as these individuals left, communication became increasingly difficult, if not impossible.

Acosta concluded, "They are fed up inside the governor's office. They feel like the president wasn't dealing with the facts and the reality of the situation on the ground in Puerto Rico."

My intention was to generalize my firm stance in defending Puerto Rico against all threats, not exclusively targeting President Trump. In hindsight, I should have been more cautious. Headlines soon read:

"Puerto Rico governor to Trump: "I'll punch the bully in the mouth."

"Rosselló warns Trump: If the bully gets close, I'll punch him in the mouth." (Figure 1)

I was frustrated and exhausted from intense weeks of work. Ideally, I should have canceled the interview.

But I didn't, and the interview happened. I thought I could just move on.

However, the reactions I received were unexpectedly diverse and extreme. On a flight to Florida, my recognition increased significantly. People approached me with various comments:

"I too want to punch him in the face!" exclaimed an older lady.

Figure 1. Yahoo news headline from Getty News "I'll punch the bully."

"I'm glad someone said what we all were feeling," a flight attendant whispered.

There were high-fives and expressions of support.

But there were also opposing reactions:

"You should face prosecution for threatening our president!"

"I'd like to see you trying to punch Trump... he'll kick your ass."

It felt like a surreal WWE event.

These interactions continued throughout my activities and meetings in Florida. The focus was on my supposed intent to punch the president, not the actual purpose of my visit.

Was my phrasing regrettable? Perhaps. But the real issue is how the media took a snippet of a conversation and incited either rage or exuberance. Most people reacted to a headline circulating on social media without watching the full interview.

"This is not an accident," says Irshad Manji. "It's designed to keep people engaged—or enraged. They do it purposefully, making a profit from it. (2020).

Polarization is profitable, but at what cost to society?

Extremism Is Growing and It Stops Progress

Polarization is not only profitable but also detrimental to the very essence of collaboration. It rewards a lack of cooperation and penalizes cross-party communication.

"Politics is very polarizing," observes Congressman Tom Davis. "People need to step out of their comfort zones and take action."

Recent studies highlight an alarming trend of increasing political polarization in the USA, now deeper than at any time since the American Civil War (Hare and Poole 2014). Political figures and the media pronounce this particular divide (Druckman et al. 2020).

Polarization involves aligning along multiple lines of potential disagreement, leading to constrained individual preferences (Baldassarri 2008). It manifests as individuals forming cohesive clusters of beliefs (DellaPosta 2020). Qiaoquiao Zhu describes political polarization as "the increasing ideological distance between the left and the right" (2021). Coupled with emotional polarization, which breeds mistrust and aversion toward members of opposing parties (Druckman and Levendusky 2019), the challenge becomes even more complex. This results in reduced interaction between groups and increased homophily—the tendency for like-minded individuals to associate more closely. This, in turn, perpetuates further polarization (Dandekar, Goel, and Lee 2013).

So, what can we do at an individual level? Professor Manji suggests a different approach to engagement: "Don't engage to change someone's mind. Engage to be the change yourself. By asking sincere questions, not to persuade but to become a better communicator, you will always gain from the conversation" (2020).

Despite over 80 percent of us not aligning with extreme views, polarization continues to grow in influence. The question remains: Will this trend ever reverse? Are there consequences for those who embrace extremism?

The Revolution Eats Its Own

"With Lin-Manuel Miranda once again as its star, the celebrated Broadway hit *Hamilton* opened for business in Puerto Rico this weekend—that business being the bolstering of the hopes and finances of a beleaguered US territory mired in debt and still reeling from the devastation wreaked sixteen months ago by Hurricane Maria" read the first paragraph of a *Washington Post* article entitled "An Emotional Opening for *Hamilton* in Puerto Rico" (Marks 2019).

What an event it was!

People from all over the world. Movie stars, sports icons, and former presidents came to see the event in Puerto Rico. Hell, they even filmed the *Tonight Show* there, and my one-year-old got to meet Jimmy Fallon (Figure 2).

The event brought attention and focus to our island when we *most* needed it.

What if I told you *Hamilton* in Puerto Rico almost *never* happened.

Late in 2018 as the planning of the event was unfolding, I received a call from Don Luis Miranda, Lin-Manuel's father. He wanted to meet. At that moment, I could not get with him, so I asked some of my key staff members to work with him.

I received a text later on from him saying: "I understand you don't want to meet because we have political differences. That's fine." He was pointing to the fact he is very much left leaning and a proponent of Puerto Rico's independence. Like him, I was a Democrat… but a fiscally conservative one. I am also a staunch advocate for Puerto Rican statehood. This would put us at very different ends.

Notwithstanding I replied, "No, Don Luis, I understood you had everything taken care of with my staff. I'll make it a point to meet."

Figure 2. Jimmy Fallon with Pedro. (Photo Credit: Magdiel Lugo)

After that, we hit it off. We met several times. He wanted to ensure a secure space for the *Hamilton* production. The event was to take place in the University of Puerto Rico's Theatre. "It is my alma mater. I want to give back," he said.

We told him we would provide him with the security detail. I also committed to helping the production with any additional needs they might have. Producing this became a priority. I was fully aware this important event could garner significant awareness of Puerto Rico, following the hurricane.

Things were moving steadily. I can say Don Luis and I—not withstanding our differences—established a relationship of mutual respect and support. At least for the time being.

And then… it happened.

"It looks like we might not be able to do *Hamilton*," Don Luis wrote.

In late November, protests broke out in the university. They stated this protest could affect *Hamilton*. "Meanwhile, it emerged that the Heend [Union] warned Luis Manuel Miranda, producer of the musical *Hamilton*, which will soon be presented at the UPR Theater, that the performances there could be affected by the university conflict" (Dialogo 2018).

This was disconcerting. What was a lead-up of several months that was to climax in a huge opportunity for the island was quickly eroding. The irony? The people provoking this were those politically aligned with Don Luis Miranda.

"Would you be willing to move the production elsewhere?" I asked. This was November 30, and the production would begin in January. We had to move fast and get creative.

His first response was no. He had high hopes to do this in his alma mater and was distraught. Just like that—the Hamilton production was about to end because of the narratives generated from a polarized ultra-minority. After the news had spread of this wonderful event globally, how were we going to articulate the cancellation? Add that to the *complex* list of things to explain.

As we were coming to grips with this, a few days later I received a message from Don Luis that out of the blue. It just said: "Where else could we do it?"

We had a shot. Reinvigorated, I started thinking of alternatives. Then it occurred to me: The government had control of Centro de Bellas Artes Luis A. Ferré. Since it opened its doors in 1981, it immediately became Puerto Rico's most important cultural center. Perfect spot.

Without checking, I proposed it. A few days later. They accepted it.

The news came out on December 23. We only had a few weeks to make it happen. Here is what the university newspaper had to say about it:

The local producer of the musical *Hamilton*, Ender Vega, highlighted that the governor of Puerto Rico, Ricardo Rosselló Nevares, made the invitation for the acclaimed musical to withdraw from performing at the Theater of the University of Puerto Rico (UPR) and moved to the Center for Fine Arts (CBA) in Santurce.

"We accepted the governor's invitation, who was the one who directly invited us and the CBA Board to move there and made it available to us. Already being that invitation, *Hamilton* ponders it, and *Hamilton* makes the decision," explained Vega, during a radio interview for Radio Isla 1320 (Colon Santiago 2018).

Notice the use of words. Notice the inference that I had provoked the move, when in reality, everything happened to *avoid* the cancellation. Yet, some activists needed to sustain their narrative, even as we were supporting them.

The *Orlando Sentinel* had it clear:

"Several weeks ago the possible cancellation of the musical Hamilton in Puerto Rico was rumored due to a possible strike at the University of Puerto Rico, Río Piedras Campus, where the theater where the famous musical would take place is located.

The production, starring Lin-Manuel Miranda, announced late Friday that it will now be presented at the Luis A. Ferré Performing Arts Center, instead of the UPR Theater, in addition to having to move the dates to accommodate the changes. Performances will begin three days later on January 11, 2019 instead of January 8" (Marcial Ocasio 2018).

"HamiltonMusical Puerto Rico is moving to @CBASanturce leaving behind a renovated first-class theater @UPRRP, fulfilling our promise @Lin_Manuel to Puerto Rico and addressing security issues," Luis Miranda posted on his Twitter account (2018).

Nonetheless, we were able to move it but not without bumps on the road.

For example, I had to ask several artists to cancel their show. Some of them were not happy. The press gave them a platform to turn on me. Polarization made a profit once again. However, thanks to the intervention of Luis Miranda and other government officials, things smoothed out with the other artists.

Majestuosa visita en La Fortaleza

Figure 3. Paper outlining a celebration we had with the *Hamilton* cast in the executive mansion (*El Nuevo Día* 2019).

"Governor Ricardo Rosselló Nevares invited us to talk with all the producers and artists with dates held between January 11 and 27 after it became known that the production of *Hamilton* moved from the UPR Theater to the Center for Fine Arts in Puerto Rico. Assuming our responsibility, we convened an extraordinary meeting of the board of directors and, fortunately, unanimously and with good faith as our guideline, we managed to ensure we could satisfy all parties with the accommodations achieved," Arosemena said in a press release (Telemundo PR 2018).

The rest, as they say, is history.

Discover Puerto Rico summarized it this way: "*Hamilton*, the award-winning musical phenomenon created by award-winning actor, composer, and lyricist Lin-Manuel Miranda, played a historic engagement in Puerto Rico in January 2019, starring Miranda as Alexander Hamilton. While the curtains closed on the historic production, the contribution of the show is still being felt across the island and will be for many years to come" (2019) Figure 3.

"There was an extra passion, pain, sadness, and beauty he brought to his character," Chernow said. "This was no ordinary performance tonight." (Kreps 2019)

The take-home message here is we put differences aside to create something special for Puerto Rico. Even then, the event almost did not happen. Political allies almost self-sabotaged themselves just because they had a minor difference. This tends to happen with extreme factions. I could have easily stood back and let them attempt to solve it themselves, but was this the best course of action for the island and our people?

Yet this is an inherent characteristic of extreme activism. They keep pulling and pulling until they tear each other apart. It is no wonder they say *the revolution eats its own.*

While all of this is happening in the front end, some lurk in the shadow—appearing one way publicly and quite another in the background.

Not All Is What It Seems

"Governor, the leader and the speaker want to speak with you," said Carlos Mercader, former head of Federal Affairs.

"Which one?" I answered.

"Both," he said.

"Okay, schedule the appointment."

We were in New York City on an unremarkable day in May 2019 at a conference to present Puerto Rico's new tourism structure and strategy. Some of my economic cabinet members attended with me. The goal was to heavily promote Puerto Rico in those days. As we were coming off the fiscal stabilization, economic growth, and rebuild after the hurricane, little did I expect to have to make an emergency stop to talk with Leader Schumer and Speaker Pelosi.

Carlos Mercader had already resigned his position but was still a close advisor. He recalls, "Jaime Lesarriga, an aid to the speaker called me. It was about 1:45 p.m. They wanted the call at 2:30. When I asked what the topic was about, I got no answer. The reason what they wanted to talk to the governor about was a mystery."

"They are on the phone *now*. They say it's urgent," a visibly nervous Mercader told me.

"Okay, I can talk… but you are coming with me," I said.

I had a feeling I needed someone to validate and listen to the conversation. His recollections on the call are here together with my own.

The manager took us to his office because there were no empty rooms. It was scruffy, the type of place where you know they get work done. Pictures of famous people who had dedicated a nice line or two to the manager filled the walls.

There, Mercader and I sat down to connect with the speaker and leader.

"Good morning, Madam Speaker. Good morning, Leader Schumer. How can I help?"

Carlos recalls, "Pelosi took the lead on the call and scolded the governor. She was unhappy that the governor kept the fight for the pensions."

The speaker went straight to the point: "We are calling you to ask you to take a strong leadership stance and support an 8.5 percent reduction in the pensions. I know it is hard, but that is what true leadership does."

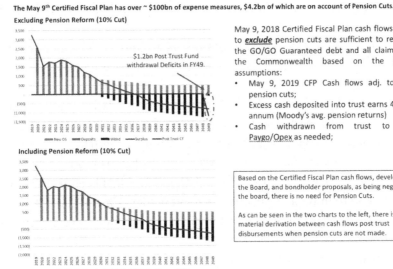

From a Fiscal Standpoint, Pension Cuts are not Needed

The May 9th Certified Fiscal Plan has over ~ $100bn of expense measures, $4.2bn of which are on account of Pension Cuts.

Excluding Pension Reform (10% Cut)

$1.2bn Post Trust Fund withdrawal Deficits in FY49.

May 9, 2018 Certified Fiscal Plan cash flows adjusted to *exclude* pension cuts are sufficient to restructure the GO/GO Guaranteed debt and all claims against the Commonwealth based on the following assumptions:

- May 9, 2019 CFP Cash flows adj. to remove pension cuts;
- Excess cash deposited into trust earns 4.14% per annum (Moody's avg. pension returns)
- Cash withdrawn from trust to finance Paygo/Opex as needed;

Including Pension Reform (10% Cut)

Based on the Certified Fiscal Plan cash flows, developed by the Board, and bondholder proposals, as being negotiated by the board, there is no need for Pension Cuts.

As can be seen in the two charts to the left, there is no material derivation between cash flows post trust disbursements when pension cuts are not made.

Figure 4. Slide presented to the Fiscal Oversight Board, denoting that pension cuts are not necessary and will not cause a material deviation, produced by Christian Sobrino.

Admittedly, this surprised me. Why would Speaker Pelosi ask for this? Did she not stand for the exact opposite? Notwithstanding, I prepared myself to battle this point. After all, I had been battling the oversight board, bondholders, and others on this issue for the better part of my term. As you may recall, I was willing to (and did) cut the budget in any variety of ways. But I was not willing to reduce the pensions on an already impoverished retiree class. The rest of the conversation was mostly one that involved me and Speaker Pelosi.

Mercader remembers my response. "When the governor responded, he was stern but respectful. He said, 'Madam Speaker, you have been given wrong advise about what we are doing in Puerto Rico."

Eagerly, I replied, "Madam Speaker, I would like to explain to you why the pension cut is not necessary." The next couple of minutes I detailed—step-by-step—why this was the case. I used the figure below to highlight my point. "In fact, eventually, it would cost *more* because retirees would be under the poverty line and would require more investment from government." (Figure 4)

"I don't think you understand," she said. "You need to cut the pensions, or they will cut it for you anyway. There is no way to sustain without a cut."

Somewhat frustrated, I said, "I don't think you understand. I work this issue on a daily basis. It is an issue that is a priority for me. I'm not just now getting a document with bullet points and asking someone to show leadership."

She did not like my response.

Her tone went up a level or two. "How condescending—I can't believe you are being this condescending," she said.

I responded: "I'm sorry if you feel that way. It was not my intent. You are getting the wrong information. I am happy to send you the data, and you can have your team evaluate it."

She interrupted, "Look, sometimes being a leader means giving bad news and doing tough things. You need to step up."

As she was saying this, I overheard someone in the background. I knew the voice. It was a leader of the teacher's union at the national level, Randi Weingarten. Aha! I was quickly able to put the invisible dots together.

Mercader later confirmed, "I learned Randi Weingarten prompted the Pelosi-Schumer call from the Pelosi staff. Weingarten was supportive of the agreement made by the FOMB and Aida Díaz, cutting teacher pensions. The governor was against cutting pensions. They figured that because he was a Democrat, they needed to support what they had agreed with the Fiscal Oversight Board and the unions."

Let's break down this complex scenario. The oversight board had been trying to buy support for the pensions cut. They were in on it. They told the bond holders they would get more money if the pensions were cut. Some of them were in on it too. Still, the oversight board needed more support. Their solution? They made a deal with the unions.

Now why would the unions and the leaders of the Democratic party be asking me to cut pensions? An issue of social justice, responsibility, and empathy with our elderly. It didn't seem to add up. But it did…

Smoking Gun

"There is a reality that no one should deny. The government debt with the Teachers' Retirement System is a debt that is not insured in the bankruptcy process," said Díaz. "Teachers cannot sit idly by and be the last in line for pay. Therefore, we sat down to negotiate a tentative proposal that is not perfect but that protects our long-term future" (*Caribbean Business* 2019).

Here's the smoking gun.

The teacher's union at the local level agreed to *reduce* the pensions for those who had already retired. Why? So they could get access to renegotiate their collective bargaining agreement, which was previously frozen.

Of course, they didn't explicitly discuss any of this on the call.

The director of the Puerto Rico Fiscal Agency and Financial Advisory Authority (AAFAF), Christian Sobrino, responded to Díaz, "(She) has indicated that it is the legal position of his organization that 'the obligation of the government with the retirement of teachers it is an unsecured debt within the bankruptcy process. Since 2017, Governor Ricardo Rosselló Nevares, the Legislative Assembly and AAFAF have argued completely the opposite. The position of the Teachers Association is equivalent to a total surrender of our pensioners in exchange for nothing. We vehemently reject the position of Mrs. Diaz and her organization that pensioners do not deserve consideration in the bankruptcy process beyond another general unsecured creditor. This position is a dangerous one that threatens our pensioners without considering the basic postulates of our jurisprudence."

Díaz was an operative of Weingarten. Weingarten had the national unions. The National Unions pressured. The Speaker responded to that pressure, asking me to do something she would never do on her own right.

All Hell Broke Loose

"Step up?" I responded. I was usually fairly patient in these encounters. Not in this one. "Have you ever had to tell people in your district that you are cutting pensions? Have you supported this publicly? More so when it is not necessary?"

Somewhat shaken, the speaker responds, "Sometimes you have to do the hard things—show leadership." This irked me. In the face of evidence that went against her ask, she diminished the conversation into a soft-thinking leadership lecture.

"Hard things?" I recoiled. "Have you ever had to cut a budget by twenty percent? I've had to. Have you ever had to close three hundred and sixty-five schools because the student population diminished by forty percent? I did and had to go to their communities and attempt to explain it. Did you ever have to endure protests and face up to them because of the cuts an oversight board was making? I've made hard choices, and still to this day I am doing so. I'm just not going to give in to my priorities and do something stupid in leu of something that's right."

"After this," Mercader recounts, "they told the governor he was 'overstepping in his quest not to cut pensions.' He was fighting with 'their people' and should let go of this fight. The governor stuck to his position saying it was the right decision, and it was his priority to protect pensions."

She raised her tone again and said: "This is incredible. You need to show leadership. I can't believe this. We will no longer be able to support you. We will have to make a statement."

Carlos left the call with an ominous feeling. "I truly believe—as I came out of that call—that this was the beginning of the effort to push for the governor's resignation."

They ended the call. She was right about one thing. They never gave the support we required.

Time Agreed with Our Arguments

The question lingered: Who was right in this debate? Was she mistakenly or intentionally crafting a narrative to support her unions, or was my explanation flawed, reflecting poor leadership? Figure 5

"The governor has very important considerations with the island's pensioners. Our group nor any GO group are asking the pensioners to take impairments. We look forward to working with the governor. The pensioners are an important part of the go-forward economy for Puerto Rico," stated Susheel Kirpalani, Quinn Emanuel Bankruptcy Chair (Bloomberg Daybreak 2019)

Even bondholder groups concurred that pension cuts were unnecessary. They recognized that such cuts would not only impede Puerto Rico's economic progress but also negatively impact their interests.

Christian Sobrino vividly remembers the situation. "Hearing about your call with Pelosi and how they threatened to withhold recovery funding if we didn't approve the pension cut, I thought it was quite bold of you to stand your ground. Now, everyone—both the public and the Fiscal Oversight Board—acknowledges there were no reductions in current pensions in the 2021 restructuring plan."

Three years after this episode, the Fiscal Oversight Board (JSF) introduced the eighth amended Plan of Adjustment. This plan eliminated cuts to the accumulated monthly pension benefits of retirees and established a Pension Reserve Fund with a supervisory board. In essence: no pension cuts.

Figure 5. Cover of *the San Juan Daily Star,* highlighting my stance against pension cuts from a rational and logical perspective (2019).

Had I yielded to Pelosi's demands and compromised my principles, retirees would have had an 8.5 percent reduction in their pensions without any significant progress happening.

Takeaways

"Some government and business leaders are saying one thing but doing another. Simply put, they are lying. And the results will be catastrophic."

—UN SECRETARY GENERAL ANTÓNIO GUTERRES

You want to move climate change policy? How about gender equality? Want to reduce taxes? Protect children? Then you need to move beyond what some politicians are *saying* and see what they are *doing.* In some instances, it is just the absence of action (e.g., climate change). In others it as simple as saying one thing and doing another.

By the same token, a leader can actually be doing exactly what they are saying they are doing, and the narrative opposes it. It is muddied waters. The key point here? If you want change and you want reform, this sort of behavior kills it in its tracks.

And bad begets bad.

What do we get with extremes?

1. **Hindered Constructive Dialogue and Collaboration**: Extreme positions and polarized viewpoints obstruct meaningful dialogue and collaboration. Governor Cuomo noted how extreme factions are more interested in the rhetorical power of an issue rather than its substantive resolution. This mindset makes it challenging to find common ground and work toward solutions that benefit the greater good.

2. **Media Amplifying Polarization**: The "I'll punch the bully in the mouth" incident demonstrates how media can amplify polarization by focusing on sensationalized snippets rather than the broader context. Such practices not only misinform the public but also deepen divisions, making it harder for leaders to bridge gaps and work collaboratively. In addition, media outlets have an economic incentive to perpetuate divisive narratives.

3. **The Singularization of Identity** underscores the dangers of reducing people to a single identity and viewing group identities as monolithic. This is happening at an ever-rapid pace. Such reductionist views can lead to exclusion, alienation, and even violence against those who don't *conform to a dominant narrative*. To counteract this, we need a broader understanding of the complexities of individual and group identities, which can help in resisting the pull of polarization and fostering a more collaborative political environment.

As if this were not enough, more and more the hindering of the overall reputation of leaders and special interests has come to the point that now everyone assumes there is an *ulterior* motive. This soft thinking is diminishing good leaders and their desire to participate in politics.

"Recent decades have seen significant declines in political participation and growing levels of political mistrust. Perhaps most disturbing, these declines have been most pronounced among young Americans. For example, according to US Census data, in 1972 nearly half (49.6 percent) of eighteen-to-twenty-four-year old's voted in the presidential election. By the 1996 election, voter turnout among this group had fallen by nearly one-third, to only 32.4 percent. Many people looking at such data believe young Americans are apathetic and disengaged from American politics" (Hamilton Survey 2000).

Do we really want this? How can we move past these limitations?

"If all we are doing is working past each other, and the side in power at the moment is imposing its solutions on the other, there is no triumph. In fact, if there is a solution, it is an illusionary one. It's a very temporary one because all you are doing is planting the seeds of blowback." Manji warns (2020).

And the seeds of blowback grow stronger every day. Aside from creating bridges, how can we establish a path to clarity?

If we don't, polarization wins. Extremes win. Inferior leadership wins. And the vast majority of people lose.

PART III

FACTORS THAT IMPACT REFORM

CHAPTER 11:

Context, Initial Conditions, and Time

The context from my governorship was very different from, say, that of the governor of Florida or New York. I had to deal with a Fiscal Oversight Board, a hurricane, and a closed market. Those provoke significant changes in timing and initial conditions. This illustration shows one of the many battles I had to wage against the oversight board. Here they were asking for furloughs, with no evidence of need. We showed it was not necessary. Time demonstrated we were right (Bayon 2017).

"Context is to data what water is to dolphins."

At least three times a week, my daughter and son ask me to sit with them just as they are about to go to bed and tell them a story. Not just any story… one with a lesson. The process has gotten more sophisticated, and now we are making stories together.

The following is a story created by Claudia and Pedro… with a little help from their old man.

Splash and Wave

Once upon a time, in the majestic Pacific Ocean, there were two identical twin dolphin brothers named Splash and Wave. Born of the same pod, they were similar in almost every way; their sleek silver bodies

Figure 1. Pedro, Claudia and I have a tradition on certain nights. We start with a book or graphic novel followed by the creation of novel stories.

cut through the waves like masterful swimmers. They were also known for their mischievous nature, often engaging in lively underwater games with each other.

However, their lives took different paths due to timing and circumstance.

Splash, the elder of the two, was adventurous and eager to explore. He left their pod at a young age, venturing into the open ocean during the stormy season when food was scarce. He was quick and agile, but his inexperience and the harsh conditions made finding food a challenge. Despite his speed, he often found himself competing with larger predators for food. His impulsive nature and the unfavorable timing of his departure made survival difficult.

On the other hand, Wave, the younger brother, chose to stay with their pod for a longer period, learning the art of hunting and survival. He ventured out on his own when the calm season arrived, bringing with it an abundance of fish. Wave was no faster or stronger than splash, but his patience and the timing of his departure during the plentiful season made hunting easier. He didn't have to compete with larger predators, and he thrived in the favorable conditions (Figure 1).

As time passed, splash, despite his early struggles, became a skilled hunter. However, the harsh conditions and competition had taken a toll on his health. Wave, on the other hand, grew stronger and healthier, his well-timed departure and favorable conditions contributing to his success.

The two identical dolphin brothers, Splash and Wave, led vastly different lives.

"What's the lesson?" she asked, as she inevitably does.

"While *abilities* and *traits* are important, the circumstances we find ourselves in and the timing of our actions can change our outcomes," I responded.

The same is true for our capacity to reform and govern.

Policy Windows

John W. Kingdon's concept of "policy windows" illuminates the fleeting opportunities in the policy-making process where conditions align, enabling advocates to advance their issues or effect changes in policy direction. These windows are transient, emerging from a confluence of problems, potential solutions, and political circumstances. When such a window opens, it presents a critical chance for policy entrepreneurs—those who champion and advocate for solutions—to impact the policy agenda.

"Problems can more readily translate into policy when coupled with solutions and favorable political forces. These three streams—problems, policies, and politics—come together at certain critical times. Solutions become joined to problems, and join to favorable political forces. This coupling is most likely during those critical times I call a policy window—those windows of opportunity when the conditions are ripe for change to occur." —Kingdon, J. W. (1984).

A classic instance of a policy window occurred in 1986 with the passage of the Tax Reform Act in the United States. The public's growing frustration with the complex tax code, President Ronald Reagan's commitment to simplification, and a bipartisan consensus in Congress converged to create an opportune moment for comprehensive tax reform.

To effectively leverage these windows, understanding the context and initial conditions faced by policymakers is essential. Time and timing are crucial elements in this process. The 1986 tax reform, which simplified tax brackets, eliminated numerous deductions, and broadened the tax base, exemplifies how various factors can converge to create an opportune moment for significant policy change.

However, without initial understanding and preparation, they might not fully utilize these windows of opportunity or, worse, miss them entirely.

Plan for Puerto Rico: Establishing Context

"How would this be different from other government platforms?" One of the twelve individuals I had gathered to craft a strategic Plan for Puerto Rico posed this question. We convened in a borrowed, partially renovated office. Dust lingered in the air, and some windows were obscured, yet the space's potential was evident. It mirrored the determination and effort required to realize our vision for Puerto Rico, setting a fitting backdrop for our endeavor.

Addressing the initial query was crucial. Why should these talented individuals dedicate their time if the plan's unique value remained unclear?

"Are you not tired of seeing every year, every candidate—without distinction—proclaiming improvements in healthcare, education, job creation… yet their platforms lack substance and action? These are passive promises. Our plan must be purposeful, well-documented, active, and executable," I asserted.

I grabbed their attention.

"But how should we do it?"

Eligio, a particularly insightful member of our group who later became secretary of education, posed a critical question: "I like the idea, but how do we implement it?" I suggested we start by thoroughly examining our context. Like *Wave*, who carefully studied and learned before diving in, understanding our context could reveal the root causes of our problems, providing a solid starting point.

Figure 2. Outlines planned objectives by year, leading up to the 2016 election. This framework helped us understand the island's context and initial conditions, maximizing our window for execution.

I cannot overstate the importance of these initial conditions. Neglecting them in the planning phase could lead to poor execution or even complete avoidance of crucial issues. Like in classical music, where musicians invest significant effort in composing and arranging before the orchestra performs, our planning required meticulous thought and preparation.

I emphasized the need for a different approach: "Let's make a distinction here. Traditional platforms tend to be mere wish lists, limited only by what the paper can hold," I said. "We need to craft an actionable document with purpose and thought. This can't just be an academic or political exercise. It needs to be a social endeavor, a journey."

I proposed a five-year journey, breaking down the plan into tangible components that would yield results:

1. Identifying the root cause problems (Understanding the real context).
2. Studying best practices from elsewhere to address these root causes (Engaging in deep thought).
3. Developing a vision and initial architecture and involving citizens in the discussion (Fostering citizen engagement; creating vision maps).
4. Conducting public hearings and reevaluating our stance based on new insights (Continuing the deep thought process).
5. Preparing an executive plan and associated legislation to ensure immediate action upon taking office (Focusing on timing) Figure 2.

"It's going to take time, but our advantage is we don't have the constraint of a specific timeframe." Or so I thought.

Reflecting on that day, Dr. Eligio Hernández said, "In that meeting, filled with candor, openness, and hope, we discussed the process of enculturation of Puerto Ricans and the possibilities of redefining ourselves through our means and convictions. The mood shifted. By the end, we were excited about starting a movement, a fight against the status quo. In a unified decision, lawyers, scientists, educators, businessmen, women and men from diverse backgrounds agreed to leave the comfort of inaction and embark on an unprecedented endeavor."

They were all committed. This was the genesis of Plan for Puerto Rico—a process of thoughtful planning, evaluation, and citizen engagement, demanding dedication and resilience. We didn't know when our policy windows would open, but we were on the right path for preparing for them.

The Island's Initial Conditions

"Are you going to eliminate the sales tax?" Junito, a sixty-something-year-old coffee worker from the outskirts of Ceiba, inquired during a public hearing in the open basement of an abandoned home. With around one hundred attendees, the atmosphere was somewhat rowdy.

"The other candidates have said they will. These taxes are killing us," he continued, referencing the sales tax imposed by the Acevedo Vilá administration. By 2015, Puerto Rico was in a dire state with a debt of $123 billion plus unfunded pension liabilities and a decade of negative growth (Gonzalez 2017), including a default on a payment.

This was a moment for thoughtful consideration.

"I would love to say we could. But right now, if I told you that... I'd be lying."

The noise subsided into an uncomfortable silence.

With a mix of nerves and idealism, I began to explain the complexity of the situation. I talked about past poor decisions and the tough choices ahead. I emphasized our current predicament was due to unfulfilled populist promises.

My detailed understanding of the issue stemmed from our team's ability to assess and comprehend our conditions. I shared a brief list of these conditions and their contributing factors:

1. Government structure: We had 132 agencies operating in silos, with employees often in a stagnant and nonproductive environment (Suarez Torres 2015).

2. Government culture: A lack of accountability and transparency. Financials and key performance indicators were either unavailable to the public or nonexistent. This led to reckless spending and an unsustainable fiscal burden, including pensions and government debt.

3. Migration patterns: A critical issue. People were leaving the island. We managed to slow this trend between 2017–2019, which might seem minor but was significant. It changed the projection of dropping to 2.5 million citizens by 2034 (preadministration estimate) to reaching that number by 2060. The book details various migration mitigation efforts, but the overarching issue remained: the disadvantages of being a colonial territory (Figure 3).

4. A welfare state culture: It's a difficult truth, but Puerto Rico has one of the lowest labor participation rates globally (high thirties, low forties, *Caribbean Business* 2018). A 2012 study found only Gaza and Moldova had lower rates. We proposed a sequenced approach to create a welfare-to-work pathway.

This context allowed me to answer Junito with intellectual honesty. As I was about to delve into these complex issues, he took the microphone and said, "Thank you for telling me the truth. Nobody else was willing to do so."

That sentiment resonated throughout the room. We realized this was what we needed to achieve during the campaign: honest, transparent communication.

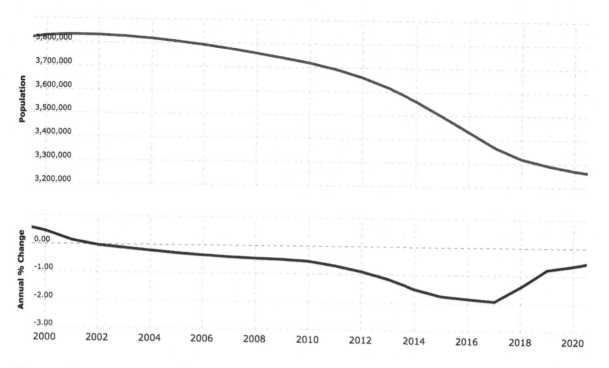

Figure 3. Shows the change in population over the past two decades, with a noticeable shift in the curve in 2017.

Why Initial Conditions Matter

Understanding our initial conditions was not just about recognizing the present state of affairs; it was also about setting the stage for future actions and decisions.

Consider the analogy of captaining a boat. It's one thing to steer a boat with basic knowledge in calm waters, but quite another to navigate through a storm without proper skills or understanding of the sea conditions. This scenario could easily fit into one of Claudia and Pedro's adventurous tales.

Applying this to governance, there's a stark difference between governing a state like Texas and governing Puerto Rico. The initial conditions are crucial; they dictate where practical priorities should lie.

Some aspects are within our control, such as preparation and understanding the landscape. Failing to do so is negligent. This phase is about identifying the conditions that will shape the most effective path forward. Will there be failures? Absolutely, but this approach offers the best chance for success. However, some conditions are beyond one's control, like Puerto Rico's colonial status or the initial state of crime. Planning must be based on the current reality, not on an idealized version of what we wish it to be.

These initial conditions act as a compass, guiding planning and decision-making. The timing of when and how to execute these plans and decisions is often a critical factor.

Overwhelmed My Opponent with Content

In February of the election year, I faced a significant challenge: gaining media coverage. The media seemed only interested in unsubstantiated attacks on my campaign, and as a result, our election polls were slipping.

"What can we do about this?" I pondered aloud in a staff meeting. The media was an uncontrollable element for us.

Then, an idea struck me. "I am going to present a new proposal from our Plan for Puerto Rico every day." I knew the media might not cover it, but we could still saturate the internet with our message.

Around this time, Facebook introduced Facebook Live, and I was among its beta testers. I seized this opportunity. Each day, I presented a new proposal, drafted a press release (despite knowing everyone might ignore it), and released a short video explaining the proposal. This was something within my control: creating content to inform the public.

My follower count surged. The message was getting through. About a month into this strategy, people began to take notice. While they might not delve into the details of each proposal, they were aware we were consistently offering solutions. This shifted the dynamics of the campaign.

Ramon Rosario, who later became my secretary of public affairs and policy and had previous involvement with my primary opponent's campaign, reflected on this strategy. "Ricardo Rosselló's lack of media coverage was a disadvantage until 2016. He overcame this by breaking away from traditional methods of presenting a government plan, opting instead to share ideas and measures daily. This compelled the media to cover him and put Pedro Pierluisi's campaign on the defensive." He viewed it as a pivotal change. "Other politicians now emulate Rosselló's approach in Puerto Rico because it successfully monopolized media attention and steered the conversation."

By the end, my videos were attracting more attention than traditional press releases. This approach helped us counteract an issue that seemed insurmountable and regain momentum at a critical juncture.

Time was our ally. It allowed me, a younger and less experienced candidate, to set the agenda against more seasoned opponents. Time spent understanding the landscape, connecting with people, and identifying talent was crucial to my success.

As chief executive, being mindful of time also propelled our initiatives forward. I delve deeper into this in chapter 15, but for now, it's enough to say we accomplished more reform in my first six months than in the previous twelve years combined. We leveraged time to our advantage.

However, time can be a double-edged sword, working for or against you.

Untimely Reform: How I Lost Law 80 Labor Reform Battle

An untimely and unpopular reform can be devastating. In addition to losing that battle, you diminish the opportunity of future reform efforts. Timing is vital.

Although times were historically tough, we prepared and executed quickly and effectively. I even got a second wave of reforms after the hurricane. A new policy window opened up for me as the devastation called for a general reboot. I soon discovered that reaching too far can be just as dangerous—if not more—than not doing enough.

JOANISABEL GONZÁLEZ
joanisabel.gonzalez@elnuevodia.com
twitter: @jgjanahisz

Luego de seis años consecutivos de desempeños negativos, el último año fiscal en que **Ricardo Rosselló Nevares** ocupó la gobernación de Puerto Rico, la economía creció en 1.5%, estableció la Junta de Planificación (JP).

Empero, el avance que habría mostrado la economía durante el año fiscal pasado, se haría agua en este año fiscal en curso y el siguiente por causa de los terremotos y la pandemia del coronavirus, alegó la dependencia responsable de medir el curso de la economía.

El crecimiento del producto bruto de Puerto Rico durante el año fiscal 2019, está consignado en el Informe Económico a la Gobernadora, documento de 288 páginas divulgado el jueves.

En el año fiscal 2018, donde se reflejó el golpe que dejaron los huracanes Irma y María en septiembre de 2017, la economía se contrajo en -4.3% a precios constantes. La cifra del año fiscal 2018 fue revisada en este ejercicio. Así pues, entre el año fiscal 2018 y 2019, el producto bruto mostró un alza de 5.8%.

Se trata de un salto no visto en tiempo reciente y que la JP también adjudica a factores externos como la economía estadounidense y a las medidas adoptadas por el gobierno para lidiar con la emergencia y aquellas "de desarrollo económico y reformas fiscales".

A precios constantes, durante el año fiscal 2019, el producto bruto se calculó en $5,825 millones. A precios corrientes, la riqueza que produjeron los individuos y empresas con sede en la isla produjeron unos $70,780 millones.

Según la JP, la mejora económica estuvo atada -principalmente- a un aumento en el gasto de consumo personal, estimado en 5.9%.

En tanto, durante el año fiscal 2018, el gasto de gobierno -como resultado de los desastres naturales- también se habría movido al alza, a razón de 13.9%.

De otra parte, a precios corrientes, el producto interno bruto de Puerto Rico regresó a los niveles previos al huracán María. Durante el año fiscal 2018, el PIB se estimó en $100,979 millones o 2.4% menos que en el año fiscal 2019, según la JP, el PIB se calculó en $104,988 millones. Al cierre del año fiscal 2019, según la JP, el PIB se calculó en $104,988 millones.

Los números provistos por la JP para el año fiscal 2019, serían el cierre de la gestión de Rosselló Nevares, quien ocupó la gobernación por espacio de dos años y siete meses. El científico se vio forzado a dejar su cargo el 2 de agosto de 2019, luego de protestas ciudadanas masivas ante los escándalos de corrupción que asediaron su administración y la revelación de un chat en el que se discutían asuntos oficiales, se trataban asuntos políticos en ho-

La economía creció antes de la salida de Rosselló Nevares

● El hito se registró al cabo de seis años en negativo, pero los terremotos y el COVID-19 anegarán ese progreso, dice la Junta de Planificación

Aunque mínimo, el crecimiento de 1.5% que registró la economía en el 2019, pasaría por alto en este año fiscal en curso y el siguiente por causa de los terremotos y la pandemia del coronavirus.

archivo / el nuevo día

LA CIFRA

EN POSITIVO

1.5%

CRECIMIENTO
de la economía registrado durante el año fiscal 2019

ras de trabajo y se compartían mofas contra figuras públicas, mujeres, periodistas e integrantes de la comunidad LGBTQ.

EL EFECTO DEL COVID-19

No obstante, en el informe a la sucesora de Rosselló Nevares, **Wanda Vázquez Garced**, la JP expone que los terremotos que afectaron el sur de la isla y la pandemia del coronavirus traerá otros dos años de contracción económica.

La JP hizo sus cálculos considerando tres extensiones distintas al periodo de la cuarentena. Los economistas de la dependencia entienden que el producto bruto de la isla vería una contracción de -3.5% en su proyección base o de hasta -5.4% en el cuadro pesimista durante este año fiscal.

La previsión de la JP para el año fiscal en curso es casi idéntica a la baja de -3.6% estimada en el plan fiscal revisado por el gobierno y ante la Junta de Supervisión Fiscal (JSF). En cambio, la diferencia es abismal en el año fiscal 2021. El plan ante la JSF contempla una baja de -7.8%. La JP estima una baja de -1.2%, en el escenario base y de -2% en su cuadro pesimista.

Las proyecciones de la JP podrían ser conservadoras. Su escenario más pesimista contempla una cuarentena entre el 16 de marzo y el 30 de abril pasados. Puerto Rico, en cambio, ha estado encuarentena desde mediados de marzo hasta el pasado 3 de mayo y esta continúa aunque con cierta flexibilización.

Entre otros factores, la JP estima que la economía estadounidense crecería 2.2% este año fiscal y el siguiente.

Figure 4. Newspaper article denoting that the economy grew for the first time in over a decade prior to my exit (El Nuevo Día 2020).

In my first month in office, we were able to pass labor reform, necessary for Puerto Rico. The results speak for themselves. We achieved the lowest unemployment rates in the history of Puerto Rico and the first year of growth in more than a decade and a half. All of this with the added insult of a category 3 and 4 hurricane walloping our island (Figure 4).

To give perspective, an article after my exit from office read "*The Economy Grew before Rosselló Left Office*" (El Nuevo Día 2020). Granted, labor reform was not popular, but it worked. Fast forward to the summer of 2018, I had been working on a potential deal with the oversight board. After much debate, we achieved an agreement that ensured maintaining of the Christmas bonus and avoiding a reduction in employee vacation and sick days to just seven days each (Rivera Clemente 2017). This was good.

One minor detail. "However, Rosselló said last night that this change was possible in exchange for the repeal of Law 80 on unjustified dismissals." (Rivera Clemente 2017). Law 80 was the last cog to a full labor reform. The prevailing legal framework provided compensation to employees based on their longevity, should they face termination in the private sector. Puerto Rico and Montana were the only jurisdictions in the US with a law like this.

While it was good for the employees as a safety net, it was an onerous unknown cost for businesses to establish in Puerto Rico. Critics would point out that it would hinder job growth because people would be reluctant to participate. I countered with the empirical evidence that most people were leaving the island. They were also moving to states that *did not* have an analogous framework to our Law 80. Quite the opposite, most were "work at will states."

Needless to say, we faced ferocious opposition from certain groups. Some of these groups had nothing to do with the workers or labor laws, but rather other affected constituents from other reforms enacted (e.g., healthcare reform, education reform, government downsizing). An aggregated effect to the opposition is a theme we'll come back to in this book.

To address this concern, we dove deep into the details. We identified the constituents most likely affected if they eliminated Law 80, which were older folks with long tenures within a company. This represented a minute fraction of the labor force. Notwithstanding—we had to find a way to mitigate this impact.

We found a way to do it. We crafted an agreement where we would create a safety net fund for people who had been in the industry for more than eighteen years. If fired, they would get the *same* compensation package from the government. The oversight board approved this. Now that we had a solution for this… smooth sailing right? Not exactly. If anything, some opponents got more vitriol.

I still did not even have the votes in House of Representatives where we owned a sizable majority (Avila-Claudio 2018). Many legislators and labor unions believed that Law 80 was a crucial protection for workers against unjust dismissal. They argued the repeal would leave workers vulnerable to arbitrary decisions by employers. Some believed political motivations and the interests of big businesses rather than the genuine interests of the Puerto Rican people drove the push for repeal. And then there was the possibility of social unrest.

Whatever the reason, they were all feeling the pressure. Since I did not have the votes, I had to meet with them individually. I went to their districts. In a very memorable encounter, I sat down with four representatives. Typically, friendly to my policies on reform, all four of them were very young. At that point, they were the last four votes I needed. Then the reasons started pouring in, and I got more clarity.

"They are coming to my house to ask me not to do it," said one of the representatives.

"People will not vote for me if I do this," said another.

I appealed to their hopes for a better Puerto Rico. That moved the needle a little bit, but not enough. So I had to play hardball.

"If you don't support this, you will be part of the reason why we won't achieve our Plan for Puerto Rico," I told them. "I'll make sure everyone knows in the next election cycle who opposed it."

Hesitantly, they accepted. Still, the margin was too thin.

In a final effort, I called upon the Legislative Assembly to make a final plea, and they granted me access to their chamber (Agencia EFE 2018). I argued repealing Law 80 would make Puerto Rico more attractive to businesses and investors. They believed the law was a deterrent to job creation and economic growth. I got a few more people on board.

It was not easy, and as if it was not enough… the media started to profile the people who would vote with my petition. Quiquito Melendez, a House Rep, publicly stated, "This is going to end up in court. This is going to the Tribunal. We go to court now or on the 20[20]."

I understood the challenges. I understood this was not a black or white situation. But I believed it was a piece of the puzzle to make things better on the island. Part of being a leader is taking unconformable positions in gray zone areas. Your judgment guides you through the often-conflicting and cluttered data.

Having to become chief communicator, I had to articulate *why* I was taking this action. "We had an in-depth discussion with the legislature and with the members of the board," I said. "This to ensure the Christmas bonus for all workers in Puerto Rico, vacation and sick leave for employees in the private sector, and the necessary funds for the municipalities, the University of Puerto Rico and for our economic development."

The repeal Law 80 would comply with the agreement with the Fiscal Oversight Board and add would add a Compensation Fund for longer termed employees (Caribbean Business 2018).

In the end, on June 14, 2018, after a contentious live vote, we were able to rally the House of Representatives with the details of the agreement and the compensation for tenured workers. The House approved it by a vote of thirty to eighteen.

The opposition intensity was growing. Now the battleground became the Senate—a place where we had a sizable majority. However, the president of the Senate was a bitter participant in my policies. His style was the opposite of mine. He cared for power for the sake of power and operated as such. More importantly, his unaccomplished goal was to hold the seat I had.

A leader of the opposition, Hector Ferrer stated "This is not only illegal and unconstitutional but also immoral." While you could argue the latter, the two former descriptors were absolutely incorrect. It did not matter. The narrative was out there again, and those *words* were winning. (Caribbean Business 2018).

The Senate president was against the repeal of the bill. After several bouts, he offered to repeal it but only prospectively (Bauza 2018). The Senate actually passed this bill. I was fine with that, but the oversight board did not accept it. In hindsight, I should have run with that agreement, but blindsided, I felt the need to protect the retirees, civil servants, and give a runway to the university and municipalities.

And so, I did not accept that bill.

This started a tussle. The Senate rejected the measure from the House.

"The Senate considers the matter of Law 80 finished. We will not repeal Law 80," exclaimed the president of the Senate.

Figure 5. Cover of the newspaper denoting that the Senate defeated my proposal again (*El Nuevo Dia* 2018).

I remember being in a car in New York, feeling dejected and disbanded. In response to the president of the Senate's unwillingness to work in the best interest of the people and succumb to political pressures, I said, "This was the time to unite and together get out of the shameful past we inherited. He chose to hinder. He chose to follow the tricks of the past that have gotten us into this situation. The president of the Senate chose a step that takes us away from heading out of this quagmire they bequeathed to us and we had already begun to dissipate."

We were so close. As a last resource, I used my State of the Union address to call the House and Senate for a special session. But once again, I failed to realize the matter was dead on arrival. The policy window closed. I had lost the support I once had to attrition and the opposition was using this to point to my loss of influence (Caro Gonzalez, Figueroa Cancel 2018).

With an image portraying me tired and dejected, headlines read: The Senate Defeats (Again) Rosselló's Plan.

They were right. I was defeated.

Real Life Splash and Wave

Mikhail Gorbachev and Deng Xiaoping were both reformist leaders in the 1980s, but their outcomes on the world stage were drastically different due to the unique contexts of their rule and the ways in which they implemented their reforms. Gorbachev, leading the Soviet Union, introduced radical and swift changes with a goal of democratizing politics and stimulating economic growth. However, his policies of *glasnost* and *perestroika* caused instability, which led to economic turmoil and nationalist movements that eventually resulted in its dissolution (Zubok 2017).

Deng Xiaoping led a period of transformation in China through reform while maintaining tight political control. His reforms proved successful due to carefully planned execution over time; some were in blitzkrieg fashion (as we'll see in chapter 15), but these gradual changes occurred during a period of relative stability, which allowed for unprecedented economic growth resulting in millions stepping out of poverty (Kołodko 2021).

Both leaders had reformist ambitions. However, their context of operation as well as timing of implementation determined whether or not they would have success or failure. Gorbachev quickly transformed a rigid political system without having enough time to properly implement his plans, leaving him open to failure. Whereas Deng took his time creating an environment where he could slowly implement necessary changes that ultimately brought immense prosperity for China.

It is a story that repeats itself. How can we grasp it better to avoid the ever-growing number of pitfalls?

Takeaways: Lessons Learned and Application to Reform

I could experience both sides of the timing and context space. On the one hand, preparing the Plan for Puerto Rico and understanding what I was getting into was super valuable. In addition, that preparation gave me the gift of time. I had the ability to execute at my highest moment of influence and being ready to do so. On the other hand, there was a lot of Splash in me as well. I proceeded to move reforms at suboptimal times and when the environment was not permissive.

Here are a few key observations:

- **The Crucial Role of Timing and Context**: My kids' tale of "Splash and Wave" underscores the profound impact of timing and context on outcomes. Two individuals (or situations) can be similar in every aspect but can experience vastly different fates based on the timing of their decisions and the circumstances they find themselves in. This principle does not just confine to stories but is a recurring theme in governance and reform. Gorbachev and Xiaoping illustrate this.

- **We Are Blind without Recognizing Initial Conditions**: Before embarking on any significant change or reform, it's paramount to understand the current state of conditions and extrapolate what got us there. Like a good piece of classical music, it requires time to prepare before the execution starts. This was a guiding principle in Plan for Puerto Rico. Identify initial conditions, assess the root cause problems, look for solutions, and implement at the best time possible... because...

- **Understanding Time: A Double-Edged Sword**: Time can be both an asset and a liability. While it offers opportunities for growth and reform, it can also introduce challenges and setbacks, as evidenced by the Law 80 labor reform saga. Leaders must master the art of discerning when to act and when to pause. In general, you have most influence in the onset. The capacity to reform diminishes thereafter unless unexpected policy windows pop open. This quantitative reality will serve as a basic assumption for our understanding of the reform dynamics developed in this book.

Hindsight is twenty-twenty. Today, I could have done several things differently. First, having the foresight to execute this earlier on. I could pass comprehensive labor reform in twenty-three days (timing), but I did not include Law 80. This could have been a missed opportunity. Second, I could have taken a smaller step. During the negotiations, I had the chance to have a watered-down version of Law 80. It was essentially grandfathering. If you can get to 60 percent of your objective, *do it*. I did not. I was too in the weeds with the proposal from the oversight board and neglected the benefits we would get from this bill. It would have been a unique opportunity to allow Puerto Rico to have a stronger positioning statement for businesses in the future.

The realization that one has lost their shine is another key moment. This is a time and place where you need to figure out how to reposition your reforms and yourself. I sustained the same strategy that worked for me in the past without noticing I had changed in the eyes of many.

There were plenty of reasons for this change, but the friction created by our reforms was a key contributor. Many times, groups will oppose your reform, not for the content of the measure, but for political or opposition-based reasons.

As that opposition grows, it has a compounding effect. This will inevitably change your context. Understanding the dynamics of the opposition is an imperative. If you don't, it will eat you up.

Can a reformer overcome this friction?

CHAPTER 12:

Aggregated Earned Opposition

Significant reforms often attract substantial opposition. This MetroPR cover illustration shows a tug-of-war with the president of the Senate and the presidents of the mayors' organizations (2019b), who were resisting the elimination of municipalities and my proposal to regionalize government. The scale of this reform was immense, and it faced corresponding resistance.

In the summer of 1999, during my father's second term and my first year of college, he surprised me with an invitation: "We are going to Cooperstown." As an avid baseball fan, I was thrilled. Baseball is almost a religion in Puerto Rico, and Roberto Clemente, a native son and Hall of Famer, inspired many to emulate his greatness. The island has produced an impressive array of talented players.

This time, another Puerto Rican, Orlando "Peruchin" Cepeda, known as "The Baby Bull," received induction into the hall. His achievements included the National League MVP in 1967 and a World Series championship that same year.

That year's Hall of Fame class was remarkable, featuring George Brett, Robin Yount, and Nolan Ryan, arguably the most intimidating pitcher of his era with seven no-hitters. Ryan, a Texan and member of the Rangers, had invited another notable figure—Governor George W. Bush.

At that time, Bush's potential presidential candidacy was just a rumor. Spotting him, my dad suggested we greet him. Despite being a Democrat, my dad had a good relationship with President George H. W. Bush, Governor Bush's father.

Governor Bush greeted me warmly, saying "Cómo *estás*, amigo?" (How are you, my friend? in Spanish). He gave me a firm handshake and posed for a photo.

My father then asked if he could sign my baseball. He agreed. But as he was signing the ball he told my dad, "I heard you are with the other guy," in reference to Vice president Al Gore.

Before my dad could say anything, he said, "I am very disappointed."

My dad responded: "I am a Democrat, and I support him, but I respect you"

An awkward silence ensued, and then, my dad asked, "How's your father?"

And Governor Bush replied, "He's disappointed too."

I laughed out loud. I like to think it broke a bit of the tension. Then we went our separate ways.

Even with amicable interactions, significant disputes and clear lines formed. The friend of my enemy is my enemy, and it's natural for opposition to amass over time.

Opposition Amassed

Ivan Rivera's reflection on the protests leading to my resignation was telling. "It was fascinating to see various groups, each distinct in their agendas, unite under the excuse of the chat scandal to demand your resignation," he said. This convergence of opposition was a pivotal moment in my political journey.

Time is the friend of the opposition. With each day that passes, the honeymoon fades, challenges become apparent, and opposition aggregates.

Why does this happen? The growth of opposition to a political leader often results from a mix of factors. As leaders make decisions and implement policies, they inevitably create both winners and losers. While supporters may celebrate the successes, those negatively impacted by these decisions grow increasingly vocal. Over time, even small grievances can snowball into significant opposition. Furthermore, the longer a leader is in office, the more likely they are to face tough decisions or unexpected challenges, providing further fuel for opposition.

I checked all the boxes.

Ivan pinpointed two primary groups that rallied against me. "First, there were the groups who historically opposed to all the reforms that Rosselló began to implement in 2017. They normally operated under the understanding that no one would dare to carry them out due to the potential electoral cost. Rosselló carried them out quickly and effectively. Second, a commercial and economic class that has historically operated as a dependent of the government, for whom said reforms created uncertainty regarding the future of their businesses. To the first group, the reforms represented a threat to their extreme ideology, and the probability of reelection was evident. The second one was willing to do anything to ensure a halt to the reforms so they could prolong the existence of their business and government dependency."

An experienced statesman once advised me, "The longer you stay in power, the more you attract discontent. It's not solely the mistakes you make; it's also the public's growing fatigue." His insight was accurate.

In politics, opposition is often a byproduct of action. If not managed carefully, it can spiral out of control, becoming unsustainable.

Too Much Aggregate Opposition

In the introduction of this book, I recounted a pivotal moment during the final days of my administration when a group of lawyers visited me. They came with the intention of convincing me to remain in office, armed with arguments about the manipulated nature of the situation (later proven true) and the

Figure 1. War room with some of my team (Photo Credit: Raymond Cruz).

absence of any legal wrongdoing on our part (also demonstrated to be true). They were confident of a decisive legal victory, should it come to that.

"It's bulletproof." "They can't remove you." "You haven't done anything to merit removal," were among the assurances they offered.

Despite their confidence, the political climate had deteriorated into an overwhelmingly toxic environment. The arrests of two former high-ranking members of my administration and the leaked chat conversations had ignited massive opposition. Even members of my own party were advocating for impeachment on questionable grounds.

After hearing their arguments, I broke the tense silence with a simple yet profound question:

"Yes, but what is the purpose?"

They stared at me at a loss for words. I'd heard enough. I thanked them, went upstairs to my chambers. I made a decision I would announce in a few days. One of the lawyers (Edwin Prado) a year later went on TV and expressed the following: "If the governor of Puerto Rico wanted to he could have appealed the case" (MetroPR 2019a).

The interviewer responds: "What did Rosselló decide at that moment when you told him these are the two cards ... he could have been litigating for eighteen months and then leave or what?

Edwin said, "I have to say the governor at that moment placed his bet on the future of Puerto Rico... why do I say this? The governor told us, 'What is the value of governing, if with me at the helm, this will become ungovernable?' Governor Rosselló based his decision on that. And the other aspect I have to recognize from the governor is..."

Ferdinand Perez (interviewer) interrupts: "Hold that thought, Prado, I have more questions for you, but I have to go to break." The interviewer rapidly went to commercials. Never came back to ask more questions. The answers didn't seem to fit his narrative.

Back to the question: What was the purpose if I wouldn't get to achieve anything in the next eighteen months? What is the purpose, if at that point, I had reached a critical threshold, where the opposition and friction to action was so big there was no turning back. What is the purpose if my goal was to reform, and I could no longer do that from the governor's seat.

This concept of the critical threshold is only relevant if your aim is to reform and be an effective executive. Otherwise, you could go the other route and stayed in power for the sake of power. At some point the mounting opposition is so big and consolidated, you will not be able to act.

This should be a concern to everyone. After all, the impedance of action eventually hinders all constituents. Lack of execution sets you in a collision course for failure and crisis. Here, you have to pay attention to the concept of mounting opposition. The idea behind it is simple. In your first efforts to reform, you will get a group that opposes it ferociously. If you pass reform, that group will have a score to settle. That means the next time you attempt reform, you will not only face the natural opponents of that effort but also the added opponents from previous reforms. The effect compounds and can get out of hand.

Misery Loves Company

Why do we resist reform? I understand not all reforms are good. Probably many of them are worse than the current situation. But here, let's examine inherent causes of this opposition. Resistance to reform often arises due to a variety of factors.

1. **Fear of Change**: It's normal. It taps into our innate human instinct to seek stability and predictability. When faced with reform, individuals often worry about how the changes will affect their lives, their jobs, and their communities, leading to resistance—in some cases, ferocious resistance. As former British Prime Minister Tony Blair once said, "The art of leadership is saying no, not yes. It is very easy to say yes." This underscores the challenge leaders face in pushing for reform amid resistance fueled by fear of the unknown.

2. **Loss of Power or Privilege**: Reforms often aim to redistribute power or resources, which can threaten those who currently hold these advantages. Those in power may resist reforms they perceive as threatening their status or privilege. A subset of these are economic reforms, especially those related to economic policy, that can lead to winners and losers. Those who stand to lose economically from the reforms may resist them. The problem is beneficiaries have less commitment than those affected. Governor Cuomo told me in our sit down, "Beneficiaries do not have the same commitment nor do they feel as vested. Theoretically, yes, I understand the benefit to me, but it's only a theoretical benefit. The opponents have a vested interest today that you're going to hurt me."

3. **Ideological Differences**: People have different beliefs and values, which can influence their attitudes toward reform. If a proposed reform conflicts with an individual's or group's deeply held beliefs, it is likely to encounter resistance. This resistance is growing increasingly large. Last April, I had a conversation with Governor Kasich. Known for his pragmatic and moderate approach to politics, Governor Kasich often emphasizes the importance of bipartisan cooperation. Among the many things we discussed, he was poignant in stating: "The main problem to the country now is we're so divided by red and blue. This does not work. I'd rather get along with people than fight with them."

4. **Lack of Trust**: If people do not trust the individuals or institutions promoting reform, they are likely to resist it. This can be particularly true if previous reforms have failed or have had negative consequences. Trust and failed reforms are the subject of other parts in the book.

5. **Poor Communication**: If there isn't clear communication about the reasons for the reform and its potential benefits, people may resist it out of misunderstanding or lack of information. This can also be intentional misdirection or miscommunication by the opposition. Creating a mess tends to work effectively.

Now envision why this is so easy to aggregate. Some reforms might lead to fear. Others to ideological differences. Yet others are constantly bungled intentionally or unintentionally, developing a problem in how we communicate them. The old saying "misery loves company" is true. Those who feel slighted by reform will tend to unite, and this effect is cumulative. I learned this the hard way.

A Mayor(s) Problem

Puerto Rico has seventy-eight municipalities. It is unsustainable.

The majority of these municipalities heavily rely on central government transfers, costing the government approximately a billion dollars annually. When the Fiscal Oversight Board recognized this, budget cuts seemed inevitable. This crisis, however, presented an opportunity to improve local governance.

They made a decision to cut four hundred million dollars from the subsidy to municipalities over a few years. As expected, the mayors united in opposition. "We have information to share with the governor and request his collaboration on the fiscal plan concerning municipalities. Losing the $410 million subsidy would put us in a dire situation, possibly leading to layoffs and insufficient resources for even part-time work," they expressed.

This challenge arose just two months into my tenure. The mayors' resistance compounded the opposition I already faced from labor reform detractors. Despite my efforts, I couldn't fully engage the mayors in meaningful policy discussions thereafter.

My proposal to consolidate municipalities and form counties aimed to (1) enhance services and (2) save $1.2 billion annually. Additionally, I planned to delegate more power from the central government to these regional entities.

"You're crazy for doing this," an advisor warned. "The mayors will never forgive you."

I argued that it was in their best interest, a path to growth for Puerto Rico, promising better services for the people. "It doesn't matter. You're taking power away from them," she countered.

She was right. The mayors became some of the most vigorous opponents in the protests against me, regardless of party affiliation.

Changing the status quo is a formidable challenge. This is partly why Puerto Rico has long endured its colonial status. Despite five hundred years of demonstrable failure, the colonial system felt... stable.

The same is true for the municipalities. Generally, they are inefficient, draining fiscal resources and providing subpar services. Breaking the status quo is difficult. Fernandez and Roderik question, "Why do governments often fail to adopt efficiency-enhancing policies?" The answer lies in the uncertainty of who wins or loses. The result is a bias toward maintaining the status quo, often at the expense of necessary reforms (1991).

The status quo hates reform...

Big Oil: Energy and Climate Change Reform

The broken energy system in Puerto Rico is the single biggest obstacle to business. It can be abusive to a citizen's quality of life. Hurricane Maria clearly unmasked the consequences of running an outdated, unmaintained energy system.

The obligatory question is: Why if this was such a broken system—and everyone knew about it— was nothing happening to change it?

Big oil.

While there are additional factors (unions, complacency, etc.), the predominant issue is energy reliance. A staggering 98 percent of Puerto Rico's energy generation depends on imported fossil fuels (oil, natural gas, and coal) with only 2 percent from renewables (solar, wind, hydroelectric) (Massol-Deya, Stephens, and Colon 2018). The result? Not only does Puerto Rico have the most expensive energy in the United States, at twice the national average, but it also suffers from the least reliability (Energy Sage 2023). This is in a territory where income levels are a third of the national average (Rosselló 2012). "Apagones," or blackouts, are commonplace with frequent power losses. This unsustainable situation necessitated broad and sweeping energy reform.

Post-hurricane, we saw a chance for change. A policy window opened, and the crisis created an opportunity. I proposed immediate energy reform, starting with privatization and leading to diversification (El Sentinel 2018).

Maria Palou, my infrastructure czar, remembers, "The energy reform answered the public's call for drastic change. The existing system's failure was evident after Hurricanes Irma and Maria. As with any reform, the main opposition comes from those invested in the current system." She highlights a time of reform challenge. "Rosselló's energy reform was ambitious but lengthy. Over time, people forget the devastation caused by an outdated system, and that's when opponents regroup. Surprisingly, movements supporting old interests have resurfaced."

Our objective was to achieve 42 percent renewable energy by 2023, a pioneering goal at the time. The announcement surprised many, including party members tied to the existing energy system, who later became major adversaries.

In 2019, we enacted a climate change reform bill with specific goals and methods, including a 50 percent reduction in carbon emissions over ten years. This was challenging, especially for big oil, who received significant aid by ending coal burning. Announcing the prohibition of coal for energy generation later that year earned me more enemies.

You would think people who had been protesting against coal burning would be supportive. Not a chance. Most of them were tangled with other agendas. Once they oppose you, it's hard to get them on board for anything.

Nevertheless, the situation was unique, with high stakes. We had substantial funds to overhaul the energy grid. My vision was to use this as an opportunity for innovative leaps, aiming to make Puerto Rico a model of resilience for the US. However, those facing losses were not receptive.

What a case study! Wanting something done by most everybody, yet nobody could do it. An internal poll from June 2018 showed the biggest issue for people was energy, and they were most looking forward to energy reform. Against plenty of big money, we were able to secure these reforms.

However, many who initially wanted a new system now opposed the changes, deeming them too slow or ineffective. Critics were adeptly attributing fifty years of ineffectiveness to the transition's growing pains.

Protests and unrest over apagones (blackouts) had become common. The reality is systemic change takes time, and opponents exploited this. If initial efforts to derail reform fail, they bide their time, waiting to incite discord.

This raises a crucial question: How can we achieve reform if those demanding change become opponents? We must consider this, especially as some people lack the democratic right to choose and face severe suppression. Attempting to assist them can attract powerful adversaries.

Humanitarian help to Venezuela.

"The Venezuelan people desperately need humanitarian aid. The US and other countries are trying to help, but the Venezuelan Army under orders from Maduro is blocking aid with trucks and tanks to transport goods," former Secretary of State Mike Pompeo said (El Colombiano 2019).

The situation in Venezuela was horrible. The protests were a series of demonstrations at the national and international level against the dictator Nicolás Maduro caused by the presidential crisis that occurred when the National Assembly appointed Juan Guaidó as temporary and interim president. Many people lost their lives in organized demonstrations in protest of the Maduro government. In the midst of this, picture people in the street desperately looking for food and medical supplies, many of them voiceless.

A member of the Venezuelan community in Puerto Rico recalled, "I have family there and they tell me of the desperation they feel because they can't buy or get anything. It's awful. You can't even imagine" (Anthony 2019).

Who would help them?

Leopoldo López, a former mayor of Caracas and political prisoner recounts in a conversation on November 2022. "There is complete censorship. There is complete contamination. And then there is

Figure 2. Image of the boat we sent to Venezuela for humanitarian aid (Photo Credit: Magdiel Lugo).

fear because there are consequences." He paused. "People express what they think of the regime, and they get killed."

It is that simple.

Worst of all, nobody wanted in. Nobody, except for Puerto Rico. Although the odds were stacked against us, we went in to help.

"Due to the humanitarian crisis that Venezuela is going through, the island's governor, Ricardo Rosselló, has ordered that, 'through a joint effort,' 'the necessary steps be taken' to send humanitarian aid to Venezuela." Those were the words of my secretary of state, Luis Rivera Marin (Cybernews 2019).

On January 30, 2019, we sent out a boat to the coast of Venezuela filled with food, medicine, and other articles of humanitarian aid. Our goal was to help people. Thousands gathered in the docks to get the supplies. Of course, Nicolás Maduro did not care.

As the boats were arriving, military personal entered and created a blockade so the supplies would not get in.

Nicolás Maduro never forgot. He saw me as an enemy. Before these efforts, I had another virtual encounter with Maduro. The Nuevo Herald reported, "Rosselló responded in this way to a journalist's question after Maduro pointed out that he carried the island 'in his soul' and that the cause of Puerto Rico remained pending on the agenda of the liberator Bolívar. Governor Rosselló replied that in Puerto Rico they value 'the fundamental principles of democracy.' 'We respect human rights and life,' he added. 'Nicolás Maduro, you are very different from the vast majority of Puerto Ricans. Our solidarity remains with the people of Venezuela'" (El Nuevo Herald 2018).

I had a powerful opponent.

So it is no surprise then that one day after I resigned, the Foro de Sao Paulo—an extreme socialist assembly—took place in Caracas. Maduro was hosting. "The almost five hundred delegates of the Sao Paulo Forum, and many other guests, celebrated the announced resignation of the governor of Puerto Rico, Ricardo Rosselló, while calling for the independence of the Caribbean Island." (Agencia EFE 2019).

Opposition might stay latent for a while, but they aggregate and align to strike a blow.

Unions

In March 2018, Randi Weingarten was to meet with me at La Fortaleza. Despite our past differences, I had made room in my schedule for her. However, at 2 p.m. that day, instead of attending the meeting, they chose to protest outside the executive mansion (Quintero 2018).

"Are they coming?" I asked my scheduler.

"They haven't checked in," she responded.

"Could you call them again?" I asked.

She returned a few minutes later to inform us there was no response.

After waiting for an hour, I moved on with my schedule. Later, to the press, they claimed, "The governor had snubbed her."

This incident typified my relationship with the unions. They consistently sought to cast our efforts in a negative light, viewing me as a perpetual adversary.

Carlos Saavedra, a skilled lawyer I appointed as secretary of labor, reflected on the challenges: "The 2017 labor reform modernized numerous labor laws, making the legal framework more flexible and empowering workers. This was a threat to unions and groups accustomed to older laws for maintaining

Figure 3. A protest involving unions (Quintero 2018).

their power. Consequently, they not only opposed the labor reform but also became detractors of other reforms, like the single employer initiative, often resorting to protests and disinformation campaigns."

Unions were among the first to feel the friction with my government. We had to implement several tough measures: (1) freezing government hiring immediately upon my term's start, (2) suspending collective bargaining at the oversight board's request, (3) downsizing government, (4) introducing charter schools and vouchers, and (5) enacting labor law reform.

However, some private sector unions supported me because of my decision to increase the minimum wage for construction workers to fifteen dollars an hour through executive order. This, in turn, garnered opposition from private sector construction groups (Agencia EFE 2018).

Public unions opposed most major reforms, even those not directly affecting them. This phenomenon—aggregated earned opposition—became a significant aspect of our journey.

Such aggregate opposition inevitably impacts reform efforts.

A Global Example

In the last chapter, we compared Gorbachev and Deng Xiaoping. Gorbachev aimed reforms at addressing the economic stagnation and political corruption that had plagued the Soviet Union for decades. However, these reforms ultimately led to a surge in opposition and resistance that contributed to the dissolution of the Soviet Union and his ouster.

Gorbachev's reforms were radical and transformative. He sought to decentralize the economy, introduce elements of free market capitalism, and promote political openness. However, these reforms met with significant resistance. Various scholars contend that Gorbachev's attempts to dismantle the Marxist-Leninist ideology and replace it with a new ideology of perestroika for the Soviet Union and the world met with resistance both domestically and internationally. Many saw Gorbachev's reforms as a threat to the existing power structures and the ideological foundations of the Soviet Union.

In his paper "Economic Reforms in the Sovereign States of the Former Soviet Union," William Hogan noted that Gorbachev's reforms led to a significant economic crisis with the central budget deficit approaching 20 percent of gross national product in 1991.

This economic instability fueled and coalesced the opposition to Gorbachev's leadership. His party split and internal opposition and resistance to Gorbachev grew from within.

Sound familiar?

Gorbachev's reforms, while intended to modernize and revitalize the Soviet Union, ultimately provoked too much resistance and aggregated opposition that contributed to his exit.

Takeaways: The friend of My Enemy Is My Enemy

1. **Cumulative Opposition Grows Over Time**: As leaders make decisions and implement policies, they inevitably create both supporters and opponents. Over time, even minor grievances can accumulate, leading to a larger and more organized opposition. This is not just about the mistakes they make but also about the inevitable weariness of the public. Those who benefit from reforms are less enthusiastic about it in their activism than those affected. As the tenure of an executive

progresses the likelihood of reform diminishes due to factors such as polarization, dehumanization, and execution errors.

2. **Reform Creates Opponents**: Reform often leads to changes that can threaten established power structures or the status quo. Those who stand to lose power, privilege, or economic benefits from reforms will often resist them. This resistance can come from various sources, including fear of change, loss of power or privilege, ideological differences, lack of trust, and poor communication. The resistance to reform is often *cumulative*, with opponents from previous reforms joining forces with new opponents to resist subsequent reforms.

3. **Threshold of Unsustainability**: There comes a point when the mounting opposition becomes so significant that it impedes the ability to govern effectively. When the opposition reaches a critical threshold, the leader may find it challenging to implement reforms or even maintain the status quo. This can completely inhibit the capacity of an executive to perform, even if they believe they are acting in the best interests of their constituents. The impedance of action eventually hinders all constituents, and a lack of execution can set the leader on a collision course for failure and crisis.

These are just a few of the examples that demonstrate a point. Opposition aggregates across time, even if the reforms benefit them and even if they have no relation to the reform. Politics makes strange bedfellows, and in this case, the enemy of my enemy becomes my friend. When making reform, it is important to be mindful of this. We will later discuss ways to mitigate this effect. But if nothing changes, your capacity to reform will be highly diminished or even completely terminated.

What was smooth operating in the first one hundred days became ever so much harder to pull as time went along. I could get a second bump after the hurricane, as people were rallying for a united effort. But it continued diminishing until my final months in office. Interestingly, two months before my resignation, I was ahead on all polls for reelection. I had the general support of the people. However, I had mounting opposition that coalesced. In addition to the traditional political opposition, aggregated earned opposition generated. The unions were against me (labor reform, and civil service reform). The teachers were against me (education reform). The mayors were against me (fiscal measures and proposal to create counties). The vast majority of the legislature was against me. The international socialist movement was against me (Maduro).

They were waiting in the wings. Every time a new reform came about, they would aggregately oppose it. There comes a point when you can't operate if the opposition friction has reached a critical level. In the end, I gave them the perfect excuse to rally together by mistake and lack of judgment on my part. I realized my family was in jeopardy and the emotional negative narrative took an unrelenting hold. At this point, I could no longer operate as an effective governor. I, therefore, resigned... for what was the purpose?

CHAPTER 13:

Magnitude of Reform

Metro featured this illustration by Nell Amador on the cover. It shows me "turning the lights off" on the old Energy Public Corporation Utility by announcing we would privatize and change the energy model from petroleum dependent to higher renewables. It was big, bold and—of course—riddled with opposition (*MetroPR* 2018).

Just a couple of months after the storm, the recovery phase was far from over. A sense of stagnation was settling into society and the government, for that matter. On January 21, 2018, I called for a special message to the people of Puerto Rico.

Speculation about the content ran *rampant*.

"Most people thought you would speak about the recovery, the challenges ahead, perhaps even an inspiring message," recalled William Villafañe, my former chief of staff. "Then you dropped a bombshell. Nobody knew about it. Nobody expected it."

"The governor of Puerto Rico, Ricardo Rosselló Nevares, announced in a message to the country the end of the Puerto Rico Electric Power Authority (PREPA) as a public corporation and revealed the plan to start a privatization process for the agency. The surprise announcement comes at a time when

Figure 1. Image from the special message on energy, telling the people of Puerto Rico that we would privatize energy and shoot for a transition to renewables.

almost 30 percent of consumers remain without service more than four months after the passage of Hurricanes Irma and Maria," said the *Orlando Sentinel* (2018).

I had told nobody about my plan. I told my press person to call the local network to transmit a message. I called the presidents of the House and Senate to come over.

"What will the message be about, Governor?" asked the president of the House.

"You'll see," I responded.

Following my message, they were not happy. They did not see it coming.

"You should have told us," said the president of the Senate. Truth is, he was *not* trustworthy. He is a beacon of the status quo (not on statehood, but pretty much everything else). Had I told him, he would have torpedoed the announcement. Why?

Because it was a major reform against *"things as they were."* (Figure 1)

Understanding the PREPA Drag

The Puerto Rico Electric Power Authority (PREPA), established in 1941, is the island's state-owned electric power company. However, its inefficiency and corruption marred its history. Known for frequent power outages, PREPA also developed a reputation for dishonest dealings (Volpe 2019).

Imagine a public corporation capable of issuing bonds for infrastructure improvements but instead using those funds for operational expenses, payroll, and benefits. This made PREPA a coveted employment destination. At every event, people approached me with résumés, hoping for a position in this public corporation.

"The benefits were through the roof," recalled Ramon Rosario.

But at what cost? The result was an expensive, unreliable, and crippling energy infrastructure.

A 2017 Reuters article highlighted the root issues: "Frequent turnover in management and board leadership, which has long failed to prioritize grid maintenance, according to reports prepared in 2015 and 2016 for utility regulators by the consultancy Synapse Energy Associates. The deferred upkeep led to a 'degraded and unsafe' grid that needed at least four billion dollars for modernization" (Brown, Respaut, and Resnick-Ault 2017).

Entrenched interests consistently thwarted efforts to reform, despite the widely recognized dysfunction of PREPA.

Recognizing a fleeting policy window, I chose to act decisively and swiftly, keeping my plans close to the vest. This approach was part of our public Plan for Puerto Rico, but few believed we would actually implement it. In my first year, we worked diligently on strategies for reform, a process both intricate and extensive.

However, the urgency became clear post-storm, revealing the fragility of our neglected energy system. The cost of inaction was too high.

My decision to push for privatization and a new energy model made me new enemies, but I saw it as a chance for fundamental change. A year later, progress was evident. Scientific American's article "Puerto Rico Pledges to Go All-Renewable by 2050" began: "Puerto Rico has ambitious plans to transform its hurricane-battered electric grid to rely entirely on renewable energy by 2050. The move is part of a multimillion-dollar program to reduce the US territory's carbon footprint and make it more climate resilient, Puerto Rican Gov. Ricardo Rosselló announced" (Cusick 2018).

This policy shift was monumental, potentially transforming Puerto Rico's energy grid from one of the most expensive and unreliable in the United States to one of the best.

Though I didn't see the project to completion, I take pride in its initiation. Despite current challenges, the reform's magnitude promises a lasting positive impact on Puerto Rico.

And I have witnessed firsthand the effect of a beneficial reform of large magnitude.

"La Tarjeta de Rosselló"

My early memories from childhood evoked the sense of reform. I lived in a house that was mostly one story, with a small room in the attic. This was my father's cave stacked with books, documents, old trophies, and pictures of our family. At the end of it stood a desk that was "chaotically organized."

My dad, a pediatric surgeon by trade, had stumbled upon the many problems in the healthcare system. He rarely had time to himself with work, family, and the sport he loved (tennis) occupying most of his time. But when he did—he would play *Beethoven's Fifth Symphony* and start writing ideas and plans to improve the healthcare system.

At that point, anyone who knew him would attest that public office was the farthest thing from his mind. He was developing this because he was an academic, who saw a problem and wanted to solve it. More so, one of our neighbors was a recognized politician who was running to be the mayor of San Juan.

"I would ask Maga to give these documents to Baltazar," he recalls, "but it was slow evolving." Eventually, Baltazar, the mayor of San Juan, tabbed him to lead San Juan's healthcare system. The rest is history…

By the early 1990s, Puerto Rico had a broken healthcare system. The public opinion polls at the time reflected the key point of contention regarding the healthcare system was the differences between the systems for the rich and for the poor.

"In Puerto Rico there were two parallel systems for healthcare. One was the private system that offered better services and treatments for those who could pay. The other was the public one. It lacked quality services and excluded people from low resources to get the appropriate treatments. It was a system that sustained medical-indigent a large sector of our population" (Rosselló 2004).

The visuals were scary. Imagine local hospitals with no medical equipment and no medicine. Imagine patients treated as if it were a DMV. There was no sense of urgency and no urgency to change. Government bureaucracy at its worst, it was unsustainable.

At that point 45 percent of the population was without insurance, which was a huge problem. It would take an enormous reform to change it. Not many people thought it could change. Nobody, until 1993 rolled around.

I asked the architect of this massive undertaking a key question: How did this reform come to fruition?

"In 1976, I returned to PR, after fourteen years of education and training , to practice pediatric surgery in an academic setting (UPR School of Medicine). There, systematically deficient and unfair treatment of children, especially infants, confronted me. This was a wakeup call for me. I had to do something," said Dr. Pedro Rosselló, who eventually became Puerto Rico's seventh governor.

"So, I took a sabbatical and concluded that a two-prong system was inefficient and dangerous. I Developed a blueprint for reform that required unification of both systems, with access it for all, on an equal basis, through insurance, to reach universal coverage," he told me with a glimmer in his eyes.

For the most part, people immediately attacked the proposal. Famously, his main opponent on the campaign trail tried to kill these reforms by saying they were impossible. To which my father responded with what became a rallying cry for the rest of his tenure "*si, se puede*" (yes, we can) Figure 2.

Once elected, how was Dr. Rosselló going to engineer this complicated reform that required significant runway?

He recalls, "It required the divestment of a large medico-hospital structure with sale of hospitals and clinical facilities and investing that spent on the old public system into obtaining insurance for more than one-half the total population who could not afford it. The government's role changed from that of a direct provider of services (public) to that of an insurer of access. From two distinct and unequal (in recourses and in results) to one system with equal access to all."

Complicated stuff. The status quo was not happy. Not surprisingly, plenty of obstacles ensued.

"First, the always present resistance in the legislative process. Opposition parties vigorously opposed its adoption. Solid support overcame this after the usual intraparty wrangling. Solid support of our majority in both chambers of the legislature overcame me. Second, the aggressive and public opposition of organized medicine, led by the PR Medical Association and other healthcare organizations. And lastly, general opposition of population to a major unknown change was also present."

Figure 2. Picture of my father, Dr. Pedro Rosselló (Photo Credit: Magdiel Lugo).

Halfway through his first term, they called him "Pedro el breve" (Pedro the brief), as an indication that he would not last very long. The changes he was proposing were too strong, evoked too much will, and provoked the ire of opponents.

Then… things started changing. He was garnering more and more support. Why? By the end of his first term, people started feeling the real effects of the "Tarjetita de Rosselló." He recalls that "over one million citizens had acquired private (although publicly financed) insurance, who previously had none."

One million empowered people felt the effects of it. Game changer. For example, in 1992 less than 40 percent of the children on the island had vaccinations; a staggering thought nowadays. By 1996, that had gone up to 75 percent, and by the end of his second term, 99.4 percent (Rosselló 2004).

In 1996 he won by the biggest landslide in modern history and—to this day—holds the record for most total votes. What was that total? You guessed it: *one million votes.*

This reform was something of *high magnitude*—a meaningful change in a severe problem. Before there were two systems: one for the rich and another for the poor. By the end of the 1990s, Puerto Rico was the first US jurisdiction to have virtually 100 percent of its citizens covered. They also had access to the same hospitals, which was a dramatic change of landscape. The effects of this high-magnitude reform set the stage for his unprecedented victory.

An important lesson: While it will be a hard path forward, making reforms can have a superbly beneficial result, not only on the people but on the prospects of a reelection.

Yet sometimes you don't get to see or feel the results of it. So what happens to those high-magnitude reforms that start but can't execute?

The Elephant in the Room: Regional Government Reform

On March 18, 2019, I called a significant meeting with every mayor and news outlet in Puerto Rico at the Pedro Rosselló Library, which boasts a comfortable, modern amphitheater. This setting was ideal for discussing issues with the depth and rigor they deserved. Once again, I did not exactly say what we were going to discuss. Otherwise, I'd be lucky if I got one or two mayors. This topic was regional government reform, essentially how to create counties and reduce the power of both central and municipal governments.

This was a continuation of my government reform efforts. We successfully implemented government downsizing measures, consolidated or eliminated government agencies, and enacted the single employer policy. We had reduced more than twenty-three thousand positions in government without layoffs, cut over two billion dollars a year in expenses, and increased revenue by a similar amount. Now, it was time to tackle vertical integration in government function.

Advisors warned me against this move. "This is a terrible idea," one said, fearing a lack of political support and potential backlash. My determination didn't waver, perhaps buoyed by our previous successes or maybe due to a bit of hubris. But there was also a rational aspect to my decision. Our projections showed that municipalities would soon be unable to sustain their fiscal burden. We had a six-to-seven-year window to transition.

"If you are the mayor of a municipality that depends 80 or 90 percent on transfers from the central government, and those transfers cease, there is a serious operating problem," I explained to the mayors (Telemundo PR 2019) Figure 3.

Let's look under the hood a bit to justify this explanation. Puerto Rican municipalities have long been dependent on financing from the central government. The fiscal crisis hit them hard, with many facing severe financial difficulties. The table below shows the impact on municipalities, considering various scenarios of central government support. Even with bailouts, several municipalities would still face closure by 2024–2025. Without them, the majority would fail (Figure 4).

When advised against this policy, I asked my team, "Do you want me to be reelected?" After affirming, I explained, "Then I need to do this because, otherwise, this collapse will happen under my watch."

Figure 3. Presenting the need for regionalization to mayors and policymakers (source: Telemundo PR).

Number of municipalities not being able to meet expenses by scenario

	Expenses that municipalities decide to pay in each scenario	2015	2016	2017	2018p	2019p	2020p	2021p	2022p	2023p	2024p
A	Debt+Capex+PayGO+ASES+Opex Payroll+Opex Other only	60	63	66	78	73	66	65	63	63	63
B	Debt+Capex+Opex Payroll+Opex Other only	45	51	61	74	62	59	59	58	56	58
C	Debt+PayGO+ASES+Opex Payroll+Opex Other only	26	32	50	68	61	57	59	58	58	58
D	Debt+Opex Payroll+Opex Other only	19	20	43	63	53	51	51	51	51	52
E	Debt+Opex Payroll only	1	0	2	3	3	3	3	4	4	6
	Debt only	0	0	0	0	0	0	0	0	0	0

Figure 4. Slide showing municipalities unable to meet expenses at the current rate.

Secretary of Public Policy Ramon Rosario recalled, "The governor insisted that creating counties was essential for the survival of municipalities. Rosselló had been warning and discussing since 2016."

I compromised with a group of mayors on a five-to-six-year runway for creating counties. During this time, the central government would cover all municipal expenses except for debt service and payroll. This would also involve delegating many central government services to the new regional governments.

I emphasized the reform was not just a fiscal necessity but, more importantly, an imperative for better community services. The county system would save more than a billion dollars annually and improve accountability and service quality (Figure 5).

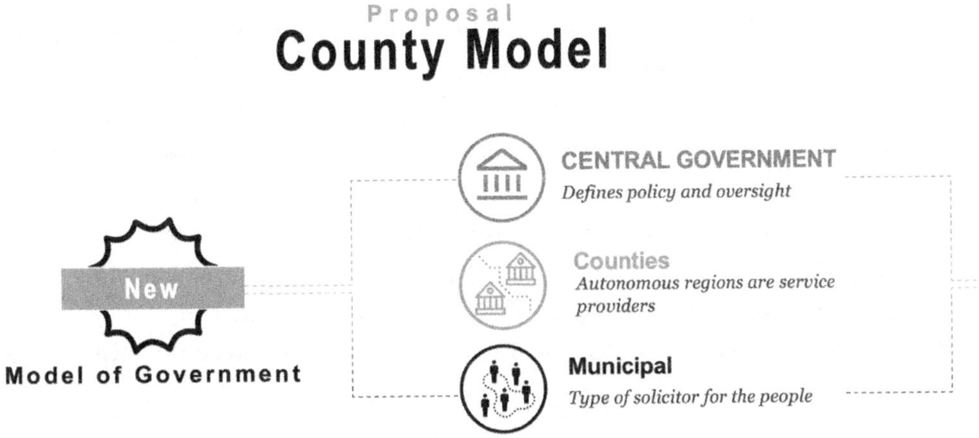

Proposal
County Model

CENTRAL GOVERNMENT
Defines policy and oversight

Counties
Autonomous regions are service providers

New
Model of Government

Municipal
Type of solicitor for the people

Figure 5. High-level slide denoting the new government model and the roles at the central, regional, and municipal levels.

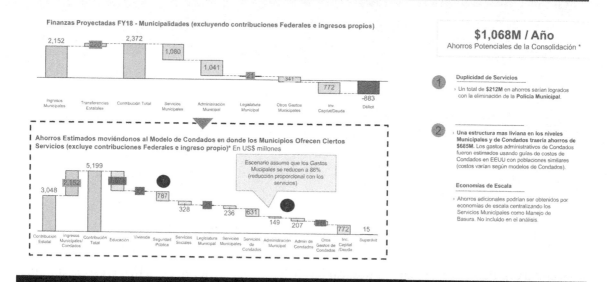

Figure 6. Slide denoting the savings from the transition to counties.

This reform would rationalize the role of government, clarifying accountability. The central government would mostly dictate policy and oversee its execution. Counties would have fiscal tools to adjust taxes and provide desired services for their region (FIgure 6).

Despite careful planning, my influence was waning. The reform threatened the power of the mayors, and they strongly opposed it. My focus on numbers and projections perhaps overshadowed the political challenges.

"At that time, given the various fronts of opposition, I suggested to the governor to pause the discussion of the municipal consortia," Ramon remembers.

In hindsight, my advisors were correct. Politically, there was very little chance I could get this done. At best, this reform was a way to create enemies; at worst, it was a suicide mission. My fixation on the numbers and the projection that came along with them clouded my political IQ.

I continued, achieving the first steps of planning a new county structure. However, the summer of 2019 brought unforeseen challenges, and the regional government reform came to a halt amid widespread protests with mayors from all parties mobilizing against it.

When I left office, the regional government reform initiative, which could have created counties, was dead.

A Small Side Story

Philippe was my secretary of public policy throughout my final year in office. He also had the distinction of having me press on him for this reform to move forward. He recalls meeting me a few days after I had announced my resignation as I was working on a transition in my absence.

"On the days leading up to the end of your tenure as governor, we met in your office to discuss pending matters you wanted to address, including pending legislative bills under your consideration. I remember you asking me if the executive order you asked for to implement the Municipal Reform was ready. This issue had moved from the priority board of your policy decisions during the month of July, 2019, mainly because of the public outcry and civil protests that led to you ending your term early.

"August 1, 2019, on the eve of you exiting La Fortaleza, we met in your office to discuss and ultimately sign this executive order. I remember you looked at peace and had on your running clothes, tennis shoes and a baseball cap. You told me you always wanted to dress informally in the Throne Room but never did due to your respect of the institution and what the office represented. Even though we both felt there was little chance that subsequent administrations would implement the executive order, you decided to sign and publish it to perpetuate all that work and what your vision was for regional governments. You planted a flag for your vision, even in your toughest time."

Here is a quirky twist of fate.

"However, the most interesting part of the story was that, due to procedural requirements, the secretary of state must sign all executive orders to properly certify enactment pursuant local law. As you may recall, you had appointed now Governor Pedro R. Pierluisi as your secretary of state to serve as your successor after your term ended.

"On August 2, close to 4:00 p.m., I went to Governor Pierluisi's apartment in San Juan, to arrange for the then secretary of state's signature so the executive order could properly publish. As history shows, just shortly after signing that executive order, at 5:00 p.m., I witnessed Pedro Pierluisi sworn in as governor. As we know, a week later the Puerto Rico Supreme Court said they did not confirm Pedro Pierluisi pursuant to the Constitution of Puerto Rico, paving the way for the swearing in of Governor Wanda Vázquez, who was next in the line of succession."

He surprised me. "There is one thing you may not know. Knowing the importance, singularity and historical context of this executive order bearing your signature and Governor Pierluisi's, I arranged for the signing of two additional mock "originals" of the executive order. I gave one to you and I kept to the other "original copy." I still hold this historic document dearly to this day in my files in my private office. It is one of the few documents with your signature as governor and with Governor Pierluisi's signature as secretary of state that exist."

It is important for him for the blood sweat and tears he went through in getting things together for this model. But more so because of the magnitude of this proposed change.

Having it signed by two governors is fitting.

Takeaways: Size Matters

High-Magnitude Reforms That Get Results Pay Off:

- **Long-term Impact**: The healthcare reform led by Dr. Pedro Rosselló had a long-term positive effect with more than one million citizens acquiring private insurance who previously had none. He had to go through some rough patches, but once it was executing, it was game-changing. This not only improved the quality of healthcare but also garnered significant public support.

- **Electoral Benefits**: Successful implementation of high-magnitude reforms can lead to electoral success. Dr. Pedro Rosselló's healthcare reforms, for instance, set the stage for his unprecedented victory in the subsequent elections.

- **Long-Term Vision**: Even if the immediate benefits of a reform are not evident, communicating the long-term vision and potential benefits can help in gaining public support.

High-Magnitude Reforms That Don't Have Enough Runway Can Be Politically Costly and Avoid More Reform:

- **Stakeholder Resistance**: The regional government reform faced significant opposition from mayors and other stakeholders. Without adequate buy-in from key stakeholders, even well-intentioned reforms can face challenges.

- **Political Costs**: Pushing for reforms without securing enough political support can lead to backlash and can be politically costly. For instance, the regional government many saw as a threat to the power of the mayors, leading to widespread opposition.

- **Potential for Unfinished Business**: High-magnitude reforms that start but can't fully execute due to various challenges leave behind unfinished business, which can be a point of contention in future political discussions. Who will own the problem?

Take Advantage of Timing and Policy Windows to Make Major Moves:

- **Seize the Moment**: The announcement of the privatization of PREPA came at a critical time when Puerto Rico was still recovering from natural disasters. This timing was seen as an opportunity to bring about significant change. Even if I was not there to see the change, I could start a process that would lead to future gains for our people.

- **Public Perception**: The context, such as ongoing recovery efforts or other significant events, can influence how the public perceives a reform. It's essential to be aware of the broader context when announcing or implementing reforms.

- **Policy Windows**: Certain events or situations create unique policy windows to possibly leverage to push for significant reforms. For instance, the aftermath of the hurricanes in Puerto Rico created a policy window for major changes in the energy sector.

The magnitude of reforms can have a lasting impact on your future capacity to execute and electoral prospects. It can, however, have significant negative effects in the execution process prior to getting results. During this phase, opponents will attempt to stop the successful implementation of the reform.

It is, therefore, critical to plan accordingly and allocate enough runway to execute. This is not enough, though. Support through these rocky times is paramount. This could be in the form of different groups explicitly supporting or the capacity to execute other smaller but beneficial acts, which will buy time and goodwill.

By the same token, making mistakes or missteps will likely be highlighted and magnified, prompting careful execution and scenario planning and reevaluation as the reform implementation process moves along.

One key observation is some reforms take a long time to achieve results, even longer than a term in office. This puts the reformer or leader in a position to choose if they proceed with the reform at the negative cost associated with the buildup or if they scrap it altogether.

Without big reforms, we can only make small tactical changes when more is necessary. If we lose the capability to implement big changes, we are likely to lose any edge within our jurisdiction relative to others who are willing and capable of doing so.

It begs the question: Why do we make it harder and harder to generate meaningful and impacting reform?

CHAPTER 14:

Bandwidth and People

This illustration has me "knighting" the members of the first congressional delegation (Plan Tennessee). At that point, it was the governor who appointed them. I was able to select three former governors, a president of the Senate, a general, a national committee woman, and a Baseball Hall of Famer. Selecting the right people is paramount to success, no matter the strength of your plans. And in government, it is getting harder and harder to do so (Bayon 2017).

"The energy or mental capacity required to deal with a situation" is the second definition Oxford Languages gives to *bandwidth*. For the most part, we have used bandwidth in the technical sense **(the data transfer capacity of a network in bits per second (Bps))**, but here we refer to it as a measure of capacity to do.

It is a way to define if leaders, governments, and institutions have the tools and capacity to get things done. The more you have of it, the better position you are in to achieve your results. This is true when speaking of reforms.

While plenty of factors might influence bandwidth, I will focus on a few: people, structural and process, and tech.

Selecting People

"Rosselló has his cabinet positions ironed out (planchao')" read the heading of a news article in *Primera Hora*, a few days prior to the elections (Figueroa 2016).

"I have in my mind a series of people who have shown aptitude and commitment for the various government secretariats," I said, reiterating there was no communication with these candidates because "I made the decision not to offer anything to anyone during the campaign."

Why was I so confident I had been able to identify these people? Answer: I had *time* in my favor. Over nearly five years of developing a Plan for Puerto Rico, I encountered numerous individuals, many outside traditional political circles. This exposure allowed me to assess their capabilities firsthand. As the movement expanded, referrals increased, providing further opportunities to evaluate their contributions at various levels.

One example was Carlos Contreras, referred to me by Norma Burgos. Norma was a powerful leader in several positions in government, including secretary of state. I trusted Norma and her foresight. "You need to meet Carlos. He is something else," she told me.

"Carlos is a brilliant engineer, but there is one detail." She paused for effect. "He is blind."

I was skeptical at the beginning. But as I got to know him better, I could connect with him while working on Plan for Puerto Rico. The man could literally see plans in his head. Clearly qualified, he knew quotes and page numbers from the sent documents. Nobody else was aware of it. Nobody expected it.

In their best-selling book *WHO*, Geoff Smart and Randy Street discuss a framework to identify the right people. Briefly, it is about: (1) being clear about what the job requires, (2) having a strong flow of candidates, (3) having the capacity to discriminate for the right candidate between similar looking ones, and (4) the ability to *keep* the best candidates (2008).

The Right People in the Right Seats... and Keeping Them There

Smart and Street emphasize the importance of having a team of A+ players, stating, "A small team of A+ players can run circles around a giant team of B and C players" (Smart and Street 2008). This principle guided my approach in selecting my cabinet and key personnel for the Plan for Puerto Rico.

I had a clear vision of the qualities needed in a leader and an A-player. Different leadership styles were necessary for different roles and at various times. For instance, I chose Manuel Laboy as my secretary of economic development. Despite being an engineer and a lawyer, not the typical profile for a chief economic promoter, his deep understanding of processes and capacity for implementing change made him the ideal candidate. His continued role in government, leading the recovery and reconstruction office, attests to his effectiveness.

The creation of a *talent bank* was instrumental in this process. It was a nuanced referral base, helping to identify and recruit exceptional individuals. As Street notes, "Referrals are the lifeblood of any business" (2008), a concept equally applicable to government.

Fun story behind my selections—very few people expected many of my appointments. The media was surprised, perhaps even stunned at not having a clue.

"'(Ricardo) Rosselló has been very careful with the appointments, he is working on that (laughs). He has a table on his computer," a source in a news article from NotiCel stated (2016).

Traditionally, the press would leak out who were the appointments before the governor would. They would cite sources and experts. This time around, it would not be the case.

"The doctor (Ricardo Rosselló), who is very meticulous, has been very zealous with the appointments," they assured NotiCel.

"Those appointments are like state secrets," said another source close to the campaign.

They speculated that it was internal bickering, but the truth of the matter was simple. I had a talent base. I had notes. I had been making an informed decision. While the previous couple of governors externalized the decision-making of the agency heads, I took it upon myself to work on it.

It had its benefits and its limitations. The benefit was I had an unbiased (or less biased) assessment of the folks I was selecting because they ran through the gauntlet in Plan for Puerto Rico. The limitation was my own personal bandwidth. I could manage some, but it is always good to get more advice on the matter.

Having the press oblivious to the appointees and wrongly speculating? Well, that was just frosting on the cake.

This worked out well at the start of our administration. We had a good stream of candidates, people like Ramon Rosario, who became an outstanding policy and public affairs secretary and a chief communicator. Itza García, an organized and talented leader, had a deep passion and understanding for the plan we were about to undertake as she assumed her role as associate chief of staff. Christian Sobrino, a smart and no-nonsense executive, could lead many of the changes as head of the fiscal entity in Puerto Rico. His leadership could overcome some of the underwhelming actions (or lack thereof) his predecessor made. Maria Palou, a quiet and highly gifted infrastructure savant, led permits and policy change as well as the execution of key strategic projects. William Villafañe, my trusted friend and a skilled orator and natural-born leader, was chief of staff and went on to be a senator in his own right.

And of course, I was genuinely lucky to marry to a person with the highest giving capacity I have ever meet—Beatriz Areizaga. As she plainly puts it: "While you were addressing some of the policy issues, natural disasters, and structural challenges, I was making sure I touched the hearts of people and saw they were getting what they needed."

These are just a few, but many others exist.

I went on a search for someone who could implement meaningful change in the education system. I looked outside the current pool as I thought the system had become to controlling. I found Julia Keleher, who despite her conviction was a brilliant and masterful executive. One thing does not negate from the other. Hector Pesquera became one of the pillars in driving down crime in Puerto Rico to historic lows. He was a strong, experienced leader during the hurricane. Both ended up with terrible public opinion numbers, but both executed at a higher level than most.

I asked Hector about this. His response: "The opposition definitely used the press to create a negative narrative around me. They had to do something because the crime plan was working, which helped you politically." He was referring to our anticrime efforts that were producing the lowest crime rates in the history of Puerto Rico. As I did, he thought results would be enough, and he did not have to

ESTADISTICAS-2018-12

El Presidente del Senado Tomas Rivera Schatz	8.91% 18	15.84% 32	28.71% 58	15.84% 32	24.26% 49	6.44% 13	202	2.67
El Senador Eduardo Bhatia	4.48% 9	17.91% 36	26.87% 54	19.90% 40	20.90% 42	9.95% 20	201	2.61
La Secretaria de Justicia Wanda Vazquez	4.95% 10	12.38% 25	34.16% 69	14.36% 29	26.24% 53	7.92% 16	202	2.52
La Secretaria de Educación Julia Keleher	7.43% 15	9.90% 20	19.80% 40	18.81% 38	39.11% 79	4.95% 10	202	2.24
El Comisionado de Seguridad Hector Pesquera	3.96% 8	5.45% 11	18.32% 37	15.35% 31	50.50% 102	6.44% 13	202	1.90

Figure 1: Internal Poll showcasing the five worst public opinion numbers for selected public servants (Internal Polls 2018).

talk about them. "I thought the numbers spoke for themselves. In hindsight, it was not enough, and I should have looked for an alternative to combat the opposition's narrative. I don't like talking about previous achievements. I'm not like that." (Figure 1)

And, along the way, I could promote some great people who showed me more once they were in office. An example of this was Ricky Llerandi, whom I tapped for imports and exports but eventually became an outstanding chief of staff for our administration. Similarly with Erik Rolón—one of the few people I did not know before tapping him for secretary of corrections and rehabilitation—a judge who became a phenomenal and thoughtful executive. I could tap him because of the referral system I put in place. He was an A-plus player.

As time passed, friction increased and attacks intensified. Good people left the administration. I was not able to keep them, breaking the fourth pillar. It got to a point where it was tougher to find substitutes. The ample bandwidth I originally had for reform and execution—thanks to good, quality A-players—started to erode.

Short Bench

Although I believe we had a great starting lineup in our administration, it is also true the bench was short. This is not to say there was a lack of talent. On the contrary, we had plenty of talented folks. The problem was severalfold. First, as discussed in chapter 9 on dehumanization, people's interest dwindled, no longer caring about holding office due to attacks and vilification. Second, competing against private sector jobs and salaries is a big hurdle.

Many shellacked me for paying some folks higher salaries. Remember what Street and Smart mentioned? Few A-players are better than many B and C ones (2018). In several instances, I consolidated positions and gave them the helm of two or three entities. Think of this also as part of a transition in the downsizing of government. By doing so, I eliminated the need for more positions. I raised their salaries, but overall, this was a reduction in expenses. And an enhancement in capacity, execution, and bandwidth.

Agency heads, whose salaries are higher, take on more responsibilities and even hold more than one top government position. Such is the case of the director of the Public-Private Partnerships Authority, Omar Marrero, who is also executive director of the Ports Authority and the Convention Center District Authority. He excelled at all three jobs. He was a talented team builder and could create more bandwidth for himself. I eventually promoted him to run the Recovery Office, and as of this writing, he is the secretary of state of Puerto Rico. Tania Vázquez, a superbly talented executive, was responsible for consolidating an agency and implementing environmental policy. They drug her through the mud for this.

Tania reminds me she "had five hats at one point because I was consolidating entities. It was tough but exhilarating politics in PR, and its ramifications complicated the work, but I understand having a clear goal helped us navigate many obstacles and chart a new way of working in government. It was hard, and sometimes I would question if it was worth it. But looking back, we made important changes, and I would not change anything." That's an A-player.

But the press was not having it. They were hellbent on defining this as a spending spree or cronyism. Headlines like "Requests That the Governor Does Not Give High Salaries" (Metro 2019).

"Undignified, as a public servant, that Governor Rosselló announces the new salary of the secretary of state is $14,000.00 per month, the same as in Education, Security, Port Administration, AAFAF and UPR among others with privileged remuneration."

I responded with facts:

"Governor Ricardo Rosselló assured today that his administration has reduced by 12.5 percent or $1.4 million the expenses corresponding to the payment of salaries to agency heads although some of these officials earn more than what their peers earned in the past four-year period," I told the *Caribbean Business* (2019).

There you could see the two worlds collide. First the salary expectation. In many instances, as was the case with Pesquera, they took a *pay cut* to come to government. Yet because the salaries were higher than expected, this was the linchpin for driving a campaign of dirt and discredit against him. They faced attack *and* they earned less.

It should therefore be no surprise we are getting a shrinking pool of potential candidates not only to run for office, but to hold executive leadership offices in government. This was a very concerning reality.

A publication by the Institute for Economic Policy Research in Stanford University found several important features:

"As running for office gets more expensive and holding political office has less appeal, moderates are less likely to run." The publication reads. coupled with "Polarization among those willing to run for office may be a more important factor in the rise of legislative division than the polarization of voters" (Hall 2019).

Polarization stems from leadership.

The conclusion? "Research suggests this growing polarization is a key reason the policy process broke down."

In the end, the shrinking pool of talent was noticeable. The bandwidth we had to execute greatly diminished. Comparing my first ninety days, where we were able to pass reform and stop the fiscal bleeding, to my last thirty—where I lost the trust of many of my constituents, and my agency heads were exhausted and frozen by personal and family attacks—got me to a point where I had essentially *zero* bandwidth to execute. This, along with my family's safety was the main reason for resigning.

If I could not execute at the level I set my standards to, I could not continue the functions as governor. I would not hold people hostage to a year and a half of little to no execution.

Clogging the Bandwidth—Misalignment:

"In 2016, Jenniffer González was campaigning against Donald Trump, after all the president's mistreatment of the island, she was 'Latinos for Trump.' How invertebrate or spineless can one be in politics, for several times?"

—ALEX DELGADO (2021).

"Governor, we should meet every week so we can keep ourselves abreast of what is happening on the island and in Washington, DC," Jenniffer González Colon, the congressmember for Puerto Rico (resident commissioner) told me in the first few days of my administration.

I happily obliged.

In Puerto Rico, the congressmember and governor are closer than in other jurisdictions. For one, they run on the same ticket. It is more akin to a vice president type of relationship than that of a member of congress.

I asked her, "When is it most convenient for you?"

We agreed on Fridays at 2 p.m. So, I separated that day to engage with her. The first two Fridays, she came in. After that, she always missed our meetings.

I kept the calendar spot open, even as I knew she would always send word if she could not make it.

A few times in the in between, I would call and check if she was coming, only for her to cancel last minute. We lost many great opportunities for collaboration. My mechanism of action was to use our PRFAA (Puerto Rico Federal Affairs Agency) office because I had otherwise no connection with our congressmember's office.

She was not happy. Every time we took an action she was unaware of to get resources and financing, she would explode on the media.

At first, she blamed my staff, venting to the media that she "did not engage with '*the help*,'" demeaning the work of some in my team. I called her and said, "Look, you have a weekly set-aside time to come and talk. What are you complaining about? If you have issues, come in and discuss them."

She then told me she could not make it on Fridays.

"Can you make it another day?" I replied.

"Mondays," she said.

And Mondays it was. Again, the first two Mondays after the change, she came. We had an agenda and discussed matters. Shortly after that, she never came back.

I continued using PRFAA. She felt I was going around her. She had her sights on my seat as opposed to her role in Washington, DC. It was a recipe for disaster.

Not surprisingly, she was the first within my party to ask for my resignation—shortly followed by her cohort of her allies. The Speaker of the House Carlos "Johnny" Méndez Núñez commenced the impeachment process with what, in hindsight, you could describe as a pure political vendetta.

One of her closest advisers describes her best in her book *Pasión de Guerrera*.

"I knew her character and style of work. She is one of those people who likes to sleep during the day to work at night… she has shown she is not very compliant with her commitment schedules. Her relatives sweat because of her lack of punctuality… I came to the conclusion she only wanted them to tell her what she expected to hear. The arrogance in her gestures and expressions were a constant insult to the dignity of the people who worked with her… that girl was sick, drunk with power, and prey to a pride never seen before…"

—ZAIDA "CUCUSA" HERNÁNDEZ (2015).

This misalignment created severe problems for our progress. Sure, when working together, as I have highlighted in this book, we were able to come out with outstanding results. But those days were few and far between. This created an environment that was toxic, with an exponential decay in trust.

Trust and Culture

During a speaking engagement in November 2022, I had the opportunity to ask Harvard Professor Frances Frei, author of *Unleashed*, about trust. Her response was enlightening: "I am more likely to earn your trust if you experience my authenticity, logic, and empathy."

This perspective on trust resonated deeply with me, especially in the context of leading and empowering a workforce and securing the support of constituents.

Dr. Frei's formula for trust is particularly compelling: "Think of trust as a 0–1 variable. It's A (authenticity) times L (logic) times E (empathy). If any of the three are missing, it breaks trust." Reflecting on my administration, I realize my strength lay in logic. I consistently relied on facts, evidence, measurements, and results to make decisions and communicate them. This logical approach, however, sometimes led to accusations of being overly verbose or even evasive, especially when I admitted I didn't know something rather than fabricating an answer.

In any event, my wabble (as Frei calls it) was authenticity. For the longest time I had trouble making some people believe the genuine interest I had in solving problems and policy measures. This was where many of my opponents attacked me. They called me *Tricky Ricky* or *robot governor* among other names. Clear dehumanization tactics in play here. Still to this day I struggle with this. An exception to this was my portrayal and communication of the vision we had created for Puerto Rico. I was enthusiastic and optimistic. I believe people felt this to be the genuine case.

Empathy, which was initially a strong suit demonstrated through the Plan for Puerto Rico and my island-wide visits, began to wane as I became increasingly engrossed in my work. Although Beatriz maintained direct contact with the people, my own engagement diminished, which, in retrospect, was a mistake. The release of the chat further eroded perceptions of my empathy and authenticity.

In hindsight, a more proactive engagement with the citizenry, similar to my approach before and after my term, could have preserved the trust that eventually crumbled.

The decline in trust isn't just a personal issue; it reflects a broader national and global trend. A Pew Research study reveals a stark reality: "Fewer than two in ten Americans say they trust the government in Washington to do what is right 'just about always' (1 percent) or 'most of the time (15 percent)'" (2023).

Two in Ten!

This is a drastic drop from the over 75 percent trust levels of past decades. Factors contributing to this decline likely include dehumanization affecting authenticity and empathy, oversimplification of complex issues impacting logic, and extreme narratives undermining logic and empathy.

And this is how bandwidth relates to people. You can augment or diminish bandwidth by structural changes in organizations.

Structural Impedance and Culture

"We can have the energy grid back up in forty-five days," Lt. General Todd Semonite told me. We were in a room at the Convention Center—the place where operations gathered. Just a few days after the storm. Eli Díaz-Atienza, Ricardo Ramos, and Hector Pesquera were with me.

Carlos Mercader recalls the state of the island at that point. "The first one hundred hours were pretty chaotic. We had 88 percent of the energy polls down; nobody had seen anything like that before."

To add insult to injury, the trust level was not high with Puerto Rico, even before the storm. Mercader recalls, "Officials in Washington were saying 'It's going to be a lot of money' That was the narrative created because of the fiscal situation other administrations left us with. Unfortunately for us, it stuck in the recovery process." (Figure 2)

FEMA, through the Army Core of Engineers, was proposing to do this for us. The federal government would pay them directly to do so. It seemed like a no-brainer. Yet there was uneasiness in the room.

"I don't trust them," Pesquera told me. Ricardo was more gentle, but in the same lines "Rebuilding the energy grid is complicated. I'm not sure they are aware."

Pesquera recalls, "The quick and effective response we had in Irma (two weeks prior) was because there was not much damage and the infrastructure remained. This is what FEMA knows. Now, Maria comes, and we end up without infrastructure. There is no water, electricity, telephone, bridges, roads, internet, workers, ports, airports, hospitals without generators, etc." The workers were with their families and couldn't get there.

Here is Pesquera's key point. "FEMA or the Army Core of Engineers had never experienced that situation in the Continental US, and they had not made plans for how to operate under those circumstances. They were very bad operationally. They did not have supplies nor enough equipment or personnel. It was a completely different level, and they were not even aware of it."

Figure 2: Image taken by our photographer a few days after the storm, in which me and my team had a conversation with the Lt. General Todd Semonite in regard to restoring energy in forty-five days.

Of course we asked them if they were aware of the challenges. They said they were. Pesquera did not buy it. "Every time I would ask the general point-blank a question, he would wiggle away. Once I asked him, "Can you do it? Yes or no?" He hesitantly responded yes. I don't think he liked that I was so direct with him."

Naturally, our team had concerns. So, I asked, "What are our alternatives?" We had none. Carlos Mercader recalls: "One of the things we learned was the previous administration did not negotiate the typical agreements with the energy sector. This further limited our moves." So, Mercader concludes, "They shoved the mission assignment because we had no choice."

We lived at the event horizon of the geopolitical blackhole.

This is a terrible position to be in when you have very few avenues to move forward. Other states could spend money however they chose because they had cash in the bank. They could spend and ask for a refund later. They have the flexibility of deciding. We could not borrow because the previous administration default on payments. And we only had about five hundred million in the bank.

This ended up being one of my biggest blunders.

Needless to say, in forty-five days they had not even started. "Two-thirds of the island's recovery on that [electricity] front is in the Corps of Engineers' hands," Rosselló said. "I have seen a lack of urgency on that, whether it is on the contracting side or the bringing materials side, which is a current problem" (Hoyos 2018).

Semonite responded, "The magnitude of the logistic and repair mission is beyond the governor's expectations." The same expectations he had given us on that fateful day... right after the storm.

Carlos Mercader was in one of those meetings and remembers, "Semonite and Long were trying to blame the governor. Instead of getting personal, the governor took on one of the screens where the maps lay. He explained in detail what needed to happen. He schooled the Army Core on what things they were doing wrong. Some of the president's own advisors, like Tom Bossert, sided with the governor."

The key lesson here is there are many systemic obstacles to bandwidth. You might have the people willing to execute, but other forces (procedural, legal, political) might keep it from happening.

This is why one of our main objectives was to restructure and downsize government. Reducing the government's size was not only a fiscal imperative but also an executional need. The government agencies became silos and were too far apart to function aptly. The bureaucratic overburden ate everything up. Changing this was imperative. And we did.

One way of achieving this was betting on innovation.

Tech Can Help

Imagine a girl standing in a long line in a DMV. We can all relate. The typical agony of waiting and not getting results. Next, imagine that same girl happily using her smart phone achieve all her DMV needs.

This was the visual in one of my ads for governor.

The DMV had become the poster child of government inefficiency. We were all tired of it. No matter how much people complained, it was never solved. It was beyond me why this was so. We placed this as a priority. And, after all, how hard could it be?

Well, it was a more challenging task than I envisioned.

Why? When in doubt… follow the money trail.

Various government contractors owned the code for the DMV's computer system. But that code consisted of patches that *fixed* the old relic of a system the DMV had used for years. Without the contractors' support, it was virtually impossible to upgrade or replace that system. To add insult to injury, many of these contractors only wanted to create more patches with the express intent of continuing to use the deficient system. They held the keys to the entire DMV. They were permanently necessary—or so they thought.

My Chief Information Officer Luis Arocho worked diligently on the matter, but there were always roadblocks. Luckily, one day my Chief Innovation Officer Glorimar Ripoll came with an idea: "Why don't we get university students to work on it."

She caught my attention. We created the Office of Innovation and Technology Service to provide the sort of roadmap and execution to identify areas of opportunity. These were for tech and other innovative designs of government. Take our executive order to recruit folks from the private sector who were experts in process engineering and 6-sigma and bring them to the government on a loan basis. Puerto Rico has a robust manufacturing sector with plenty of expertise in this area. Yet, our government is significantly lacking this high-efficiency mindset. This is the type of opportunity we need to be considering.

Back to the DMV. Glorimar told me: "Let's have an internship. Have them try to tackle it. This way we avoid all the big contractors and finally get things done."

I asked Glorimar about this, and she said, "This was bureaucracy hacking at its best! I had to first understand all the challenges and limitations. One was untampered and talented resources. Then, on January 2018 we engaged students from the University of Puerto Rico, Bayamón Campus and five MIT students doing their internship."

With her guidance, the students immediately grasped how to incorporate the concept of innovation to complete the Digital CESCO. This meant we were not digitizing obsolete processes and experiences but innovating to deliver better services to the people we served in a way relevant to citizens' expectations in our digital world.

And we got things done. Young talent overcame the big hurdle. Thanks to the computer science students in the University of Puerto Rico *Bayamón Campus.*

The results?

"The end of long lines in the DMV (CESCO)" raved one headline at Wapa TV (Vázquez 2019).

The quantitative results a few months after the application was 59,000 hours less in line and 2,445 less days in government offices. A game changer impacting thousands of people (Micro Juris 2018).

"The CESCO Digital application is part of the multiple initiatives of the governor (Ricardo Rosselló) to modernize the government with technology, to provide a better service to citizens." Read the papers.

Once that leap was done—others could follow. To this day, the Digital CESCO keeps adding value and reducing cost and bureaucracy, using technology to facilitate things.

Technology is a powerful force to facilitate activity in government and, therefore, reform. With technology, and the people and bandwidth to implement it, we can adapt to the times and facilitate the workflows that might have blockage elsewhere.

Speaking of adaptation…

The Environment of Change

In November 2022, Heather McCohen explored the dynamics of change and adaptability in leadership. "You need knowledgeable people," she said, "but they must also be able to unlearn and relearn for whatever job comes next. Hiring for cultural fit, cultural evolution, and learning agility is crucial."

This book emphasizes an evolving environment where change is constant, making adaptability an essential aspect of effective leadership. Post-storm, this became even more evident. Some team members, despite their talents, struggled to adapt to the rapidly changing, high-stress environment. Their inability to adjust under these new pressures highlighted a critical aspect of leadership—the capacity for agility in the face of change.

Conversely, individuals like Alfonso Orona, Maria Palou, Glorimar Andújar, José Marrero, Surima Quinones, Carlos Flores, and Tania Vázquez exemplified this adaptability. They not only adjusted to the new reality post-storm but also excelled beyond their previous performance levels. José Marrero, my OMB director and a numbers and energy savant, became instrumental in navigating the complexities of FEMA. His insights were pivotal in our swift actions to secure more than seventy-nine billion in recovery funding for Puerto Rico.

Alfonso Orona adeptly managed the dual roles of communications and legal advisor, consistently rising to the challenges presented. Beatriz demonstrated remarkable adaptability and capacity to innovate. "Something clicked in me," she told me. "As I was waiting to have Pedro... I was nesting. Then after the storm, every child I saw became my own. I could not rest until every child was safe." And she did not. She orchestrated efforts to feed more than one hundred thousand people daily, provided shelter, coordinated logistics for basic needs delivery (even before FEMA's involvement), and more (Hernández 2017). Her maternal instinct extended beyond our family, as she saw every child in need as her own, tirelessly working to ensure their safety.

Beatriz's words: "Something clicked in me... every child I saw became my own," encapsulate the essence of adaptability and empathy in leadership. The ability to adjust and expand one's bandwidth is not just a desirable trait but a necessity in today's world, especially under extreme conditions. This capacity for adaptability and agility separates effective leaders from the rest in times of crisis and change.

Takeaways: Look to Amplify your Bandwidth

1. **Bandwidth Is Directly Proportional to the Capacity to Reform**: The more A-players, proper systems, and enabling tech you have, the better. Trust is a key driver. Trust, built on authenticity, logic, and empathy, is foundational for leadership and governance. The level of trust leaders command directly influences their capacity to reform. Bandwidth gets obstructed when trust dissipates. The portrayal and interpretation of a leader's actions and decisions in the media shape public perception. This perception, in turn, affects the leader's bandwidth and their capacity to implement reforms. When I lost the trust of the people, I had no bandwidth to execute.

2. **Bandwidth Is Increased with A-Players**: Spending time selecting the right people for the right positions is a savvy investment. Identifying and selecting the right candidates for leadership roles directly impacts the bandwidth available for reforms. Referrals and firsthand evaluations are crucial in this process. Within the pool of referrals, A-players, or top-performing individuals, are essential for increasing bandwidth. Their presence in a team ensures the planning and execution of reforms effectively.

3. **Technologies and Processes are Bandwidth Multipliers (or Obstacles): Structural Impediments**: Systemic obstacles—whether procedural, legal, or political—can hinder the reform process. We had to face these as a colonial territory of the United State in the rebuilding after the storm. Recognizing these impediments is crucial to enable effective reform. Similarly, as we showed with our digital DMV, technology can facilitate and amplify bandwidth obstacles standing in your way and pave the way for effective reform. The ability to adapt and make informed decisions is vital for reform. Rigid processes or over-reliance on external entities can reduce bandwidth and hinder the reform process.

When I was in office and during Plan for Puerto Rico, I had a rubric whereby I would evaluate my team. I used a wide variety of criteria to evaluate: leadership, alignment, execution, projection, expertise, bonus for complexity, capacity to communicate.

This helped me, but I must admit, it became somewhat cumbersome. In the end, I realized these were the key parameters: alignment (loyalty to the cause) and capacity to execute. You can learn everything else, and everything else is manageable.

You need people who align with your core values, goals, and objectives. And you need them to have the capacity to do the job. This amplifies bandwidth and allows you to execute to the maximum of the capabilities.

To allow the people to flourish, you must evaluate the systemic restraints and compensate for those. These changes can happen with reforms such as our New Government Reform, Energy Reform, Education Reform, or with novel innovative pathways, as the digital DMV was.

Once you have the conditions to establish a powerful culture, people will feel supported by the system. If they feel supported, they will trust your structure or government. Establishing that trust requires results (logic), empathy (deep understanding of how people feel), and authenticity.

Without people, there is no bandwidth. Without trust, there is no bandwidth. Without bandwidth, there is no execution. Without execution, there is no reform.

PART IV

STRATEGIES TO REFORM

CHAPTER 15:

Blitzkrieg

I love this illustration depicting my ceremonial swearing in. I'm standing with Beatriz and my daughter Claudia, the chief justice reading the oath, and the outgoing governor and his wife packed for a vacation. The image depicts me as a tiny guy ready to go to battle. After hearing my message and seeing the actions of the first twenty-four hours, the message of swift action penetrated even to the cartoons (Bayon 2017).

Blitzkrieg (definition): an intense campaign intended to bring about a swift victory.

A few weeks before my inauguration, I asked for an audience with the chief justice of the Supreme Court. When I visited her chambers, I noticed that books and documents filled the room. It was the well-organized environment you'd envision from the top legal powers from the area.

There was a nervous energy between her staff and mine. "I would like you to swear me in," I told her.

This surprised everyone. My predecessor appointed her. As such, she identified as an opponent of my party. "I'm surprised," she said, "but it would be my honor."

"On one condition," I said.

She looked at me as someone waiting for the other shoe to drop. Expecting some sort of extravagant and impossible request.

"What would that be?" she asked.

"That you swear me in at 12:01 a.m.," I said.

Figure 1. My swearing in by the chief justice alongside Beatriz at 12:01 a.m. (Source: *El Nuevo Día* 2017b).

She agreed.

That's right. *12:01 a.m. (Figure 1)*

On January 1, 2017, I took a nap from 8 p.m. to about 10:30 p.m. We left my house around 11:40 p.m. and went to the Supreme Court chamber. There, I had the chief justice of the Supreme Court to swear me in.

Why? "We want the people of Puerto Rico and the board to know we have not waited a minute to start working. At 12:01 a.m. From his first day in office, the governor signed the first executive orders to address the fiscal crisis, and it has continued like this for ten days," said Ramon Rosario, secretary of public affairs (*Caribbean Business* 2017).

Immediately after the swearing in, we had a short ride to the secretary of state, where I signed six executive orders to set the tone of the actions against the fiscal crisis we were facing (Micro Juris 2017).

- Reduced 20 percent of political appointments and an immediate 10 percent reduction on all agency budgets
- Create the Federal Funds opportunity office, to maximize more than one billion dollars left on the table
- Infrastructure emergency, to push forward a mechanism for the stagnant development in the past decade
- Create a zero-based budgeting mechanism, as the official policy for the administration
- Ensure transparency and anticorruption actions
- Proactively augment the participation of women in government

Before people had awoken to my inauguration day, we had already made meaningful policy changes. One headline read: "The Swearing Ceremony that People did not see: Breaking with tradition, the governor swore in at 12:01 in the morning of January 2" (*El Nuevo Día* 2017b).

The blitzkrieg had begun (Figure 2).

Figure 2. Cover of *El Vocero*. Denoting the ceremonial swearing in where I established our blitzkrieg agenda (2017).

The idea here is quite simple: Start quick and take advantage of the high influence runway. The opposition will be disorganized, members of your own party are more inclined to support, and most constituents want to see action. This momentum diminishes quickly as time goes by.

Implicit in my strategy was recognizing that my highest level of influence was in the early days of the administration. Prepare thoroughly and strike fast at the initial conditions of the most critical problems. In our case, it was the fiscal challenges and government reform. If I wanted to get some of these complex reforms done, I would have to get them through within the first one hundred days.

The next morning, as I was getting ready to give my inaugural address, all the talk was about the executive orders and the actions taken. Current senator and former chief of staff William Villafañe recalls, "I remember this stunned everybody. They did not expect quick and decisive actions. We had told them for the longest time we had preparations and were ready. I believe most people thought it was just political promises and that we were too young and had too little experience to proceed."

Once again, I set the tone in my formal inaugural address: "During the next one hundred days we will be able to implement specific plans aimed at regaining the confidence of the financial markets and the federal government. We are going to act immediately to ensure no interruption in pension payments. Let's protect the most vulnerable. I will not leave you alone."

In doing so, I was not just doing lip service. I submitted eleven bills that morning to the legislature that would be reforms. These included:

1. Public-private partnerships reform
2. Government reform as a single employer
3. Creation of the socioeconomic and self-sufficiency office
4. Tourism reform: the creation of a direct marketing organization (more on this later)
5. Investment reform: The creation of Invest Puerto Rico (externalizing investment to stakeholders)
6. Law for medical professional retention, granting them the most competitive tax consideration in the nation
7. The creation of the office of the inspector general—to battle corruption in real time
8. Bill of rights for the elderly—a necessary policy to protect our most vulnerable
9. Amendments to protect women from domestic violence abuse
10. Law to create the fiscal entity that would empower fiscal reform
11. Labor reform

This was not without opposition. Leaders who used to critique lack of action were now opposing the "speed" at which things were about to unfold (Figure 3).

Figure 3. Spread from *El Nuevo Día*, outlining several of the key steps that took place in the blitzkrieg of the first one hundred days (*El Nuevo Día* 2017).

"We are facing a new way of doing government. This is outrageous… a completely antidemocratic strategy and against all the principles of transparency. The parliamentary process is to differ, to debate," said Tatito Hernández (*Caribbean Business* 2017).

Ramon Rosario notes, "Unlike other administrations, Ricardo Rosselló presented a package of measures from his Government Plan on the same day officials swore him in as governor. This proved to be a fundamental game changer."

All in a day's work. They all became law. Many of these bills are yielding positive results. Blitzkrieg accomplished.

Blank Canvas: Adjusting after the Storm

"Devastation also means a chance to reimagine things as the island rebuilds, and the thirty-nine-year-old is casting Puerto Rico as a *blank canvas* for innovators to come and experiment," *Time* magazine said in an interview with me about nine months after the hurricane devastated the island (Steinmetz 2018).

I have already spoken about the pain and suffering we all went through. The powerlessness brought by the largest natural disaster in the modern history of the United States, but also the powerlessness embedded in our colonial situation and inherent in our second-class citizenship.

Adjusting needs to happen fast. The process to reassess our current state and forecast the level of catastrophe that could ensue, happened a few days before Hurricane Maria. After all, we had already passed through Hurricane Irma only two weeks prior. For Irma—a category 3 hurricane—we had preparations, we executed, and we helped more than five thousand citizens stranded on other islands. Even the opposition gave us great grades.

But Maria was a different level.

"Everyone, we are facing a game-changing situation. It is important we change our mindset. What we were working on before is going to completely change. There will be a pre-Maria Puerto Rico and a post-Maria Puerto Rico," William Villafañe recalls me saying in a meeting with all heads of agencies within the government.

"We will have three work streams that are parallel to each other," I told our team "The first one will be the emergency phase, which I define as a moment to save lives. The second one is the recovery phase, which I define as our path to reach normalcy. By this I mean that schools will be running again, businesses will be open, and the restoration of energy will occur. The third, the rebuild. This is the unique opportunity we will have to remake and rebuild Puerto Rico with all the resources we will get and all the understanding we have of the global needs and changes."

And so, we did. The emergency phase was brutal. Whereas in other places it would take a few days to surpass, the emergency phase in Puerto Rico lasted at least three months. The recovery phase—reaching normalcy—was about a year in length. During this grueling and painful process, many people did not have access to energy, schools, modes of communications or jobs; things we tend to take for granted.

After Maria, the rebuild had to be visionary and inspiring.

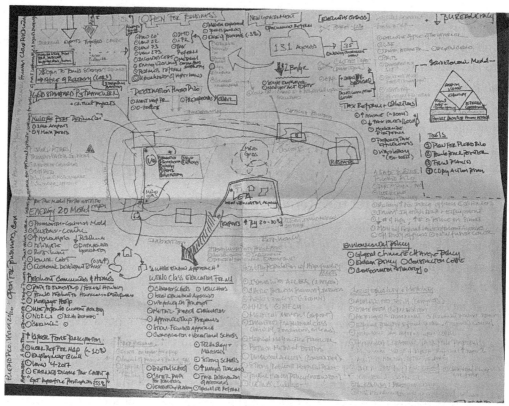

Figure 4: Vision map I prepared post-Hurricane Maria. It denotes the efforts to fix the fiscal situation in Puerto Rico along with maximizing the window to create a new energy paradigm, education reform, environmental policies, labor reform, and criminal justice shift.

As with other moments during my journey, I went to my drawing board to intake all the information we had, see what challenges lay ahead, and capitalize on the opportunities. Below is the handwritten map I developed. It helped me organize the vision and details. It also helped me communicate the next set of actions and the why (Figure 4).

I showed this to Pamela Patenaude. She was the sub secretary of HUD for the Trump Administration and quite possibly the most helpful hand throughout the recovery process. "I vividly remember the first time you shared the very impressive Puerto Rico recovery vision map with me. I encouraged you to share your vision for the island's recovery with senior administration officials, including the White House, OMB, and the HUD secretary. I believe the vision map played a critical role in communicating how Puerto Rico would utilize the historic disaster recovery funding to rebuild the island."

Our first step was to create the Central Office for Recovery, Reconstruction and Resiliency (COR3). The goal was to establish an entity that could work transparently with the federal government to manage the billions of dollars of aid. I recognized the government of Puerto Rico historically had a bad reputation for managing funds. If we did not drastically change this model and perception, we would find ourselves stuck in a stagnant rebuild subject to corruption and failure. Our *bandwidth* would have limitations at best. So we defined the COR3 with the following vision:

"My concept for Puerto Rico's recovery is built around the four core principles of (1) promoting effective governance and transparency, (2) investing in building capacity we need both for reconstruction and for the future of Puerto Rico, (3) incorporating resiliency into everything we build and do, and (4) pursuing innovation in our recovery wherever possible."

Very quickly, we adjusted.

The crisis provided a path toward embedding these four core elements into our operational culture. Even after a devastating blow, we needed to have the foresight to rebuild. It was the time to reevaluate our conditions and vision. People wanted action. This presented a second opportunity for another blitzkrieg.

Updating the Vision

The Plan for Puerto Rico had provided a thorough roadmap for us. Along the way, some of those conditions changed—some for the worse while others presented unique opportunities. Upon that reality, we choose to reevaluate the plan's vision and modify it (Figure 5).

Figure 5: The five pillars of a vision for Puerto Rico under my administration.

The updated vision for Puerto Rico included these five points:

1. **Home of the Human Cloud**: Puerto Rico aims to be an ideal home for professionals, both locally and globally. The goal is to export services from the island, creating a "Human Cloud." We would make efforts to enhance the island's appeal for living and professional growth.

2. **Open for Business**: Puerto Rico seeks to be a business-friendly environment. We aimed to attract businesses and entrepreneurs to the island. Supporting economic growth and investment is a key objective.

3. **Connector of the Americas**: Geographically located in the center of the Americas, Puerto Rico aims to become a bridge connecting cultures, economies, and diplomacy. We would emphasize on our bicultural heritage, with English and Spanish spoken.

4. **Island of Innovation**: Puerto Rico's fundamental goal is to leapfrog into innovation, giving people the tools to be creative and establish ourselves as a global center of innovation. Focusing on technological advancement and creativity is a priority for our long-term success.

5. **Empowering State**: Puerto Rico aims to empower its citizens. Ensuring *access to opportunities* for people of all backgrounds is a key objective. By doing so, we aim to improve the quality of life and well-being of our residents.

The goal was to channel people's aspirations toward tangible results. All these crystallized after the hurricane. And with it, our commitment to execute it.

More Reform, More Opponents

"Our people have faced situations of great sacrifice and together, with great effort, we are overcoming the effects that Hurricane Maria left us. We still have a long way to go on the road to full recovery, but overcoming adversity also presents great opportunities to build a new Puerto Rico."

This is how I started a televised message to the people of Puerto Rico a few months after the hurricane. As I mentioned in a previous chapter, it was an unexpected announcement. The opportunity presented itself and we had to act swiftly. A natural *inertia* develops from dealing with the energy issue. It's been decades since the decay of the grid and very little was done structurally to change it.

This was our opportunity.

"We have a generation system that is twenty-eight years older than the average for the electric power industry in the United States. We have a dependency on oil that makes it more and more expensive, more polluting and less efficient… The Electric Power Authority will cease to exist as it currently operates deficiently. During the next few days, the process will begin where PREPA assets sell to companies that will transform the generation system into a modern, efficient, and less expensive one for the town," I said.

As expected, opposition mounted. "The privatization of [PREPA] is putting the economic development of the country in private hands. The authority will serve other interests," said the mayor of San Juan Carmen Yulín. Leader of the independent movement Juan Dalmau wrote "Privatization is not necessarily a sign of efficiency or savings." Yet others could not argue against the merits of the proposal, so they used the current state of devastation to deviate from the proposal (*Primera Hora* 2018).

This was deliberate. The time for discussion had passed. It was time to execute. The policy window was just slightly open.

The situation with energy was onerous. The vast majority of Puerto Ricans wanted change. More than 70 percent of Puerto Ricans understood the energy system was not working and they would be willing to privatize (NotiCel 2016). Even after I resigned, when I had my worst possible numbers, there was broad support for our privatization efforts. The positive delta was 30 percent (Figure 6).

Why did this not happen before? There was just no political will to do it. The conditions would not allow it. Policy windows were small, and folks did not take advantage of them. Whether it was the unions or big oil or Maduro… opponents were always ready to shut the window down.

The storm created a broader runway to execute. People were without electricity for so long in large part due to the deteriorated and antiquated system we had. They wanted change. We needed to act swiftly to bring it about.

The *Orlando Sentinel* called it "a surprise announcement" (2018). They were right. It was a *blitzkrieg*.

The new environment presented the opportunity to do the same with another core promise of our administration and a critical cog in the future of Puerto Rico—education reform. I address education reform elsewhere. Suffice it to say now this was a hurdle just as big as energy reform. Without the capacity to adjust, our timing might have been too late, and education reform would not have gone through. Which, by the way—also had a positive delta (44 percent) regarding the voucher system we implemented.

The windows are brief and often unexpected. Acting swiftly was a must.

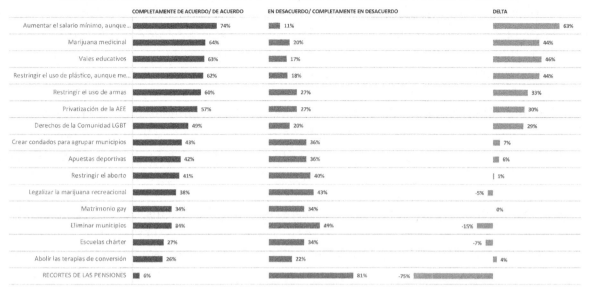

Evaluación de Asuntos – Quick Poll – Octubre 2019

	COMPLETAMENTE DE ACUERDO/ DE ACUERDO	EN DESACUERDO/ COMPLETAMENTE EN DESACUERDO	DELTA
Aumentar el salario mínimo, aunque...	74%	11%	63%
Marijuana medicinal	64%	20%	44%
Vales educativos	63%	17%	46%
Restringir el uso de plástico, aunque me...	62%	18%	44%
Restringir el uso de armas	60%	27%	33%
Privatización de la AEE	57%	27%	30%
Derechos de la Comunidad LGBT	49%	20%	29%
Crear condados para agrupar municipios	43%	36%	7%
Apuestas deportivas	42%	36%	6%
Restringir el aborto	41%	40%	1%
Legalizar la marijuana recreacional	38%	43%	-5%
Matrimonio gay	34%	34%	0%
Eliminar municipios	34%	49%	-15%
Escuelas chárter	27%	34%	-7%
Abolir las terapias de conversión	26%	22%	4%
RECORTES DE LAS PENSIONES	6%	81%	-75%

Figure 6: Internal polls from October 2018, displaying different issues and their deltas. In the case of privatizing the power authority, it had a +30 percent delta. (Internal Poll 2019).

Back to Deng

How was Deng Xiaoping different from Gorbachev? One difference was his swift execution of milestone initiatives. Deng assumed leadership in China in 1978, surprising the world with his swift and decisive implementation of economic reforms. This was very much opposite to what his predecessor Mao Zedong, who maintained a centrally planned economy, had done.

Deng introduced a series of economic reforms akin to a blitzkrieg in their speed and impact. He opened up China's economy to foreign investment, decentralized economic management, and introduced market mechanisms, effectively transforming China's economy from a planned economy to a *socialist market economy*.

"When Deng Xiaoping initiated a series of economic and social reforms in 1978, rural society reorganization constituted a critical first step. To quote Barry Naughton, 'It was in the countryside that reforms succeeded first, and it was the dramatic success of rural reforms that cleared the way for continuing and progressively more profound change' (Vendryes 2010).

Deng implemented these reforms with such speed and decisiveness they caught many both inside and outside China by surprise. Many credit this action with putting China on a path of rapid economic growth, transforming it from an impoverished nation into the world's second-largest economy in a matter of decades and laying the foundation for China's economic miracle.

Takeaways: Maximize Your Time with Influence

- **The Importance of Swift Action**: To successfully implement reform, it is imperative to take quick and decisive action to seize opportunities and maximize the chances of success. This is particularly true in the early stages of an endeavor. An example was my decision to swear in as governor at 12:01 a.m., immediately followed by the signing of multiple executive orders and policy changes within the first hours of taking office.

- **Utilizing Policy Windows**: Be mindful of moments when conditions align favorably for the implementation of significant reforms or changes. Acting swiftly during these windows is crucial. We had a policy window open up after Hurricane Maria. The public's desire for change after a natural disaster created the opportunity to implement significant reforms in energy and education, capitalizing on a broader policy window.

- **Execution is Key**: Planning and preparation are essential (more on this soon), but execution is equally important. Taking action, even in the face of opposition, can lead to successful outcomes, especially when there is a clear vision and public support. Deng Xiaoping in China laid the foundation for its rapid growth, illustrating the importance of effective execution in achieving desired outcomes.

The key is to kickstart change and reform when your influence and capacity to execute is at its highest, which for most people will follow the election of selection to the position of power. The problem is many of those elected are not ready to execute immediately. They waste valuable time in figuring out what they will do and how they will do it, and when the moment comes, support dissipates and friction increases.

El Vocero newspaper: You have had one hundred days to learn more about the political, economic, and social reality of the country you administer. Is there any aspect of the political reality of Puerto Rico that you have underestimated?

Ricardo Rosselló: No, we anticipated it was a situation of great challenges but also of great opportunities. Today, twenty-one pieces of legislation have already become laws, twenty-nine executive orders, and countless actions have resulted in savings in hiring and appointments of trust. We have been able to have a certified fiscal plan because we anticipated this. If you compare with the previous administration, which could not have a certified plan with all the time in the world, and we could do it in fifty-eight days, you see a difference.

I had plenty of challenges, mistakes, and failures, but Blitzkrieg worked for me. We were also able to adjust when another opportunity arose.

Blitzkrieg is not without challenges. It will raise challenges of transparency (even if you have signaled), bypassing the legislative process, and ultimately may lay the foundation for having your governance deemed undemocratic. While the blitzkrieg approach to reforms can lead to quick wins, it can also lead to resistance from those negatively affected by the changes. This resistance can slow down or even halt the reform process.

The speed and sequence of fiscal adjustment and structural reforms are key to their success. A blitzkrieg approach can help to overcome resistance to reform, but it may also exacerbate social tensions and even lead to a backlash against reform.

While I understand all these concerns, they pale in comparison to not acting and sustaining the status quo. This accentuates when states are failing.

It is also important to state that blitzkrieg only works temporarily. You cannot govern at that pace. I found that out the hard way. Eventually friction overcomes the capacity to do, and you have to step back and reevaluate your environment. This is where other strategies need to come into play. Alternatively, other events may happen, whether provoked or not, that will present an opportunity to adjust.

Whatever the case may be, blitzkrieg is a strong temporal strategy that can help you get your actions for change moving. But preparation, anticipation, and capacity to adjust are critical, as the windows of opportunity rarely stay open.

Be prepared. Be aware. Have a sense of timing. Strike emphatically. Blitzkrieg and adjust.

CHAPTER 16:

Priority Setting and Preparation

Illustration of me as a school principal, with my plan in my pocket. You cannot understate the value of planning and preparing. I like the imagery for this chapter, as it encompasses planning, and education—two of the main themes (Bayon 2017).

One teacher can change the life of a person. *Just one.* How do I know? Because it happened to me.

"I didn't really get into math. I thought I was very bad at mathematics," I told Scott Jacobsen of *In-Sight Journal* (2021). "I can clearly state I didn't get into mathematics or had any interest up until the first two months of ninth grade, where I had a serendipitous event."

I was an okay student *before* the ninth grade. I did not pay too much attention to school because I largely focused on sports and socializing back then. But math… math was my Achilles heel. Or so I thought.

I had this one teacher. His name was Jorge de Jesus. For some reason, I fell into the advanced mathematic class. I felt unqualified. In fact, fear seeped into me when I found out I would be in this class. After all, this guy was notorious for calling out people. He was a guy who trained mathletes. And on a family level, his class was the main reason my older brother was not *valedictorian*. (Don't shed tears… he was still *salutatorian*.)

I can remember looking at him that first day of class. He looked back with a stare that screamed "*You don't belong here.*" The first few weeks I was quiet and attentive. I knew I could not make one single wrong move.

A few weeks passed, and I got a bit more relaxed. I said something to a classmate as he was writing something on the blackboard. I can still remember him looking at me through the corner of his eye…

"*Rosselló!*" he said. "Are you nervous because of your dad's debate?" Referring to a much-awaited debate my father—newly minted governor—was about to have on the status of Puerto Rico.

Like a predator—he identified the moment to strike… and so he did.

I was silent. Petrified even.

"Why don't you come up to the blackboard and solve this problem." Zoinks!

I was afraid. But I went up there anyway. Somehow, I looked at the problem and I could see the moving parts. I worked through it… and solved it. This surprised many of my classmates… but not more than I was.

Interestingly, this didn't surprise my teacher. He just said, "Hmmm. Rosselló, stay after class to talk to me." His tone went down a few notches.

Turns out, the problem on the board was *not* a ninth-grade mathematical problem. It was a problem from the International Mathematical Olympiad. He sat me down and said, "We have this math club. I would like you to come by."

It was completely surreal. I had no business being in this conversation. I really had big lagoons on basic mathematical operations, and so forth. But thanks to his mentorship, I could thrive.

A few years after, he became an important figure in my life. I asked him to be the godfather in my Christian confirmation.

So yes. It takes one person. One single teacher was so influential that encountering him was probably was the main reason I chose a professional path in engineering and science. What engineer can do without math? That, in turn, led to other decisions that allowed me to be a scientist… and so on and so forth.

Prioritizing Education

Reflecting on this transformative experience, I prioritized education in our Plan for Puerto Rico and beyond. As I noted in my book, *Un Mejor Puerto Rico es Posible*: "The early education of a people is one of the two most important sociopolitical parameters; the other being public health. The effect that education can have on the individual reflects in the collective" (2012).

Implementing this goal in Puerto Rico was a formidable challenge. The statistics partly illustrate the situation:

- Ninety-nine percent of students in the private system graduate, whereas only 42 percent in the public system.
- Almost 100 percent of all students from private schools went to college, yet only 2 percent (from those who started) public, would make it there.
- In 2011, only 5 percent of students performed at a basic level while 95 percent of them performed at sub-basic.

Figure 1. Signing education reform (Photo Credit: Magdiel Lugo).

This is a clear and present problem.

In her book *Student Centered School Improvement*, Dr. Amiee Evans, an experienced education researcher, practitioner, and school improvement specialist, describes my path to set education as a priority. "Five years before his election, Rosselló went on a journey to identify the root causes of these issues, study best practices worldwide, and then engage with the communities to present his ideas and get the communities' feedback. 'The year leading up to election, we had the bills drafted. It wasn't just ideas; we had everything put together. In hindsight, that was the first thing we did well. We were very prepared, and we didn't have to improvise or guess.' This was important, as Rosselló shares because the 'windows of opportunity that an elected official has to bring forth new priorities and legislation are very short'" (2023, 225) Figure 1.

In my second year in office, we passed education reform, a priority from the start. This enabled the establishment of charter schools, regional accountability, baby bonds, a voucher system, and increased salaries for teachers and principals, granting tenure to thousands and providing new books and electronic tools. However, such reforms require time. While we saw modest improvements in a short period (NAEEP scores rose from 5 percent basic to 8 percent basic and 1 percent proficient), the full impact of these significant reforms will take years to manifest (US Department of Education 2019) Figute 2.

Why wait for the second year to start education reform? As one can imagine, reforming education has many roadblocks. Many in the administration felt our observation that "kids before administrators" was a direct attack on them. We had vehement opposition from the unions and other sectors. It would have been easy to postpone the reform and go onto other easier issues. We kept pushing only because it was a true north of the administration. Otherwise, we'd be lost.

Headlines denoting the changes we were providing for education reform.

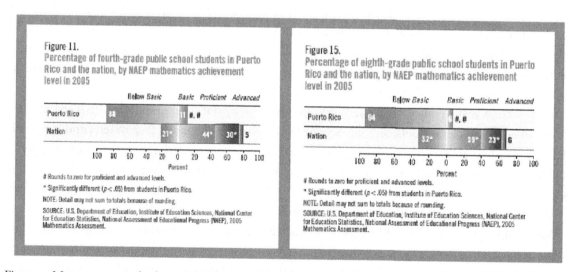

Figure 11.
Percentage of fourth-grade public school students in Puerto Rico and the nation, by NAEP mathematics achievement level in 2005

Figure 15.
Percentage of eighth-grade public school students in Puerto Rico and the nation, by NAEP mathematics achievement level in 2005

Figure 2. Most recent results from the NAEP tests, displaying a modest improvement, but very much below the objectives for our island. These numbers demonstrated major reforms needed to take place (US Department of Education 2019).

Why Prioritize?

The truth of the matter is everyone would love to do everything. Yet it is not a realistic view. How often have you heard politicians say what they think about an issue, and they always respond with: "Is it a priority"?

When everything is a priority, nothing is.

The hard truth: Priorities discriminate between different issues or actions, so you know where to put your resources. It may not sound pretty, but it will help you get things done.

"The truth is you have limited resources, and you need to ration them appropriately," my father told me. "This is where priorities come in."

In the education system reform, I prioritized the students over keeping dysfunctional schools open. It was a hard action, but I was clear on the objective. I had to close schools, 365 of them. My priority was not to keep half-empty buildings open when our student population had decreased by 40 percent. My priority was to give all kids full faculties with a path to a better education.

The word priority can't be just a tag line. Otherwise, it loses its true meaning.

Jim Collins, author of *Good to Great: Why Some Companies Make the Leap and Others Don't* famously said, "If you have more than three priorities, you don't have any." Collins emphasizes the importance of focusing on a small set of priorities to achieve results and excellence. Having too many priorities can lead to scattered efforts, difficulty in selection process and diluted results (2001).

This sort of mindset allows you to face challenges in uncertain and chaotic times.

Facing Chaos by Preparing and Prioritizing

"I brought order to what was a very chaotic, dysfunctional system," Governor Cuomo told me, reflecting on his most significant impact as governor. He cited budget deficits, economic challenges, political corruption, and gridlock as key factors contributing to this dysfunction. "I wanted to bring functionality and professionalism to our government. That was my priority. I prepared for it. That is what we accomplished."

"The state government must pass a budget annually by April 1. The state government never achieved this by April. To me, this was a clear sign of incompetence and arrogance. It is a requirement that citizens pay their taxes by April 15. But as governor, failing to meet the April 1 budget deadline every time? That was unacceptable and needed to change. It became my priority."

In an environment rife with chaos and complacency, Governor Cuomo successfully introduced professionalism and efficiency by focusing on preparation and clear priorities. (Figure 3)

Shortly after assuming office, I confronted similar chaos in Puerto Rico, characterized by poor fiscal management and execution. I aimed to redefine these areas. However, the oversight board quickly outlined their expected results and demanded actions to achieve these goals. Key highlights included:

- "Reducing payroll costs by approximately 30 percent through substantial position eliminations and other reductions in public labor compensation, including consolidating and significantly reducing nonessential government services."
- "The Board believes the government of Puerto Rico should implement measures in the fiscal plan to generate annual healthcare spending savings of one billion by fiscal year 2019."

Figure 3. Meeting with members of the oversight board (Photo Credit: Magdiel Lugo)

- "To ensure the financial sustainability of government pension plans, a reduction of approximately 10 percent in pension costs and related expenses may be necessary."
- "The government can achieve approximately $0.3 billion in annual savings by reducing subsidies to UPR."

In simpler terms, these suggestions/requirements from the Fiscal Oversight Board (FOMB) meant:
- Laying off forty-five thousand government employees
- Removing healthcare access from five hundred thousand Puerto Ricans
- Pushing 60 percent of pension recipients toward poverty
- Significantly cutting education spending

These were the *suggestions* or *requirements* I received from the Fiscal Oversight Board (FOMB) on my second week in office. Due to the inaction of previous administrations, Puerto Rico hit mismanagement levels so high that we were in a very precarious position. Seventy-three billion dollars in debt, fifty plus billion in unfunded pension liability (Stojanovic and Wessel 2022). These were the conditions, and the solution was cuts.

I responded with a letter to the oversight board a few days afterward and stated: "It is my view, that any fiscal plan premised exclusively on a reduction in the health, well-being, and living standards of the people of Puerto Rico through healthcare delivery cutbacks, current retiree pension reductions of our most vulnerable segments of the population, and layoffs is by its nature unacceptable."

This by itself might seem like a cop-out, taking a stand to avoid cuts. I was very mindful of the cost-reduction efforts we needed to employ. But they did not need haphazard performance. On that same letter, I go on to state: "Our government has put forward a plan... detailing the requisite policies that underlay the actions we have already undertaken and support our approach to the development of a fiscal plan. While we agree with your assessment of the magnitude of the crisis, our approach is in sharp contrast with some of your proposed initiatives."

In other words. I recognized the magnitude of the problem. I actually ran a campaign on addressing the fiscal challenges. The key difference here was recognizing we had worked for five years to tackle this problem in a thoughtful and meaningful way: *preparation*.

During our efforts in Plan for Puerto Rico, we were able to establish solutions for the fiscal situation, debt crisis, and unfunded pension liabilities, all while providing functional necessities for our people. Our path took us through an examination of root cause problems, best practices, formal presentation of proposal, civic engagement, and bill drafting. We were ready from the get-go.

As part of the preparation process, we had to weed out—out of the many things we could do—what was most important: *priority setting*.

And it came down to the last minutes…

Cigarettes Save the Day

On the evening of March 1, 2017, I had a deadline to fulfill a challenging fiscal plan. The setting was an unutilized room in the residence floor of La Fortaleza. This became my makeshift call center to finalize the fiscal plan. For about forty-eight hours, I practically never left that room. By that point, the walls were lined with papers, charts, and numbers… just about anything that could give me the insight to arrive at a certified plan.

A few weeks prior, and after much deliberation with the oversight board, we had agreed on a number: $9.6 billion budget for that fiscal year. There was a tug-of-war with back and forth between the oversight board's team and my own that spilled to the media. In between barbs here and there, we were inching closer.

But time was not our friend…

That night around 8 p.m., we were still forty million dollars off. I attempted to close the deal with our number a little bit off. At that point, it was down to me and two other people working the numbers and policy considerations. Luckily, they were among the brightest and most effective.

"No dice," said one of them after talking with the oversight board's team. "They want us to get to the number."

I looked at the walls and saw nothing.

I asked our team, who came back with a few ideas, but those would not move the needle. If I did not have this done, the oversight board might come back with a plan to cut access to healthcare. This was against our principles and priorities. We could not allow it.

At 10 p.m., we checked in again and still had nothing.

Suddenly, as I was about to consider other courses of action, I see a picture of me and my friends, celebrating one of their birthdays in a refurbished tobacco plant in Durham. Around 10:45 p.m., I called Pedro Soto and Edward Calvesbert.

"Did we look at taxing cigarettes?"

One of them said, "I think someone in the team had looked at it, but we did not follow through because the high-level ask was no more taxes."

Energetically, I said, "Check what they have. I'll check the elasticity in pricing." As it turns out, Puerto Rico had a relatively low tax on tobacco products. "What's the highest taxing rate for cigarettes in the states?" I asked.

"New York," they replied.

"Let's get up there—maybe a tad higher." We ran the model one last time. Eureka. The numbers matched.

The oversight validated It.

We had a fiscal plan. We did it while keeping our priorities intact. Temptation and doubt swirled, but clarity on priority prevailed.

"Wise are those who learn that the bottom line doesn't always have to be their top priority." These words from William Ward rang so true. We *understood* Puerto Rico was in a cataclysmic fiscal scenario. But the priority was always to provide a better quality of life for our people. In doing so, we were mindful of what we had to do fiscally, but we had to get creative to build better systems and find savings. Not a simple task, and one that required plenty of planning and discernment.

Sounds like a challenge? It was. But we *prepared*.

New Healthcare Model

Prioritizing healthcare access was crucial. The idea of depriving half a million people of healthcare, as suggested by the Financial Oversight and Management Board, was not in the cards.

Remarkably, we managed a plan to sequentially cut one billion in healthcare costs without denying access to five hundred thousand citizens. In fact, we expanded coverage. Our goal was to provide healthcare access to all, necessitating a thorough examination and improvement of the existing system.

To achieve this, we delved into the intricacies of Puerto Rico's healthcare model. We noted that health insurance companies were minimally accountable, with the island divided into eight regions, each served by a single insurance carrier.

Our solution? Consolidate into one region, allowing patients to choose their provider. This approach enabled effective cost control and service delivery. The crux was twofold. Insurance companies would face accountability and competition, and they could participate only if they provided comprehensive services at a fixed cost (per member, per month). I will detail the development of this proposal in a subsequent chapter (Figure 4).

This reform, like many, faced skepticism and challenges. One major hurdle was obtaining federal approval, which many believed was unattainable. Yet we succeeded. The result was the introduction of *Vital* as the new healthcare model for Puerto Rico, enhancing patient empowerment, service quality, accountability, and transparency, all while reducing expenditures by one billion and ensuring universal healthcare access.

Figure 4. Slide illustrating the proposed healthcare model

"We continue the renovation and recovery of the island as well as the guidance on the benefits to which citizens are entitled. Today from the western part of Puerto Rico we remind you that with the new Vital health model, beneficiaries will have mobility and greater options to receive better services since it establishes a single region for the entire island" (Telemundo Houston 2018).

This achievement was possible because we identified healthcare as a priority. We dedicated significant resources to this reform, including enacting laws to attract more doctors to the island, establishing the medical assistant profession under Dr. Rafael Rodriguez Mercado's leadership and implementing electronic systems for accountability and fraud prevention, among other initiatives.

Without prioritizing healthcare, we might not have invested the necessary time to uncover and address systemic flaws. The potential consequence? Hundreds of thousands of Puerto Ricans without coverage today.

Smart Government Cuts

To implement our priorities, we had to have our fiscal house in order. With more than $120 billion in debt and liabilities, a multitude of strategies and tactics were necessary to maintain stability. A priority was therefore to transform government expenditures into efficiencies.

The opposition reacted strongly. Colberg, a chief strategist from the opposition, warned, "Teachers, social workers, corrections employees, special education employees, those in school canteens already know if this individual wins, they will be fired."

Vega Ramos, a house representative said, "Since last year, candidate Rosselló told the press that he would eliminate forty agencies. He never produced the list. Prior to the debate, he spoke of a percent cut in the consolidated budget. He has refused to do the breakdown. That reality was evidenced by saying he is going to indiscriminately remove thousands of parents from the government because Ricky Rosselló's priorities are inverted" (Jover 2016).

Despite these accusations, our priority was clear: reform government, reduce cuts, and protect the vulnerable. Contrary to Vega Ramos's claims, we had a well-defined strategy. This allowed us to counter the oversight board's demands for layoffs and furloughs.

Our approach included turning government into a single employer, freezing government hires, reducing political appointments, offering early retirement options, and facilitating transitions to the private sector or nonprofits. We also reformed the pension system with a pioneering pay-as-you-go model. These were among many other initiatives.

In two years (Rossello 2019), we were able to: (1) reduce payroll by twenty-three thousand without having to lay off anyone (Agencia EFE 2019), (2) reduce the number of agencies in government by forty-two (NotiUno 2019); doing more in two years than what Mr. Vega Ramos mocked we would not be able to do in four), (3) reduce spending in government (Cartwright 2017), (4) save the retirement system (Telemundo 2021)).

Luis Ramos, a civil service employee, shared, "Single employer was a game changer. It allowed much-needed simplification and flow. In my agency alone, folks like me were getting lower end of the scale and could not move. They reclassified and promoted others. This uplifted morale. They could use the experiences they had learned in other venues." For those dissatisfied with their classification, options included appeals, transfers, or transition programs to the private sector. Luis concluded, "In my opinion, the single employer was a powerful tool for fiscal responsibility, but it also gave our civil service more options for growth. It set the tone for a much better HR model."

From my budget presentation statement in 2019:

"My administration has faced unimaginable challenges. Thanks to our commitment to sound financial discipline coupled with a clear set of priorities that address the will of the people, the signs of progress are clear."

With a blueprint and a north star, no matter how dire, the sky's the limit.

Takeaways and Another Story from My Kids

- **Without Preparation, There Is No Reform**: Timely preparation sparks the reform process. Preparation is not just about gathering resources or setting up infrastructure; it's about understanding the nuances, challenges, and potential roadblocks that might come up during the reform. With strong preparations, one can anticipate these challenges and address them proactively. For instance, having foresight about the necessary cuts allowed us to avoid more draconian measures proposed by the oversight board, and enabled us to create a new healthcare model.
- **Blind without Setting Priorities**: Setting clear priorities is crucial for the success of any reform. Without clear priorities, efforts can become scattered, and we might waste resources on less impactful initiatives. By identifying and focusing on the most critical areas first, one can ensure the reform

process is efficient and effective. Here, we highlight education and healthcare reforms as key priorities that would have otherwise died out if we had not provided the appropriate bandwidth and effort.

- **Interplay between Preparation and Priority Setting:** Preparation and priority setting deeply interconnect. Proper preparation can inform priority setting by highlighting the most pressing issues. Conversely, having clear priorities can guide the preparation process, ensuring that we direct resources and efforts toward the most important areas.

Once again, I asked my kids to create a narrative for preparation. Here is what they came up with (with some *minor* edits).

Bob, Alice, and Charlie were three friends on an epic cross-country road trip. Bob, the speed demon, wanted to get there as quickly as possible; Alice, the romantic traveler, preferred the scenic route; and Charlie, ever the pragmatist, suggested a cost-effective option. After some lively debate, they settled on a reasonable compromise: semi-fast travel that was still picturesque and affordable.

The next part of their journey required some preparation. Alice brought along an extensive year-long packing list while Bob packed light with just a toothbrush and a change of clothes. Practical Charlie made sure to bring along a first-aid kit, toolkit, and enough snacks for a zombie apocalypse!

At last, they were ready to go in Charlie's trusty old car. Along their travels Alice realized she had forgotten her camera. Much to Bob's chagrin, he found himself shivering in his summer clothes during a sudden cold front. This led to many humorous moments between them all. Fate then struck when their car ended up having mechanical problems. Thankfully, Charlie had his toolkit and saved the day.

Despite all the minor bumps in the road—literally and figuratively—Bob, Alice and Charlie eventually arrived at their destination full of laughter and memories that would last forever. It was unanimously deemed "the best road trip ever!"

Greg Shindler always told our team, "We are on a twenty-mile march. Our priority is to reach our spot in twenty days. We made a plan. We march through it. There will be good days and bad days, but we keep our priority clear. Every day, we wake up, we execute, and we will reach our goal."

Greg always evokes grit as a key success metric. *Merriam-Webster's* dictionary defines grit as firmness of mind or spirit: unyielding courage in the face of hardship or danger. It is one of his core values. And there is a reason for it. According to Angela Duckworth, author of the book, *Grit: The Power of Passion and Perseverance*, it is the number one criterion for success. Not IQ, not EQ, not Smarts, not talent. Grit (2016).

Connecting this to planning and priority setting—a lot of grit is involved in getting them done. Preparation is hard work. The payoff is down the line. It is an investment so your future can be more successful. And priority setting is a subset of that.

Looking at it from the perspective of factors, preparing and priority setting enables you to maximize the use of your time. If you know what your best moments for implementation are (heavily relying on the beginning), you can execute in those moments. Similarly, preparation enables you to search for A-players and useful tech that will enable higher bandwidth.

So, if there is no substitute for grit… there is no substitute for preparation and setting your goals and priorities. Yet in politics and reform-making, it is something typically left to decipher after the elections. This takes up valuable time, and of course, you could be facing serious challenges that require immediate action once in office. Without proper preparations, you don't have a vision and a path forward, and you risk becoming a day-to-day manager as opposed to someone who can provoke change.

In that same spirit, priority setting is fundamental. You need to know what you want to do and how to stack it relative to everything else. In a chaotic space, you need to understand what your focus is so everyday fires don't derail you. Priority setting is key because although we would want to affect every facet of government and society in the most positive of ways, it is unlikely one will have the bandwidth or the resources to do so. This important concept requires tools for proper execution.

I made mistakes in my tenure, but thankfully we could excel in this area because it was the difference between people having access to healthcare or not. Likewise, provoking a shift in the education system, greatly needed to break the inertia, was the difference between laying off people or not. And it was the difference—as we learned in chapter 10—that even with pressure from the highest places, the pensioners did not have to succumb to poverty. They were always a priority.

CHAPTER 17:
Coalition Building

In the aftermath of Hurricane Maria, a powerful call to action bound people together. This coalition of people, from all walks of life and parts of the world, helped conjure a powerful response. This illustration showcases that imagery of collaboration and that—even under the most challenging circumstances—great things can happen (Bayon 2017).

The atmosphere was tense. As part of our Plan for Puerto Rico—I committed to getting policy measures for LGBTQ and faith-based communities. I had representatives of both sides staring at each other. I was in the middle. You could cut the tension with a knife.

I did this because we had a crazy and wildly unpopular opinion: Both communities have a lot to add.

My view was we could not do it in silos. Somehow, we had to work on it together. Doing it separately would only foment the dehumanization between the two that was already pervasive. So I got leaders from both sides in the same room together.

For the longest time, these sectors battled each other, dehumanized each other—perhaps inadvertently—to have their position prevail. In most cases the extreme factions of each were doing most of the talking and the hurting.

Does it have to be that way? I wondered. I wanted to test it out. "Today, I have asked for your collaboration to achieve concrete actions for the Plan for Puerto Rico. While I have a few already established, I want your aid and support in figuring out what the best path forward is."

Separately, we had determined a wish list from each of the communities. They reduced their wish lists to fourteen action items. I asked them to present it in the following way:

"State an issue that is of utmost importance for your community and propose a solution. Once you have done this, the other community will respond. They will have to say if they can support it or—at the very least—live with it."

This commenced a process that lasted about ten hours. Tensions flared a few times. People had to leave the room. It got testy. As the meeting ended, we achieved our goal: A proposal that contained tangible action items for *both* communities.

Marybell Rivera was in that room. She helped run faith-based initiatives for me. "I did not think it would work. But I trusted (Rosselló's) leadership, so I went along with it. In the end, it stunned me to learn both communities were agreeable on most everything they wanted."

What's more was the people in the room no longer saw each other as cartoons or ugly villains. They were able to minimize the dehumanization by just having a conversation. Creating a *space* to communicate is a powerful thing—one we have lost along the way.

Getting people to sit down together and have those conversations can be difficult, but it is essential. I had the privilege of teaching a course with Congressman Tom Davis. He is well-known for his efforts to bridge gaps and arrive at consensus building. Speaking about this, he points to the new challenges in Congress:

"We used to have bipartisan retreats where we would take members up with their families... but the ethics rules down so they can't even do that anymore... We lost that opportunity for a face-to-face to get to know each other to get more personal in terms of their relationships. It makes it harder to attack them if they do that."

During the 2016 Party convention, I unveiled the Plan for Puerto Rico. Most of the conversation centered on two things:

(1) It was the first time the New Progressive Party had a section for LGBTQ community.

(2) Members from both LGBTQ and faith-based communities were speaking *together* about this.

I had my coalition. It was small, but strong. Cecilia La Luz and Johanne Velez were spearheading the LGBTQ community while Hector Albertorio and Marybell Rivera, were moving the faith-based—all known and respected personalities in their niches (Banucci 2016).

Of course, more extreme factions (or political opponents) on both sides attacked me:

Figure 1: Signing executive order for the LGBTT council with Cecilia la Luz and Johanne Velez. (Photo Credit: Magdiel Lugo).

Pedro Julio, an LGBTQ activist, said: "I don't recognize anything new on this platform for the LGBTQ community." Reverend Heriberto Martinez, faith-based activist: "There are many serious problems the country has that we have to pay primary and priority attention to. I am not going to be spending at all discussing things that are not really the reason for our crisis."

Both opposed my administration. Both were opposed here, but the strength of their rhetoric was weak.

"With the announcement of the creation of the LGBTQ Advisory Council, the general reaction of the community was very positive. For the most part, it was met with congratulations and a desire that we continue forward. Extreme lefties and haters disapproved, mainly because it was a Rosselló who created it." Cecilia La Luz, founder of the LGBTQ community center in Puerto Rico (Figure 1).

Some of the opposition was not having it. You have to factor that into your equation.

And so, I had the foundation of support that allowed me to move forward with these much-needed actions for both communities. The end result? We were able to achieve twelve out of the fourteen commitments for both communities in the span of two and a half years. I would not have even gotten half of those done if there was no strong coalition behind them.

Coalitions Trump Opposition

Recall the aggregate effect of opposition? The true power of coalitions comes from the synergy of diverse perspectives and the ability to present a united front. This unity can often derail opposition by presenting a broad-based consensus that is difficult to argue against. But it can also be a mitigating factor against the inherent aggregated resistance.

Coalition building is a potent tool in the political arena, serving as a means to consolidate power, unify disparate groups, and drive forward legislative agendas. By bringing together diverse stakeholders with shared objectives, coalitions can amplify their collective voice, making it harder for opposition groups to dismiss or sideline their concerns.

When multiple groups unite under a common banner, they not only pool resources but also create a more formidable front that can challenge even the most entrenched opposition. This fact alone helps mitigate the impact that a strong force such as the aggregated earned opposition can pose.

Coalitions can act as a counterbalance to inertia in government, ensuring that action is taken even in the face of significant resistance. Coalitions don't just battle explicit opposition, but they can be very useful to tackle the inherent immobility in governments.

Taxis versus Uber

One of the most potent coalition builders I know was my good friend and chief of staff, William Villafañe. William has poise and is thoughtful and patient. He would balance out some of my more stubborn tendencies.

In May 2017, taxi drivers held a strike in protest to the new rideshare technologies. William recalls, "When I served as chief of staff early in 2017, the debate began on the introduction of Uber and other shared service technology platforms. Taxi drivers quickly called a strike as a form of protest, which turned out to be a crucial mistake."

I saw an opportunity for blitzkrieg. Strike swiftly and powerfully.

"The taxi drivers left several critical points without service, including places as important as the international airport. Given complaints from citizens, the governor acted immediately and opened the new shared service modality to ensure the continuity of passenger transportation. His decision almost unanimously praised—even from opposition."

But we had work to do. Here is where William's magic came in. Instead of striking and moving to the next item, he told me, "I want to engage the taxi drivers, make them be part of the change." I was skeptical.

William worked with another talented member of my administration, Luis Damian Garcia. He recalls, "After establishing a frank dialogue with them, I convinced them they were acting against their own interest, we reached multiple agreements that allowed us to guarantee certain advantageous operating conditions, allowing them to compete without limiting the incorporation of modern services, which already had the support of the clients and citizens in general. After long hours of conversation, the strike ended. Taxi drivers returned to work and companies like Uber began to offer their services in Puerto Rico."

William saw the opportunity to create a coalition where I had just blazed through. We established a fairly good relationship with the taxi drivers group. This important lesson would serve me well later on in the administration.

This is the mindset we took to Congress after Hurricane Maria.

We went in with no political power, in a split bipartisan environment for Puerto Rico. Not the best initial conditions. Our only chance was to bring together different groups to collaborate.

$19.9 Billion Reasons for Bridge Building

Puerto Rico was at the end of the road. We had just had the most devastating hurricane in the history of the United States, and Congress seemed to be side-stepping us to focus on other matters. The main enabler? The powerlessness provided by virtue of being the oldest and most populated colonial territory within the largest, most prestigious democracy.

In our search for emergency funding, we had to compete with other states who also needed that funding. Not a good position for the powerless to be in. A hurricane had hit Texas and Florida a few weeks before Maria hit Puerto Rico. In Texas, it was Hurricane Harvey; in Florida, it was Hurricane Irma, which also slammed through the northeastern part of our island. Because of the devastating toll, Congress was about to embark on a bill to provide recovery funding.

Here's the catch. They were ready to do so, but *not* for Puerto Rico.

Their excuse? The hurricanes had passed before in Texas and Florida, so they would address that matter first. In subsequent bills, they would look at Puerto Rico. More specifically they were citing the lack of data and damage assessment. In fact, a specific memo running in the Office of Management and Budget (OMB) stipulated as much.

I'm sure it had nothing to do with the fact that (a) Florida and Texas are two of the biggest states with some of the highest number of representatives in Congress (where Puerto Rico has none) and (b) the governors of those states were Republicans.

What were we to do? No time to feel sorry... we acted. We created an assessment team head and shoulders above everyone else. We placed it as a *priority* for these teams to provide data and help (Rosselló 2017). New York stepped up in a big way. On the one hand, Governor Cuomo was helping with expertise, support, and aid. On the other hand, Senate Minority Leader Charles Schumer was establishing a commitment with his colleagues.

The outcome? By November, we were able to produce more advanced and detailed damage assessment than both Florida and Texas. I went to Washington, DC, with the damage assessment. OMB director Mulvaney, and his team met with us in a small office adjacent to the White House. They were surprised to see the advances we made. "This is good. This is good. Let me see what we can do," he said. "If not, I am sure we will tackle this in *the next* recovery bill. I have to go now. You are in good hands." And he stood from the meeting and left.

Of course, the next recovery bill never happened. Out of sight—out of mind. The momentum was there for us *now*. Otherwise, Congress would forget. This is particularly true of a colonial territory with no representation. On to the next crisis. Leadership knew this.

We used all venues to communicate the need for implementation with the Whitehouse, but to no avail. A bill submitted to Congress had more than seventy billion in recovery funding and $0.00 for Puerto Rico after the largest natural catastrophe in the modern history of the US.

The bill passed the House. Our resident commissioner could not stop it or get Puerto Rico to be included in the bill. It was a sobering moment. All the effort we had established to sort of see it fall through. To their credit, leaders from Florida and Texas lobbied to include Puerto Rico in the bill. To no avail.

Figure 2. Sitting down with Leader Schumer, as he committed to stopping any bill that would not include clear aid for Puerto Rico (Photo Credit: Magdiel Lugo).

Did we have any options left? Our Hail Mary consisted of a collaboration effort between strange bedfellows. The first part was working with Leader Schumer. I went to visit the leader in his office and explained the situation. He was aware of the recovery situation. He has plenty of constituents from the island in New York (Figure 2).

"Leader," I told him, "there is no reason for this bill to pass without Puerto Rico. Everything Florida and Texas requested, we exceeded. We need your intervention." Luckily for us, the bill contained other issues the leader did not like.

"This is not fair. This will not pass the Senate as is. I give you my word if there is no money for Puerto Rico, the Senate will not consider this." He was true to his word. Although the Democrats were in minority, the Senate needed a sixty-vote majority to pass these bills. They could not do it without Democrats.

As promised, the leader delivered. This was a tough sell, as it would leave stranded the people from Florida, Texas, and other states benefiting from the bill—at least temporarily.

What ensued was a surprise. Instead of waiting for the House to redo a bill, the Senate stepped in first and created a bill, which included many of the petitions Leader Schumer had, including directed funds for Puerto Rico. This was a huge step. Now the challenge was getting a vote to pass it.

Parallel to this effort, I spoke to President Trump. "Some don't want to pass this now," he said. "But if you get support from your party, I will make some calls. We'll get this done."

We needed some bipartisan support in this bill. The senators from Florida and Texas were on board, as it benefited their states (that's four Republicans). But it was not clear who else would come in and make it happen.

Lastly—and most importantly—I collaborated with our resident commissioner (a nonvoting member of Congress) so we could build bridges that would be paramount to the success of the bill. She's a Republican with some ties in the House as I was a Democrat with ties in the Senate. We understood from the get-go we had to work together, and if this would pass, it would be with subtle dance to leverage bipartisan support in a divided Congress.

On February 9, the bill finally came down, at about 1:30 a.m. I met with several Senate leaders to push this bill forward. "Senate Leaders Announce Two-Year Budget Deal." Read the headlines. It was a split vote. The final tally was seventy-one to twenty-eight, but the win was bipartisan in nature with thirty-five Republicans and *thirty-six Democrats* (eleven Democrats, seventeen Republicans against). So in the Senate, the Dems spearheaded the way with Schumer's leadership (Fox, Mattingly, and Barrett 2018).

We had passed the bill in the Senate! But still the House was looming. We did not know when they were going to take a look at this bill. What's more surprising was those self-proclaimed supporters of Puerto Rico, like Nydia Velázquez, Luis Gutiérrez were *against it* (NotiUno 2020). This made it more challenging. They rallied support from Speaker Pelosi as well.

A little after midnight, we get word the vote would come down that morning! *"At this point, we expect next votes in the House to occur at very roughly 3:00–6:00 a.m.,"* House Majority Whip Steve Scalise's office says in email to lawmakers.

However, in the House, our resident commissioner worked the votes from the Republican side. The House brought down the bill a few hours after passing in the Senate. There was no clarity as to what would happen. But it seemed the Democratic support seen in the Senate would not translate into the House.

The resident commissioner and I spoke at around 3 a.m. as we were rallying the votes. She said, "You got the votes in the Senate... I'll get the Republican support. You just need to get *some* support from the Dems. Nydia is pushing hard to stop this bill." Recalling that different from the Senate, the Democrats had majority in the House.

As inconceivable as it may seem, not only were they against the bill, they were doing everything in their power to prevent Puerto Rico from receiving the funding. This required the creation of a proxy war room to rally enough support.

The vote came down early in the morning at about 5:30 a.m. We were anxiously awaiting the results in a small room with cold pizza and coffee. The walls were a mess as we had drawn an impromptu whip board. It looked like something out of the movie *A Beautiful Mind*. We were hopeful, but not sure. Having the Speaker rally against the bill was never a good thing.

And then... the results came in: 240–186. Different from the Senate, this time, the driver was the Republican minority. One hundred and sixty-seven Republicans in the House voted for the Bipartisan Budget Act of 2018 (sixty-seven against), and only seventy-three Democrats voted for it (119 against).

Here's what *Politico* had to say:

"The House vote, around 5:30 a.m., was 240–186. House Minority Leader Nancy Pelosi (D-Calif) had urged her members to oppose the bill over the GOP's failure to resolve the standoff over 700,000

Dreamers, but her efforts ultimately fell short. Seventy-three Democrats ended up backing the bipartisan package, which came after months of closed-door talks. The defeat was a bitter one for Pelosi and other top Democrats, who have sought for months to tie a resolution of the fight over the Deferred Action for Childhood Arrivals program to the budget caps negotiations" (Bresnahan, Scholtes, and Caygle 2018).

I recall feeling jubilated. This was no small accomplishment with plenty of hurdles making it an improbable event. I grabbed my phone and tweeted about the extraordinary moment and how team work and coalition building won the day.

Later that day, President Trump signed it, and the Bipartisan Budget Act became Public Law No: 115-123

A *New York Times* article read:

"Puerto Rican officials have for months denounced the federal government's response to Hurricane Maria, urging for more attention and action to help the island's hard-pressed storm survivors. This week, island leaders declared a rare victory when Senate leaders folded disaster relief funding into a two-year budget deal to avert a government shutdown. Puerto Rico, along with the United States Virgin Islands, certainly has reason to cheer: The deal includes $4.8 billion to replenish dwindling Medicaid funds, two billion dollars to restore the shredded power grid and nine billion dollars for housing and urban development projects" (Mazzei 2018).

In Puerto Rico—the aftermath and bewilderment at the lack of support from Velázquez and Gutiérrez was evident:

In Senate Resolution 621, the New Progressive Party (NPP) legislator opined that both congressmen "turned their backs on their fellow Puerto Ricans, by voting against the funds allocated for the government of Puerto Rico, which will result in benefits for the entire island."

Later on, a HUD press release read "The US Department of Housing and Urban Development (HUD) today awarded a record $18.5 billion to support long-term disaster recovery in Puerto Rico following Hurricane Maria. HUD's Deputy Secretary Pamela Hughes Patenaude announced the disaster recovery grants with Governor Ricardo Rosselló." Secretary of HUD, Ben Carson said, "We are making a historic investment to support our fellow citizens in Puerto Rico. These grants will rebuild homes, restore businesses and the people they employ, and address infrastructure needs" (HUD 2018).

Without a doubt, this complex scenario had many ways to fail. In my view, this is an example where everything had to go right for the enactment of the policy. We had to have the foresight and execution on the front end to achieve what others had not with the damage assessment. We needed to identify a leader (Schumer) who would stop an inadequate process. Collaboration was paramount, and we had to reduce media bickering under the negotiation timeline. Strategic, bipartisan alliances saved the day on the vote.

The highly criticized relationships fostered with the president (good at that time) as well as those with the Senate Democrats and House Republicans by our team are the reason today the colonial territory of Puerto Rico got $19.9 billion earmarked and access to more, instead of getting $0.00 and playing politics.

After the storm, now we could get things moving. It was all possible because of strange bedfellows and rare cross-party coalition building.

Coalition Building Opportunity Building a DC-PR Coalition

One of the great coalition opportunities before us in this election cycle is the chance to show the world that the US treats minorities with equality and dignity by offering statehood to Puerto Rico and Washington, DC. In doing so, the United States would demonstrate that it wants to create equal partnership with a district whose population is mostly black (44.5 percent) and a colonial territory whose population is almost completely Latino (more than 98 percent).

Now is the time to take action.

Naysayers abound, of course, as they have for years (and as they have for most of the territories that eventually became states). In the case of Puerto Rico, the island has had two plebiscites in the past eight years, and it is about to have another. In both, Puerto Ricans voted overwhelmingly for statehood. Some are now trying to delay the move toward statehood by proposing a constitutional assembly. The question is why propose a convoluted method when the will of the people of Puerto Rico is already clear? There is no greater, more open decision-making path than the direct vote of the citizens of Puerto Rico.

Similarly, in DC, some are arguing that because it is a federal district, established by the Constitution, it has constraints to becoming a state. Here a solution is simple: Redefine "the district" to be the congressional campus and White House while allowing the rest of the citizens to have active participation in the process.

In addition to equality, the problem we are tackling here is one of democracy. How can we justify three million US citizens in Puerto Rico and more than 750,000 in Washington, DC, disenfranchised and without full representation?

In both cases, politics plays a role although it should not. The last two states to join the union were Alaska and Hawaii. Critics insisted we could not add two noncontiguous states. What really drove the resistance, however, was one state would lean Republican and the other Democratic. Interestingly, both sides were wrong about which state would be blue and which one would be red.

In a televised conversation with several governors and President Trump, I told the president the people of Puerto Rico "did not want to be a territory anymore. We want to be a state." adding, "In your words, sir, you want to make America great again. I think we could make it greater expanding it to include Puerto Rico as the fifty-first state" (ABC News 2018).

He replied with by saying, "Thank you, Ricardo, very much, and Ricardo is going to guarantee us two Republican senators." He quipped, "I might make that process very quick" (2018).

Clearly, the president was sending a message: If it's not going to be a Republican state, don't bother. The flaw in that reasoning is assuming the new states will behave one way or another. In truth, we don't know.

It is time for leadership from both Washington, DC, and Puerto Rico to establish a coalition to make this happen. Working together will enhance the probability of success. Specifically, the six million Puerto Ricans who live stateside should use their power in critical states, such as Florida, Ohio, and North Carolina, to enlist support for this coalition.

The decision is much greater than adding two states. This will define to the world the true position of the United States in the coming decades. Do we want the perception of a democracy with different castes of citizenships that mostly exclude minorities? Or do we want the world to know that embedded in the DNA of our nation is a true notion of equality that does not distinguish by ethnicity or by tier of citizenship and that portrays America as a mosaic of many cultures brought together to work for a singular dream?

What we do know is the previously perceived distant, nontangible paths to statehood for Washington and Puerto Rico can now become a reality. The House of Representatives has already passed a bill to make Washington, DC, a state. In 2022, the House did the same for Puerto Rico. From there, it's a matter of working together to get these two jurisdictions incorporated as states of the union. It's the will of their people. Polls show the majority of Americans support this move.

It's time to end the unfinished business of American democracy and live up to the ideals we have long espoused. It's a matter of civil rights. It's a matter of human rights.

Takeaways: The Sum Is Greater than the Parts

- **Space Creation Reduces Dehumanization:** Coalition building creates spaces where diverse groups can interact, leading to mutual understanding and reducing the chances of dehumanization. The sum is greater than the parts. The soft coalition between the LGBTQ+ community and religious groups allowed for dialogues that broke down barriers and dispelled myths, leading to a more inclusive understanding of each other. It allowed us to achieve most of their priorities.
- **Coalitions Can Overcome Aggregate Resistance:** By bringing together multiple groups with shared interests, coalitions can muster greater strength and resources to counteract resistance from powerful entities or the status quo. In our efforts to achieve a recovery bill, we were battling opposition that had aggregated over several issues. Finding partners—such as Leader Schumer, Florida and Texas reps, and the Whitehouse—helped us overcome.
- **Coalitions as a Powerful Tool to Defeat Government Inertia:** Governments often resist change due to bureaucratic inertia. Coalitions, by presenting a united front and pooling resources, can apply pressure and drive reforms more effectively. It does not get more status quo than the colonial territory. To defeat this inertia and get over the hump, we must find ways to aggregate support from different sectors.

"If you want to go fast, go alone. If you want to go far, go together" (African Proverb).

Without a doubt, many issues have an urgent feel to them. These need to happen quickly. But as we often said in the cabinet room, "The urgent is rarely important, and the important is rarely urgent." Having that in mind, it is important to cater relationships to be able to create great coalitions. I have been on the right and wrong end of these.

As leader of Plan for Puerto Rico, I could—with time and care—create a coalition that spanned beyond my party and allowed me to win the election. It was a coalition based on goals (getting a thoughtful plan together), shared interest (the commitment to participate and add value), and values (grit, innovation, and the understanding that may the best idea or proposal win).

Once in office, while I could conjure a few examples of collaboration, I veered away from that element of time investment in people. People will help you create those coalitions. This provoked my opposition to grow much faster than my support.

Needless to say, I made my fair share of mistakes as well as was apparent with my push for Law 80 (chapter 11). I did not spend enough time connecting with some in the legislature and at the mayor's office. This was a lost opportunity.

The coalition-building effort may seem like a long-term investment and—in some cases—a waste of time. But it will bear fruits given the appropriate dedication, foresight, and understanding of goals. It is something I am now using for our effort to build a coalition with the extended congressional delegation for Puerto Rico statehood.

A well-structured coalition can present a narrative that is both compelling and hard to refute, making it challenging for detractors to maintain their stance. But alas, without it, you'll be standing alone. As I was in 2019.

CHAPTER 18:

Narrative Setting

One of President Trump's biggest assets was the way he could direct the narrative to different directions. This is a powerful skill. This illustration displays all hell breaking loose behind him while the front man has another story… It's fine (Bayon 2017).

"I can't accept your premise" became one of my unintentional catchphrases.

It emerged from the necessity to navigate the complex dynamics of media interaction. Picture the scene: a small, antiquated room in the oldest executive mansion in the Western Hemisphere, crowded with journalists. Here, I held four to five press conferences weekly, countering the approach of my predecessor who had become notably absent in the media. My rationale was clear: to effectively communicate the intricate situation of the island, I needed to be a proactive communicator-in-chief.

However, these press conferences, often marathon sessions lasting one to two hours, revealed a challenging aspect of media engagement. Some in the press, at times, seemed less interested in our announcements and more in advancing their own agendas. A single misstep could become the headline, steering the narrative away from our intended message.

Journalists often craft questions to fit a particular narrative. My response, "I can't accept your premise, and here's why," was not just a rebuttal but a strategic tool to deconstruct their questions and clarify the underlying issues for both the media and the public. This approach was crucial in maintaining control over the narrative and ensuring we could communicate our actions and changes effectively.

Ramon Rosario, my top evangelist, shared, "The strategy I always used was to remove the loaded question posed. Then, I could inform. Many spokespersons and politicians fall into the trap of answering what the media or journalist wants to hear to create a headline. These politicians do so in the hopes they will receive better treatment from the press. Yet others never quite had the ability to recognize the loaded question from the beginning."

Admittedly, this approach yielded mixed results. In general, I never had a positive relationship with the local media. I was not good at it, nor did I desire it. Even if I did, plenty of activism manipulated the narrative in the newspapers. I don't think I would have been able to stop it.

With that in mind, let's examine someone who actually could.

TRUMPing the Narrative

In chapter 3, *Ten Hours with Trump*, I talk about President Trump finally accepting General Kelly's recommendation to fly over Puerto Rico during his one-day visit on October 3, 2017.

As we flew over Puerto Rico in the Marine One helicopter, observing some of the disaster that had ensued, most of the people in the helicopter marveled at the awesome destructive power of Hurricane Maria. But the president had had enough.

Trump had tried to change the topic from the disaster on many occasions. I figure, it was to sort of take a mental break from the issue of Puerto Rico, which was not a particular favorite of his. He tried to shift the conversation to talking to me about his *genius uncle* who went to MIT or complimenting some members of his cabinet for outstanding work they had done.

During that helicopter ride, I got a first glimpse at Trump's key acumen. This man was a specialist on shifting attention. It was like a savant's sixth sense. Every time he had no control over the conversation, or did not like the topic, he would throw a figurative bomb and make it bend to his will. And the media ate it all up.

Bottom line: Donald Trump used the power of words to rally people behind them in ways that others couldn't.

Within my interactions with Trump, we had four press conferences or media events. In all of them, he posed a question to the group after the end of the media intervention.

"What Do You Think the Headline Will be?"

These words rolled out of his mouth as he pointed out around everyone left in the room. Heads of state, security personnel, assistants, even a waitress. In all of them, he calmly and confidently heard everyone's answer. After which, he would either nod in approval or dismiss you completely.

On October 17, 2022, just under a month after the hurricane hit the island, a group of my top executives traveled with me to Washington, DC, to have several meetings in the Whitehouse with the president's team. We had no expectation of seeing the president at that point, but key items needed attention, and they assured us these meetings were important. Carlos Mercader was among the members of my cabinet who were there with me.

The first meeting was set tangential to the West Wing. Twenty top-level executives from the Trump administrations greeted us in a large room in the far end of the broad corridors of the Eisenhower Executive Building. The meeting started. As I was finishing my introductory remarks, I could hear the echoes of fast-approaching footsteps getting louder and louder. Someone rushed into the room abruptly.

"*The big guy wants to see him,*" said then OMB director Mick Mulvaney. By *him*, he meant me. Several of the officials gesticulated as he repeated "I don't know... I don't know... Now. Let's go."

I was very much surprised. I did not expect to see the president. Nor did I expect an interruption of this important meeting for a simple meet and greet. I presumed this was a quick photo op and I could get back to business.

My team stayed behind with the rest of president's executives. Mulvaney rushed me to the Oval Office with my press secretary Yennifer Alvarez, Carlos Mercader, and my assistant Raymond Cruz. All of whom were working hard and diligently to help Puerto Rico. He paused to catch his breath.

"*One minute,*" he told me.

I wondered, why are they sending the OMB director to run around the Whitehouse and usher people around? This started to get surreal. But not even the tip of the iceberg.

As we were ready to step into the Oval Office, someone at the reception asked my team to stay behind.

It was my first time in the Oval Office. For a few seconds, I marveled at the history-rich room. Countless number of world-changing events and images. Such awesome gravitas generated from a physical location. It was actually much smaller than I expected! Still, this is the true definition of a home-court advantage.

At the end, behind his desk, was President Trump. With a big charismatic smile on his face, he said, "Governor Rosselló, how are you?"

I went into the Oval Office and shook the president's hand. I figured it would be a short photo op at the time. I thanked him for his quick disaster designation for Puerto Rico. And while I was getting mentally ready to leave his office and head back to the Executive Building, he sat down.

"Stand back there. Let's take one more picture."

Gently, he passes his hands across the desk. "This is a nice desk," he told me. "Don't you think?"

I nodded.

"Maybe, some day you will be sitting here," he told me.

I processed a million responses in a millisecond and could only muster this: "No, Mr. President, this desk does not suit me. My focus is Puerto Rico. The desk suits you."

He smiled. I mean, genuinely smiled. As if I had passed some sort of initial basic test. Not intellectually but intuitively.

"Come here. Let's get ready."

Ready? Ready for what? I wondered.

Figure 1. Image from the impromptu meeting with President Trump in the Oval Office (*PBS NewsHour* 2017)

He went to the side of the Oval Office where there is a tiny bathroom. He had A few dozen spray cans in there neatly organized. I know it sounds cartoonish, but I could not make this stuff up. He picked one up and combed his hair.

"Let's sit and talk." And we did. We sat down at the two chairs typically reserved for international heads of state. Once again, my mind went to the power of that place. I got the sense that what was going on in our island merited the full attention of the US and possibly the globe.

Finally! I thought. *The moment I've been waiting for. The opportunity to spell out what we needed, the obstacles we had, and a path forward for Puerto Rico.* Up until this point, the president and his team had been very open to conversations, and there was a willingness to help. But it had been hard to spell out specifics and get action items going (Figure 1).

As I started making my case, the president said, "Call Mike. Have everyone come in." The vice president, Tom Bossert, one of the most effective people handling the issue of Puerto Rico, Brock Long, Mick Mulvaney and a few members from my staff sat on the red sofas adjacent to the chairs. They also brought in Director of Federal Affairs Carlos Mercader, who had been doing an outstanding job.

"Let them in. You know what, let the media in," the president remarked with a hand-waving gesture.

"The governor looked at me with a look as if to say, 'This is happening.' I remember Justin Clark (one of the aids) was baffled," Carlos Mercader told me. "One thing that amazed me the most: Nobody in the White House knew this would happen. The president started to call General Kelly and others into the room."

Turning the Tables

The media rushed in like cattle. There must have been thirty-some member clumped together in a small space. Mercader described the chaotic scene: "If you have not seen a press conference from the Oval Office, it can be intimidating. Picture this, out of nowhere, you have a herd of twenty to twenty-five people fishing into a small space."

What transpired is still surreal to me to this day. We had a thirty-five-minute impromptu press conference in the Oval Office, where the president and I addressed the issue of Puerto Rico.

The president addressed other issues such as Ukraine. Halfway through, Mercader notes, "I remember at like minute twenty-one, the press staffer came in and said, "Carlos, please tell the governor to stop this. I responded. You tell the president. I am not interrupting this."

With its highs and lows, I thought the photo-op-turned-meeting-slash-press conference was going fairly well. Until, of course, the very end. As the media were about to leave, the president went off-the-cuff and decided to ask me a question. Here is transcript of exchange.

Trump: Governor, I just want to maybe ask you a question because for the spirit of these people that have worked so hard and so long, like Tom [Bossert] and like Brock [Long] and like so many others. Did the United States, did our government—when we came in, did we do a great job? Military? First responders? FEMA? Did we do a great job?

Rosselló: You responded immediately, sir, and—and you did so. You know, Tom and Brock, they have been on the phone with me essentially every day since the disaster.

We recognize there are some logistic limitations in Puerto Rico. We didn't have the ports open for a couple of days. We didn't have the airports working [at] full capacity until about a day or two ago. Some see this as a limiting step, a very limiting step, but even with those obstacles, we got about fifteen thousand DOD personnel, about 2,000 FEMA personnel, HHS, and others in Puerto Rico.

Do we need to do a lot more? Of course, we do. And I think everybody over here recognizes there's a lot of work to do in Puerto Rico. But with your leadership, sir, and with everybody here, we're committed to achieving that in the long run (Delkic 2017).

The exchange was about to go *viral*. While nobody back home was aware of it (90 percent of people still did not have electricity), it made it everywhere in the states. Media and pundits analyzed and explored every angle. Hell, experts even evaluated our body language:

"Moreover, Trump's position on the right-hand side of the 'stage' (Oval Office) allows Governor Rosselló to then have the more alpha position. Rosselló's hand, from our view, covers Trump's hand. The governor amplifies his alpha status further by grabbing the president's elbow with his left hand. Although Ricardo Rosselló is subordinate to Donald Trump, the governor's body language during these moments were significantly more alpha than the president's" (Brown 2017).

Yikes! My bad.

The *Washington Post* wrote:

"Rosselló is a politician, and judging only by this answer, he's a pretty good one. Trump put him on the spot, asking him a direct question and hoping Rosselló would provide him a full endorsement.

But then Rosselló… didn't. The things he said weren't critical and won't cause problems with Trump (which Rosselló seems to be studiously trying to avoid), but his response was also hardly a full-throated bit of vouching for the federal response. Trump asked him if the federal response was "great," and Rosselló's response was not "yes;" it was basically commending the federal government for recognizing the situation right away and communicating effectively" (Blake 2017).

Trump and others saw it the same way. After the press conference concluded, and the media left the premises, the president crossed his arms, shifted ever so slightly to give me his back and said:

"I'm not happy. I'm not happy with you, Governor." He went on to say, "I put myself out there. I asked myself, 'Should I ask him?' This is going so well… What the hell, I'll ask him. And then oh no… I should not have asked him. He let me down."

Not good position to be in for a governor of a colonial territory.

I told him, "Mr. President, what would you have me do? Say that everything is fantastic as people are still having a really hard time? It is just untrue."

Still bothered, he looked at the vice president and said, "Mike, what do you think?"

Mercader remembers that moment: "Mike Pence explained he believed the governor gave a thoughtful answer. He went on to explain it was because he gave the administration cover. There were hundreds of reporters on the island, which would refute any notion that things were going well."

The VP saved me. No doubt about it. Without his intervention, this could have spiraled negatively.

Calmed down, the president responded, "Well, Mike, you are probably right. You are a politician. I'm not a politician." As he was about to say goodbye, he looked at us and said, "But you know what the headline will be—'Trump gives himself a ten, and the Puerto Rico governor does not.'" Most people tried to reassure him that that was not the case, but he was right. He knew it was not a good look for him. He knew that would be the narrative he would have to work with.

However, knowing this, having this keen intuition about what moved the narrative, gave him a powerful advantage over any political opponent. It is a big part of what made him—and still does—a formidable opponent. What's surprising is people *still* underestimate him.

This same thing happened during the three other times we had media interactions, and he was right on all of them. In those cases, he could move the story in his desired direction.

For instance, on June 21, 2018, President Trump invited a group of governors to the Whitehouse for a work-lunch. As the only Democrat invited, I held a good relationship with many of them. At that point, I think the president had a somewhat favorable impression of me.

"What do you want to talk about?" asked President Trump. He went around the table. The chief focus of the conversation for most governors was workforce reform. My turn came along, and this was the exchange (Figure 2):

Rosselló: "I see Puerto Rico as a place for equal treatment. Everybody sitting on this table—mostly—all governors are governors of a state. Except for me. I am the governor of a territory. And it is important, Mr. President, for you to know our people have chosen twice in the past five years to become a state. We want equal treatment. We want one American citizenship. And I think it would be a great legacy

Figure 2. Work-lunch with President Trump, his staff, and a group of governors, when I addressed Puerto Rico's status issue (personal photo).

that your administration could pursue, that would give a path forward to the people of Puerto Rico so they could finally have equality and end the unfinished business of American Democracy." I finished with: "Your words, sir, you want to make America great again… we could make it greater by expanding to include Puerto Rico as the fifty-first state."

Trump: "Thank you very much, Ricardo, and Ricardo is going to guarantee us two Republican senators. Is that correct?" He smirks. "It might be a very quick process."

I respond: "I guarantee Puerto Rico will be a battleground state" (Delgado 2018).

As the media left, the president did ask his usual: What do you think the headline would be? Here, it amazed me to see everyone in the room got it wrong. We are talking high-level political operatives, federal executives, and of course, governors. This time, I was aware of the game. I felt I knew the answer.

"You are all wrong." With a smile hi said, "It will be Puerto Rico. Good job, Governor!" . He pointed at me as he dismissed everyone and said goodbye.

Some headlines from that day: "Puerto Rican Governor Wants Equal Treatment" (ABC News 2018), "Rosselló asked Trump to push statehood for territory" (Olorunnipa and Levin 2018), "Rosselló advocated for statehood" (Delgado 2018).

Again, he was right.

Houdini-like Moves

On the morning of September 13, 2018, I was in a small house adjacent to the executive mansion. I recall my in-laws came in to help us with baby Pedro. That little house was great to detach for an hour or two while still five minutes away from my desk. You could see the whole of Old San Juan and hear the people and water down at the bay. For the most part—an unremarkable day. Until my phone started vibrating nonstop.

I stepped outside to see what the fuss was about. The president started bashing Puerto Rico, seemingly out of nowhere. My press secretary wondered, "Why the hell would he do this now?" Nobody was picking a fight with him. Things were slowly moving along…

He threw the content-bomb… and the media went wild.

"Three thousand people did not die in the two hurricanes that hit Puerto Rico. When I left the island, after the storm had hit, they had anywhere from six to eighteen deaths," read the tweet (Edelman 2018).

Even some of his staunchest supporters, like then Governor Rick Scott—who had been very helpful to Puerto Rico—had to stand in front of it.

"I disagree with POTUS—an independent study said thousands were lost and Gov. Rosselló agreed. I've been to Puerto Rico seven times and saw devastation firsthand. The loss of any life is tragic. The extent of lives lost as a result of Maria is heart-wrenching. I'll continue to help PR." (Scott 2018)

Why would he pick that day to raise the issue of Puerto Rico? It made no sense,. Was he genuinely erratic or was there more to it? At that point, I'd gotten to know the president more. My gut told me it was not a random occurrence. I had seen him shift the narrative several times before.

And then, the answer became clear. About an hour after the tweet, a news story came out with the heading "Paul Manafort and Special Counsel Close to Deal for Guilty Plea" (Perez and Polantz 2018).

After months of speculation, it seemed like there would be an indictment for his longtime advisor and campaign director. Sure enough, the next day "Paul Manafort Pleads Guilty and Agrees to Cooperate with Mueller Investigation" (Polantz 2018).

This was a major news story, one that would occupy all the air in the room. Yet by striking first with another narrative, Trump could mitigate it. Within the clutter and chaos, he could orchestrate words that would move the conversation elsewhere. "Trump Falsely Claims Nearly 3,000 Americans in Puerto Rico 'Did Not Die'" read the headline that shared the spotlight that day (Klein and Vazquez 2018) This is a powerful skill, and one his opponents always seem to underestimate.

Trump could double down on everything. He could use words that ranged from flawed to fully false, and he could repeat them, ignite emotion, and stir them in a direction that best suited him. This was his unique talent as a politician, and unfortunately, he didn't always use it for the best.

The sad reality is the actual truth or deeds did not matter. Words did. Words that evoked emotion over reason. Words that facilitated demagogy over science. The president achieved his sole goal: *To rally his troops.*

"We Can't Seem to Stop Talking about Him"

That *him* is Trump.

Those were the words of former President Bill Clinton when he came to visit Puerto Rico with Hillary, for the Clinton Global Initiative. We were discussing the current state of the Puerto Rico recovery—particularly energy—and the topic of the president came up.

Figure 3. Conversation with the Clintons in the Throne Room in La Fortaleza (executive mansion). (Source: Magdiel Lugo)

"I ask myself," said the president, "why we can't seem to stop talking about him." This is an important statement coming from President Clinton. After all, in my view, he is one of the smartest presidents we have had and one of the most cunning.

We all looked at each other across the seats in the governor's office in Puerto Rico. And I blurred (Figure 3).

"Well, why don't we just stop?"

The Clintons gazed at me with a confused look on their faces, as if asking me to develop what seemed a trivial yet impossible proposition.

I added, "Why don't we establish a viral effort not to talk about Trump for five days. Good or bad. Resist the urge."

They smiled.

I concluded, "I bet if we don't talk about him, he won't be able to do much harm. It will drive him nuts."

"This is a great idea," Clinton said. "I wonder if we could pull it off."

Of course, it never happened. But the core of the idea is what I want to elaborate here. Words can only impact over action if you infuse them with enough energy (positive or negative, but typically negative), they brush rationality out of the room. If the constant flow of superlatives is not thrust upon us, we might have a chance to look at the fundamentals.

Rafael Cerame a talented communications expert, friend, and advisor told me, "Contrary to the way we analyzed and developed news twenty-five years ago, where, for example, a front page of a newspaper or a prime-time news program marked the media attention for the rest of the day, currently the massive flow of information on digital platforms means that news events develop minute by minute. Whoever has the ability to maintain a narrative wins."

When thinking about how this impacts reform, a famous ethical conundrum comes into play: If a tree falls in the forest and no one is there, does it still make a sound? Analogously if a reform gets results, but nobody knows about them... is it effective? Narrative is key to reform, no doubt about it.

Yet there are also moments when narrative loses its pull.

When Narrative Gets Trumped

Cerame astutely observes, "The success of effective communication lies in the credibility that you manage to maintain in front of that large audience. In the world of politics, when you lose credibility, you lose the ability to interact with people, and when that happens, you lose."

Consider Trump's approach. He was known for his unwavering stance, epitomized in a viral video where he asserts, "Nobody knows this stuff better than me. Nobody knows more about taxes than I do. Nobody knows more about construction than I do. Nobody knows more about campaign finance than I do. I know more about drones than anybody. Nobody knows much more about technology... than I do" (NowThisNews 2020).

This pattern of doubling down, never admitting fault or apologizing, largely worked for him. I contend that, had it not been for the devastating impact of COVID-19 and his lackluster response, he might still be president.

However, things took a different turn.

The initial signs of trouble appeared in 2018, with the disbanding of the White House pandemic response team. Trump's dismissive attitude toward the emerging crisis became evident. "We have it totally under control. It's one person coming in from China. It's going to be just fine," he declared on January 22, 2020.

By early February, his tone remained unchanged: "We pretty much shut it down coming in from China."

As the situation escalated, so did his assertions. "CDC and my administration are doing a great job of handling Coronavirus," he claimed in late February.

Then, from the man who boasted about his unparalleled knowledge, came: "I like this stuff. I really get it. It surprises people I understand it... Every one of these doctors said, 'How do you know so much about this?' Maybe I have a natural ability. Maybe I should have done that instead of running for president."

This downward spiral created an opening for an effective communicator to fill in the leadership void. That was Governor Andrew Cuomo.

"COVID-19 was the extreme." Cuomo emphasizes, "There's a communication and then there's the leader. For the leader, it is probably a question of character more than anything else. In that moment, you either rise to the occasion or flow down the stream."

He reflected, "When I went down to Puerto Rico and saw you handling Hurricane Maria, the occasion was just as big as COVID-19. What training did you have? You didn't. You just had it. You can't train somebody. It was a question of your character, integrity, and strength. To say yes, I'm scared. Yes, this is catastrophic. But damn it, it's my job to stand up and lead… and that's what I'm going to do. And that's just the character of leadership. People capable of charging into battle and leading the way. You did that in Maria. You showed great leadership and resolve. The president could have done the same. He did not."

Cuomo acknowledges the challenge of communication in such circumstances: "It is difficult because the cynicism is so high because you're a politician. And people don't tend to believe politicians."

Yet, he overcame this hurdle. When I asked how, he said, "I would say to people, let's discuss facts first. Forget that I'm a Democrat or New Yorker. Facts are facts. My opinion you can throw in the garbage. These are facts you have to know." He identified a fundamental issue. "So much of our political system now is opinion-based. I wanted to reverse that. I said, here are just facts. Here's a graph. It's boring. Here's a chart or numbers, pictures. Here's evidence. I'm just giving you facts to inform you so you can make your own judgment because I respect you."

His observation and conclusion are noteworthy. In challenging times, he adhered to facts, respecting his audience's intelligence. This approach fostered trust in leadership. "I want you to have the information that's right for you and your family. And I will separate my opinion from that distinctly."

Thus, the narrative evolved to having a communicator-in-chief, calmly providing essential information, not just opinions. Leadership abhors a vacuum, and when President Trump ceased to inform on the pandemic, Governor Cuomo stepped in, offering the clarity and direction that both New Yorkers and the nation needed.

Double-Edged Swords of Narrative

Narratives wield immense power, capable of both forging and obstructing paths for reformers. Consider Angela Merkel, chancellor of Germany from 2005 to 2021. Renowned for her strategic narrative use, she effectively implemented significant economic and immigration reforms. She crafted a compelling narrative highlighting Germany's historical responsibility, moral duty, and the economic benefits of welcoming refugees and immigrants. This approach not only garnered widespread public support but also facilitated comprehensive immigration and integration reforms, addressing labor shortages and enhancing social cohesion.

Conversely, Silvio Berlusconi, Italy's prime minister and a media tycoon, often manipulated his media empire to control the narrative around his leadership. His charismatic, flamboyant persona served as a smokescreen, diverting attention from Italy's pressing economic and corruption issues during his tenure. Berlusconi's narrative, portraying himself as a self-made billionaire and successful leader, overshadowed his failure to enact meaningful economic reforms, contributing to Italy's economic stagnation.

The case of Nicolás Maduro exemplifies how narrative can severely impede reform. Under his rule, Venezuela has grappled with profound economic and humanitarian crises. Despite international efforts to assist, Maduro's resistance was palpable. He has consistently spun a narrative portraying himself as a staunch defender of socialism and a victim of foreign meddling. This narrative, resonating with some Venezuelans, has hindered opposition groups from garnering broad support for reform. Consequently, while Maduro's narrative has helped him retain power, it has simultaneously led to Venezuela's downfall.

Moving Furniture

["nosotros decidimos el tamaño del cuarto y el gobierno decide cómo acomoda los muebles en ese cuarto"]

Narrative was to present itself in a very critical way during my administration. We had the unprecedented task of working with a poorly designed Fiscal Oversight Board. A few days after the election, I sat down with the president of the oversight board. After some pleasantries, we got into the thick of things.

José Carrion III told me, "We want to work together with you to make these changes."

I agreed. Just one sticking point. I wanted to make clear we were in charge of policy—not them.

"For this to work, you have a job. I have my mandate. Yours is to make sure we are fiscally responsible. Mine is to implement our plan. We will make the adjustments to meet the numbers."

And here is where things changed. I used an analogy.

"You decide the size of the room, we move and decide on the furniture."

I saw it in his eyes. It clicked.

He agreed. We shook on it. A couple of week later, he was publicly using that analogy in various public appearances (Torres Gotay 2018).

And so, the narrative was set.

This would be useful later when the board attempted to take control of government policy issues. In a murky scenario, with little clarity, the fact we agreed on a narrative locked their potential intervention down. We used their own words against them.

Recall in chapter 16 when we were able to take their policy recommendations to reduce costs and reject them for our own policy on reduction? What enabled that window was the agreement of the narrative had sunk in. It was hard to back out now—even if the federal law was very scant one way or the other.

I know this was the case because later we were able to avoid usurpation of power by the new board-appointed executive director, Natalie Jaresko. A skilled former minister in Ukraine, she wanted to have her hands in policy matters. We were able to prevail when she crossed the policy barrier such as trying to take control of the Power Authority and stop us from reducing sales tax (for food) as part of our policy measures.

While other factors also played a role, the narrative decided the limit to the board's reach in government. This worked well for us, but imagine being at the wrong end of the narrative?

Takeaways: Like It or Not, Narrative Is King

I've had a growing sense of the importance of narrative. Originally, I believed the data spoke for itself. It does not. But it was not until a few years ago when I met Laquita Claire that it really struck me. She gave me and a group of executives a workshop on storytelling that was thorough and compelling.

She was kind to offer her insights on this topic: "Storytelling makes people relate. If you're purposeful about your words, they can lead to certain outcomes in real life."

- **The Power of Narrative in Shaping Perceptions**: Narratives, when skillfully crafted and communicated, can shape people's perceptions and influence their understanding of complex issues. Leaders like President Trump used narrative to control the conversation and guide public opinion. Leaders like Governor Cuomo used it to declutter the noise and focus on the facts. The narrative can either reinforce or challenge prevailing beliefs, impacting the direction of reform efforts.

- **Narrative Cuts Both Ways**: Narrative can have both positive and negative consequences. It can be a valuable tool for advancing reforms, but others sometimes use it to distract from critical issues or spread misinformation. The example of Silvio Berlusconi illustrates how a charismatic leader's personal narrative can become a distraction from important economic and political challenges.

- **Hard to Reform Without the Right Story**: The narrative is not just a complementary element but a necessity for any reform strategy. It can make complex issues more digestible and relatable to the public, helping build support for reform initiatives. In other chapters, I demonstrated how I used our vision as a narrative to get people on board for reforms.

Creating the right narrative is like tuning the strings to your guitar. You may be able to know the exact notes to play, the greatest of all songs. But if you don't have your strings in tune, it will be suboptimal at best; noise and chaos at worst.

Likewise, there are limits, and if the notes are horrible, no amount of tuning is sufficient. Or at least, one would hope so.

Still, words are powerful, and the correct sequence of those words creates a storytelling environment that connects with people at a deeper level. This is a premium and a necessity to move the agenda. Laquita reflects, "If we think about the power of story, it is for good and for bad. A story can spread and cause a huge amount of harm as well. And sometimes the squeaky wheel gets oiled first."

So how can we use it for good?

LaQuita suggests that addressing complexity is one such example. "Storytelling helps the issues become more digestible. If I'm talking to you about data, and I'm throwing you a bunch of different figures and data and numbers, that doesn't allow you to absorb the information. If something has no human face to it or no human element, we don't connect to it."

So narrative can address one of the key issues we have addressed in this book—namely simplifying complexity. It can also help avoid dehumanization and polarization. To battle the extreme and toxic side of narratives, one could always aim to avoid it or focus on crafting one that debunks it and makes it tone-deaf.

In the end, our focus is on reforming. And what is pretty clear is there can't be a reform strategy without a narrative strategy woven into it. The tighter it is, the better the path to execution.

The question remains, is narrative enough to push reform? And more importantly, should it be?

CHAPTER 19:

Sequencing

While not directly related to the topic, I found this illustration to be humorous and showcasing a point. President Trump receives a letter from me. He has an idea. He is cold, so—instead of reading it—he uses it to prop up his fireplace. A sequence (Bayon 2017).

"We have not passed labor reform in thirty years and you want to start with this?" an aid told me a few days after my inauguration after I proposed labor reform.

"It's suicide," he said.

I countered, "If we want to achieve the goals we've set for the economy, we need to sequence our reforms logically."

As you can probably tell from previous stories, this was one of the few times I could beat political conventional wisdom.

During Plan for Puerto Rico, I proposed labor reform. On January 23, 2017, amid opposition and protest, we were able to pass it. I recognize Labor Reform is not the most beautiful of proposals, but something had to happen to open the door for future efforts (EFE 2017) Figure 1, 2.

Opposition abounded, even within my own party. "The labor movement demands the elimination of the false labor reform and the restitution of the rights taken from our private company workers," said one of the leaders of the Unions.

Ramon Rosario said it surprised the opposition that "In record time, and in the same month the governor took office, the measure became Law No. 4. These measures to reduce expenses for the businessman and to reduce bureaucratic requirements were not understood by many, in Puerto Rico and at the national level. They did not understand how a Democratic governor insisted on measures

Figure 1. Introduction of labor reform on January 9, 2017 (*El Nuevo Día* 2017).

to reduce spending and business freedom. However, the approval of this measure immediately demonstrated a reduction in unemployment in Puerto Rico and an increase in jobs on the island despite the bankruptcy of the government."

At that point, the situation in Puerto Rico's labor and economic market was dire. Unemployment was at a whopping 12 percent, GDP growth was at -3.2 percent. You can see other parameters in table 1. As previously stated, the ill-advised policies were based on an end, with no path toward achieving it (Figure 3).

How could we change this course? Based on our work in Plan for Puerto Rico, we have identified the root causes for economic downturn to be (1) labor laws, (2) expensive and unreliable energy, (3) a weak permitting framework and (4) a heavy tax burden at the local level. Evidently, these items are very distinct and don't always have a solution with one fell stroke. We had our vision (image below) but how would we tactically execute each piece?

Economist Nicolás Munoz, speaking about the first piece in the sequence, concluded: "In summary, the proposed labor reform makes the labor market more flexible in times of economic crisis to stimulate the growth of employment opportunities and facilitates the employer-employee relationship in the

Figure 2. Signing Labor reform on January 26, 2017 (Source: Magdiel Lugo).

employment contract to give breathing space to companies, particularly small ones. The unemployed person who does not have a job today does not lose what he does not have and the worker who is currently employed does not lose what he acquired in his current employment contract because the changes in the law do not apply to him" (2017).

	By January, 2017 Garcia Padilla	By August 2nd, 2019, Rossello	Change from AGP to RRN	As of January 2nd, 2021 Vazquez	Change from Rossello to Vazquez
Unemployment rate	11.70%	7.50% *	-3.50%	8.90%	1.40%
Employment claims	95,272	76,376	-18,896	351,353	274,977
Total employed	987,000	1,009,075	22,075	956,078	-52,997
GDP growth	-3.20%	1.50% ***	4.70%	-6.00% **	-8.50%
Total public debt of the Government of PR	71,353,228	63,566,939 **	-7,786,289	64,866,939	1,300,000
Average Income per household	20,830	20,166	-664	18,826	-1,340
Labor participation rate	40.60%	41.70%	1.10%	40%	-1.70%
Homeowner rate	63.90%	68.10%	4.20%	62.90%	-5.20%
Poverty rate	43.5	43.1 ****	0.40%	N/A	N/A
Government payroll expenditures	3,427,216,000	2,744,401,000	-682,815,000		
Government operational budget expenditures	7,747,050,000	6,889,594,000 #	-857,456,000		
Number of public employees	146,097	122,668	-23,429	128,355 *	5,687
Cash flow	390,000,000	7,417,000,000	7,027,000,000	7,796,000,000	-5.20%
Defunding pensions	-3,270,000,000	1,400,000,000	1,400,000,000	-4,200,000,000 ***	-4,200,000,000
Total Tax Relief per year	-1,900,000,000	2,000,000,000	2,000,000,000	N/A	0
Total revenues to the general fund	9,815,000,000	11,376,000,000 ##	1,561,000,000	9,300,000,000	-2,076,000,000
Average time for construction permits	92 days	20 days	72 days less	N/A	
Average time for use permits	23 days	7 days	15 days less	N/A	
Number of transactions to get permits	23, licences, certifications and permits	1 unique permit	22 less transactions		
Permits given per month	879.4166667	1532.916667	Increase of 653 permits/month	1248.428571	284 permits per month less
Number of govetnment entities	123	89			

*	Lowest levels of unemployment rate in the history of Puerto Rico
**	First time in the modern history of Puerto Rico that the debt is reduced
***	Largest economic growth in 15 years
****	Lowest poverty rates in the history of Puerto Rico
#	Single largest budget cut (year to year) in the history of Puerto Rico
##	Single largest year in revenues (FY19) in the history of Puerto Rico

Most favorable
Most favorable change
Most unfavorable

Figure 3. Highlights some economic and fiscal parameters before, during, and after my administration. Blue denotes a more favorable result, and red denotes unfavorable.

And so with opponents and all, we placed the first cog in the machinery of our "Puerto Rico Open for Business" objective. "This new law lowers the costs of doing business and will help expand local companies like mine and the arrival of new capital," said the owner of the small business, Gerónimo Guevara, who had been struggling to keep afloat. Check.

"We have chosen a multistep strategy to promote economic development," I said as legislators from his party, agency heads, and representatives of different private sector industries accompanied me.

Translation: *Sequencing*.

Chain Reaction: The Art of Sequencing Reforms

"Sequencing reforms is a critical aspect of policy implementation. It's about the implementation order of reforms," explains Clare Lockhart, author of *Fixing Failed States: A Framework for Rebuilding a Fractured World* and director of the Institute for State Effectiveness (ISE). Lockhart and ISE played a pivotal role in guiding us through asset mapping and policy-based budgeting.

Their Reform Sequencing Tracker, encompassing more than fifty thousand reform actions in more than seventy countries, underscores the importance of the sequence of implementing reforms. "The sequence of implementing reforms can significantly impact their success. It's not just about what reforms to implement, but also when and in what order," Lockhart emphasizes (Figure 4).

Labor reform was the first domino to fall, a move the opposition keenly focused on to thwart subsequent reforms. Two years later, former representative Burgos criticized the reform. He went to say I was "irresponsible, insensitive, and a liar" (Hernández 2019), claiming a reduction in employment—a statement contradicted by BLS data showing employment growth and historically low unemployment rates. This was a classic example of soft thinking and demagoguery, aiming to portray policy failures.

Figure 4. Snapshot showcasing our economic development model.

Our preelection plan was sequential. We knew our next steps. After labor reform, we targeted permit processes. Labor law signaled change, but without streamlining permits, new businesses would hesitate to engage, rendering subsequent reforms ineffective. Historically, Puerto Rico's sluggish permit process deterred businesses with many abandoning plans due to prolonged waiting times and running costs.

Maria Palou, my infrastructure czar, reflects, "This process was our chance to establish an agile, fair, transparent, and advanced permitting process in Puerto Rico."

In February 2017, shortly after signing the labor reform, I announced our initiative on permits. *Caribbean Business* reported, "Ricardo Rosselló, flanked by private sector representatives, outlined the bill, highlighting a Unified Information System for all permit processes, automatic permits for certain uses compliant with qualifying district parameters, and a unified, standardized permit requirement system." (Caribbean Business 2017)

The challenge here differed from the labor reform. Instead of countering narratives of antiworker sentiment, we confronted governmental bureaucracy and environmental concerns. "An agile system doesn't equate to environmental neglect. Convincing certain groups that efficiency and environmental protection can coexist was always challenging," Maria reiterates.

This phase underscored that reform alone wasn't sufficient; we needed to bolster our bandwidth with the right people to drive these changes effectively.

Challenges of the Permanent Government

A story will help clarify this idea. Consider my experience with the implementation of the new "automatic permit." As the name implies, once you requested it, with certain documentation, it would have automatic acceptance. I began to receive permitting data. It did not add up.

"Why, do we have two hundred automatic permits less executed than requested?" I asked Secretary of Economic Development Manuel Laboy as we were sitting in my office—a royal fishbowl-like room that had visibility over several businesses in the Old San Juan area.

He looked at the Key Performance Indicator tab that he had just given me. He paused and thought about it for a few seconds. "This should be a typo," Manuel said. "Let me confirm."

A few days later, surprise, surprise, it was *not* a typo.

How can a permit—which by definition needs to be automatic—have two hundred more requests than those given?

The answer: The traditional government machinery had stopped this from happening. "But how could they do it if it's automatic?" I asked.

Simple. It was automatic, *but* someone in the office had to press a button to recognize the documents and forms came in. They added this process in the parliamentary process. Someone wanted to either create a new position or wanted the power to halt the process.

So halt the process they did. How? They simply left that position vacant.

This reminded me *of The Simpsons* episode where Homer realizes all he has to do is press yes or no on the key board. Then realizes all he has to do is press Y or N, and he tripled his productivity. He goes one step further and substitutes his labor with a "typing bird" that just presses Y.

PERMISOS DE CONSTRUCCIÓN			
Año	Tiempo promedio	Solicitudes recibidas	Adjudicadas
2015	98 días	2,874	2,812
2016	92 días	2,642	2,627
2017	98 días	1,966	1,931
2018	58 días	2,405	2,306
*2019	20 días	878	668

*Primeros cuatro meses.

PERMISOS DE USO			
Año	Tiempo promedio	Solicitudes recibidas	Adjudicadas
2015	23 días	8,893	8,829
2016	23 días	9,063	9,047
2017	16 días	6,685	6,668
2018	14 días	8,200	8,149
*2019	7 días	2,950	2,578

*Primeros cuatro meses

Datos: Departamento de Dessarollo Económico y Comercio. **ARTE | METRO**

Figure 5. Denotes the increase in speed in permits given (source: Metro 2019)

Of course, it ended poorly for Homer. But for us, it would have been a great idea! All we needed was Homer's typing bird, and we would have complied.

To me this illustrates the importance of people working together and sequencing on a smaller scale. Just one cog severely reduced *bandwidth*. You are as strong as your weakest link. We had moved about 90 percent of the elements that were necessary for this reform, but the bottle neck was rendering it inoperable. Soon after we fixed it, things started flowing.

They hired a person as well as making other changes, and we reduced the time wait on permits by 500 percent. This had a powerful impact on our economy. Labor reform, check. Permits reform, check. Two obstacles down. Next one in sequence (Figure 5).

Tax Reform:

The next domino was tax reform. Puerto Rico has a unique status as a foreign tax jurisdiction within the United States. What does this entail? It means individuals pay zero income tax at the federal level. However, Puerto Rico had the highest local income tax bracket in the United States (PwC 2023).

Tackling this issue wasn't just about adjusting numbers to lessen the burden. The real challenge lies in enhancing transparency in the system and boosting revenue returns. Our historically low tax collection meant an uneven fiscal burden. Some evaded taxes, forcing others to pay more. This imbalance led to chronic underfunding, persistent deficits, and the government's inability to pay contractors and suppliers promptly. Consequently, contractors inflated their costs by an additional 20 to 50 percent to offset expected payment delays or defaults by the government.

Addressing this issue was paramount; without it, broader tax reform would make no sense.

While implementing labor and permits reforms, we took decisive executive action to rectify these issues. We identified noncompliant taxpayers, developed innovative methods to monitor supplier payments, issued long-withheld tax returns (dating back to 2014), and streamlined our operations. The result? Increased tax compliance and a record-breaking revenue surge for the treasury—a 22 percent increase, amounting to more than two billion dollars more than the previous year, even post-hurricane (Hacienda 2019a).

Effective sequencing often involves initiating reforms that yield immediate, positive outcomes, thereby setting the stage for more comprehensive changes. In this case, we leveraged other necessary benchmarks to deliver quick, tangible benefits to the people.

This success provided the essential funding to tangibly impact people and businesses. Subsequently, we introduced more than two billion dollars in direct tax cuts and credits for businesses and individuals (Hacienda 2019b). These benefits varied, putting hundreds to thousands of dollars back into the pockets of our citizens. With money circulating and confidence restored, we launched a third initiative to further reduce taxes for businesses and individuals, introduced earned income tax credits (previously unavailable in Puerto Rico), and decreased the sales tax.

Three reforms completed, one remained—the most challenging yet.

The Inertia of Energy Reform

This was the elephant in the room. This is the third time we tackled this issue in this book. The truth of the matter is energy reform requires several chapters. It's multifactorial in nature. You have the unions. You have the broken-down system. You have excessive debt. You had people claiming it was a *national heritage* (I kid you not, this was an actual reason for keeping the Power Authority in public hands). On top of that, 98 percent of the energy was generated by fossil fuels. We had the highest cost in the Americas of any energy provider. and the highest unreliability rate of anywhere in the US. Should I go on?

While we tackled all those issues, some with more success than others, here we focus on the last two: Cost and Reliability. These were the key drivers limiting our growth and the capacity to create a buoyant environment for businesses to come over.

Moving Energy reform and attending to those issues was like moving an oil rig. It's hard to get it going, and you'll face many obstacles, but once you start, it gains momentum. In our case, we sped up reform right after the hurricane. We adjusted. And thankfully we did because I did not end up having four years to achieve this. Due to its complexity, we had to break down energy reform into two parts. The first part established the legal framework to (1) empower the user to choose their energy and (2) allow privatization.

Opposition was coming at us from diverse places—the unions, the political opposition, some entrenched government employees, the petro cartel, lobbyists, etc. But because people saw what happened to our old, ineffective, inefficient energy system during the storm, we had their support.

"Selling PREPA is part of the plan the government and the fiscal control board have to sell the country as they want to do with the beaches, the schools, the highways, and the university, among others. PREPA is not for sale, and neither is Puerto Rico," said the leader of the union, Angel Jaramillo. The effort was to create a narrative that would enrage people because we were "selling their national heritage."

They merged every cause into theirs to *aggregate opposition*. The constant wave of dehumanizing attacks eventually worked against me. But the pain due to the power outages before and after the hurricane told a stronger story. And while this cog will likely take years to gain full traction, it needed to begin. It will likely result in more protest and short-termism, in an attempt to bring PREPA back to government. The next administrations will need to work through these.

But it is necessary to remember that "Businesspeople in Puerto Rico have long complained of obstacles with obtaining permits, property registrations, filing taxes, energy reliability and other operational hardships, which slow down the level of economic activity needed to boost growth" (German Ojeda, 2022).

Underlying all this was the effort to stabilize the fiscal conundrum. Our fiscal team was very conscious of the sequencing that had to occur on that front. Although we discussed this at further length in chapter 8 it bears noticing that with restructuring of the debt, we also sequenced.

Christian Sobrino, who spearheaded the restructuring efforts notes, "Restructuring Puerto Rico's debt wasn't like restructuring real estate. Here everything's involved with policy, and you have to start thinking of what it's going to look like a couple of years ahead. And I would say the clearest, most important part of the whole process was we knew exactly where we wanted it to get to and they did it. While others had an Excel spreadsheet, you actually had a plan."

We tackled all our goals. They worked synergistically. They were yielding results. (table 1)
Four out of four. *Checkmate.* Time to create a new economic environment.

Creating New Markets

With our sequencing strategy, we tackled the foundational challenges facing businesses, paving the way for new opportunities.

"The reform of permits and the flexibility of the labor framework is already a reality. The fourth area is the new tax model we present to the Legislative Assembly to address the four components all studies point to as our impediment to achieving economic growth," I declared after signing the first leg of the energy reform.

This groundwork laid the fertile soil for growth. We were ready to plant seeds that would soon yield abundant crops.

These seeds were at least five new markets we created, including medical cannabis, e-sports, sports betting, hemp, and blockchain. I saw these as thrilling opportunities to generate revenue and address other societal issues. I often said to my team, "We need to stop being spectators of the global economy and become innovators and set the tone."

Naturally, disruptive markets attract opposition. Skillful sequencing was essential to navigate these challenges.

Medical cannabis was our first market (Bernal 2018). Leveraging the momentum from earlier reforms, we successfully implemented it, despite resistance from socially conservative members of my own party.

I had to go one-on-one to convince legislators this was the path. We were only able to push it through in large part because we set our *priorities* and *prepared* to accomplish them. I reminded them they signed a document pledging to follow through on Plan for Puerto Rico. Herb magazine highlighted our efforts:

"This advanced legislation recognizes medical cannabis as an alternative medical treatment while maintaining all safeguards to protect the general public. Rosselló Nevares was a scientist before becoming governor of Puerto Rico. He said the law addresses an important public health issue. 'As a scientist, I know firsthand the impact that medicinal cannabis has had on patients with various diseases. The time has come for Puerto Rico to join the flow of countries and states that have created similar legislation.' The bill survived a contentious debate in the National Assembly" (Herb 2017).

The debate continued, but we gained support from key figures like Secretary of Agriculture, Carlos Flores, who enthusiastically backed our hemp and cannabis initiatives.

Next, we focused on bitcoin, blockchain, sports betting, and e-gaming—industries adding value in line with our mission. Our reports indicated sports betting could generate $44 to 62 million annually in new revenue with national projections reaching $3.1 billion by 2023 and $8.1 billion online (Spectrum Gaming Group, The Innovation Group). E-gaming, including the rapidly growing e-sports sector, also held immense potential. Recent data ranked e-sports second only to the NIL in the US (MBA@ Syracuse 2021) Figure 6.

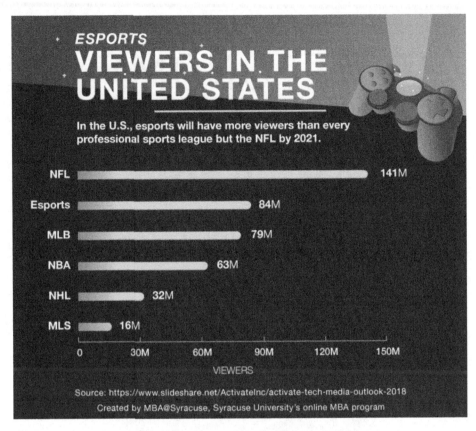

Figure 6. Growth of e-sports in the United States, 2018 (MBA@Syracuse 2021).

We also embraced cryptocurrency and blockchain, aiming to be innovators rather than bystanders. "We would … like to take advantage of blockchain because it has transformative and disruptive components for business and government," I mentioned in a CNBC interview, leading to executive actions and orders (Picker and Giel 2018).

Resistance persisted, particularly from far-right groups opposed to medical marijuana, sports betting, and e-gaming as well as from far-left groups opposing blockchain and cryptocurrency.

Metro Newspaper captured the essence of this opposition: "Public hearings on Governor Ricardo Rosselló's project to authorize and regulate sports betting met with resistance. As with past advanced measures that could benefit the economy, opposition often stems from ignorance." (Metro 2019).

The last sentence applies to most reforms and changes.

Despite these challenges, we successfully implemented many of these initiatives with the results speaking for themselves.

In a story by *Caribbean Business* entitled "Rosselló twenty months on," the paper noted that "Even with obstacles, improvements are present… We see improvements in unemployment with a decrease in 24.7 percent in the past twenty months, increased participation rate, and increased household income. The GNP showed growth, reflecting a much better performance than the previously projected -13 percent" (Rodriguez-Castro 2018).

CARIBBEAN **BUSINESS**   Thursday, November 15, 2018

ECONOMY

THINKING STRATEGICALLY:

Rosselló
20 Months On

Even With Obstacles, Improvements
Are Present; On Agenda: Hurricane Relief,
Healthcare Parity, Reconstruction Funds

BY FRANCISCO RODRÍGUEZ-CASTRO
www.birlingcapital.com

Takeaways: Many Hits over Big Swings

- **Pitfall: Pursuit of an End without a Strategy**: Pursuing specific policy goals without a well-thought-out and strategic plan is a dead end. It is important to have a clear strategy and sequencing of actions to achieve desired outcomes effectively. García Padilla's government may have pursued economic goals, such as a job creation target of fifty thousand new jobs, without a clear and coherent strategy, leading to unfavorable economic conditions, high unemployment, and other challenges. This illustrates the potential consequences of pursuing an end without a well-defined plan or sequence of actions.

- **Strategic Sequencing of Reforms**: This theme highlights the importance of strategically planning and sequencing reforms in a logical order to achieve specific goals or objectives. Here, we emphasize the order in which we implement reforms can significantly impact their success. An example is when we first proposed labor reform, recognizing it as the initial step in a sequence of reforms aimed at addressing various economic challenges in Puerto Rico. Permits, tax, and energy reform followed, each building upon the previous one, creating a comprehensive strategy for economic recovery.

On May 2020, the newspaper read: "After six consecutive years of negative performance, the last fiscal year in which Ricardo Rosselló Nevares held the governorship of Puerto Rico, the economy grew by 1.7 percent." (El Nuevo Dia 2020)

This was highest number in the last fifteen years" (World Bank 2023).

I had already resigned at that point. The actions might have not helped retaining my seat, but they certainly helped the economy and the fiscal health of Puerto Rico. Table 1 showcases several key performance indices from the administration that preceded me, my own, and the one that immediately followed.

In virtually all categories, from unemployment, total employment, GDP growth, poverty rate, etc., we outperformed by a wide margin the bookend administrations. While there were many factors, being able to sequence policy and reforms was one of them.

The takeaway here is severalfold. First, you must have an overall objective you want to achieve. This is important but is not sufficient. "Home runs are good, but hits are better!" someone once said, and in this case, it applies figuratively and literally. García Padilla had an overall objective of creating fifty thousand new jobs. Great for a headline, but there was no substance and no execution behind it.

The newspaper headline read: "Governor Hits First Home Run with 10,000 New Jobs!" This, just two weeks after taking office. The article goes on to say, "The jobs we announce today, there are all kinds of jobs because there are people of all kinds looking for work" (NotiCel 2013).

He did these announcements accompanied by future baseball hall of famer, Edgar Martinez. They stood, alongside other members of his administration, on stage with bats at hand. The message: We are hitting it out of the park!

Of course, at the end of his tenure, far from getting fifty thousand new jobs, there was a total *loss* of more than forty thousand. It is therefore important to have an understanding of the underlying problems and to have a plan to tackle each of these. He clearly did not.

But even with the right understanding and actions, sometimes you can get thwarted if you don't pursue them in the right, thoughtful order. This is the last layer of strategic execution: Sequencing.

How you actually ascribe a sequencing approach is a subjective matter. One can still extract some general observations. First, embedding short-term resulting policies on the front end, alongside other longer-term components. This is to demonstrate to your stakeholders that results follow your actions. This gains the reformer credibility and trust for your next steps. Second, careful consideration of the more complex policies should implement first, at the highest point of influence. This was apparent in chapter 15 about blitzkrieg. Third, continuity matters. In our case, once I left office, some neglected these items, pushing the economy back down, unemployment up, and a precipitous job collapse during Wanda Vázquez's administration.

One final thought: Take intermissions after an established period of time to evaluate the policies, engage citizenship, and make any corrections necessary. I did not do this adequately, and I recognize now this will give you an opportunity to gain more support and identify shortcomings before they become a big problem.

In the end… sequencing hits are better than hoping for home runs…

But how can we effectively assess if we are sequencing correctly?

PART V

PUTTING IT TOGETHER

CHAPTER 20:

Reform Dynamics

Curiosity is one of the attributes I value. It is what drove me into science in the first place. I have applied it in every aspect of my life. Already a politician by the time of this illustration, it showcases me experimenting. This chapter contains a model shaped by my experiences and produced by the curiosity to understand the dynamics of reform (Bayon 2016).

The temperature in the room was cold. The jubilation of swearing in as governor had quickly shifted into the staunch reality of the critically damaged system we had inherited. Concerned looks were prevalent in my close inner circle. We were sitting down in what we would eventually call *"the Roberto Clemente room;"* a cozy area where I would meet with several of my top officials to discuss matters with a beautiful view of the San Juan Bay.

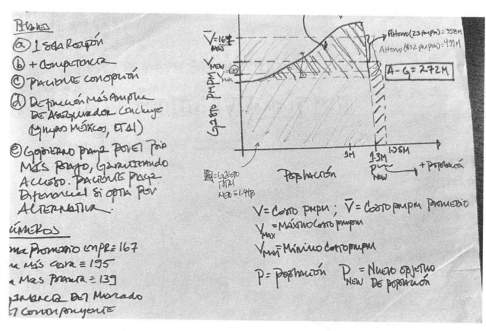

Figure 1. Napkin where I drew out the new healthcare model for Puerto Rico. Here, I found the limitations, inefficiencies, and drawbacks to the current system. We also had a limitation in expenditures that would have been catastrophic if the old model sustained.

"The oversight board wants to reduce one billion dollars in spending… That would mean several hundred thousand without access to healthcare immediately," my chief of staff told me on January 26, 2017.

"No, it does not," I responded as I pulled out a paper with my hard-to-read notes. As I scribbled, many on my team stood there confused. It would not be the last time.

"If we change the model, we can provide quality health care to everyone and still reduce expenditures." (Figure 1)

On one old napkin (image), I had changed the healthcare model. Of course, this is literally a back-of-the-envelope exercise, but it provided the framework to dive in deep and find opportunities.

We had a healthcare system divided into eight regions. Each region would request a proposal from insurance companies to provide the coverage. Once the region awarded the contract, the insurance company had the monopoly. The outcome? A high cost per member per month, low accountability due to the monopoly, and undesired patient outcomes.

"What if we change this regional assumption," I asked the group "Why not have everyone compete in one single region?"

Luckily—a few months prior, I had sat down with my father—an expert in healthcare systems, and we were able to start playing around with assumptions. I came to him with my idea for a new model and he said, "That should work." This was important to me because we would not be changing just any model. We would be changing the model he created for Puerto Rico in the 1990s—one that became the first to give 100 percent access to all its citizens in the United States.

"Every reform has its lifespan," he said. "Then you need to see what the new problems are and tackle those."

The model I proposed had the same purpose: Giving everyone access to quality healthcare. But now restraints were coming left and right with the budget, the lack of visibility and accountability, unequal treatment based on the region the person lived in, and the comfortable monopoly position of some healthcare companies.

"Think about it," I told my team. "One region giving access everywhere. Because we will have several insurance companies bidding, we can have them compete against each other. This will create different choices for the people. They will have the opportunity to choose among the insurance companies. They could also change their insurer if they are not satisfied."

Some liked the idea. Others challenged saying it would be too costly. I again went back to my napkin.

"Actually, we can reduce the cost by almost a billion dollars," I said pointing at the area under the curve that represented savings. "We even have a little bit to spare to expand access to groups that don't currently qualify (about fifty thousand)."

We could—and we *did* (Figure 2).

The take-home message here is that fundamental reform for healthcare started with that basic model. After working on it several times, trying out new variables, we were able to make it click. It's never lost on me that in the beginning… it was just scribbles on a napkin.

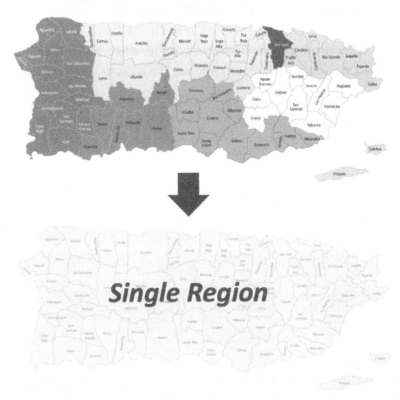

Figure 2. Conceptual slide I prepared to showcase the foresight to change a fragmented system, into a single system, which put the patients in the driver's seat.

From Healthcare to Reforming

Lets do a similar back-of-the-envelope exercise and turn our attention to reform dynamics.

Typically, we define a math model as a simplified representation of certain aspects of a real system. They capture the essence of the system. The more robust and complex the model, the more knowledge of the variables and their control, the better the outputs.

In this book, we have showcased several factors that affect the capacity to reform. In general, we saw as *time* passes, it becomes *harder* to reform. The *bigger*, more *impacting* a reform, the *better* the outcomes. That opposition aggregates as one reforms, and these reforms only matter if you can execute upon them.

The observations, from my experiences and others throughout the book, support these assumptions. But they are just that—assumptions. They can fail, break, and there can be better ones.

To understand reform dynamics, it would be interesting to see what happens when we stress test these assumptions and place them together into a model.

The first thing to do is set our axis. We want to see how the capacity to execute reform changes as a function of time. So, x-axis is time. Y-axis is capacity to execute reform. Within it, some sort of reform dynamics will occur (Figure 3).

The *initial conditions* will be very different in different places and moments in time (chapter 11). An example was when hurricanes hit Florida and Puerto Rico at roughly the same time. The initial conditions fiscally were quite different. While Florida had billions of dollars in the bank, Puerto Rico was going through a fiscal crisis with barely anything. This created a huge deficit for immediate response. To aggravate this, during the recovery phase, Florida could spend its money knowing FEMA

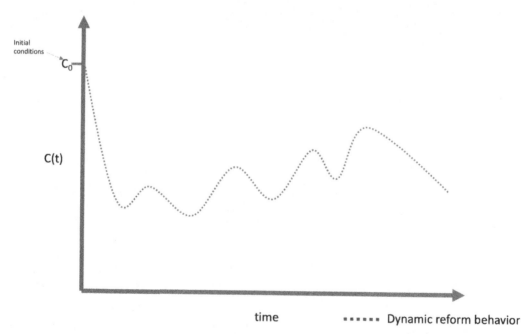

Figure 3. Showcases the cartesian coordinate system where the reform dynamics will unfold.

Once a month, I would make it a point to separate from everything for 12 hours and see the big picture. This is how I could assess how the items we were working one where having an effect. I could meassure the variables. Occasionally, I would have the help of my kids (Pictures by Beatriz Rossello)

would eventually reimburse. While we had the same consideration, to reimburse you need money to spend in the first place.

Geography was also very different here. The day after the storm hit Florida, aid rode in through interstate highways. In the case of Puerto Rico, we had to wait for boats sent with the requisite support.

So, initial conditions matter and need consideration in any model.

The hurricane also provides an important analogy to the *time* (chapter 11) dependency of execution. In the hours and days after the storm, everyone pledged support. A few weeks to months after, the support significantly dwindled. The focus had shifted. The momentum had died down. The *policy window* closed.

Similarly with leaders, maximizing the earlier phases of a term provides the best breeding ground to move reform and execute (chapter 15). Recall I was able to pass comprehensive labor reform in twenty-three days, but when I attempted to work with one single provision of labor laws a year and a half after, I was railroaded.

Bandwidth (chapter 14) manifested itself in a variety of ways during the hurricane compared to other states. Puerto Rico had limited bandwidth with a collapsed infrastructure. The better A-players, systems, and technology one has, the higher the impact on executing reforms.

And the magnitude of the reforms (chapter 13) can be a double-edged sword. If you can overcome the initial hurdle of systemic opposition (chapter 12), negative narrative (chapter 18), and inertia, you can showcase results that are meaningful to a large group of people. This was the case with energy reform (partially), government reform, my father's healthcare reform, Governor Cuomo's gun reform and marriage equality reform. However, if you are not able to overcome this, you will have gained all the opposition and negative projection, without any of the potential outcomes for a result. This was the case with my regional government reform. Then there is another scenario where you can achieve the reform, yet the results don't come in quickly enough to get you on the positive side of things. This was the case with my education reform (chapter 18). Those likely need to be sequenced (chapter 19) with other smaller reforms to sustain headwinds.

Why model anything?
Nerd alert

Once upon a time, in the vibrant city of Numeria, there lived an extraordinary chef named Fibonacci. His restaurant, "The Golden Ratio," filled with customers eager to taste his unique and delicious dishes. Fibonacci had become renowned for his secret method of cooking—something no one could figure out.

One day, a young apprentice named Euclid came to Fibonacci asking him to teach him this secret method. Fascinated by Euclid's ambition and drive, Fibonacci agreed. He revealed that his secret not only involved cooking but also the application of mathematical models.

Fibonacci explained, "Each dish we create in this kitchen is like a complex system. The ingredients act as variables and the cooking process acts as equations that determine the outcome—the taste of the dish."

Euclid was curious as to how mathematics could help them cook better. To demonstrate, Fibonacci chose their signature dish, "the pi," and created a mathematical model representing its ingredients and process. The model predicted it would be delicious. However, when they tasted it, it wasn't quite as good as the model predicted. Rather than feeling discouraged, this excited Fibonacci. He said, "This is why mathematical models are so powerful. When our predictions don't match what happens, we can revise them and improve our outcomes."

So they began making adjustments to their model—changing quantities and altering processes—until eventually they created a 'the pi' that was delectable beyond belief!

Euclid now understood the power of mathematical models. Not only do they enable us to predict outcomes but also provide us with a systematic way of improving processes. From then on, he applied mathematical models to all his cooking endeavors, eventually becoming a master chef known for his innovative culinary creations and exquisite dishes—all thanks to Fibonacci's teachings!

Here's the important lesson: In life, just like in cooking, mathematical models are powerful tools capable of turning uncertainty into understanding and mystery into knowledge!

It may not be perfect, but it helps us make sense of things.

Another Napkin Creation

We have our culprits and our objectives. You can see assumptions here:

Our model aims to track how the capacity to reform (C, y-axis) is affected as a function of time (t, x-axis), when reforms of a particular magnitude are inserted across time ($[R]i,ti$).

We have developed the concept that certain variables, assumptions, and actions affect the outputs. Assumptions:

1. Keeping everything constant, the capacity to reform (C) will fall down as a function of time. It could be a nonlinear decay or linear. (Figure 4)

2. We assume rational behavior of the society, therefore the higher the magnitude of the reform, the harder it will be to achieve. As time goes to infinity, easy reforms with high outcomes go to zero.

3. We assume that opposition to reform is aggregate. That is to say, the opposition to [R]1,t will be p1. Then the opposition to [R]2,t2 will be p1+p2. (Figure 4; dotted circle comparing dotted lines)

4. The effect of a reform [R]i,ti will have a negative term to denote the time where implementation is ongoing and opposition is in full effect. We will call this the "runway" term. There will be a positive term to denote the effects after t,r (time of results), where the effect of the reform starts taking place. We will assume the behavior of the positive effect will be an s-curve behavior (low effectiveness in the onset, inflection point, and stability).

5. Higher bandwidth allows you to achieve faster, more effective results on your reforms. (Figure 4, red line comparison)

6. Initial conditions have an inherent quality to them (namely, the previous administration's impact) but can alter with preplanning and early recruitment of people (A-players). Therefore, you can evenly treat a model even at t<0 for proper efforts in planning, recruitment, and coalition building. (figure 4, green line comparisons)

7. Coalition building is a net positive and it counteracts resistance pi.

8. All things being equal, the higher one of any of these qualities, the more rapid the natural decay of capacity to execute: dehumanization, soft thinking (demagogy, ideological zealotry), extremism, and polarization. (Figure 6)

9. All things being equal, a positive narrative will expand the time frame to execute while a negative one will shorten it.

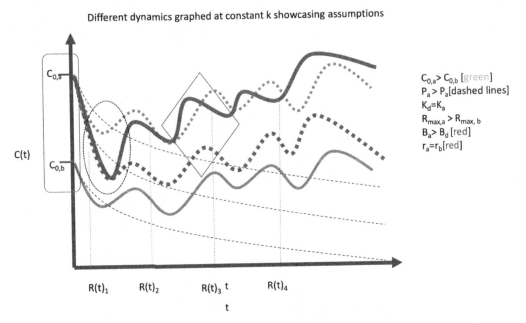

Figure 4. A variety of dynamics occurring with different shifts in parameters. Here we showcase the sensitivity of the model.

The variables:

[R]i,ti = Reform magnitude (i) on capacity to execute at time (t). = -[runway term]+[optimal reform output]

C= Capacity to Reform (as a percentage 0–100 percent).

t= Time

p= Opposition friction/resistance

Bandwidth to execute = f(people, tech, systems, inherent initial conditions) ~ (tr-ti)/[R]i, where tr is the time where the reform yields results and ti the moment when the reform (R)i starts. Please note the function f(people, tech, systems, inherent initial conditions) is not developed at this stage, rather we will use the difference between inception and time of results over the magnitude of the reform as a proxy for this value.

[R]i,ti = -[runway term]+[optimal reform output] = -[(tr-ti)*(1+ SUM[pi])] + Rmax(ti, tr, trmax)

Co= Capacity to Reform initial conditions at t=0.

After building this, I called my friend Dr. Tomas de Camino—a scientist, musician, and expert in biological mathematics and dynamics.

I pulled out another napkin. He said, "There is something here. I have yet to have seen these dynamics modeled. Let's take a look." Unlike my team when I wrote out the healthcare plan in a napkin, here we had a high level of energy and discussion.

"To model reform capacity, we use a dynamic model to simulate reform capacity over time as a function of executing reforms under different levels of opposition, or 'friction,' as you have stated and the other parameters you mention. Some of them can even be consolidated," he said.

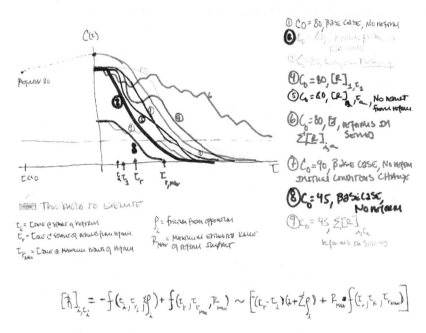

Figure 5. Napkin containing some of the original behaviors with the factors we have described in this book.

After a lot of math, I could land the plane. How did we model the factors toward the reforming landscape?

$$\frac{dC(t)}{dt} = [(w + \mathbf{r}(t))C(t) - wm](1 - C(t))$$

This mathematical model seeks to describe the change in reform capacity over time. As previously mentioned, the capacity for reform tends to decline over time, which is represented in the equation by a negative w. Reforms are denoted by r, which is the rate at which reforms occur and are applied over time. The multiplying term is simply to express the change in reforms as a value between 0 and 1, which cannot exceed a reform capacity of 1, the maximum capacity for reform.

First, let's reexamine the culprits we have discussed throughout the book: Magnitude of reform (chapter 13), time of execution (rate of reform, chapter 11), bandwidth (chapter 14), resistance to reform (chapter 12), and inherent conditions to the system that may provide an underlying effect on reform (chapters 6–10).

With this in mind, we aim to discover the behavior of each reform and their overall impact to future reform possibilities. We call the last factor C(t); probability of reforming.

The first observation: Time is an enemy of reform. To model this, we assume the probability of reform will decrease. There, of course, are different variations here. The graph below shows four different scenarios (Figure 6).

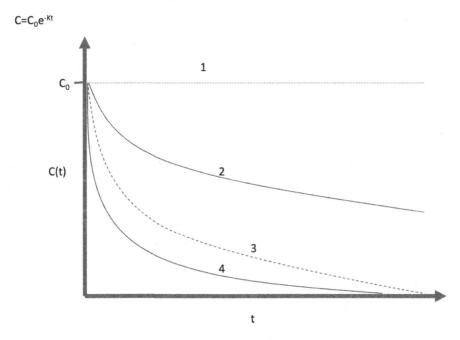

Figure 6. The effect of time on probability of reforming. The figure showcases four examples. The quicker the dip, the more factors affecting the environment and prompting less receptivity to reform and executive changes.

Case 1 is an extreme case where time has no effect on the probability of reforming. We venture to define this as a scenario where there is an autocratic dictator with no resistance to his will. Case 4 is one where the social conditions established in part two and three of this book crater the tolerance of society, and the decline is very sensitive to time or a system where one branch of government is at odds with the other, a severe lack of mobility on issues to reform. Think of a country like Peru, where dehumanization and polarization have been at high levels, and where the legislative body operates in complete odds to the executive.

This is a baseline for the *probability* of reforming.

A second consideration would be the initial conditions. It is not the same thing to propose and execute a reform in a country or jurisdiction that is prone to allow executive action versus one that does not. All other factors staying constant, higher initial conditions buy the reformer a runway to execute and a higher tolerance to resistance. We need to evaluate those initial conditions (Figure 2).

A third factor is the reform itself. And what effects does starting a reform in a particular moment in time have? Based on what we have constructed here, we know:

Reforms effects are *negative in relation* to p (resistance), time, and k (inherent conditions). the bigger these two are, the harder it is to reform. That is, the more resistance to reform, the more toxic the environment, and the more systematically permissive obstructive paths, the harder it will be to reform.

Reform effects are *positive in relation* to rate of reform, magnitude of reform, the rate of reforming, and the bandwidth. The more impacting the complete executed result of a reform is, the better for future prospects of reforms. The faster you can execute the reform, the quicker you can move on to other reforms and hit your maximum results. The better your bandwidth, the more reforms you can actually do.

Following the model, we can see an added reform scenario and the potential effect it could have.

Our model can now see the dynamic effects of reforms added as a function of time and their effects on the *capacity to reform*. For now, we will assume the ultimate outcome of a reform will be positive although we know this is not the case in reality. Figure 3 shows how the initial implementation phase of the reform brings with it challenges and obstacles. A good example was the labor reform discussed in the sequence chapter (19). Here, the negative effects of opposition resistance, the runway to get results, and the inherent expectations of inertia and inaction bombarded me. After the unemployment numbers started going to historic lows, this provided a bump of trust or credibility, allowing other reforms to have a higher chance of execution (Figure 7).

Yet the reality is there will be several reforms with different dynamics. For example, my tax reform had a relatively quick runway, as people felt the money in their pockets in short order in the form of sales tax and income tax. Education and energy reform, on the other hand... those take years. I was never able to see or lead the results of these two reforms. Yet others don't work and have a negative outcome. Figure 8 mimics an example of a sequence of four reforms versus just one reform and zero (Figure 8).

But let's go back to figure 6. Notice how a system with absolute power from the leader has no inherent conditions (outside of the reform itself). The implications are quantitative and qualitative. The leader on the extreme case of absolute power, does not have to worry about the moment of implementation.

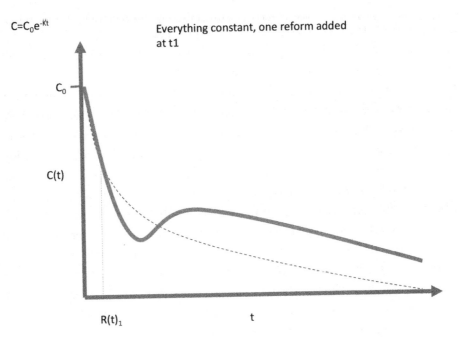

Figure 7. The dynamics of a system after the implementation of one reform.

She only needs to concern herself with actions that will enable the reform to move forward. The one on slope number 4, knows her time is limited, so she needs to act fast and effectively.

But is that enough?

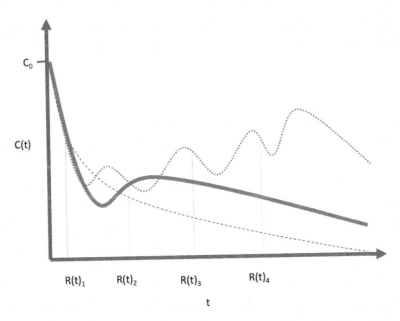

Figure 8. Dynamics of several reforms and the effect on the capacity to reform. Each reform alters the natural tendency for reforms to execute.

Implications on Autocratic versus Democratic Regimes

Let's look at three countries we have explored in this book. Take, Singapore, the United States, and Peru. What would their ease of doing reforms be?

I would argue that Singapore ranks easiest among the three for implementing reforms. The city-state operates under a parliamentary republic system, where the People's Action Party (PAP) has been in power since independence in 1965. This political stability, coupled with a high degree of control over the legislative process, allows the government to pass reforms relatively easily. Moreover, even though there are elections, things have not changed in close to sixty years. There is a low tolerance for dissidence and a high level of trust. Singapore's k-value is not zero, but it is very low.

What about The United States? Right now, it would likely be somewhere in the middle. The US is a federal presidential constitutional republic, where power divides the federal government and the states. We characterize the political system by checks and balances, which means that reforms often require negotiation and compromise between different branches of government and between different political parties. By design, within this framework, the more extreme the players get, the less capacity to achieve anything. Relative to say, Singapore, the process of passing reforms is more *complex* and *time-consuming*. As discussed, time is not on our side.

However, the US also has a long history of political stability, which can provide a supportive environment for reforms. Public opinion plays a significant role in the US, with reforms often subject to intense public debate and scrutiny. We have shown in previous chapters how trust in the government has decreased significantly in the past decades, providing even more challenges for reform.

Peru is the most difficult among the three for implementing reforms. The country operates under a unitary presidential republic, where the president serves as both the head of state and head of government. However, Peru has experienced periods of political instability, with frequent changes in government, which can disrupt the continuity and implementation of reforms. The balance of power within the Peruvian Congress can also affect the ease or difficulty of passing reforms. Public opinion in Peru can be volatile with large-scale protests and social movements sometimes leading to the reversal of proposed reforms. Words, narrative, dehumanization, extreme politics, and the oversimplification of complexities have all played a role in this volatile environment.

Therefore, a combination of factors, including the structure of the political system, the level of political stability, and the role of public opinion influence the ease of making reforms. Polarization, dehumanization, oversimplification, and the wrong narratives can affect all three (Figure 9).

What if we add China?

The Chinese government has a high degree of control over the country's political, economic, and social affairs. This means if the leadership decides to implement reforms, they can do so relatively quickly and efficiently due to the centralized nature of the government. However, the process is not without challenges. The government must balance maintaining stability and control with the need for reform and modernization. Recently, there have been more threats to the control, but it still remains very high. China also establishes a path forward with their five-year plan, which is the basis to undertake the actions and reforms.

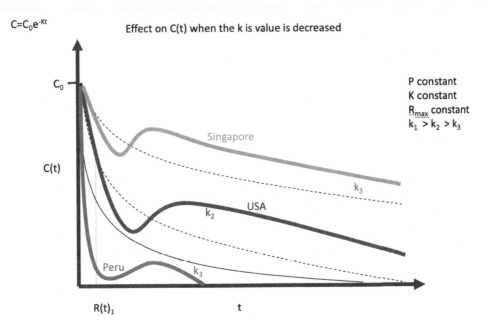

$$C = C_0 e^{-Kt}$$

Effect on C(t) when the k is value is decreased

P constant
K constant
R_{max} constant
$k_1 > k_2 > k_3$

C_0
$C(t)$

Singapore

k_3

USA

k_2

Peru

k_3

$R(t)_1$

t

Figure 9. Denotes a model with constant characteristics, except the value of k. The outcomes from implementing similar reforms are quite different as well as the expectations and possibilities for future reforms.

If we were to add China to the hypothetical ranking, it would likely rank high in terms of the ease of implementing reforms due to its centralized government structure. Higher than the US.

So, what does this mean for the future?

What we have seen in figure 9 is just one example with one reform in a period of time. It gets compounded as you add more and more reforms. The beneficial effects start adding up. The benefits of acting fast will accrue. As technology and societies evolve, governments will have to adapt. Those that don't will likely be in a weaker position than those who do. These rapid changes will only accelerate. The small gaps today can become monumental shifts in the future.

Two Interesting Proxy Values to Consider

Looking at the dynamics, two values can be insightful when assessing strategy. One points to getting the most reform possible in the time cycle, the other to finishing with the highest value of reform capacity (Figure 10).

1. **The Aggregate Value of Reform Potential**: You can estimate this by amassing the area under the curve and subtracting it from the baseline value of decline. While this value is really the aggregate value of reforming capacity over time, it is a good proxy to assess what the impact of the reform was. This means the higher the value under the curve, the higher the impact due the reform implemented.

2. **The Optimal Ending Cycle Value**: We are assuming these timeframes for reform are finite and can cycle. As such, the capacity to reform at the end of the term or timeframe represents a proxy for the present moment evaluation of the leader that got them to that point.

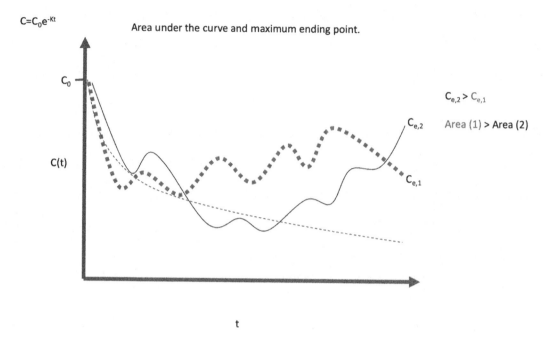

$$C = C_0 e^{-Kt}$$

Area under the curve and maximum ending point.

C_0

$C(t)$

$C_{e,2} > C_{e,1}$

Area (1) > Area (2)

$C_{e,2}$

$C_{e,1}$

t

Figure 10. Plot derived showcasing two scenarios. One with a higher cycle endpoint value (black) and the other with a higher aggregate value of reform potential (red).

Assuming the validity of these proxies, we can see the strategy a leader employs will be different depending on his objectives. For example, a leader might want to attempt the biggest impact of reform, even if at the end his perception is not good (red curve). Alternatively, a leader might want to time the optimal ending cycle value for maximization to enhance their probability of reelection (black curve). And of course, there are variations in between. Of course, these require deeper analysis, but I wanted to point them out to the reader for their evaluation.

Takeaways: Reengineering Democracy?

When asked what advice he would give policy makers in the face of economic uncertainty, former head of the Fed Larry Summers replied, "Arithmetic is arithmetic." Using those same concepts, we can build a model to understand the flows, tendencies, and opportunities.

By no means do I claim this will be an exact science. By definition, a math model is a simplified representation of certain aspects of a real system. The aim is to capture the essence and be able to detect trends or make predictions.

Here, I compiled my own experiences with those of other people who have attempted to lead and reform to assess what factors would be critical to reforming. Based on those discussions, we established a framework by defining the capacity to execute and see how it would vary across time with de addenda of particularly defined reforms (their magnitude, time to execute, etc.).

Within this framework we are able to account for many of the observations that are spread out, and here is what we find:

- For most cases, the early stages of an administration present the highest capacity to execute.
- Reforming in strategic sequence is more effective than at random.
- There is a threshold where capacity to reform will diminish beyond repair.
- While you can't control for initial conditions, actions such as preparing, planning, and key stakeholder participation can enhance your outcomes.

And perhaps the most troubling of all:
- Holding all constants equal (and assuming correct intent), a totalitarian system is in a better place to execute than a democracy. This distinction becomes bigger as some of the observed factors that counteract reforms increase. Bandwidth starts decreasing, execution diminishing, rampant opposition evolving.

What can we do about it?

There is near-universal agreement that our system is not working well—in particular, that it is not delivering the results people want. This is troubling because most people value democracy for its fruits, not just its roots.

"Based on six high-quality surveys conducted in the last year and a half, support for democracy as the best form of government remains overwhelming and mostly stable across party lines. However, about one in five Americans have views that make them at least open to, if not outright supportive of, authoritarianism" (Galston and Kamarck 2022).

That keeps developing worse initial conditions for the following governments, and so on and so forth. What can we do about it?

A clear area of opportunity stares us in the face when observing the diminishing impact and participation of what we tend to call the *middle*. As this happens, it becomes easier to overcome some of the factors that have been affecting democracies through the rise of polarization.

Can we redefine this middle, not only to become a political force but—more importantly—to tackle all the glaring limitations that are inhibiting our capacity to execute and effectuate change?

PART VI

RADICAL MIDDLE

CHAPTER 21:

Reimagining Our Notions of the Middle

When things don't work, we need to pursue new ideas. This cartoon depicts the start of my administration. Understanding things were not working, I had to get to work. Is the same thing happening to our political system? (Bayon 2016).

Tony Robbins's words at the AC360 conference (2023) resonated deeply: "We're equal. Therefore, I treat people that way... We can have different points of view but still get along. It's insane and stupid to feel unsafe because someone has a different opinion. Our kids are learning that bullshit."

This intolerance is a disconcerting force in the US and other democracies, leading to mediocre progress or a complete standstill. The current political climate, with its extreme polarization, prompted me to delve deeper into the dynamics hindering reform and action.

One culprit? We have segmented society into three broad identity clusters: the left, the right, and the middle. The left and right are drifting further apart, leading to:

1. More extreme discourse gaining media attention (Padgett, Dunaway, and Darr 2019).
2. An expanding middle, as traditional left and right members feel alienated or expelled from their groups.

The extremes demand complete adherence to their identity characteristics, leaving people with two choices: conform to the extremes or join the undefined middle.

The perception of the political middle, the largest group, is indecisive and lacking clear values or priorities. This perception, whether accurate or not, has become the reality.

Jake Dunagan, director of the governance futures lab, emphasized, "We don't need to compromise to the least common denominator. Splitting the difference between extremes often fails to solve problems. It is a mistake to think a rational strategy would be to just split the difference between two extreme positions in the hopes of finding some acceptable middle ground. Most often that does not solve the problem."

Nor does it inspire folks. But is this truly what 84 percent of the people are? Or are they just stuck in a sort of limbo space with no binding characteristics? This predicament definitely benefits the extreme agents. "But there is also an opportunity," Dunagan tells me. "There's also a sense of a *shared space* and a kind of a kind of rational middle in that sense for the future."

A kind of rational middle. That's a good place to start.

Irshad Manji talks about this type of space: "You can stand your ground and seek common ground simultaneously. It's about expressing your beliefs while creating space for others to do the same. To be heard, you must first be willing to listen" (2020).

This idea of a *shared space* is a key concept—a place where dialogue can happen. From that dialogue, the environment created is one more permissive to develop, innovate, and to build. The current environment seems to be going in the opposite direction.

Governor Eric Greitens recalls a story that illustrates the nature of this space:

"One of the people I worked with most effectively was a black, Democratic antipolice representative from St. Louis, Missouri, named Bruce Frank. I was obviously a pro-police Republican governor. And the reason I loved working with Bruce was everything that came out of his mouth was true. He believed what he was saying. Of course, we had times when we were having meetings, and Bruce was standing up screaming at me a few feet across. I always believed if I'd grown up the way Bruce Franks had—having lost many friends—I would probably believe what Bruce believes, and that we can learn from each other."

Learn from each other. What a powerful concept. I asked him what the requirements were to participate in this space?

"You must have the humility to believe other people have something to offer. You must have the curiosity and interest in what they learned from their life experience. You must have the care for other human beings that motivates you to do that."

This *space* is getting smaller and smaller. Consider what happens if this space disappears. Could we get anything meaningful done as a people?

In these short words, we identified a few culprits to the current toxic environment. So how can we begin to organize these observations and place them in a logical structure to provide an alternative for a wide-ranging group of citizens?

An Example Close to Home

Many viewed me as a centrist, but that label doesn't quite capture my approach. I wasn't seeking the lowest common denominator, nor was I perceived as lacking strong positions on issues. On the contrary.

Achieving tangible results by gauging the initial conditions and idiosyncrasies grounded my actions. This approach led some to brand me as an extreme fiscal conservative, given my actions like slashing the budget by more than 20 percent, downsizing government, restructuring debt, and reforming. However, others saw me as a social liberal, evidenced by my veto of a restrictive abortion bill and a guns bill, prohibition of conversion therapies, and healthcare reforms.

My decisions did not root in a belief of knowing all the answers. I based them on comprehensive planning and research, an understanding of best practices, and collaborative discussions with our citizens. It was a decision-making framework designed to give our island the best chance of success.

Were some of my decisions mistaken? Absolutely.

But in those instances, I relied on a rational process and self-evaluation to correct the course. Self-evaluation thrives when there's *space* for it.

However, today's political landscape often lacks this nuance. You're either left or right, with judgments made based on the viewer's perspective, often without regard for evidence or results.

And if you don't fit neatly into these categories? You're in the middle, making you a prime target for attacks from both extremes. This dynamic is peculiar. While the extremes engage in mutual attacks, they remain largely impervious to each other's rhetoric.

Former Congressman Tom Davis highlighted a crucial point: "While political leaders fear compromise and cater to their bases, they need to understand that failure to produce results threatens the whole system" (2011). This lack of space for producing results sets us all up for failure.

Despite the high stakes, this polarization doesn't seem to shift the needle. Instead, it has led to more polarized political figures than ever (Theriault 2008). Why? Because of pragmatism. Statements from one side are often predetermined as falsehoods by the other, even before they're fully articulated.

The end result? Extreme politicians maintain their base, and their extreme base continually support them, regardless of outcomes. This dynamic allows them to further divide consensus and remain electorally successful.

But what about those striving for reform, rationality, and dialogue across differing views to achieve results?

The focus shouldn't be on moving left or right, but on moving forward.

"The extremes and the extreme left in my party opposed me in the elections and were a major block in forcing me to resign," recalled Governor Cuomo in our interview.

If the majority remains silent, extremism will dominate, halting progress.

How do we overcome this daunting challenge?

Breaking the Cycle: Boricua Ahora Es!

"I want you to meet a friend," José Elias Torres Montalvo (may he rest in peace) told me after I had an interview with him. He is what I believe to be one of the last great professional journalists on the island. In fact, prior to his passing, we were discussing writing a book together. José Elias and I had just finished our conversation on his old-school radio station. The scenery was very different from the modern, big stage setup of the larger island-wide radio stations. This was in Ponce in the south part of the island. The room was small and cold with big 1970s equipment everywhere. The feeling was more like being at a barber shop. Whether intentional or not, it gave the sense that the content of the discussion was far more important than the visual output (Figure 1).

On that day I spoke about an idea I had. In essence, I wanted to bring together people who wanted independence for Puerto Rico, free association *and* statehood.

Plenty of skepticism met the idea. Perhaps even total dismissal. As I have illustrated before, these three sides have always been at odds with one another. Many would say they have been on opposite sides of the spectrum.

Indeed, that was the perception, which, of course, became a reality. And with that came the slander and dehumanization of groups that just couldn't stand each other... or who learned to believe so.

As someone who strongly identified with the statehood movement, I was hitting roadblocks to get people behind this concept. *Why are independence supporters and statehooders fighting with each other instead of fighting together against the colonial regime?* I wondered.

Figure 1. Picture taken during an interview with Jose Elias Torres Montalvo (Photo Credit: Beatriz Areizaga).

This was in the face of a new proposed plebiscite where the people of Puerto Rico would be able to choose if they wanted to continue as a colonial territory of the US or not. My position was to create a coalition that would give us an opportunity to have a clear result as opposed to the ambiguous ones we had gotten in the past.

It hit a chord with José Elias. I could see it in his eyes. He understood what I was proposing and had a much deeper understanding than I did at that time of the implications.

You see, José Elias was an unapologetic supporter of the island's independence. Such had been the case that he could write an interview book of one of the most notable figures in the armed independent movement—Filiberto Ojeda (Torres 2006). However, he also had the breadth of perspective to do the same with my father, quite possibly the biggest statehood figure of our modern times.

After the interview, he reached into his scrawny bag and handed me two books: *Nacionalismo Revolucionario Puertorriqueño, 1956–2005: La Lucha Armada, Intelectuales y Prisioneros Políticos y de Guerra* and *A Plena Voz: Nuestra Resistencia 2005 2010*, both by Dr. Michael González Cruz.

"He is a friend. I want you to meet him. I think he will find what you are proposing compelling." Compelling? A man who wrote about the armed fight to attain independence? Hardly… Now *I* was skeptical. Funny how the tables quickly turned. He challenged my own view and raised the ante.

Somewhat unsure, I accepted—if only because of the respect I had for José Elias.

A few days later, I met Dr. Michael González Cruz at the entrance of that same radio station. He was the very image of an academic intellectual. I was nervous, but that feeling quickly subsided. His demeanor struck me. He was soft spoken but very clear in his beliefs, very respectful nonetheless. Not at all what I expected.

"Ricardo," he said. "I think what you are proposing is very interesting. And it would not be the first time." He then went to rattle off stories about the *actual history* of collaboration between the father of statehood for Puerto Rico (Dr. Celso Barbosa) and Eugenio María de Hostos, a notable hero of Puerto Rican history—and supporter of the independence movement.

Dr. González Cruz recalls, "We talked about the background of our movements, and we highlighted our commonality to the model of the League of Patriots founded by Eugenio María de Hostos. Together with the annexationists Roberto H. Todd and Julio Antonio Henna, he advocated for a plebiscite and for a decolonizing education for Puerto Rico.

League of Patriots proposed to President McKinley in 1899, a plebiscite enabling the people of Puerto Rico to choose between being a Federated State of the North American Union or an independent Republic to put an end to the military regime arguing the young North American nation violated its Democratic and Republican principles."

After listening to him, I asked, "So… are you in?"

"I'm in," he said.

That moment, and some creativity on the part of my wife-to-be Beatriz (she conceptualized the name), was the birth of the Movement *Boricua Ahora Es*.

Boricua translates to—It's time!

And time it was to let go of an old way of looking at things and forge a new path.

Different Is Better than Better

"Insanity is doing the same thing over and over and expecting different results."

—GENERALLY ATTRIBUTED TO ALBERT EINSTEIN

Our movement's foundation wasn't rooted in past alliances or impulsive political leanings. It stemmed from recognizing a profound flaw in how we discussed Puerto Rico's status. Despite clever discourse, progress was minimal or nonexistent.

Dr. González Cruz observed, "Independence supporters and statehooders locked into a fierce battle, overshadowing the real issue: The colonial territory, known as ELA. Boricua Ahora Es (BAE) aimed to change this dynamic."

This initiative faced significant resistance. Critics within my party accused me of siding with the enemy or even supporting independence. It was much worse for Dr. Michael González Cruz. Labeled a traitor by some, he remained undeterred, focusing on BAE's mission.

He explained, "At BAE, we united pro-independence supporters in an educational campaign against colonialism. Rubén *Berríos* had warned against diverting the independence fight to attack statehooders, calling it a colonialism-enabling distraction. BAE provided an inclusive platform, focusing on decolonization rather than ideological divides."

Our efforts began modestly, speaking to small groups across the island in universities, backyards, anywhere we could. Gradually, we gained support from diverse ideologies, including Joel Isaac and Luis Delgado, who supported free association.

Ivan Rivera, a proponent of free association, initially viewed the movement with skepticism. He recalled, "The buzz about people from all ideologies uniting was everywhere. I was skeptical, suspecting personal agendas, but my perspective changed after seeing the movement's genuine focus."

His skepticism shifted after discussions with Luis Delgado, who passionately advocated for BAE. Rivera noted, "Delgado's enthusiasm and the movement's inclusive nature, giving voice to leaders like him, convinced me of its significance. I could internalize what was important about the movement because it gave *space* and voice to people like Luis Delgado, selfless leaders who fought for the decolonization of Puerto Rico out of conviction and principles. BAE united people across decolonization methods, transcending personal agendas."

It-Gave-Space. Something special was brewing.

Hard at the Beginning... Worth It at the End

As we were putting together this movement, a poll came out on the plebiscite. It was a demoralizing blow.

At one point, polls had the support for the colonial territory at more than 60 percent. Later in March 2012, a survey by *El Nuevo Día* showed that 29 percent supported the no vote while 50 percent supported the yes vote. (*El Nuevo Día*, March 2012). What was worse was even within the Statehood party, 32 percent wanted to retain the current colonial status (Figure 2).

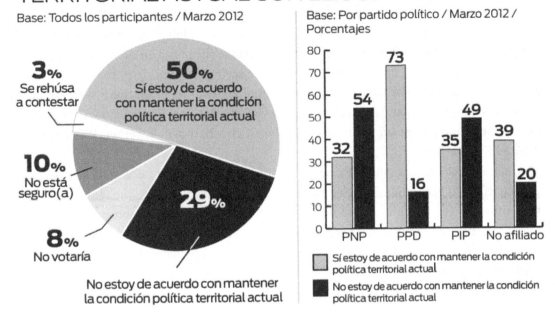

MANTENER O NO LA CONDICIÓN POLÍTICA TERRITORIAL ACTUAL CON EE.UU.

Base: Todos los participantes / Marzo 2012

3% Se rehúsa a contestar

50% Sí estoy de acuerdo con mantener la condición política territorial actual

10% No está seguro(a)

29%

8% No votaría

No estoy de acuerdo con mantener la condición política territorial actual

Base: Por partido político / Marzo 2012 / Porcentajes

	PNP	PPD	PIP	No afiliado
Sí estoy de acuerdo con mantener la condición política territorial actual	32	73	35	39
No estoy de acuerdo con mantener la condición política territorial actual	54	16	49	20

Sí estoy de acuerdo con mantener la condición política territorial actual

No estoy de acuerdo con mantener la condición política territorial actual

Figure 2. Public polls published in *El Nuevo Día*, showcasing the twenty-point-plus lead the acceptance of the colonial status had over its rejection (*El Nuevo Día* 2012).

This provoked many from the New Progressive Party (the party that supports statehood) to distance themselves from this question. "They did not want to catch a blow. A defeat. They were happy with Rosselló taking the fall," an insider from the 2012 campaign told me.

Perhaps with a combination of youthful exuberance and naivete… we moved forward. A critical moment was when I received an invitation to the New Progressive Party convention in 2012. The governor at the time called me. His numbers were not too good, and the projection was he'd lose to García Padilla by a sizable margin. On top of that, he had estranged a large number of the constituency from the party who had supported my father because he referred to my father as a cancer. (Burgos 2014).

"Ricardo," the governor said over the phone. "Can you give a talk on the plebiscite for our convention? It would be on the plebiscite and statehood."

"Yes," I said, somewhat surprised to receive his call. "Only one caveat. I am taking people from other parties to participate." There was a long pause.

"Let me think about it. We'll call you back," he said.

Mixed emotions engulfed me. On the one hand, I had an opportunity to communicate something very special and important on a big stage, where I felt the message would flow through. On the other, I had to look past the governor's past digressions still painfully tattooed in my heart.

A few days after, I received a several phone calls attempting to dissuade me from my ask. I did not budge.

A week later, "You can do it with whomever you want," the campaign aide told me, reluctantly.

So, we prepared a town hall type of event, where three of us: Dr. Michael González Cruz (Independent), Joel Isaac Diaz (Free Association) and me (Statehood), would talk about the focus at hand. Also accompanying us was **Ramón** Luis Rivera Padre—a long time mayor of Bayamón and an icon of the statehood movement. He would later become the president of my campaign.

The vibe was something different as if people were seeing or listening to something they never gave consideration. This sentiment started spreading like wildfire. From there, we went and gave talks together across the island. We celebrated the day of a national figure who was also the father of the statehood movement on the island—Dr. José Celso Barbosa—together. We scrapped, and we debated (Figure 3).

Alas, the idea of Boricua Ahora Es was a rousing success. I think because of the novelty of it, people started paying attention. Novelty alone would only carry us so far. The idea behind it would push us through. The thought we did not have to conform to the preestablished battle lines. We could have people who thought *passionately differently* come together for a greater cause.

That was all well and good, but we still had quite a massive challenge. How did we turn a twenty-point disadvantage into a victory?

Short answer: We had to sweat it out.

Figure 3. Picture with the three founding members of Boricua Ahora Es from different ideologies and political parties. Dr. Michael González Cruz (middle), Joel Isaac Díaz (red shirt), and me. In the background, is Luis Delgado (green shirt), a staunch supporter of free association, credited with collaborating in this effort (Photo Credit: Beatriz Areizaga).

Breaking preconceived notions is not an easy task. So we started going door to door with a model ballot and explaining little by little why this plebiscite was so important. We had to break down one by one the colonialists' arguments. We had to debunk the myth that voting for the territory was the only way to assure US citizenship. This was geared toward the statehood vote. We also had counter the belief that voting for the territory would assure our Puerto Rican heritage.

If you are confused. You are not alone.

This stems from the reality that the colonialist movement based it's branding on having the "best of both worlds." For more than fifty years they repeated this until it became a base assumption.

We needed to *break* that assumption. We needed to demonstrate that it was not only contradictory, but that it actually brought about the *worst* of both worlds. People started to open their eyes. While it was not a reform in policy, it was certainly a reform of mindset. Only that mindset shift would allow for us to commence the most critical reform of all on the island—Decolonization.

That's when the polls began to shift.

A Seismic shift

As the election approached, my task was to participate in the only debate on the issue of the plebiscite. I was thirty-three years old at the time. I would face an established leader from the territory supporting party. Hector Ferrer was a skilled debater and polemist. I was not. He had been president of his party and candidate to the highest offices.

My only advantage? I felt the highest conviction that I was armed with the correct arguments. I had been able to deliver them throughout the island in a grassroots effort. As long as I didn't let the noise and pageantry of the debate distract me, I could precisely convey the message.

The debate started, and Hector poked at me. But I was not having it.

When I was young, I became a tennis champion—not by virtue of my talent, but by the strength of my focus and mental toughness. I applied those same principles in the debate.

The message got across: Why get distracted and divided by the colonialists if we have this single opportunity to come together and defeat what we all oppose.

November 2012. The results came in. And while the pro-statehood incumbent governor lost a close race, the people of Puerto Rico rejected colonialism with 54 percent of the vote.

Dr. González Cruz recalls, "Boricua Ahora Es publicly promoted #5101, that is, statehood or independence and for a record we mobilized 910,970 citizens who voted *no* to the territorial status of the commonwealth. From that victory we began to take the results to various educational forums, the US Congress and the United Nations Organization."

We achieved a new milestone and gained a new perspective. And the rest is history.

A Parallel to the Extreme Control over the Middle

The current political landscape bears striking similarities to the situation with colonialists in 2012 and earlier. I also see parallels between what we term the "middle" and the movements in Puerto Rico that sought change from the status quo. Here are a few shared characteristics:

1. A smaller group often controls the narrative of a larger constituency.
2. This narrative gains traction because it is built on false assumptions.
3. It relies on soft thinking and demagoguery, and it is driven by dehumanization.

I discussed these concerns with Yascha Mounk, professor of the Practice of International Affairs and author of *The People vs. Democracy*, particularly about the extremes' control and the resulting impediment to collaboration. His response was enlightening:

"All of that is very, very concerning. So, what can we do about this polarization? One is for moderates to speak up and get off your high horse. I know for most people it is really scary to enter the fray." His words were like a bucket of cold iced water—powerful and awakening.

Research supports Mounk's claim. It suggests moderates are increasingly hesitant to engage in political discourse. "Although the costs of seeking office and the benefits of holding office might accrue equally to all types of candidates… models… suggest why more-extreme citizens may be more willing to bear the rising costs and falling benefits than more-moderate citizens" (Hall 2019).

With Puerto Rico's colonial territory issue, we achieved a breakthrough. Are there lessons here for the middle?

In Puerto Rico, we successfully rebranded a faulty narrative that had previously held us back. This required concerted effort, coalition building, and patience. It wasn't an overnight success and still demands ongoing proactive action.

Michael González often describes his efforts as a *revolution* or *radicalizing*. There's a potential parallel here in energizing the middle. Can we radicalize the middle?

While radical often equates with extremism, its true meaning is quite different. Being radical involves addressing the fundamental nature of something in a far-reaching or thorough manner.

Wouldn't it be a fundamental and far-reaching effort to unite all those who wish to move forward and add value to society through rational collaboration, thoughtfulness, and engagement?

I believe it is… but the question remains: How do we even begin?

Horseshoe Approach

Understanding the current political landscape is crucial. We find ourselves in a narrative dominated by extremes, who control the media despite being a minority. You can visualize the commonly perceived political spectrum as follows: (Figure 4)

In 2021, in the US, only about 16 percent of the population identified as progressive liberals or faith and flag conservatives. This suggests the middle encompasses a significant majority, ranging from 60–84 percent (Pew Research Center 2021). Moreover, major network and cable TV news outlets

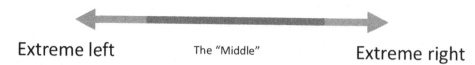

Extreme left   The "Middle"   Extreme right

Figure 4. Diagram illustrating the conventional gradient of the political spectrum.

have disproportionately featured members of Congress with the most extreme views, giving undue representation to partisans on both ends of the spectrum (Padgett, Dunaway, and Darr 2019).

This scenario raises a critical question: How does a small minority manage to suffocate or intimidate the vast majority?

"The extremes control a majority of the media and the message. They are powerful performers. This is what both parties have done professionally. Democrats should have learned from what the Tea Party did to the Republican Party a few years ago," reflected Governor Cuomo. The Tea Party's influence reshaped our understanding of intraparty dynamics. "We saw how the Tea Party forced the Republicans to marginalize themselves by catering to the extreme. Now, the Democratic Party faces a similar challenge with its far-left faction. They're socialists. But one cannot govern as a socialist in a capitalist nation."

Both sides employ similar tactics: pushing, intimidating, dehumanizing, using demagoguery, and bullying.

They weaponize identity, and as this identity narrows, ironically, it diminishes the diversity that many of these extreme groups claim to champion.

Extremes thrive on simplistic rhetoric, which helps them navigate complex issues. They wield words as weapons, dehumanize opponents with ease, and often masquerade as something they are not. This aligns with the toxic environment we've identified, resistant to change and reform.

How do we tackle this?

The Radical Middle

Professor Yascha Mounk's response to my question about fostering a new middle ground was insightful: "We need to get along and not live in fear of a loud minority who denounce each other or engage in intimidation." He's right, but the challenge is how to unite and stand up against this.

The middle, as it currently stands, needs a complete overhaul. It's reminiscent of Puerto Rico's Statehooders versus Independents narrative with the middle trapped in ambiguity. The colonialists, though fewer and with a weaker proposition, survived by diverting their opposition's focus. Similarly, vocal minorities at the extremes dominate today's political landscape, leaving the majority in a vaguely defined middle, resulting in inaction.

The middle is a mix of diverse views, lacking cohesion, clear messaging, and leadership. But there's a way out of this cycle.

First, we must define the extremes. They are more alike than different, driven by control, dogmatism, and a belief in their sole ownership of truth. They refuse dialogue, dehumanize opponents, and oversimplify complex issues.

Both extremes, regardless of left or right, exhibit similar behaviors: dogmatic, unclear, uncompromising, emotionally driven, power-hungry, and ideologically rigid. They have a symbiotic relationship, each feeding off the other, opposing the majority who don't adhere to their rigid views.

Instead of a disjointed middle, we need a group characterized by rationality, clarity, dialogue, fact-driven approaches, and innovative thinking. This group, which I'd term *rational* or *civilized*,

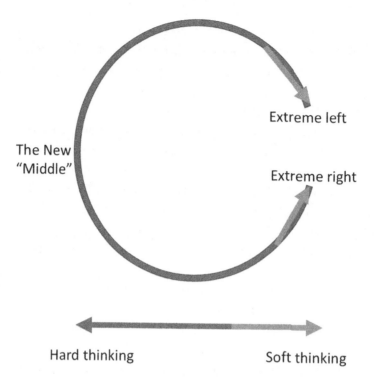

The New "Middle"

Extreme left

Extreme right

Hard thinking   Soft thinking

Figure 5. Proposed horseshoe approach to political counterparts, graded on a hard-thinking scale.

truly opposes the extremes, embodying reason and humanity. Not everyone in the middle fits this description, but hopefully most do. The extreme right and left, contrary to popular belief, represent the same disruptive force (Figure 5).

This concept mirrors our approach with Boricua Ahora Es, where we recognized that independence and statehood, despite their differences, perpetuated colonial status by opposing each other. To overcome colonialism, we needed unity.

Why can't we apply this understanding to the far left and right, merging them as polarized demagogues, and reshape conventional wisdom about political opposition?

They are the same.

On the other end of the spectrum, let us look at all of those who *don't* feel compelled to identity by intimidation and who want to look for ways to improve, even if it requires debate and collaboration. Those who look at the extremes and *know* what the vast majority has expressed in countless polls: Things will not end right if we let polarized leadership take hold.

In a way, this is what José Elias taught me. By many accounts, José was someone that people would generally associate with "extreme factions," but he was actually one of the most reasonable among us. He looked for ways to connect. To find common ground. To improve and dive deep into how we could do it.

A few years ago, José Elias passed away (Munoz 2021). Here is what I had to say about him at that point:

"A great journalist, a great human being. Always prepared, always with questions of thematic depth. He continually worked to perfect his craft and lived with a passion to teach what he knew to a next generation. His motivation was a genuine curiosity to know the truth and understand his interlocutor. For this reason, he could connect with figures as different as Filiberto Ojeda and Pedro Rosselló. I say goodbye and celebrate the life of a friend who thought very differently from me on multiple issues, but where respect and cordiality always prevailed. After all, more unites us than divides us."

I hope we can all learn from his example and understand where the true divide is.

On the one side, the extremes. On the other the rest of civilized society. One who pursues progress through rationalization, innovation, and collaboration. It is the opposite to extremism, yet it is a radical idea at its core.

A new radical middle.

The writing is on the wall. But are we hearing the signals?

CHAPTER 22:

The Writing Is on the Wall

A few weeks before I resigned, it was hard to fathom. The economy was moving in the right direction, polls had me winning by a landslide. As it turned out, I missed some very powerful signals. Missing out on these can be catastrophic. The writing was on the wall. I just could not read it (Bayon 2019).

"Diana, this makes no sense," I told my pollster after I compared the public polls, my internal polls—which all had me winning by a landslide—and the qualitative focus groups, which were very negative.

"How do we make sense out of the polls against the focus groups?"

"These are signals," said Diana.

And signals they were.

At the time I did not get it. You see, in May, 2019 the main newspaper's traditional *year-and-a-half-prior-to-the-election* poll came out. For some context, every incumbent in the past twenty years was losing by double digits by this juncture. In Puerto Rico, it is a rarity the incumbent gets reelected, at least in this millennia.

Yet, the headline read "Rosselló Has Little Electoral Competition." Pitted against six opposition hopefuls, I was leading all the ones that had declared by 15–20 percent points. "This was something unexpected and unseen in decades. Amid the fiscal and economic crisis, the hurricane, Rosselló was leading the polls," analyst Luis Davila Colon stated on one of his radio programs.

The quality-of-life perception more than doubled as well. In 2016, only 17 percent thought quality of life was good or great. By 2018 that increased to 39 percent (Cortes Chico 2018).

A month later, in June, we performed our internal polls. This time, I also asked for a *qualitative study*. They both came in. To my surprise, they seemed… *contradictory*. The quantitative poll showed almost the same results as those published in the newspaper. A few of those snapshots below (Figure 1).

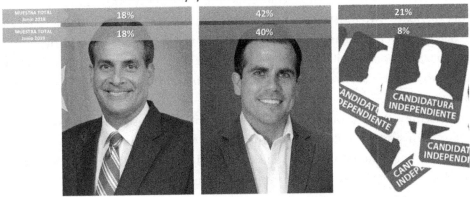

Candidato que escogería si las elecciones para la gobernación fueron hoy y los candidatos fueran…

Figure 1. Internal polls demonstrating significant leads over my closest competitors in the race for governor (Internal Polls 2019).

In essence, I was ahead by about twenty points from my closest competitors. The polls showed other interesting bits of insight. First, the poll evaluated my *qualities* (Figure 2):

Briefly, the strongest quality people saw in me was my work ethic. I had a delta of 42 percent. Second, they saw me as smart or intelligent (a delta of 41 percent). The third quality, "He worked well during the hurricane," had a positive delta of 24 percent. The next couple of positive deltas showcased that I was innovative (14 percent), understood the problems of the people (14 percent), and was honest (12 percent). We'll get back to the *honest* piece later.

I thought these were all very good indicators. Comparing those numbers with my predecessors, they had all negative perceptions in most of these areas. The attrition and friction of governing affected them much more than they did me… or so it appeared.

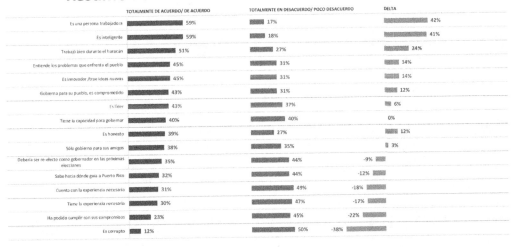

Resumen cualidades: Ricardo Rosselló – Junio 2019

	TOTALMENTE DE ACUERDO/ DE ACUERDO	TOTALMENTE EN DESACUERDO/ POCO DESACUERDO	DELTA
Es una persona trabajadora	59%	17%	42%
Es inteligente	59%	18%	41%
Trabajó bien durante el huracán	51%	27%	24%
Entiende los problemas que enfrenta el pueblo	45%	31%	14%
Es innovador /trae ideas nuevas	45%	31%	14%
Gobierna para su pueblo, es comprometido	43%	31%	12%
Es líder	43%	37%	6%
Tiene la capacidad para gobernar	40%	40%	0%
Es honesto	39%	27%	12%
Sólo gobierna para sus amigos	38%	35%	3%
Debería ser re-electo como gobernador en las próximas elecciones	35%	44%	-9%
Sabe hacia dónde guía a Puerto Rico	32%	44%	-12%
Cuenta con la experiencia necesaria	31%	49%	-18%
Tiene la experiencia necesaria	30%	47%	-17%
Ha podido cumplir con sus compromisos	23%	45%	-22%
Es corrupto	12%	50%	-38%

Figure 2. Summary of qualities those polled saw in me (direct answers) on June 2019 (source: Internal Poll).

From the negative deltas, we could see the most negative areas were: knows where he is taking Puerto Rico (-12 percent), has been able to achieve his promises (-23 percent), and a combined challenge to my lack of experience (two questions, -18 percent and -17 percent). The final one was not surprising. Experience had always been a handicap for me. Most of my opponents utilized their resources to showcase my *inexperience*. In spite of having addressed a fiscal calamity, having economic growth, and handling two mayor disasters, this tag still stuck—something to think about when discussing branding and narrative setting.

Not having achieved my promises was something of a surprise. We were actually ahead of schedule with reforms implemented. Several third-party entities denoted that we did more reform in those two years than the previous decade combined. The problem was the perception these reforms had. I was losing the battle of *narrative* by a landslide, and it was getting personal. This should have been a clear signal.

Check out the negative deltas I had on these specific issues (Figure 3):

Energy: -18 percent delta. This after we passed two energy reform bills, many of which were hailed as leading initiatives at the national level (Ellsmoor 2019). Yet the narrative had evolved around the blackouts and the time without energy after the Hurricane.

Economy and employment I had a delta of -22 percent. What? I was really losing the narrative battle. This was even more surprising as we had just had nine months in a row where we charted the lowest levels of unemployment in the history of Puerto Rico. That year, we also had the first year of meaningful economic growth in fifteen years. But labor reform and a couple of failed efforts with other initiatives provoked this type of perception.

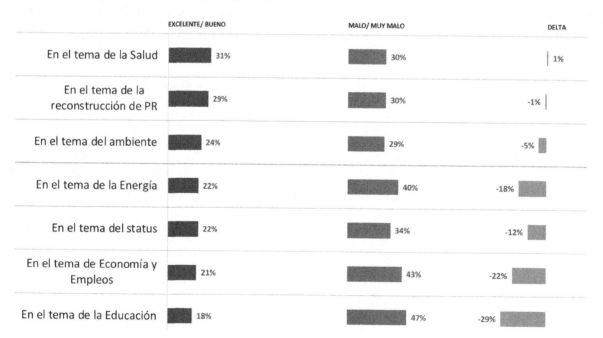

Figure 3. Shows negative deltas on certain topics (Source: Internal Poll).

Lastly, as expected, was education. The bet always was short-term pain for longer-term growth. This is an example of the challenges to a lengthy process of reform. Everyone wanted to change the education system, but the process was not pretty. I promised the inclusion of charter schools, a priority-based budget, transparency over finances, vouchers, baby bonds, computers for every kid… we delivered on all of that! Yet the changes had to include school closures, which are tough, even if the motivation was to give kids complete faculties. The student body population had diminished by 40 percent in fifteen years on the island, and we had schools virtually without faculty. Although I was cognizant this would happen, my expectation was people would see the results in the mid- to long-term. For now, I had to hold the fort. But it was not pretty: I had a -29 percent delta.

Even with these apparent incongruences, I thought overall things were looking good. On the surface, people had some good and bad opinions of me. The opposition was naturally rallying against it. But we were still prevailing electorally and functionally.

That is when the qualitative assessment (or focus groups) shook my view of these conclusions. This was the high-level summary from the qualitative assessment on how people felt on three top-of-mind issues:

Economy: weak and broken, in the opinion of the participants, shows no sign of to get better. With job instability that leads them to live in fear of losing their homes, assets, livelihood, and health.

Education: coupled with the lack of values that should be the basis of any society leads them to fear for the direction of the country in which many are still raising their children.

Security: The concern is not only at the country level. It is at the community, home. Lack of respect for life. No longer safe in home. It's a low point where citizens are afraid to leave their house.

This was frightful to say the least. Here are a couple of quotes from the participants:

"A carousel, sometimes up sometimes down."

"I don't have a job. I have to invent them— making cakes, empanadas, giving tutorials."

"Young people do not want to study. They don't see the value."

"Very bad, there is no security. Criminals can rob you at night, and if you don't let yourself be robbed, they'll kill you."

"It hasn't improved. I'm in the same situation. I hit the ground and I won't start."

These, my friends, were signals. I focused too much on the drivers. On the fundamentals. On all three of these items, we were doing *quantitatively better.* Here are just a few of those:

- Crime reduced to lowest levels in modern history (Estadisticas PR 2018)
- For two consecutive years, murders reduced by 7 percent, the third-lowest figure in the modern history of Puerto Rico (Policia de Puerto Rico 2019)
- 2,558 temporary teachers given tenure (Hernández Pérez 2019)
- Achieves the lowest unemployment rates in the history of Puerto Rico (The three years, 10.8, 9.2, 8.19 percent respectively) (PRFAA 2018)
- People return to PR: The first reported increase in people returning to Puerto Rico in decades at 100,000 (Cortes Chico 2019)
- The lowest level of poverty recorded in history at 43.1 percent (Redaccion SinComillas 2020)

- The debt lowers for the first time in the history of Puerto Rico (Bradford 2019)
- The largest (municipal) debt restructuring in the history of the United States occurs (Reuters Staff 2019)
- Collections reach record figure, *without* tax increase at $11,376 million (Hacienda 2019)

These were *quantitative realities.* Yet none of it mattered. None of it was seeping into the core of people. They still had concerns and fears that were mounting. The narratives chattered the results. These were strong signals, and I missed them.

Adding insult to injury, when asked who they would vote for, I received a whopping 15 percent! In some head to heads I was third place. Compare this to the two quantitative assessments that had me winning by landslides and way beyond the margin of error (Figure 4).

So what was going on here? Perhaps Dr. Lyn Jeffery, an expert in future foresight, can lend some insight into this. "One of the biggest traps is over-reliance on quant metrics: The more precise the

Candidato por el que votaría para la gobernación

Candidato por el que votaría para la gobernación

Figure 4. Percentages from the focus groups participants in terms of their votes for governor. Notice the enormous gap between these numbers and those from the quantitative polls (Source: Internal Polls).

numbers, the more precise they may seem. It makes it hard to think how things can be different. example When Donald Trump won, all the polls showed that he would lose easily to Hillary Clinton" (2022).

She says with the drivers of change, like the quantitative data I had, we can see them, understand them. Signals, on the other hand, are a different story. "[It] is harder to take on because most of us are trained to deal with things that are not anecdotal. This (signals) are the real vivid transformations in the world. As we train ourselves better, we start noticing new and unexpected experiences" (2022).

I did not have clear training to see them. I was focusing on the drivers too heavily and overlooking small micro trends that could develop into seismic changes. In the end, another evaluation criterion showed what people thought of me. In reading it, particularly, the weaknesses part was telling, almost ominous.

How do you view Ricardo Rosselló? Look at the chart below:

Positive characteristics:

A family man

Hard worker "Everyday he is doing something."

A fighter "He inherited a tough time."

He battles against the oversight board and his own party.

An innovator. "He has new proposals and ideas."

Some of the prevailing quotes.

"He's always out there".

"He's had a tough moment to govern—oversight board and the hurricane."

"People are betraying him."

"He did very well with the hurricane."

"He is very intelligent and has new ideas."

Weakness

Lack of maturity

Inexperienced

Does not show confidence in decisions

Stay away from the corrupt. He is not transparent.

His aides bring him down.

"He's a liar because he knows what is happening and says he does not know."

"He is worthless, lack of honesty."

"I don't believe him."

"It's only a matter of time before we get him out of La Fortaleza."

What a signal. This was barely over a month before I decided to resign. The environment was littered with a perception of *corruption* and *lack of honesty* because of a *lack of maturity* on my part (exhibited in the chat), where aides brought me down. I apologized but the prevailing sentiment was "I don't believe him."

All the negative attributes augmented more than ever. All positive ones disappeared in the chaotic environment that ensued. I became a caricature of my negative traits. And in the end, it was a matter of time before they got me out of La Fortaleza.

Broader Signals Out There

Ray Dalio, a billionaire investor, hedge fund manager, and author of *Principles: Life and Work* and *Principles for Dealing with the Changing World Order: Why Nations Succeed or Fail,* shared some profound insights at a YPO Edge event. "The most powerful empires in the world followed this cycle for more than five hundred years, and every time they did, it was a sign of the changing world order," he stated (Dalio 2022)

Dalio is adept at identifying what he terms *forces* and analyzing their impacts. He delves into the mechanics of significant changes, such as the unprecedented levels of debt production and monetization we're witnessing. "We have a level of debt we're producing and then monetizing. That debt and other central banks are buying money to monetize the debt in amounts that have never existed in our lifetimes before. So how does that work? What are the mechanics of that? And that is reverberating through the system, it changes, and we can go into what that looks like."(Dalio 2022).

Puerto Rico serves as a microcosm of these global reverberations. We had to overhaul local and federal frameworks, establish legal precedents for debt restructuring, and implement major fiscal cuts. These actions not only impacted Puerto Ricans but also sent shockwaves through the US municipal bond market and pension systems.

Imagine this occurring on the scale of the entire US?

Dalio further observed: "The second is internal conflicts within countries. We can see it particularly in the United States. We have the largest wealth gap differences, the largest values differences, and we're producing populism of the left and the right. Populism didn't exist earlier in our lifetimes. And a populist is an individual who will win at all costs for a side, it's one side against another. They won't resolve irreconcilable differences, and they'll have a clash." (Dalio 2022).

This notion of populism, emerging from both the left and the right, echoes the extremism we've been discussing. It's characterized by a divisive, win-at-all-costs mentality, fostering irreconcilable differences and clashes.

The Blinding Signal of Polarization

"The United States is increasingly and sharply polarizing politically."

—MIRON KAUFMAN

"Rapidly increasing political polarization threatens democracies around the world."

—GINSBERG

Polarization—one of the key factors we discussed in part 2—drove a wedge into our political conversation and seems to hamper any real possible progress. What's more, our political realities are reaching an absurd outcome because we have let polarization roam uncontrollably.

A pew research study showed that in 2020 both Biden and Trump supporters said the victory of the opponent would result in "lasting harm to the country." Specifically, 89 percent of Trump's and 90 percent of Biden's supporters said this.

This is nuts.

We found ourselves in a position where virtually nine out of ten of each of the leading candidates' supporters feel the *other* will *destroy* the country. This premise alone signals the lack of collaboration. It signals the higher hurdles toward reform as a byproduct of this enormous gap between sides.

And we seem to be talking about it a great deal but *doing* very little. Barack Obama said,

"We can accept a politics that breeds division, and conflict, and cynicism. We can tackle race only as spectacle — as we did in the O.J. trial — or in the wake of tragedy, as we did in the aftermath of Katrina, or as fodder for the nightly news. …

We can do that.

But if we do, I can tell you that in the next election, we'll be talking about some other distraction. And then another one. And then another one. And nothing will change." (Obama 2008)

His predecessor George W. Bush tackled the issue by stating, "Too often, we judge other groups by their worst examples while judging ourselves by our best intentions."(McGregor 2017).

What's worse is the problem is *growing* by leaps and bounds. This signal points to an inevitable conclusion—eventual standstills in the efforts to reform and the breakdown of any sort of functioning government.

Polarization is turning into more than a *signal*. It is the elephant in the room. We see it. We talk about it, but no one is doing anything meaningful to slow its growth. Is there a way to overturn this tendency? I believe Ray Dalio provides a hint.

Innovation and Adaptability

"And then, number five [of the forces], the most important over time is adaptability and innovativeness technologies. The capacity to invent and adapt and make solutions the way we did with the vaccinations, for example," Ray Dalio stated in his message to the YPO Crowd (2022).

The capacity to identify a problem at the edge of the precipice.

South Africa, particularly Cape Town, faced a severe water crisis in 2018, termed as "Day Zero," the day when the city's water supply would have completely run out. The crisis was a result of a prolonged drought, population growth, and an underprepared water infrastructure. The situation was so dire the government asked residents to consume a maximum of fifty liters of water per day and implemented measures such as banning car washes, swimming pools, and fountains.

However, the city managed to avert "Day Zero" through a combination of stringent water restrictions, public awareness campaigns, and infrastructural improvements. As the former mayor of Cape Town, Patricia de Lille, stated, We can no longer ask people to stop wasting water. We must force them," (BBC 2018).

Moreover, the crisis led to a shift in the mindset of the residents, who started treating water as a precious resource. As a result, water saving became a part of the daily routine for many households. Behavioral change became their strongest action against the drought.

Day Zero was a wakeup call, but it also demonstrated what we can accomplish if we set our minds to do it. If people can overcome the looming unsustainability of a future without water, why can't we do it to prevent the collapse of our society?

Brief Takeaways

1. Connecting invisible dots: Detecting signals when there is a notable discrepancy or misalignment between different types of data, such as public polls, internal polls, and qualitative feedback. It underscores the need to reconcile conflicting information and think deeply if there are any hidden signals.

2. Perception versus Reality (data): We focused on the importance of recognizing and addressing signals that indicate a gap between public perception and quantitative realities. We emphasize the potential consequences of ignoring negative public sentiment and concerns. I ignored some of these signals, much to my demise.

3. Rising Global Challenges: We need to recognize and act upon global signals and challenges. These include increasing debt levels and political polarization, which can have significant impacts if not detected and addressed promptly. Political polarization seems to be a clear-cut culprit of hazards that await in the future. It underscores the importance of tackling it before it becomes untenable.

Day Zero for Democracy

Signals are ever-present around us. They are pre-indicators of underlying realities. Some might be obvious. Others might not.

The toxic environment generating in many of our democracies is a signal we should all be paying attention too. Symptoms like demagoguery, polarization and dehumanization are telltale signs that things are heading in the wrong direction.

These factors all lead to decreased capacities to make change in the form of sustained and executable reforms. The sentiment that this is disastrous seems to be present, but the urgency to solve it is not. We appear stuck in a sort of no-man's-land where most of society feels pigeonholed into inaction while the extreme factions take hold.

What's it going to take for us not to only see the signals but also to take action upon them?

As governor, I was given signals and ignored them. And it was to my detriment.

Let's not make the same mistake as a society.

It is time for something *radical* to happen…

CHAPTER 23

Creating the Radical Middle

During the five-hundred-year storm that passed through the island, challenges abounded. After the storm, it was time to build, imagine, and create. It was time to roll up our sleeves. This illustration depicts me multitasking after the storm to get things under control and create something new. Same is true for the radical middle (Bayon 2017).

Let's delve into a proposed definition for the radical middle—a movement that fosters an open space, uniting individuals who may not align on all issues but share core values and a collective aspiration to solve problems.

This concept of the radical middle is not just about finding a middle ground; it's about creating a dynamic space where the vast majority of us can entertain diverse ideas and perspectives to turn them into meaningful action.

When I initiated Plan for Puerto Rico, it started as a simple idea. We recognized the primary issue in Puerto Rico's governance was a lack of clear direction, rigor, and execution. The question was, how could we address this root problem?

"We needed to have a set of core values and a roadmap," stated William Villafañe, who spearheaded the effort and later became my chief of staff. "This would be our key differentiator."

He was spot on. With this approach, we began by establishing core values for our movement, the foremost being inclusivity. The prevailing polarization had reached a point where dialogue, let alone consensus, was impossible across party lines. Our solution: to create an inclusive space where *anyone* could contribute meaningful proposals to enhance Puerto Rico.

But could we truly achieve such inclusivity in a highly charged environment?

In Ceiba, a northeastern town on the island, Santiago, a member of the Popular Democratic Party, stood up in one of our workshops and offered a small business proposal. The respect and attention he received were palpable. At the event's conclusion, he expressed, "I just want to thank you for letting my voice be heard, even if I am not from your party." This moment marked a shift. Attacks ceased, engagement flourished, dehumanization vanished, and complex discussions became possible.

Creating such a space opens endless possibilities.

Governor Greitens highlighted the importance of this space with an analogy: "Imagine an incredibly talented painter, capable of creating sublime works. Then you ask them to paint something beautiful on a greasy, broken hamburger wrapper. You're not giving them the space. Similarly, trying to have a meaningful conversation in the current political environment is like trying to paint on that greasy wrapper. There's no space for something compelling or intellectually interesting. The media is largely to blame for this."

Many, like Santiago, were seeking this space. Carlos Ruiz, a member of the pro-independence party, also participated, bringing forward proposals for cultural preservation and promotion.

"By being open to everyone, the platform allowed voices to be heard and facilitated tracking of executed work, allocating resources to comply with it—all in line with the plan," Carlos explained to me.

I appointed him as the director of the Institute for Puerto Rican Culture, a position he still holds.

"This approach led to transparency and established a coherent playbook for different sectors. It enabled holding the government and leaders accountable to the plan voted for by the constituents," he added.

Many embraced this new space while others hesitated, perceiving it as risky or superficial. Overcoming these obstacles requires time and patience, but the foundation for success is present.

It's crucial to note that *inclusivity* has become somewhat politicized. True inclusivity means welcoming anyone willing to participate, not just those who align with every belief you hold. Beware of false inclusivity, as it fosters the very environment we aim to avoid.

Made-up Minds

Governor Kasich, a Republican renowned for his centrist and problem-solving approach, shared a poignant story during a class I taught at George Mason University, which resonates deeply with our current discussion.

"We face significant violence in Ohio, not just in Cleveland but statewide, particularly affecting African Americans. The situation escalated tragically with the shooting and killing of fourteen-year-old Tamir Rice by police while he was holding a toy gun," Kasich recounted.

He continued, "The atmosphere was tense. I met with three or four African American women legislators, all Democrats, who proposed a comprehensive study to examine these issues in depth. I opted for immediate action instead. We formed a coalition to address these concerns directly, deliberately including diverse voices and avoiding those with rigid, activist mindsets."

This concept of a *made-up activist* epitomizes the culture of polarization. Such individuals offer quick, individualistic gains but lack substantive, long-term solutions. Their presence can derail constructive dialogue, and it's crucial to engage with those open to collaboration, not just those intent on dismantling the efforts of others.

Kasich elaborated, "We sought a broad spectrum of expertise, including law professors and law enforcement, to swiftly identify necessary actions. When asked when we would start, I said, 'Tomorrow.' The following day, we held a press conference, initiating this collaborative effort. John Born, a member of my cabinet and former head of the Highway Patrol, played a pivotal role. His rapport across various groups was instrumental. State Senator Nina Turner, initially one of the legislators seeking a study, also became a key figure. Despite her role as Bernie Sanders' campaign chair in Ohio, she worked effectively across party lines with Born to pursue our shared objectives."

Governor Kasich's approach highlights the importance of transcending party politics to address societal issues. Inclusivity, as demonstrated in this instance, is central to the philosophy of the *radical middle*. Bringing diverse groups together to tackle significant challenges is the first and most crucial step.

From Root Cause to Execution

In Plan for Puerto Rico, our *second* and *third* core values were to *understand the root causes* of the ails of Puerto Rico, *using science and evidence* to support our claims. In policy, a position is rarely unanimous. Doing research and learning from it makes that position much stronger. By doing so, we were able to articulate our positions more effectively and learn from mistakes. This framework makes it harder to resort to demagoguery or soft thinking.

Our last core value was a *commitment to execute*. By that we meant that anyone could put on a piece of paper ideas that might seem coherent. But can you actually get them done?

And so the Plan for Puerto Rico went on with a clear vision. Those core values allowed us to establish a timeline and a roadmap to success. We patiently worked on them for five years.

Year 1: Identify the root cause of the main problems on the island.

Year 2: Study best practices elsewhere to utilize to tackle those root cause problems.

Year 3: Develop a vision and engage citizens in the discussion.

Year 4: Have public hearings and reevaluate our position based on new information.

Year 5: Prepare an executive plan and prepare the legislation associated to execute from day one (Figure 1).

Can we apply these principles to the predicament of the lost middle? At the very least, with a clear vision, core values, and a roadmap, we can start giving the middle some much-needed direction.

Figure 1. Visual outline of the Plan for Puerto Rico set out in 2011.

The Flywheel Effect: Building Momentum in the Middle

Jim Collins, in his influential book *Good to Great: Why Some Companies Make the Leap and Others Don't*, introduces the concept of the flywheel, a powerful metaphor for the cumulative momentum organizations gain by consistently aligning actions with core principles and strengths. He asserts, "No matter how dramatic the end result, good-to-great transformations never happen in one fell swoop. In building a great company or social sector enterprise, there is no single defining action, no grand program, no one killer innovation, no solitary lucky break, no miracle moment. Rather, the process resembles relentlessly pushing a giant, heavy flywheel, turn upon turn, building momentum until a point of breakthrough, and beyond."(Collins 2001).

The parallels between the flywheel concept and the strategies we employed in the Plan for Puerto Rico struck me.

Collins contrasts the flywheel with its antithesis, the *doom loop*. This counterproductive cycle occurs when organizations frequently launch new, often flashy programs that fail to yield lasting results. They shift directions erratically, never gaining sustained momentum, ultimately succumbing to what Collins terms the doom loop (Collins 2001).

This scenario mirrors the challenges faced by centrist and alternative political groups within our current political landscape. Often, these groups become paralyzed by inertia or misdirect their efforts, failing to address issues effectively. To counter this, establishing and adhering to strong, consistent values is crucial for nurturing the growth and impact of these movements.

Crafting a Value Proposition for the Radical Middle

President Lincoln, in his final speech three days before his assassination, profoundly stated, "... We simply must begin with, and mold from, disorganized and discordant elements... that no exclusive, and inflexible plan can safely be prescribed as to details and collaterals... Important principles may, and must, be inflexible." These words align with our current endeavor to foster unity amid diversity.

The challenge we face is significant: bringing people together in an increasingly polarized environment. Yet unity demands a set of core values, a compass to guide us through the chaos. Without this, we risk disintegration.

This leads us to a critical question: Can we prevent the collapse of government under extreme ideologies? And if so, how?

A 2014 Pew study reveals a shocking dynamic: "Both the left and right ends of the spectrum, who together comprise about 20 percent of the public overall, have a greater impact on the political process than do those with more mixed ideological views" (Mitchell et al. 2014). It's perplexing that 20 percent can overshadow the voice of the 80 percent. This majority, not aligning with the extremes, is evidently seeking an alternative.

Herein lies a significant opportunity. Nature abhors a vacuum, and the radical middle could be the force to fill it. To establish this, we must counterbalance the extremes, which often resort to dogmatic and dehumanizing tactics.

We should ground our approach in reason, critical examination, and a commitment to problem-solving, steering clear of dehumanization.

Jeff Dungam from the ITFT suggests a nuanced approach: "For this to work, the middle can't just be 'compromise agents.' It needs to be more." Indeed, the "radical middle" should not merely be about compromise but about defining itself through values like common sense and a shared understanding of the rules.

Dungam adds, "The key is not defining it by its relation to other things, like the left or the right, but defining by what it is, like common sense, law, even things like agreement on the rules."

Ah! Common sense. Add that to our list of foundational values.

The radical middle might start with an agreement on the rules and adherence to them. It's a call to action for the majority to establish a foundation, preventing the extremes from dominating, as they currently do, despite being minorities.

How do we initiate this movement?

Answer: The creation of *common space* governed by shared *rules*.

This was the essence of the Plan for Puerto Rico, a platform welcoming diverse perspectives, focused on collaborative learning and progress. It was a space where left or right leanings were secondary to the collective pursuit of solutions.

Learning from Global Best Practices in Creating Common Spaces

The journey toward creating a common space for dialogue and progress need not start from scratch. We can learn valuable lessons from existing models, such as Singapore's successful initiative, "Our Singapore Conversation." (Swee Keat 2014).

Launched in 2012, this national initiative aimed to engage Singaporeans in shaping their country's future. It was a platform for citizens to express their views on critical issues like healthcare, education, housing, and employment. More than forty-seven thousand Singaporeans participated through dialogues, online forums, and surveys, contributing to a rich tapestry of perspectives.

The initiative's impact was tangible. The insights gained from citizens directly influenced policy changes, enhancing support for special needs students, and strengthening the social safety net for

Figure 2. A photo from my visit to the Singapore Centre for Strategic Futures, showcasing a presentation on Our Singapore Conversation.

low-income families. These policy shifts, informed by the people's voices, significantly improved many citizens' lives (Figure 2).

Former Prime Minister Lee Hsien Loong highlighted the initiative's success in fostering national identity and pride, demonstrating the government's commitment to citizen engagement in decision-making. Similarly, former Minister of National Development Khaw Boon Wan emphasized its role in promoting empathy and understanding, treating people as individuals with unique perspectives.

The core values identified through Our Singapore Conversation emerged from a year-long dialogue, encapsulating the diverse aspirations of Singaporeans:

- **Opportunities:** A desire for broader opportunities in education, career, and personal growth.
- **Purpose:** A call for a society driven by more than material success, seeking a deeper sense of purpose.
- **Assurance:** A need for more security in healthcare, housing, and employment.
- **Spirit:** An aspiration for a stronger community spirit, emphasizing inclusivity, empathy, and mutual respect.
- **Trust:** A requirement for enhanced trust between society's different segments, including between the government and its people.

This initiative stands as a testament to the power of collective dialogue in bridging diverse backgrounds and viewpoints.

As we envision the formation of a "radical middle," can we draw inspiration from Singapore's approach? Let's explore potential pillars for our own movement.

Proposed Core Values for the Radical Middle:

As Lincoln pointed out, "These need to be inflexible principles." Jim Collins bases most of his learnings on the need for core values. He states, "Core values and purpose, if properly conceived, remain fixed. Everything else—your practices, strategies, structures, systems, policies, and procedures—should be open for change" (2001).

Therefore, core values should (1) be timeless, (2) be discoverable, not set, (3) drive alignment and (4) be lived.

- o **Timeless**: Core values should be enduring and unchanging over time. They should serve as the foundational beliefs and guiding principles of an organization or individual, regardless of external changes or challenges. In a rapidly changing world, having timeless core values provides stability and direction. They act as a compass, guiding decisions and actions even when the external environment is uncertain or volatile. In the realm of governance, the principle of justice remains a timeless value, ensuring all citizens receive fair and equitable treatment regardless of changing political climates. Even as political ideologies shift, the pursuit of justice remains a constant guiding force in policy decisions. In Plan for Puerto Rico, we aimed to have real inclusion and critical thinking as two of our core values.

- o **Discovered, Not Set**: You should not arbitrarily choose or impose core values. Instead, you should discover them through introspection, reflection, and understanding the true essence of an organization or individual. Discovered values are more genuine and authentic. They resonate more deeply with members of the organization and members are more likely to embrace and uphold them. As an example, over the years, many democratic nations have discovered the value of transparency as a cornerstone of good governance, not because they imposed it but because history showed its importance in building trust. Policymakers didn't just decide on transparency. They recognized its significance through the consequences of its absence. Transparency was a big issue on the island with the finances. People complained. We unveiled the numbers.

- o **Drive Alignment**: Core values should serve as a *unifying force*, aligning the actions, decisions, and behaviors of all members of an organization or group. Think of the preamble of the Constitution and its emphasis on union. Misalignment drives confusion so faulty narratives and demagogues can flourish. When everyone in an organization aligns with the same set of values, it creates cohesion and unity. This alignment ensures that everyone is moving in the same direction, leading to more efficient and harmonious operations. In a diverse political landscape, the core value of public welfare drives alignment among various parties, ensuring the crafting of policies with the well-being of citizens at the forefront. Even with differing ideologies, when all parties prioritize public welfare, they can find common ground to collaborate on impactful legislation.

    ○   **Lived**: It's not enough to simply state or list core values. You must actively practice and embody them in daily actions and decisions. This action makes them real and tangible. It reinforces their importance and ensures they are not just empty words on paper. This can easily degrade into polarized demagoguery. When we live our values, they become ingrained in the culture and identity of the organization. As an example, a government that professes a commitment to environmental conservation must actively implement and uphold policies that protect natural resources and reduce pollution. This is why priorities are critically important. Merely stating a dedication to the environment in political campaigns is insufficient and favors the script of the *extremes*. The tangible actions and policies truly reflect a government's commitment.

Why is it important to hammer this down? Another Pew Research study in 2020 showed that "Roughly *eight-in-ten* registered voters in both camps said their differences with the other side were about core American Values" (Dimock and Wike 2020).

Clearly, we have some work to do. To create a radical middle, we have to establish those core values and principles that represent what the middle stands for.

Those principles aim to tackle the underlying problems we have seen throughout the book, and they will become the bedrock for these proposed solutions. Based on this, I drafted a set of core values that could represent the radical middle.

Starting Point

These are just a few suggested starting core values to evaluate. There are likely more and better, but these fit the bill by contrasting the polarized extremes' implicit core values.

1. **Treat People as People**: I asked Pamela Patenaude, former undersecretary of HUD why she helped us so much—even coming from a Republican administration to the aid of a Democratic governor. Her response: "Our different political affiliations never crossed my mind or influenced my actions in response to the hurricanes. Disaster survivors deserved the respect and access to available resources that any American impacted by a natural disaster should." Her quote embodies this core value. Recognize the inherent worth and dignity of every individual, regardless of their background, beliefs, or status. Engage with others with empathy, respect, and understanding. There is no space for destructive behavior. Contrast with polarized extreme that dehumanize individuals leading to dogma and steering away from unity.

2. **Open Space and Open Mind**: Foster environments that encourage free expression, dialogue, and exploration of diverse perspectives. Maintain a mindset that is receptive to new ideas and willing to challenge one's own beliefs. Even if we don't achieve agreement, respect should always win. Contrast to the polarized extreme that is a closed echo chamber where we only amplify one perspective and suppress and ridicule dissenting views.

3. **Embrace Complexity**: Understand multifaceted issues and challenges rarely have simple solutions. Approach problems with nuance, considering all angles and implications. Embrace the complexity

to communicate these and avoid demagoguery for the exclusive gain of power. Contrast to the polarized extreme where oversimplification of issues, promoting black-and-white thinking and ignoring the nuances and intricacies of challenges is the driving force.

4. **Think, Plan, Execute, Evaluate, Adjust, Repeat**: Adopt a systematic and iterative approach to problem-solving and decision-making, ensuring continuous improvement and adaptability. Let's regain our national talent for problem-solving. It starts with a proven framework. Compare to polarized extremes where there is rigid adherence to a single strategy without room for reflection, evaluation, or adaptation, leading to stagnation. This provokes folks to double down on mistakes, making a bad situation worse.

5. **Always Look to Innovate**: Innovation is happening at an exponential level across the globe. Let's embrace this reality and continuously seek new and better ways of doing things, challenge the status quo, and embrace change for the betterment of society. Adding foresight capabilities will help governments be better prepared and reduce the anxiety of an uncertain future. Compare to polarized extremes where there is an inherent resistance to change and clinging to outdated methods or traditions, even when they are no longer effective or relevant.

6. **Deep Connections to Further Effective Communication**: Build meaningful relationships based on trust and understanding, facilitating open dialogue and collaboration. Recognize the importance of emotional intelligence in communication. Apply thoughtful analogies and examples to communicate. Engage thoroughly with citizens to achieve results. Compare to polarized extremes that stand on superficial interactions and unquestioned bullet points that prioritize agenda over genuine connection, leading to miscommunication and mistrust.

I am not claiming these should be the final core values; these are just an example of what could start the process. Plenty of committed minds should work together to develop these values, and they should actively resist the four conditions producing a toxic environment: dehumanization, soft thinking, demagoguery, and polarization. All of these conditions breed distrust and immobilization and cause our k-value in our model to provoke a rapid decline in the probability of reform.

A Small-Scale Example [Delegation]

"Now what?"

I was just elected as a congressional delegate. A position I did not run for, nor aspire to have. It happened two years after I resigned as governor. One year removed from the exoneration (PR News Wire 2020). And two days after I actually thought being a write-in candidate might just happen.

It was a powerful mix of emotions. On the one hand, I felt honored and grateful voters felt so strongly about what I had done in the past that they decided to write my name in. On the other, it was not long ago I had left office under undesirable circumstances.

Soon thereafter, though, reason and logic started zipping in.

What now? What would I do as a shadow congressmember once I swore in?

In an odd twist of fate, this story does have relevance to our idea of crafting a radical middle.

Mindset and Tools

I quickly realized the delegation itself—in addition to having *no* political power—had no resources. There was a flaw in the bill creating the delegation. There was no support (administrative or otherwise), nor was there even any indication of compensation.

I took some time to myself to gather my thoughts. "I have it," I told Beatriz.

I moved quickly after and asked the other members of the elected shadow delegation for a meeting.

There, I proposed a *vision* and a *mission* for our delegation. What was a weakness in the bill, was a strength to give us flexibility to design *how* we would achieve our objective. As we have mentioned countless times, words matter. Language can be the key to creating the architecture for the future.

My proposal to them was as follows:

Vision: To achieve equality and a better quality of life for the US citizens living in Puerto Rico through statehood.

Mission: To apply *external pressure* on the Congress of the Unite States to provoke a mechanism that offers statehood for Puerto Rico in a binding way. In doing so, we will also create a national network that supports statehood and equality for all Puerto Ricans.

Create external pressure?

"Think about it," I told them. "Why do the same thing over again with little results? Moreover, in this scenario now with little to no resources? If we don't push hard, they won't respond."

I went on to tell them a short story about my visits and meetings with members of Congress. "When I was governor, holding the most powerful seat on the island, I would visit congressmembers. I would talk to them about the issue. They would, for the most, part be very gregarious and kind. 'I got married in Puerto Rico' or 'I love San Juan' or "My aunt lives in so and so." Yet I would leave, and they would never commit. Why? Because we held no power over them. And to avoid getting into contentious topics, they would just punt it."

Now we had a different path.

"If we have 3.2 million residents on the island, but 5.3 million Puerto Ricans in the states… Why don't we organize them to help us be our muscle and exert external pressure," I concluded.

The vision and mission helped us define our scope and our narrative. Anything beyond this mission was not within our purview. Establishing those guiding parameters also differentiated our path. Typically, the efforts for decolonization and statehood happened through direct conversations and lobbying with congressmembers. It was the expectation of the delegation to move forward with this failed strategy—even being derogatorily called *lobbyists*.

You see, congressmembers don't really have to respond to Puerto Ricans because they are not constituents. Think about the urgency a congressman in Florida will have to solve a local problem in Idaho. Likely, very little.

On top of that, because Puerto Rico does not have congressional representation, we don't even have bargaining capacity with our own votes to rally support. Historically, moral pleas and fundraising efforts gathered the support.

"Our delegation would span beyond that and tackle their voters," I told them. Remember what I proposed when I clashed with Marco Rubio? We would now put this idea into action. "Congressmembers respond to their voters and their fear of losing their seat. This will be the new added value we bring, and it will be game-changing."

As with Boricua Ahora Es, by verbalizing this change, we inspired a shift in action and attitude.

We were now able to engage folks from the mainland (any of the fifty states) to advocate for Puerto Rico. The big difference? They had the political power the residents of the island lacked. Roberto Delgado, a Puerto Rican who is now a Virginia resident said, "I have always been a statehood supporter. But since I moved to the states, I had a hard time finding a group with a purpose. The extended delegation provided that vision. Now it was a matter of executing and recruiting."

Our mission and vision secured and clear, we had to see how we were going to achieve our goals. I went on to propose several objectives for the delegation. My quarterly report described these as: "The vision of our office is to provide equality to the United States citizens who reside in Puerto Rico. Our mission is to exert external pressure on Congress to induce an action that will end colonialism and provide the binding choice of statehood to Puerto Rico. Those actions, in short order, are: (1) district organization, (2) congressional efforts, (3) coalition building, (4) civic and constituency engagement, (5) event planning and execution, (6) media and messaging, (7) legal path, (8) forum participation (Rosselló 2021) Figure 3.

"These all seem good," said one of the delegates. "But how are we going to accomplish these objectives without any money? We don't even have a budget for an assistant."

I responded, "I have a plan for that."

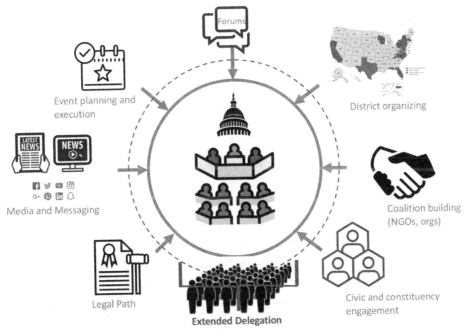

Figure 3. Slide created to showcase the objectives of the extended delegation.

Key Step: Extended Delegation

"Why have only six delegates when we could have one hundred… or a thousand or more?" I asked my fellow elected delegates as we continued to discuss the agenda.

"I propose we create a structure that will empower folks to become delegates. All they have to do is swear in the same oath we did, and they are part of it. It will empower them as volunteers. This will mitigate any shortcomings we had on the funding side."

Three out of the five other delegates agreed. In that moment, the extended delegation started. One of them was Shadow Senator Melinda Romero. Melinda has been a staunch supporter of statehood and has deep insights in our cause. "The extended delegation has become an integral part of our fight to achieve statehood, and its relevance will only grow as significant primaries and elections get closer. This idea caught on, and we need to maintain to nationalize the fight for Puerto Rico statehood. Ricardo Rosselló hit the mark with the initiative and garnered new found support among all the statehood champions in Puerto Rico."

Since the extended delegation started in 2021, we have more than twelve thousand delegates across the US. They have been working diligently on direct communication with congressmembers and other leaders (Perez Pintado 2023).

What's the key difference? Vivian Moreno, a very active delegate from Rhode Island stated, "We have political power, where our brothers and sisters on the island do not. We will be their muscle."

In March 2022, a group of delegates went to Washington, DC, from twenty states. The shocking moment came when I went with Ignacio Ros, Yadira O'Farrill, and Mario Solano to an office to ask for an audience.

As we entered, a nice young man at the reception greeted us by saying, "Sorry, the senator is busy today, but you can leave a message."

Ignacio replied, "It's a shame. I am a constituent of the senator. I also lead another organization with more than a few thousand members in his state."

The look in his eye immediately changed. "Um… hold on," he nervously replied. "Can you take a seat for a minute?"

There was movement in the bullpen. Literally, everyone in the office was shuffling. A few minutes later, the reply came. "The senator will see you shortly." We took pictures and listened attentively to the petition. The game had changed.

This was a very different feeling from the meetings I went to when I was the governor. Those were, well, mostly pleasantries without the risk of the congressmembers losing anything. This one had a key difference—a constituent. A vote. Political power.

We knew we had something special brewing. Ignacio Ros recalls, "It was a 180-degree shift. When they made the connection that we were Puerto Ricans and constituents… they were amazed." This is a key point. As documented before, there are more Puerto Ricans in the states (more than five million) than on the island (just over 3.2 million). "Their position on the matter shifted quickly and the rest is history."

But what would bind this group would be the critical part here, requiring us to break certain norms. Our organization would include both Democrats and Republicans. We needed a *space*, with common rules and objectives to propel unity. People who thought differently? We would acknowledge and respect those differences, but for this endeavor, they would need to put that aside.

"Republicans or Democrats—we would pledge our votes to those who would support the will of the people of Puerto Rico and provide a path to statehood. This was a priority."

—ZORIADA VELEZ, A VERY ACTIVE LEADER FROM THE FLORIDA DELEGATION.

Did it have growing pains? Of course. It still does. As I write this, the group has small tussles here and there… but we have a common core set of values, a mission, and a vision forward. We always have that to come back to.

Keeping with our identity, we have been able to support Democrats and Republicans as an organization. Very simple: You support equality and statehood. You have our support. You oppose it. You have our resistance.

"This is a fundamental shift in how things operate with the issue of Puerto Rico," said Roxana Soto Aguilu from the Puerto Rico Chapter.

And we need a fundamental shift to create a radical middle.

Flip the Tables

Great advice from Francis Underwood in the Netflix political thriller *House of Cards*: flip the tables. If you don't like how things are set up, look for a way to change them.

This is what we did with Boricau Ahora Es. This is what we are doing with the extended delegation. I believe we can do the same thing to create a *radical middle*.

Will it work? Who knows… in politics there are wins and losses. What I know is an opportunity exists—a big one at that.

My experiences with Boricua Ahora Es and the extended delegation are examples showcasing that we can do it. We broke down old models. We allowed disarticulated majorities to regain their direction and strength.

We can do the same with the radical middle.

It is a matter of recognizing that extreme positions are winning, even if they are less. They are doing so following a very predictable script. They make us believe the two sides are fighting against each other when in reality they *need* each other. How do we break this cycle? Flip the tables.

A Call to Action

Ample research shows political polarization has profound and negative social and economic consequences (Zhu 2021; Baldassari and Gelman 2008; McCoy and Somer 2018). It harms democracies. It leaves societies at a standstill at best, reversal at worse.

There is space to build the radical middle. There is a space. To start, you need to identify the problem, assess the purpose, and imprint the core values. Although I suggest some of these immutable principles, they should be the byproduct of Our Singapore Conversation type of approach.

On a small scale, Greitens imagined what it would be like. "Ricky, I have no doubt that no matter what the policy, if somebody put you and me in a room and threw policy x into the room and said 'figure it out' we would do it. You are a Democrat, and I am a Republican. But we would come to a space and think about it. I envision asking, 'How do we take this apart? From whom do we need to learn? How do we set the approach to figuring out?' We lay it out. We put it up on a whiteboard. We have a conversation about it. That depth, and that willingness to go deep is something that works directly contrary to the current media environment, and that is zipping into many in society."

I agree. I lived through it before.

I have had the blessing of participating in two efforts: Plan for Puerto Rico and the extended congressional delegation. In both I have seen a shift both quantitative and qualitative in nature. Opening spaces up for folks, giving it a runway so the natural defenses and preconceived notions subside can be game-changing. In my case, it helped me identify some preconceived notions I had of my own. The opening of these spaces and the demonstration of sustainability generate hope. And— used appropriately—that hope can generate important action.

In both cases, there was a clear signal and condition that provided the opportunity to create the space. Plan for Puerto Rico originated from the absence of strategic planning and a cohesive vision forward. The extended delegation stemmed from the understanding we had millions of potential advocates unutilized in the US.

And what about the redefinition of the middle? The best initial condition is that the vast majority of people would likely qualify in some way shape or form to be part of this radical middle (from a pool of more than 80 percent of us). These people sense the importance. It spans more than just creating a political core for the purpose of winning and sustaining power. Its creation will be at the core of innovating to improve our quality of life and avoid the fragmentation of polarization.

It's the eleventh hour. Are we going to answer the call?

CHAPTER 24:

Democracy 3.0

Democracy is a powerful idea but maintaining a system that sustains the core principles is ongoing work. We need to be mindful of the signals that demonstrate the systemic cracks, and adjust and innovate to make sure democracy flourishes (Javier 2017).

Recent reports paint a concerning picture for global democracy.

"Global democracy weakens in 2022" (International IDEA 2022).

"Just 4 percent of US adults say the political system is working extremely or very well; About six in ten (63 percent) express not too much or no confidence at all in the future of the US political system" (Pew Research 2023).

This is alarming.

These trends are not isolated incidents but part of a historical cycle of power shifts, as Ray Dalio highlighted at the YPO EDGE in 2022: "The circumstances we are now facing have occurred repeatedly, signaling shifts in the world order."

The concept of a "radical middle" is crucial not just for electoral success but for implementing fundamental changes to adapt to these inevitable shifts and enhance quality of life.

This ties directly to the idea of Democracy 3.0. While there is overwhelming support for democracy in the US, there's also a strong desire for fundamental change (Wike et al. 2021). However, about 60 percent believe the system is incapable of change, with only 18 percent believing in its potential for transformation (Figure 1).

Startlingly, about one in five Americans are open to authoritarianism. The likely culprit? People just want to get things done. The Institute for Democracy and Electoral Assistance's report, "Half of the democratic governments around the world are in decline while authoritarian regimes are deepening their repression," reflects this trend (International IDEA 2022). Scholars attribute this to dysfunction, polarization, threats to civil liberties, legislative gridlock, and historic lows in trust. These factors not only hinder democratic action but are also characteristics of autocratic states. (Nayak 2022)

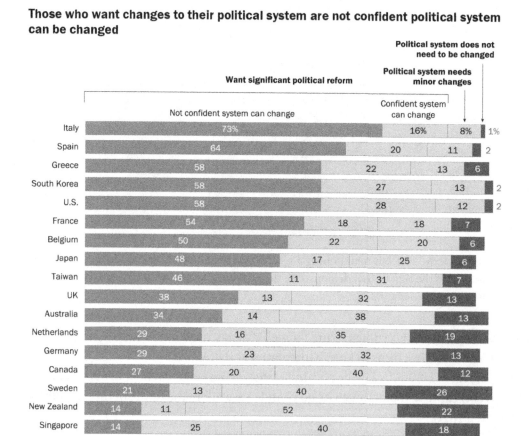

Figure 1. Low confidence in capacity to change among those desiring change. (Source: Pew Research 2021).

Do these seem familiar? Let's revisit some of the conditions we have highlighted:

- Words speaking louder than actions → speaks to dysfunction, politization, distrust and gridlock.
- Oversimplification of complexity → promotes demagoguery over a capacity to actually do. Leaders promote dysfunction because they don't understand or don't care to understand the nuance and complexity.
- Dehumanization → the clearest driving force in my view. Promotes otherisms and the most severe version of polarization.
- Extremes are winning → polarization that breeds distrust (Figure 2).

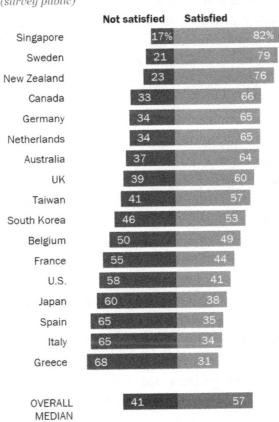

Assessments of how well democracy is working vary widely

% who are ___ with the way democracy is working in (survey public)

	Not satisfied	Satisfied
Singapore	17%	82%
Sweden	21	79
New Zealand	23	76
Canada	33	66
Germany	34	65
Netherlands	34	65
Australia	37	64
UK	39	60
Taiwan	41	57
South Korea	46	53
Belgium	50	49
France	55	44
U.S.	58	41
Japan	60	38
Spain	65	35
Italy	65	34
Greece	68	31
OVERALL MEDIAN	41	57

Note: Those who did not answer not shown.
Source: Spring 2021 Global Attitudes Survey. Q3.
"Citizens in Advanced Economies Want Significant Changes to Their Political Systems"

Figure 2. Assessment of how democracies are working. You can observe a wide variance. Staples of democracy like the USA are showing that more than half of society is not satisfied. (Source: Pew Research 2021).

Example: Looking Back at America's Core Values

One of the reasons people are losing faith in democracy is one of eroding core values. Let's consider what made the United States of America special. We inherited parts of the government from predecessors.

- **Branches of Government:** We inherited the idea of three branches of government from Rome, that there'd be an executive branch, the legislative branch, judicial branch.
- **The Idea Nobody Is above the Law:** Laws needed to apply equally, even to kings.
- **Rational Inquiry:** Greece not only gave the concept of democracy, but actually of rationality and rational inquiry. This was an integral part of the founding of the United States of America. There is a reason Thomas Jefferson, Benjamin Franklin, George Washington, and John Adams all disagreed among themselves, but they all agreed that every citizen had to be *capable* of *rational inquiry*.

So, if you lose *rationality*, and you don't have *trust in the justice system*, how do you settle differences? I asked Eric Greitens about this. "What's become strikingly obvious to people now is they will deploy the exact same arguments for the exact same behavior against one person who's their political enemy, but not a fight to somebody else who is on the other side. And what that's done is destroyed confidence in the ability to actually solve problems rationally." He brings up John Adams as an example. "As a lawyer, he represented the British soldiers who were responsible for the Boston Massacre. Why? He believed the justice system needed to make sure everyone had a fair trial, especially the people who you most violently disagree with. He later became the second president of the United States."

This rarely happens today.

It is no wonder then that the perception is that democracy keeps failing. It is an important and strong signal we need to evaluate. The authors in a recent paper in *Science Magazine*, entitled "Political Sectarianism in America," put it like this. "The rise of hate: othering—the tendency to view opposing partisans as essentially different or alien to oneself; aversion—the tendency to dislike and distrust opposing partisans; and moralization—the tendency to view opposing partisans as iniquitous" (Finkel et al. 2020).

An additional problem arises from this distrust and dysfunction: a lack of continuity in governance. This leads to destructive cycles undoing progress, akin to taking two steps forward and three steps back.

I witnessed this firsthand. After reducing Puerto Rico's government payroll and employee base significantly, my successor quickly reversed these measures, adding five thousand government jobs and reinstating part of the original problem. This not only undermined previous fiscal control efforts but also burdened future generations. It's disheartening to see hard-won progress undone for political reasons.

Similarly, we altered our labor reform, which had significantly reduced unemployment, to reintroduce previous conditions. These reversals occurred not only within opposition parties but also within my own party.

This trend of reversing progress for political gain is not unique to Puerto Rico and could become a broader issue in the rest of the US.

Understanding Anti-Incumbency

In 2021, Americas Quarterly highlighted a significant trend in Latin American politics: "Every time a Latin American country goes to the polls, some analysts suggest the region is taking a turn to the left or right, depending on who wins the election. A closer look at recent election results—especially those that have occurred since the pandemic began to ravage the region—tells a much simpler story: People are consistently voting against incumbents" (Navia 2021).

This phenomenon, I believe, isn't only in Latin America but is evident globally. In Puerto Rico, for instance, they haven't reelected any government since 1997. But what drives this pattern of anti-incumbency?

Negative narratives often overshadow positive ones. Complex policies, difficult to communicate and easy targets for misinterpretation by extremists, lead to populist promises. Once in power, these leaders struggle to deliver, paving the way for an opposite yet equally populist extreme. This ping-pong of power, focused more on maintaining control than solving problems, can be a precursor to autocracy.

In parts of Latin America, under the guise of extreme left ideologies, narcos are gaining influence. Their goal is not ideological advancement but power acquisition and retention. A recent example is Peru, where President Castillo, a radical left candidate, won the presidency but faced a nonmajoritarian Congress, corruption charges, and multiple investigations. His response was an attempt to dissolve Congress and establish authoritarian rule.

"In a televised address to the nation, Castillo had decreed a 'government of exception' and issued an immediate nighttime curfew for the country. The president said they would call legislative elections to elect new members of Congress, who would approve a new Constitution. They issued message, described by his own supporters as a 'coup d'état in progress,' hours before Castillo was set to face his third impeachment vote" (Gomez 2022).

The rising discontent in Latin America is a harbinger of a broader, global trend:

"The number of backsliding countries—those with the most severe democratic erosion—is at its peak and includes the established democracy of the United States… Globally, the number of countries moving toward authoritarianism is more than double the number moving toward democracy." (International IDEA 2022).

To address this worrying trend, I believe we must look both to the past for foundational principles and to the future for innovative solutions.

Rediscovering the Foundations of Unity

Gleaves Whitney, in a discourse on the constitutional convention, eloquently stated, "And so they practiced the art of compromise, accommodation, flexibility, all the things you need to negotiate, and they thereby became a model for what Americans can be" (Hauenstein Center 2011). This reflection on the birth of our nation underscores the enduring power of unity.

One of the most influential people in my life was my tennis coach, Ana Aleman. Hidden behind observations for the sport I loved, she always had insightful lessons for life. One example was every time I was playing poorly, she would remind me to "go back to basics." In the context of democracy,

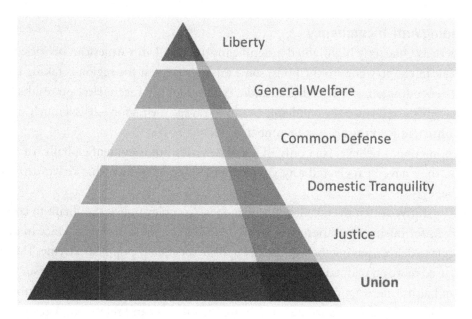

Figure 3. A slide illustrating the six premises of the preamble, highlighting Union as the foundational element.

this means revisiting our foundational principles. Let's consider the US Constitution, particularly its preamble, which I believe is a masterful expression of our nation's objectives.

"We the People of the United States, in Order to form a more perfect Union, establish Justice, Insure domestic Tranquility, provide for the common defense, promote the general welfare, and secure the Blessings of Liberty to ourselves and our Posterity, do ordain and establish this Constitution for the United States of America" (National Constitutional Center, n.d.).

These fifty-two words are the subject of countless theses. To me, they represent a mission statement outlining six key priorities, forming a pyramid of foundational values (Figure 3).

Union is the bedrock upon which other elements like liberty and justice are built. It's the unifying groundwork essential for achieving these objectives. However, polarization poses a significant threat to this foundational union.

Yuval Noah Harari, in his book *Sapiens: A Brief History of Humankind* (2015), notes, "Large numbers of strangers can cooperate successfully by believing in common myths. Any large-scale human cooperation—whether a modern state, a medieval church, an ancient city, or an archaic tribe—is rooted in common myths that exist only in people's collective imagination."

Without a shared sense of union, democratic values and liberty struggle to take root. This lack of foundational unity has led to the failure of democratization efforts in regions without a unified belief in this governance model.

Are we, too, at risk of losing our sense of unity? Signals suggest we might be heading in that direction.

A worrying signal is the evolution of political competition. What was once a hallmark of a healthy democracy has deteriorated. "Researchers have identified a second type of polarization, one focusing less on triumphs of ideas than on dominating the abhorrent supporters of the opposing party" (Finkel et al. 2020).

The end of this road is where unity goes to die.

How do we confront this critical issue? Let's pause here and consider the future of democracy in our next discussion.

Evolutionary Steps for Democracy

The United States practices a modern form of democracy, distinct from its early iterations in two key aspects. First, it allows people to elect leaders for set terms, during which these leaders govern without constant public input, unlike in early democracies. Second, it broadens political participation, including previously marginalized groups like African Americans, women, and nonproperty owners. These developments, seen as enhancements to democracy, form the crux of our discussion.

For clarity, let's label the initial democracy concept as version 1.0 and the current form as democracy 2.0.

How can democracy evolve from these versions while adhering to the principle of "the people holding some form of power"?

One area for improvement is the gap between elections. Currently, elected officials have years to implement their agendas, potentially disconnecting from public input. Could there be methods for more direct, ongoing citizen engagement with the government?

Another critical issue is political participation. In the US, there is a divide in opinions on voting rights. A 2021 Pew Research poll revealed a partisan split: 78 percent of Democrats view voting as a fundamental right for every US citizen while 67 percent of Republicans see it as a privilege with limited responsibilities. This distinction is delicate.

I align with the view that voting is a fundamental right of US citizens. While initially limited to white male landowners, the trend is toward inclusivity. However, disparities remain, as exemplified by Puerto Rico.

Puerto Rico, a US colonial territory, received US citizenship for its residents in 1918. Yet, it has consistently lagged in social parameters (income, education, health, etc.), partly due to its citizens' political inactivity (Rosselló 2012).

My father, former Governor Pedro Rosselló, described Puerto Rico as the "unfinished business of American democracy." In his book, he argues for the recognition of Puerto Rican political rights and voting rights in US elections. He views resolving Puerto Rico's political status as vital to completing American democracy.

Considering these systemic deficiencies and challenges of trust and polarization, what are the next evolutionary steps for democratic societies?

Leveraging Technology for Enhanced Governance and Democracy

We have extensively discussed the negative impact certain communication applications can have on polarization, trust, and other key factors for an effective governance and democracy. Can technology help mitigate that?

We need not look any further than *start-up behavior* and *cloud governance* for clues.

Figure 4. Personal picture of my visit to the Urban Redevelopment Authority in Singapore (2014)

Cloud governance in government contexts involves creating policies for managing cloud services and data securely and efficiently. While typically focused on companies, you can adapt these principles to improve democracy. Effective cloud governance can increase agility, reduce costs, enhance security, and promote transparency, participation, and accountability—all crucial for the health of democratic governance.

Civic technology is a key concept here. It encompasses digital tools that enable citizens to engage with governments and communities. You can use these tools for various purposes, such as mapping public issues, generating solutions, gathering input for government decisions, and facilitating community coordination. Civic tech promotes transparency, accountability, and participation, empowering citizens and strengthening democracy.

Examples of civic technology include Open311 and SeeClickFix. Open311 allows citizens to report nonemergency issues like potholes and graffiti while SeeClickFix enables reporting a broader range of community issues. These platforms provide direct engagement channels between citizens and local governments, fostering active community improvement.

These examples illustrate how technology can bridge the gap between periodic electoral participation and continuous citizen engagement.

Max Borders, in "The Evolution of Governance in 9 Stages," highlights that the start-up nation "will provide better governance options than otherwise available. As the world's complexity increases, we'll see more entrepreneurial solutions" (2019).

By establishing platforms with expertise that remain unaffected by the fluctuations of electoral politics you can significantly enhance the approach to addressing complex issues and scenarios in governance. A prime example of this is the foresight function for future planning, as discussed in the previous chapter. Another notable instance is the Singapore's Urban Redevelopment Authority (URA) Figure 4.

My visit to the URA was enlightening. Imagine a government office showcasing a 3D model of present-day Singapore. My host, Hannah, directed my attention to a video illustrating Singapore's remarkable growth over the past fifty years, both economically and physically. "Compare it to how it was fifty years ago," she told me. The URA, as the national planning and conservation authority, not only plans but also executes. What stood out was their long-term vision.

Hannah then led me to another room featuring a structural model predicting Singapore's landscape in fifty years. This forward-thinking approach starkly contrasts with the short-term, budget-to-budget planning often seen in other democracies, where strategy shifts are subject to political volatility, leading to inefficiencies and lost opportunities (Figure 5).

Embedding this concept of future planning within democracies is crucial. I believe the radical middle, with its core principles, ideally positions itself to implement these essential changes for the next phase of democracy. But the question remains: How can this be achieved effectively?

Figure 5. Personal picture from my visit to the URA in Singapore. Observing the mock-ups of future developments for the island-country.

[C]ounter Intuitive Combination

"Working with people with a vague idea of your goal dilutes the clarity of what you need to achieve it"

—JOHN SANEI, *FORESIGHT* 2019

In the risk of oversimplification, I see two areas that at first glance might seem like opposite tracks but taken together can become a powerful combination.

1. Empowering the experts: *Reducing* the accountability of the voting public and relying more on experts in subjects that should not be in the whims of the political sphere.
2. More continuous interjection of people in decision-making. Elections are done in cycles, and—within those cycles—democracy somewhat dampens. Are there areas where we can have more continuous participation from stakeholders?

Teaming up with experts allows things to flow more fluently and elegantly. Giving people the chance to interject more frequently than election cycles on meaningful decisions empowers diversity and the core of democracy.

Let's first tackle the idea we need to hand off more of our *democratically* appointed endeavors to experts and protect that from the whims of political change. Garret Jones argues for reduced accountability to the voting public in some areas and having that shifted to experts and elites in his book *10% Less Democracy* (2020).

"Rather than be governed by the masses of Boston or by the professors of Harvard, I'd far rather be governed by the engineering faculty of MIT," he states (Henderson 2020).

Jones develops the idea that—even as dictatorships are evil—how even a small amount of democracy can effectively neutralize the negative aspects of these autocratic governments. He further emphasizes the importance of having longer terms in office, central bank independence, judicial independence, and epistocracy to ensure a more stable and effective government.

And research supports the idea that longer terms in office can lead to more effective governance (Besley and Reynal-Querol 2014). A study by the National Bureau of Economic Research found that longer-term limits for elected officials lead to higher levels of investment in public goods and a decrease in corruption.

This is no small result. So could we do this in certain areas? How would we couple the participatory element to it?

Discover Puerto Rico

"If we win the election, the budget for tourism is going to go to an external entity," I told the people handling my publicity in my campaign for governor.

They agreed. Although deep down inside, I think they thought I would not go through with my proposal for a destination marketing organization (DMO), eventually named Discover Puerto Rico (2021).

Might seem a bit trite. But here is why. Every time I participate in some sort of economic forum or YPO event, and the issue of Puerto Rico comes out. Someone invariably says "Yes, it's a wonderful place. We loved it. Great for tourism."

At the risk of seeming facetious, I typically ask: "What part of the economy would you think tourism represents for the "Island of Enchantment"?

Numbers typically range from 20–45 percent. Then, I would give them the answer.

Seven percent.

Incredulous reactions tend to follow.

This compares abysmally with other Caribbean neighbors that carry anywhere on average 18 to 32 percent their economy (Acevedo, LaFramboise, and Wong 2018).

The reason? The government of Puerto Rico managed Puerto Rico's promotional budget. And within it was a lofty one hundred-million-dollar contract (four years) to manage the promotions. Historically, the publicity people from the incoming governor would receive this bounty and change the vision.

Not this time. Here is what we had on our Plan for Puerto Rico.

"For many years, Puerto Rico's definition as a tourism product and its promotion on a global level has changed, depending on the vision of each administration in office. This has caused a lack of consistency in marketing Puerto Rico as a tourism destination because many present it in radically different ways… We will create a nonprofit private corporation that will act as our DMO. This DMO will serve as an official reference point for planners, tourist guides, and visitors, and it will entice business travelers and vacationers alike to visit our historical, cultural, and recreational sites. This organization will have broad and representative participation from the private and public sectors in the community, the local industry, and other interested parties, with the goal of attracting not only tourists in general, but investors as well. In addition, the DMO will professionalize and bring consistency to our brand, turning Puerto Rico into the main tourism spot in the Caribbean, recognized as a first-class destination" (Rosselló et al. 2016).

Translation: Government has severely mismanaged the promotion of tourism. It is time to put it in the *experts'* hands with some help and participation from all stakeholders.

One government came in with a vision, and the next one would completely thrash it to impose theirs. On top of it, the people receiving the contracts saw it as a prize, and their execution was always lackluster. We were stuck in a vicious cycle that needed to change. Promptly.

This was one of the first measures I submitted, and by March 30 of my first year—taking advantage of the timing element—I signed it into law.

"Governor Ricardo Rosselló met one of his campaign promises Thursday with the signing of the law creating an independent destination marketing organization to handle branding and marketing efforts for Puerto Rico as a tourism destination. The private, nonprofit entity will run with a twenty-five-million-dollar annual budget drawn from the hotel room taxes formerly channeled to the Puerto Rico Tourism Co. for marketing efforts. The DMO duties call for developing a permanent destination brand, promoting Puerto Rico, attracting visitors, and increasing the island's global exposure" (Kantrow-Vázquez 2017).

Support from the tourism industry was there.

"We can react quicker to world events to make sure we can impact the markets we want to, when we want to. We have to spend our money well, especially in times of crisis," said Miguel Vega, chairman of the Puerto Rico Hotel and Tourism Association.

"The brand will be the result of professional and permanent decisions that can be efficient and produce more visitors, more occupancy and an economic impact," Milton Segarra, CEO of Meet Puerto Rico.

Needless to say this was met with ferocious opposition.

The press did their part. Headlines like "They are investigating for corruption the designated director of the DMO" (Metro 2018) and "Former press secretary of Rosselló already has a job in the DMO" (*Primera Hora* 2018) portrayed the DMO as a center for corruption. Similar stories have been told. It is a heavy lift to try to battle all these negative narratives when attempting to implement a novel solution. Although I was successful here, it was not the case with the Institute of Statistics… As I will soon describe.

Back to the DMO. In 2021, Angel Matos, an opposition legislator who brands himself as a tourism expert, asked: "What is the brand? What is the strategy? What is the branding? What is the promotion? Where is the achievement of the DMO?"

Well, addressing this recently Fast Company named Discover Puerto Rico one of its ten most innovative travel hospitality companies of 2023.

"This destination marketing organization's 2022 advertising campaign made a conscious departure from the Caribbean's typical selling points—oceans, beaches, and warm weather—and instead, focused on the island's people and distinct culture. The result was Live Boricua, a campaign based on Puerto Rico's original name, given by the indigenous Taínos who inhabited the island well before the Spanish arrived" (Kelso 2023)

And the results?

"Total lodging revenue was up 56 percent from 2021 and hotel rates were also 57 percent higher. Of equal importance, Live Boricua has served as a source of pride for the island's residents and wide diaspora and is a meaningful nod to Puerto Rico's native history" (Kelso 2023)

This is an important story because it showcases a few things. First, making change, *extracting* power from government is a very hard task. I could accomplish it here, but recall, I failed with the county proposal that aimed to redistribute government power. The second is in some instances, it is in the best interest of society and citizens to take away some power from an elected government to achieve better outcomes.

Brad Dean has been heading the DMO/Discover Puerto Rico ever since. I asked him to reflect on transition. "Challenging the status quo is never easy, so we knew changing the strategy, approach, and methodology of tourism marketing in Puerto Rico would be an arduous task. But the opportunity was too big and the need for progress was too compelling to let the island's potential be untapped."

And the key observation is that although rhetoric can point out that this has *less* democracy attached to it, the reality is it has more expertise and more participation.

"It was evident from day one the industry was ready for change, so our biggest challenge was aligning the opinions, perspectives and needs of six thousand plus businesses involved in the visitor economy, most of whom were facing dire circumstances," Dean recalls. This system now provides much more participation than the one that was ran by the government.

Recently, in a piece by economist Gustavo Velez titled "The Miracle of Puerto Rican Tourism," he outlines how this sector grew significantly in the past five years. He states that the "industry got strengthened and diversified" by key factors (most of which were done in our administration, including the incentives code and STRs we previously discussed). The first factor? "The creation of the organization known as DMO—now called 'Discover Puerto Rico' in 2017. With that step, the government passed to private hands the action of marketing and promotion of the destination—looking to provide more stability and continuity of efforts to attract more tourists" (Velez 2023).

Promotion of tourism is one. Many areas could absolutely benefit greatly from this shift.

Importantly, more delegation to experts *and* more participation. Both can coexist—and should. This is only a microcosm. How about on a bigger scale?

Participatory and Policy-Based Budgeting

On June 9, 2019, about a month before my resignation, I announced a groundbreaking approach to budgeting in Puerto Rico. "By July, we will introduce a system allowing citizens to track every tax dollar, understand its impact, and engage more actively," I declared (Gonzalez 2019). Amid a thriving economy and record-low unemployment, this initiative aimed to revolutionize the nexus of policy, participation, and budgeting.

I expressed my aspiration. "This new budgeting method should serve as a tool for participation and accountability."

Over two years, our team, in partnership with the Institute for State Effectiveness, developed a Production and Participatory based budget model (Figure 6).

This innovative model was designed to fill gaps in the existing budget process:

- A robust accountability mechanism
- A framework for strategic planning
- Transparent decision-making processes
- Opportunities for stakeholder participation
- A system rewarding results

The need for this overhaul was evident. The current budget model was complex and nontransparent, challenging even for experts to track spending. It lacked outcome measurement, leading to inefficiency and public disengagement (Figure 7).

Figure 6. Newspaper coverage of our initiative to reform the budget model (*El Nuevo Día* 2019).

Our analysis identified several deficiencies:

- Poor comparison of budgets year to year
- Lack of monitoring and accountability
- Poor forecasting
- A significant lack of transparency

The proposed changes aimed to rectify these issues, envisioning a model that would enhance these critical aspects and integrate a citizen-centric approach to policy development.

We weren't pioneers in this field. Brazil's Rio Grande do Sul state has implemented participatory budgeting for more than two decades. Their online platform "The Government Asks" allows citizens to propose and vote on policy ideas, with more than 360,000 votes cast for approximately 3,600 citizen-developed proposals in three years (Avritzer 2010).

Our goal was twofold: (1) to ensure policy visibility, accountability, execution, and measurement with expert input and (2) to boost public understanding and involvement in policy making.

Before fully realizing this vision, my term ended though I am optimistic about its future adoption. And speaking of the future...

Foresight Function

My visit to Singapore on November 7, 2014, profoundly reshaped my understanding of governance. While attending the International Society for Stem Cell Research Conference, I received an invitation from Richard O'Neil and Clare Lockhart, key figures in our asset mapping efforts in Puerto Rico. Clare suggested I delve into the Singaporean government's operations, an experience that turned out to be transformative.

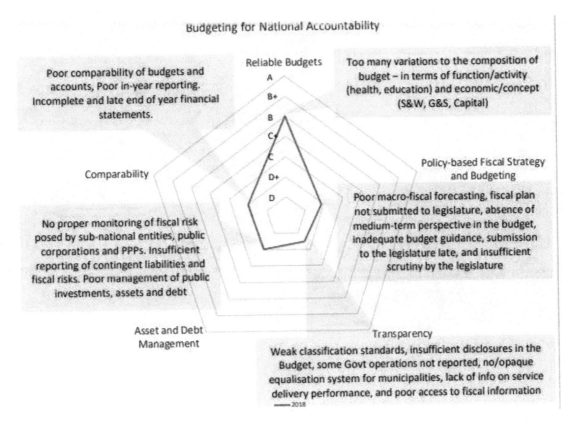

Figure 7. Analysis by the ISE and our Office of Budget Management, assessing Puerto Rico's pre-reform budget and outlining postimplementation goals (Government of Puerto Rico 2019).

"I've been in touch with the URA and the Centre for Strategic Studies in the Prime Minister's Office. They want to meet with you," the email detailed.

My previous interaction with the Urban Redevelopment Agency (URA) had been impactful, revealing their far-reaching vision. Yet, I wondered about the genesis of their insights.

The Centre for Strategic Futures (CSF), part of the Singapore government, specializes in preparing for a complex, rapidly evolving world. Since its 2009 inception, the CSF has focused on uncovering blind spots, long-term research, and pioneering foresight methodologies.

Upon arrival, two forecast analysts greeted me (Figure 8).

"We are enthusiastic about the future," one analyst said. "We aim to lessen its uncertainty."

This perspective inspired me to envision a significant administrative shift: evolving a data-centric entity into a dynamic, independent organization focused on future trends, signal detection, and governmental planning.

Interestingly, Singapore and Puerto Rico share several parallels. Both are small islands with limited natural resources, situated strategically between larger powers. In the 1950s, Singaporean leaders, inspired by Puerto Rico's success in attracting foreign investment and becoming a manufacturing and trade hub, saw a potential model for their own development.

Figure 8. A personal photograph from my visit to the CSF in Singapore in 2014.

While our paths diverged in subsequent years, the inspiration Singapore drew from Puerto Rico during that era was pivotal in its economic evolution. Could this historical influence have reciprocation?

My Singapore experience highlighted the integration of science, technology, and policy in governance, offering a new direction for Puerto Rico.

Can't Make an Omelet...

In our Plan for Puerto Rico, we proposed the creation of the PRoactive Institute (emphasizing 'PR' for Puerto Rico). The outline for the institute's goal is as follows:

"We will establish the Proactive Institute, a quasi-public entity to develop projects leveraging future socioeconomic opportunities. It will forecast future conditions and devise avant-garde, strategies" (Rosselló et al. 2016) Figure 9.

The vision was to create a Centre for Strategic Studies for Puerto Rico. However, the foundation of this entity required reliable data, which was a significant challenge. The Institute for Statistics was supposed to clarify island data, but many key parameters were missing. Our solution involved externalizing data in collaboration with the federal government and involving a third party for credible statistics, forming the backbone of the PRoactive Institute (Victoria840 2016).

Resistance to this initiative was substantial:

"The Association of American Statistics pleads Rosselló not to dismantle the Institute of Statistics." "Rosselló gains control over the Institute of Statistics" (NotiCel 2018). "Ricardo Rosselló is accused of violating laws of the Institute of Statistics" (Univision Radio 2019).

Proactive Institute Center for Government Innovation and Forecasts

The Government of Puerto Rico's current crisis is due to constant improvisation in decision-making. The government has not been able to maximize opportunities and has been reactive to circumstances instead of proactive, as we propose.

We will establish the Proactive Institute, a quasi-public entity that will develop distinct projects to take advantage of future socio-economic opportunities. We will establish a mechanism to develop forecasts of future conditions, and be proactive and avant-garde in the development of preventive strategies.

The Proactive Institute will rely on statistical data to develop a scientific plan to meet global, regional, and local challenges and risks. In addition, it will develop the capability and expertise that will prevent improvisation and enable proper and well thought-out decisions. This will position Puerto Rico as a jurisdiction with innovative processes and an avant-garde government that is focused on continuous improvements. This could be developed in partnership with private entities, the academia, or the third sector.

Figure 9. Description of our PRoactive Institute from our Plan for Puerto Rico. (2016).

Interestingly, the Institute of Statistics had in its own press release (January 2018) the root cause and justification for taking action. "The government of Puerto Rico has a long history of producing, disseminating, and presenting rigged, outdated, misinterpreted, and incomplete statistics, and then does not provide access to information sources verify the information, either by the citizen or by a congressman."(Instituto de Estadisticas 2018)

This is precisely what was happening under their watch.

As expected and detailed in this book. The narrative campaign started to unfold with weak, simple arguments: "Rosselló wants to control the institute so he can control the data." What data? "Rosselló wants to use this for his cronies." How and why? All these stories clutter the real focus.

Our real focus was to get Puerto Rico in a position not to dwell on the past and react to the present without a path forward but rather to anticipate the signals in the future and help the government create smart, hard thought, compelling policy.

In the end, the resistance gathered. It became one of those issues where aggregated opposition members—including the media—bound together and lost the opportunity. Admittedly, I was not effective in crafting a narrative on my own for the importance of this institute. Perhaps the support of experts will at least glean some insight into it.

State of Collective Shock

"Two numbers that really stunned me when I first calculated them; two numbers that feel something," said Jane McGonigal, IFTF's director of game research and development and author of *Imaginable*. She has been using her knowledge in gaming to help craft futures.

"Since the start of the year 2020 There have been more than two and a half million news headlines and stories with headlines stating the word *unimaginable* and there have been more than three million news stories and headlines with the headline *unthinkable*" (McGonigal 2022a).

"The fact that these words: unthinkable unimaginable are so ubiquitous in the stories gives us a clue to our global condition. We are in a state of collective shock," she points out at YPO Edge 2022 (McGonigal 2022b).

This is quite a *signal*.

Why is this relevant? By exploring the future, even if it does not happen as predicted, diminishes anxiety. Just the fact that one can explore beyond the immediate provides a much better prepared society.

Yes! The US has said institutes. They are independent, and I think this is valuable, but I believe the merger with government in a more formal role is critical. Jake Dungan thinks the city level is a great way to start.

"We often think about starting new policies at the national government level. However, city governments, I think are a really great place to try new things. To integrate new experiments or new kinds of institutional policies around foresight to the midstream of consciousness. The need for social foresight is one of the terms we use, or public foresight maybe is extremely important. So is finding ways to do it institutionally."

Whatever the way, the institutional foresight function can provide tools to create a space where people can work together to battle dehumanization, soft thinking, demagogy, zealotry, and extremism.

The silent majority should stay silent no more. It's time to raise our voices and be a part of the effort to depolarize societies and—ultimately—help democracies.

Step past the divide and solve the *Reformer's Dilemma*.

CHAPTER 25:

Parting Note

This illustration holds a special place in my heart. It has all my immediate family (Pedro is in Beatriz's belly). While it was done to illustrate the moment that Trump decided to come to the island, it could very well have been any other moment when I had an urge to do something and my family was always there to support or to give me clarity (Bayon 2017).

"I love what I do. I get up at 3:30 in the morning to work. These are times of great challenges, but also of great opportunities,"

SAID THE GOVERNOR WITH HIS BROAD SMILE (QUINTERO 2017).

I am grateful. I am grateful for the opportunity to learn from my past. I am grateful to have had a number of great leaders share their stories with me. I am grateful for a loving and supporting family. I am grateful to the countless many who helped me give different perspectives to this book. I am grateful to the people of Puerto Rico for giving me the opportunity to serve as their governor. I am grateful for my election by direct nomination to serve as a shadow congressmember for my island.

I am grateful to be able to share all of this with you. And I am hopeful it can be of value.

Discussing the extent of the next steps for democracy will take volumes, and profound expertise I don't have. Quite frankly, my goal with this book was to show some of the huge challenges to reform I and others faced and have some documented stories—from my perspective—for my kids. By doing this, the idea was to create a framework that would give policy makers and citizens alike a model that would help them better understand the conditions to further reform.

I thoroughly enjoyed making reforms, thinking about change and then executing to enable it. It was the life blood that allowed me to sustain many challenges. Even with everything that happened, it still motivates me to this day. Tatito's experience when I was nineteen gave me a glimpse. Now, through education, energy, economic, healthcare, workforce, government, fiscal reforms… I have a deeper understanding of what it means.

When I was nineteen… I felt conflict about whether I should engage in politics or not. I leaned toward the latter, as the dirt, mud, blood sweat and tears invariably will accumulate. Even after going through fiscal crisis, hurricanes, and a personal crisis that ended my tenure, the question remains: Knowing all of this… would I do it again? Absolutely.

Like the bricklayer, even if dirty, tired, and crumpled, we can say that *we have built.*

Yet. I understand why this is such a tough decision. Why people wrestle with it. Why increasing numbers eventually say no. My goal was to provide an account accessible to all people and give a little bit of context and inspiration to aspiring policy makers. Because of this, I used firsthand experiences, stories, interviews, and my scientific background to set it up. I attempted to be as candid as possible about what I perceived were some of my attributes and victories but also my flaws and defeats. One can definitely learn more from the falls than the celebrations.

Herbert E Meyer wrote in his book *Hard Thinking: The Fusion of Politics and Science,* "The fundamental difference between science and politics is that in science, results count and being right matters" (1993). This intersection—my preparation as a scientist, and the good and bad experiences I had as a chief executive in the political realm—have provoked me to develop a few themes for the reader that may challenge conventional wisdom.

The Reformer's Dilemma

As in Puerto Rico, the global environment calls for change. Whether it's climate change or social issues, people are clamoring for it. Yet what is the path forward for the reformer? What can she expect in the steps ahead? Woven amid my experiences as well as others, I would like to convey the possible outcome of reforming or not reforming: Crisis.

Why is this relevant? At the current change of pace (and reform) it will take ninety-five years to achieve the goal of gender parity in global politics (NDI, n.d.). This is just one example but think about your internal expectations on this front. Did you really expect one hundred years to go by to achieve this? Think about other outcomes. How people have been clamoring for change yet very little actually happens.

Words Speak Louder than Actions

"Actions speak louder than words," says the old adage. It's so traditional we rarely consider a fault in it when it rolls off our tongues. It is time tested and seems—in a way—just.

I have challenged this notion.

I believe one of the key challenges we face is words indeed have more impact than the fundamentals (e.g., results and actions). Words are beautiful. They make us imagine and dream. They are an essential tool of what makes us humans. We need words. We just can't afford to completely substitute words for necessary actions. This is—in my view—partially due to the victory of rhetoric, dogma, extremes, and fear-based emotions over hard thinking, science based, and self-evaluation.

We should concern ourselves about the environment we create. Studies have shown that all major networks and cable TV news outlets have given the most airtime to members of Congress with the most extreme views. This stands in contrast with a Pew Research poll showcasing that only 16 percent of the population lies in the most extreme sides of the right and left spectrum (Pew Research 2021). This means the news is focusing on what one out of six people consider is the path forward. What about the remaining 84 percent of us?

Recently, Elon Musk tweeted an intuitive observation: "The far-left hates everyone, themselves included, but I'm not of the far right either" (2022). Whether you like him or not, I would venture to say many feel the same, but they just don't have a way to say it or feel the inevitable attack from both ends is not worth expressing the sentiment.

The clear and present danger of polarization is there, but I would argue that it is much greater than how we are treating it.

The Radical Middle

This is when my book took an unexpected turn. After examining the implications of this model, it left me cold. By hindering the capacity to reform, we are hindering our capacity to progress and innovate. This leaves our current system in a precarious situation and, in my view, at a disadvantage against other types of regimes. The journey, it seems, was not only about the lessons of the past but also about projecting and foreseeing bigger, broader challenges in the future.

It appears the major disadvantage out of all the variables discussed between autocratic regimes and democratic ones is the intrinsic value of deterioration (k) and the effect of the mounting resistance. Assuming all other variables stay the same, the conclusion is the gap between the capacity to reform will expand between the two regimes as a function of time (Figure 1).

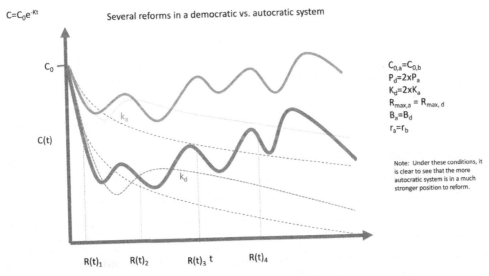

Figure 1. Comparing reform dynamics in democratic and autocratic states.

Threshold

The world currently is accelerating in many different key areas such as artificial intelligence, longevity, space travel, quantum computing and others. Envision a scenario where these technologies and their stacking offer enormous benefits for our society. One that is around the corner is self-driving vehicles.

Once we cross a specific threshold, automatic driving vehicles will be a reality. How will different jurisdictions react to this possibility. A jurisdiction with high k and resistance will likely see a few of the following things unfold. Despite all the evidence supporting the benefits of autonomous vehicles, some jurisdictions will see a coalition of groups on the fringe that will vehemently oppose the adaptation. These fringe groups may include those who are anti-tech, those who support drivers' unions, and some who believe this new technology is a conspiracy to control individuals. As they say, big brother is watching.

Invariably, this will become a political issue. A small, but strong, dogmatic group will emerge in Congress. This group will have the capacity to delay or buffer the impact of this technology by procedural handicaps such as committees and task force groups. The issue gets muddled. Laws may pass, but Frankenstein-type arrangements severely limit the impact.

Then, as the technology is unfolding, an accident happens. No matter the reality that for every—say one thousand accidents by humans on the road, there is one by automated driving. Media covers it as a polarizing issue. Groups continue to divide.

What was once a promising technology to help society now becomes a wedge political issue. The impact is tempered at best, nullified at worst.

Meanwhile, other jurisdictions with a smaller k and lower resistance can push forward. They see the impact of the technology. They understand it is not perfect, but it is a vast improvement on what we have. They get it done.

With other innovations going through the gauntlet, similar procedures unfold and the differences between the two jurisdictions compound and can grow exponentially. In addition, k and resistance factors continue to increase, providing a starcher divide.

Is there a way to detain this?

In the book, we explored a variety of strategies to reduce k, and resistance.

- Blitzkrieg: Allows changes to happen at the highest opportunity windows, which tend to be the very onset of an administration. This requires preparation and priority setting. To have both, you must invest time a priori, giving clarity and direction, which is a strong way to identify people along the way who can enhance your bandwidth.

- Sequencing: Strategically choosing a pattern of reforms that will allow the optimization of present and future success is a key action that can help overcome fast sloping k-curves and earn trust. By enhancing trust, you enhance bandwidth. By choosing to sequence, one buys oneself a runway to execute reforms that have a higher magnitude but are slower to yield results. In other words, you get runway into the long term.

- Civic engagement: A great way to drive a wedge in polarization, find common ground, and reduce dehumanization. We can build trust and strategic plans as well as strengthen the concept of democracy, by making democracy something that is more continuous than just an electoral event every two or four years. This is also the way one allows and respects the majority rule while involving minorities in the democratic process. Technology can be a game changer here.

If we take a closer look at our variables, they can be sensitive to these strategies. Certainly, reducing resistance through civic engagement, maximizing the optimal times with blitzkrieg and being thoughtful and strategic about deployment helps move these variables in a direction that enhances the capacity to reform. However, even employing these, there seems to be a disadvantage against autocratic regimes. Can we Identify another lever?

Bandwidth is that lever. Recall we defined this characteristic as one that helps reforms (or any action, for that matter) to flow more effectively. Broadly speaking, A-players, high tech, and correctly functioning institutions, processes, and systems impact your bandwidth. What are a few things that can help us with said bandwidth?

- Embracing education: We need to look at education in the broadest sense—from early schooling where you have the highest impact on a child's development to refurbishing talent that needs a new platform to excel. This is a long-term proposition, but the reverse engineering of this view is essential.
- Taking a "less democracy" approach to enhance democracy: Certain items, delegated to experts, can stay out of the whims of the populus. While the approach is likely to cause staunch resistance in the onset, it is a way to take important issues out of the political spectrum where things will more likely than not become polarized. In many instances with no real rational justification.
- Enabling foresight capability: This function gives governments a tool to battle short-termism and dogma with expertise, analysis, and a capacity to story tell. Future crafting is not only about predicting, but more so about being aware of the possibilities ahead. In that way, we reduce the uncertainty and tackle the anxiety of the "unimaginable." Foresight can help with all three variables: Creating and training A-players, identifying novel technologies and processes, and conducting a continuous improvement model on the handicaps of government. It can also facilitate a conversation that could breed trust and civic engagement.

With this, we have tinkered with our model, and proposed a reduction in resistance and k to just 20 percent greater than that of an optimized autocratic regime. By implementing strategies such as civic engagement, preparation, and foresight functions, we can optimize sequencing over the alternative state. The k change occurs if bandwidth becomes significantly higher. The plot below shows these dynamics (Figure 2).

For these outcomes to happen, a force must emerge. In the final part of this book, I articulate the concept of a radical middle as a means of achieving these goals, starting by understanding more people want this to happen than don't. Let's review the numbers:

- **We Are More:** In the US, only 16 percent of the population was progressive liberal or faith and flag conservatives and the *middle* is anywhere from 60–84 percent of the population (Pew Research 2021).

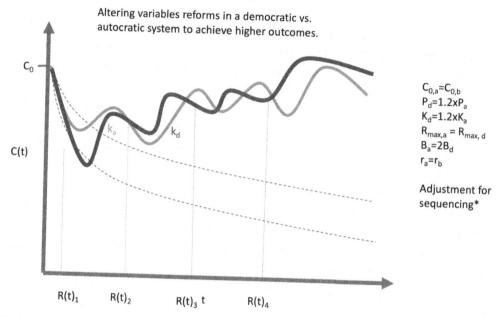

Figure 2. Reducing k and enhancing bandwidth provoke a system where conditions in democracies are more favorable than autocracies.

- **People Love Democracy:** Support for democracy as the best form of government remains overwhelming and mostly stable across party lines (Wike et al. 2021).
- **But They Feel It Is Failing:** There is near-universal agreement that our system is not working well—in particular, that it is not delivering the results people want (Galston and Kamarck 2022).
- **People Want Reform:** Across advanced economies, 56 percent believe their political system needs major reforms (Wike et al. 2021) in the US alone 80 percent feel it needs major or complete reform.
- **But More than Half Feel It Is Capable of Reform:** 58 percent of US citizens have both a desire for change and a lack of confidence and only 28 percent believe it can change (Pew Research 2021).

The ingredients are there. People (more than 80 percent) and purpose (to sustain and grow democracy while achieving results). Along with the establishment of strong core values and driving the core message that extreme constituencies pose an existential threat to progress and our way of life, a radical middle could be that agent of change.

But we need to move quickly. We must get back to the basics by highlighting the importance of the union and unity and looking forward with foresight.

The signals are ever so clear.

Four Days

As I was finalizing the edits for this book, two significant events occurred almost simultaneously, highlighting the pervasive nature of extreme polarization: the ouster of Kevin McCarthy as Speaker of the House in the US (October 3, 2023), and the Hamas attacks on Israel (October 7, 2023).

The removal of Speaker Kevin McCarthy is a stark example of the challenges posed by extreme polarization in politics. McCarthy's struggle to unify the divergent factions within his party epitomizes the difficulties faced by leaders in today's polarized environment. Hardliners often criticized his efforts to make pragmatic decisions, leading to his eventual ouster. This event symbolizes the broader issue of governance in an era where ideological purity often trumps collaboration.

Former Congressman Tom Davis shared his insights with me: "They do not reward compromise. They punish it. Members told me their calls were running 100–1 to dump McCarthy. Unsaid was that Democrats provided *96 percent* of the votes to oust him after working with them to keep government open. But Democratic primary voters were not going to reward a Democrat who voted to help a Republican speaker who launched an impeachment inquiry against their president."

Davis also noted the impact of primary elections and media consumption on political polarization: "Over 80 percent of the Republican Conference has no meaningful chance of losing to a Democrat. Their only real obstacle to reelection is their party primary. The inability of political leaders to work together across party lines is exacerbated by the way each party's voters receive their information."

The Hamas attacks on Israel, occurring less than a week later, further illustrate the global reach of polarization. The long-standing conflict between Israel and Palestine, fueled by deep ideological and historical differences, has led to a cycle of violence and mistrust. This polarization fosters a process of dehumanization, where adversaries are no longer seen as individuals but as symbols of an opposing force, making violence seem more justifiable.

These events underscore the pervasive and transformative effects of polarization, both domestically and internationally.

To address these challenges, several factors must align: effective leadership, a compelling message, strategic branding, and conducive conditions. Without these, we risk perpetuating the cycle of division and conflict.

The Paradox of Choice in American Politics: Biden versus Trump II

Gilbert García captured the current political sentiment succinctly: "We don't get close to unanimity on anything these days, so it's vaguely impressive that Americans are uniting behind the idea that they don't want these two elderly guys together on the debate stage again... But whether we want it or not, we're probably going to get it. A Biden-Trump rematch has the odor of inevitability right now" (2023).

In my discussions about President Trump, I strived for objectivity, neither praising nor demeaning. The same approach applies to President Biden.

As I write, polls indicate a likely Biden versus Trump rematch in the upcoming presidential election, presenting a paradox:

- The expectation is for Trump to win the Republican Primary, with 70 percent support even post-indictment (Murray 2023).
- The projection is Biden as the Democratic nominee (Axelrod 2023).

However, polls also reveal:

- Seventy percent of Americans, including 51 percent of Democrats, do not want Biden to run (Allen 2023).
- Sixty percent oppose Trump's candidacy, with a third of Republicans included (Doherty 2023).
- Only 5 percent express interest in seeing both Biden and Trump run in 2024.

With headlines like "Nearly half of voters have ruled out supporting Biden and Trump" proliferating, the likelihood of their matchup seems to increase.

"It's a sad fact, however, that even in a society with free elections, the public frequently gets what it doesn't want," observes Gilbert García (Garcia 2023).

This situation exemplifies the paradoxes within modern democratic elections. Despite the overwhelming majority opposing both candidates, we seem to be heading toward a showdown between them.

Interestingly, in hypothetical matchups, both Biden and Trump fare poorly against other potential candidates. For instance, polls show Nikki Haley leading Biden by four points (Blanton 2023). Previously, candidates like Gavin Newsom were ahead of Trump. Yet, as of October 23, Real Clear Politics aggregates show Trump and Biden in a dead heat.

Observation: (1) Both would likely lose to other opponents, yet (2) they stand the best chance against each other.

Conclusion: They seem to need each other, mirroring the symbiotic nature of political extremes.

Ultimately, "That means it will probably come down to who the American people distrust the least." (Garcia 2023). This raises a critical question: Is this the true spirit of democracy? And if not, how can we shift this trajectory?

Reform as a Precondition for a Successful Democracy

My journey in writing this book started as a curious search into the forces that hamper reform and led me to identify some factors I hope policy makers and citizens in general can use to gauge the capacity to execute reform. In this process, we found out that reform is the lifeblood that allows democracies to stay afloat. Reforms affect critical factors in governance such as institutional flexibility, public engagement, rule of law, measures of accountability and transparency. Without it, democracies stand to slow down or stop altogether.

The mixture of dehumanizing, extremism, demagoguery are strong opponents to progress. They limit the runway to execution and have our bandwidth clogged with unimportant aspects.

The model spells it out clearly… and if we continue on this path, things look bleak.

But if there is *one* lesson to learn from this it's that we *do* have the power to change these things. A vast majority of us feel unsatisfied with the current inaction, extremes, and state of democracy. If we can leverage that untapped power into action, we'll find a path to a better democracy.

Recognize the extremes should not represent all of us.

Recognize we are all human, and as such, we should treat everyone with a base level of respect.

Recognize curiosity and ingenuity took us to the highest levels in the past—and we must harness that same spirit for the future.

Recognize the sooner we wake up from being a slumbering majority—call it *radical middle* or otherwise—the better prospects for the future.

Otherwise, it could severely hamper our capacity to progress in a democratic system. "If all we are doing is barking past each other and the side in power at the moment imposing it's solution on the others, there is no triumph, there is no solution," Manji concludes (2020).

As Nobel Peace Prize Laureate Maria Ressa said, "Democracy, you still are you are in the last two minutes… to move away from that angle, collaborate, collaborate, collaborate."

Nobody else will do it for us.

It's up to us. The power is in our hands.

Acknowledgments

This book was born out of a small, hopeful idea (Bayon 2017)

It was the middle of the pandemic and I had been getting several offers to write my book. More specifically, to write a memoir. After all, I had gone through several very public and tantalizing events. Potential authors would come and ask write it—or at the very least, cowrite my memoir.

But that did not feel right. I did not *just* want to write a memoir… I wanted something *more*.

I postponed my project until I received an email from YPO, "*How to Write & Launch a Great Book In 2022 with Eric Koester.*" I signed up. I listened compellingly. It was game-changing. And I knew what I had to do. Thank you, Eric.

This process was not without bumps and stoppages. It's been quite a roller-coaster ride. So let me first acknowledge anyone who sits down to read this whole book. I am grateful and cognizant that you are sharing the gift of time to come along this journey with me. As I mentioned, I did not want to write a memoir. I wanted to go a different route. So, I chose to tackle a question that is near and dear to my heart, use *some* of the experiences I've had—good, bad, and ugly—and follow a process of examination and analysis.

To dive in deeper, I relied on the expertise of many published authors, scientists, and experts, some of which I was honored to interview. In that spirit, I would like to thank all those who set aside time to answer some of my questions: my parents—Pedro and Maga—whom I admire and love dearly. Governor Cuomo a great, insightful leader and friend; a true reformer. Special thanks to Governor Greitens, Governor Kasich, Governor McDonald, Pamela Patenaud, Ivan Rivera, Prof. Yasha Monk, Dr. Michael González Cruz, Peter Miller, Aaron Bare, Roxana Aguilu, Leopoldo López, Jake Dungan, Laquita Claire, Clare Lockhart, the RMI family, members of the extended delegation and Congressman Tom Davis. Members of my administration who shared their perspectives: Hector Pesquera, Maria Palou, Ramon Rosario, Glorimar Ripoll, Edward Calvesbert, Senator Gregorio Matias, Christian Sobrino, Marybell Rivera, Philippe Mesa, Luis Daniel Davila Pernas, Tania Vazquez, Carlos Ruiz, Cynthia Rivera, Ricky Llerandi, Melinda Romero, Carlos Mercader, Cecilia La Luz, Senator William Villafañe, Carmen Colon de Armas, Rafael Cerame, Erik Rolón amongst others. Your stories give diverse perspectives to the events cited. And thank you to all, especially Magdiel Lugo and Mariel Falero, who allowed me to use their photographs and illustrations to bring life to the stories I shared.

Because this book was created from the ground up, I would like to acknowledge the folks who stepped in and helped by preordering the book.

Aida L Prieto, Aimee Evan, Alberto Cruz, Alberto Carrero Jr., Alejandro Ramos, Alexis Berrios, Alpidio Rolon, Amneris Soto, Ana Presno Alemán, Ana Gonzalez, Ana Ivelisse Homs, Anabel Rivera, Andres Guillemard, Andrew Cuomo, Angel Rosado Quinones, Angel Salgado, Angel M. Martin, Antonio Pabon, Arturo Huertas, Braulio Mejia, Carlos Esteva Oliver, Carlos Padilla, Carlos Salgado, Carlos Contreras, Carlos Baez, Carlos Saavedra, Carlos Perez, Carlos Quinones-Capacetti, Carlos Vazquez Pesquera, Carlos Gonzalez, Carlos Hermida, Carlos A. Flores Ortega, Carlos Ramos Ruiz, Carmen A. Costa, Carmen M Colon, Castor Bayron, Cesar De Jesus, Christian Kerkadó, Dania Carpena, David Tirri, Delimary Maldonado, Denisse Tejero, Denisse Rivera, Dennis Gonzalez, Dennise Perez, Digna Acevedo, Domingo Nevarez, Dominik Raginia, Doris Vaughan, Dr. Dolly Garcia-Ramiu Bocachica, Dr. Vidal G. Hernández-Rivera, Ed Sosa, Eddie Moreno, Eduardo Rivera, Eduardo Mattei, Eduardo Bonar, Edward Torres, Edwin Rivera, Edwin R. Carreras, Efrain Delgado, Eloisa Cid, Eric Koester, Erik Rolon, Erwin Ferri, Felix Alemar, Ferdinand Ocasio, Francisco Ortiz Berlingeri, Gerardo Toro, Gisela Mercado, Gladys Caraballo, Glorimar Andújar, Gretchen López De Victoria Rivera, PhD, Gustavo Meza Buelvas, H. M. Pesquera, Hector Tirado, Helen Wilkinson, Hilda Marie Rivera Colón, Homero Gonzalez, Humberto Ramos, Idalia Borrero, Ignacio Ros, Ilia Rivera, Irma Rodriguez, Isaias Sanchez, Isamar Colon, Israel Ramirez Sanchez, Itza Garcia, Ivan Rivera, Ivelisse Garcia, Ivette Georget, Ivette Chardon, Ivonne Martinez, Jaime Barreto, Janet Riefkohl, Janice Negron, Javier Castro, Javier Torres, Jeanelle Alemar-Escabí, Jesus Nunez, Jesus Velez, Jesus Ramos, Jocelyn Flores, John Nevares, Jorge Aguila, Jorge Colon, Jose Morales, Jose Rivera, Jose Rodriguez, Jose Nieves, Jose Alvarez, Jose Maldonado, Jose Yglesias Cumpiano, José Rosselló, José Saavedra, Jose "Rafuchi" Nazario, José Che Perez, José F. Aponte-Hernandez, Jose N.

Vazquez Figueroa, Josephine Cortes-Torres, Josue Rivera, Joyce Martinez, Juan A. Rivera Nuñez, Juan Jose Diaz Diaz, Juan M. Mendez Rosa, Juan R. Jimenez-Velez, Julian Soto, Julio Rodriguez, Krystall M. Molina Gonzalez, Leila Rolón Henrique, Linda Laras, Lis Rodríguez, Louanson Alers, Luis Garcia, Luis Davila Pernas, Luis Ramos, Luis Pacheco, Luis Defendini, Luis Berrios-Amadeo, Luis Benitez, Luis M Rosado, Luz V Rivera Andaluz, Luz (Lucy) Arce, Maggie Ramos, Manuel Almeida, Manuel Herrero, Manuel D Lopez Alamo, Maria Cabrera, Maria Rivadulla, María Cristina Mayoral, Maria del C Perez Iglesias, Maria E. Guadarrama, Marilyn Colon, Mario A. Solano, Maritza Santos, Matilde García-Arroyo, Mayra Rivera Ramos, Mayra Enid Gonzalez, Michael González, Miguel Rodriguez, Miguel Santiago, Miguel Valdés Morales, Miguel A. Mejias Maldonado, Milagros de Lourdes Rivera Rodríguez, Mildred Perez, Milton Maury, Miriam Perez, Mohammad Yassin, Monica Cintron, Nancy Martinez Rosa, Neftalí González Santiago, Nestor Mejias, Nilsa Caraballo, Ninoska Bonnelly, Norma Serrano, Nydia Valentin, Olga Garcia, Olga Berrios, Omar Negron, Omar Marrero, Orlando F. Morales Guzman, Oscar Soto Irizarry, Paola Adorno, Pedro Marrero, Pedro Dedós, Pedro Manzano, Pedro Zorrilla, Pedro Rodriguez, Philippe Mesa, Ramon Vazquez, Ramon Lopez, Raul Zayas, Raymond Cruz Hernandez, René E. Moscoso, Rev Carmen Hernandez, Ricardo Tormos, Robert Bithorn, Roberto González Rosa, Rosa M. Velez Fernandez, Rosalinda Rivera, Sandra Repollet, Sandra Amadeo, Santos Cordero Rivera, Sarai Lastra, Saul Suarez, Shirley Monge, Sidney Baron, Soeli Velázquez, Tere Riera Carrion, Thelma Roquettes, Valentin Del Rio, Vangelis Vergetis, Vernisse Ortiz-Martinez, Victor Añeses, Vivian Rivera Moreno, Waldemar Rivera, Walter Caraballo, Wanda Beltran, Wilberto Guzman, Wilfredo Cordero Cruz, William Villafañe, William Diaz, William Velez, Wilmer Reyes Berríos, Xinjin Zhao, Yadira O'Farrill, Yamil Jaskille, Yesenia Diaz-Roman, Yolanda Perez, Zoraida Rodriguez, Zulma Rosario.

You were a driving force to finish the book; without you—this would have never been possible.

While I wrote this book independently, it was not without support. I'd like to thank the Manuscripts team for their amazing feedback. The journey started with the insights and observations from Zach Marcum. David Grandouiller and A.E. helped me remove some of the clutter, and Natalie Botero encouraged me to dig deeper into the emotions and insights from every experience. Without the patience and thoughtfulness of Chrissy Wolfe, this wouldn't be possible. Lastly, my copy editor Leah Pickett, marketing support, and art team. This was a team effort.

Most importantly, I want to thank my wife and soulmate, Beatriz. You inspire me. Every day. We are a team throughout this story.

And to my amazing wonderful kids, Claudia and Pedro. I created this book not only to share your old man's stories but also to open a window into the way I see things.

Image of Beatriz lifting up a sign that stating "they buried us without knowing we were seeds" (Photo Credit: Mariela Falero)

Appendix

INTRODUCTION

Bernal, Rafael. 2018. "Puerto Rico Reports Lowest Unemployment in 50 Years." *Latino* (blog), *The Hill*. August 17, 2018. https://thehill.com/latino/402376-puerto-rico-reports-lowest-unemployment-in-50-years/.

Bernal, Rafael. 2021. "Puerto Rico's Former Governor Stages a Comeback." *Latino* (blog), *The Hill*. May 21, 2021. https://thehill.com/latino/558587-puerto-ricos-former-governor-stages-a-comeback/.

El Vocero. 2012. "Reconocen a Ricky Rosselló por su Trabajo Científico." *El Vocero*. August 21, 2012.

Grens, Kerry. 2013. "Bird, Fish, and Fly Cells Reprogrammed." *Daily News* (blog), *TheScientist*. September 5, 2013. https://www.the-scientist.com/daily-news/bird-fish-and-fly-cells-reprogrammed-38738.

Guevara, Orlando. 2020. "El Hombre de Alma Baja no Puede Compartir la Virtud." *Marzo* (blog), *Ciudad Sin Cerrojos*. March 19, 2020. http://ciudadsincerrojos.blogspot.com/2020/03/el-hombre-de-alma-baja-no-puede.html.

Jardim, Daniel. 2019. "El Huracan Politico que Golpea a Rosselló." *Caricaturas* (blog), *El Nuevo Herald*. July 13, 2019. https://www.elnuevoherald.com/opinion-es/caricaturas/article232955967.html.

NotiCel. 2023. "Fuerte Preferencia PNP por Rosselló para Comisionado Residente." *Politica* (blog), *NotiCel*. October 23, 2023. https://www.noticel.com/politica/elecciones/20231019/fuerte-preferencia-pnp-por-Rossello-para-comisionado-residente/.

Panel Sobre el Fiscal Especial Independiente. 2020. "In Re: Ricardo Rosselló Nevares, et al. 2020. DI-FEI-2020-0005." November 23, 2020. http://panelfei.com/wp-content/uploads/2020/11/Resoluci%C3%B3n-del-Panel-In-Re-Ricardo-Rossell%C3%B3-Nevares-et-al.pdf.

Pew Research Center. 2021a. *Beyond Red vs. Blue: The Political Typology*. Washington, DC: Pew Research Center. https://www.pewresearch.org/politics/2021/11/09/beyond-red-vs-blue-the-political-typology-2/.

Pew Research Center. 2021b. *Citizens in Advanced Economies Want Significant Changes to Their Political Systems*. Washington, DC: Pew Research Center. http://www.pewresearch.org/global/2021/10/21/citizens-in-advanced-economies-want-significant-changes-to-their-political-systems/.

Rosselló, Ricardo. 2012. *Un Mejor Puerto Rico es Posible, Vol. I*. Puerto Rico: Editorial de la Universidad de Puerto Rico.

Rosselló, Ricardo, Chun-Chun Chen, Rui Dai, Jason Howard, Ute Hochgeschwender, and Erich Jarvis. 2013. "Mammalian Genes Induce Partially Reprogrammed Pluripotent Stem Cells in Non-mammalian Vertebrate and Invertebrate Species." *eLife* 2 (2013). http://dx.doi.org/10.7554/eLife.00036.001.

Rosselló, Ricardo, Zhuo Wang, Eddy Kizana, and David Kohn. 2009. "Connexin 43 as a Signaling Platform for Increasing the Volume and Spatial Distribution of Regenerated Tissue." *Proceedings of the National Academy of Sciences* 106, no. 32 (August): 13219–13224. DOI: 10.1073/pnas.0902622106.

Santiago, Iris. 2009. "Experts: Study May Be Key in Treating Cancer, Heart Disease." *The Daily Sun*. August 9, 2009.

Slavin, Robert. 2018. "Puerto Rico Governor Introduces Bill for COFINA Restructuring." *Promesa* (blog), *The Bond Buyer*. October 11, 2018. https://www.bondbuyer.com/news/puerto-rico-governor-introduces-bill-for-cofina-restructuring.

The World Bank Group. 2023. *GDP Growth—Puerto Rico*. Washington, DC: The World Bank. https://data.worldbank.org/indicator/NY.GDP.MKTP.KD.ZG?end=2020&locations=PR&start=2006.

CHAPTER 1

Awasthi, Puja. 2023. "July 2023 Is the Hottest Month in 1,200,000 Years." *News* (blog), *The Week*. July 23, 2023. https://www.theweek.in/news/india/2023/07/28/july-2023-is-the-hottest-month-in-120000-years.html.

Bayon, Miguel. 2016. "Una Peticion." *El Nuevo Dia*. November 12, 2016.

Bomey, Nathan, and John Gallagher. 2013. "How Detroit Went Broke: The Answers May Surprise You—and Don't Blame Coleman Young." *News* (blog), *Detroit Free Press*. July 18, 2018. https://www.freep.com/story/news/local/michigan/detroit/2013/09/15/how-detroit-went-broke-the-answers-may-surprise-you-and/77152028/.

Brown, Nick. 2016. "Puerto Rico's Other Crisis: Impoverished Pensions." *Reuters Investigate* (blog), *Reuters*. April 7, 2016. https://www.reuters.com/investigates/special-report/usa-puertorico-pensions/.

Collins, Susan, Barry Bosworth, and Miguel Soto-Class. 2016. *Economy of Puerto Rico:Restoring Growth*. Washington, DC: Brookings Institution Press.

Comisión Estatal de Elecciones. 2016. *Gobernador Resultados Isla*. CEEPR. https://primarias2016.ceepur.org/PRIMARIAS_LOCALES_2016_PNP_50/Escrutinio_75/index.html#es/default/GOBERNADOR_Resumen.xml.

Council on Foreign Relations. n.d. "Greece's Debt Crisis." Council on Foreign Relations. Accessed August 14, 2023. https://www.cfr.org/timeline/greeces-debt-crisis-timeline.

Czachor, Emily. 2023. "Canadian Wildfire Maps Show Where Fires Continue to Burn across Quebec, Ontario and Other Provinces." *CBS News*, July 19, 2023. https://www.cbsnews.com/news/map-canadian-wildfires-2023-where-are-the-fires-ontario-quebec/.

Eckstein, David, Vera Künzel, Laura Schäfer, and Maik Winges. 2020. *Global Climate Risk Index 2020*. Berlin: Germanwatch.

Galston, William, and Elaine Kamarck. 2022. "Is Democracy Failing and Putting Our Economic System at Risk?" *Research* (blog), *Brookings*. January 4, 2022. https://www.brookings.edu/research/is-democracy-failing-and-putting-our-economic-system-at-risk/#footnote-6.

Goodell, Jeff. 2018. "Puerto Rico Gov. Ricardo Rosselló on the Recovery, Climate Change and Trump." *Politics* (blog), *Rolling Stone*. September 20, 2018. https://www.rollingstone.com/politics/politics-features/puerto-rico-ricardo-Rossello-hurricane-maria-726605/.

Gramlich, Edward M. 1976. "The New York City Fiscal Crisis: What Happened and What Is to Be Done?" *The American Economic Review* 66, no. 2 (May): 415–429. https://www.jstor.org/stable/1817255.

Guadalupe, Patricia. 2016. "Who Are the Members of the Puerto Rico Fiscal Control Board?" *NBC News Latino* (blog), *NBC News*. August 31, 2016. https://www.nbcnews.com/news/latino/who-are-members-puerto-rico-fiscal-control-board-n640811.

Independent Evaluation Office (IEO) of the IMF. 2023. "The Role of the IMF in Argentina, 1991–2002." *Ongoing Projects* (blog), *International Monetary Fund*. July 2003. https://www.imf.org/external/np/ieo/2003/arg/index.htm.

Kaske, Michelle. 2016. "Puerto Rico's Development Bank on Brink as Debt Gambit Goes Bad." *News* (blog), *Bloomberg*. April 6, 2016. https://www.bloomberg.com/news/articles/2016-04-06/puerto-rico-s-development-bank-on-brink-as-debt-gambit-goes-bad.

Kwong, Emily. 2020. "What Would It Be Like to Fall into a Black Hole?" *Short Wave*. Released May 27, 2020. 14 minutes. https://www.npr.org/transcripts/859158971.

Phaneuf, Keith. 2023. "New CT Debt Report Offers Sobering Look at State Finances." *Money* (blog), *CT Mirror*. May 12, 2023. https://ctmirror.org/2023/05/12/ct-pension-debt-report-budget-retirement-health-care-pew/.

Rosselló, Pedro. 2005. *The Unfinished Business of American Democracy*. Puerto Rico: Public Policy Institute.

Rosselló, Ricardo. 2012. *Un Mejor Puerto Rico es Posible, Vol. I*. Puerto Rico: Editorial de la Universidad de Puerto Rico.

Schipani, Vanessa. 2017. "Land Loss in Louisiana." *SciCheck* (blog), *FactCheck.org*. March 20, 2017. https://www.factcheck.org/2017/03/land-loss-in-louisiana/.

Staletovich, Jenny. 2023. "Surging Growth in Florida and Rising Seas Equal Big Land Loss by 2040." *State News* (blog), *WFSU Public Media*. March 23, 2023. https://news.wfsu.org/state-news/2023-03-23/surging-growth-in-florida-and-rising-seas-equal-big-land-loss-by-2040.

Steinmetz, Kathy. 2018. "Governor Ricardo Rosselló: Puerto Rico Is a 'Geopolitical Black Hole.'" *Politics* (blog), *Time* magazine. May 10, 2018. https://time.com/5271767/puerto-rico-governor-donald-trump-statehood-hurricane-maria/.

CHAPTER 2

Bayon, Miguel. 2017. "Vicios de Construccion." *El Nuevo Dia*. September 30, 2017.

BBC. 2017. "Huracán María en Puerto Rico: Así Quedó una de las Comunidades Más Golpeadas por el Ciclón." *Mundo* (blog), *BBC*. September 22, 2017. https://www.bbc.com/mundo/media-41364183.

Boteler, Cody. 2017. "The 500-Year Storm: Quantifying Maria's Destruction." *Deep Dive* (blog), *Smart Cities Dive*. October 5, 2017. https://www.smartcitiesdive.com/news/the-500-year-storm-quantifying-marias-destruction/506588/.

Burnet, Erin. 2017. "Erin Burnet Outfront." Aired September 2017 in CNN Studios. Television. 1:00:00. http://www.cnn.com/TRANSCRIPTS/1709/20/ebo.01.html.

Caban, Lopez. 2017. "Rosselló Pasa con Buenas Notas Su Primer Huracán." *El Nuevo Dia*. September 9, 2017.

COR3 and Ricardo Rosselló. 2018. *Transformation and Innovation in the Wake of Devastation*. Puerto Rico: Government of Puerto Rico.

Dropp, Kyle, and Brendan Nyhan. 2017. "Nearly Half of Americans Don't Know Puerto Ricans Are Fellow Citizens." *The Upshot* (blog), *The New York Times*. September 26, 2017. https://www.nytimes.com/2017/09/26/upshot/nearly-half-of-americans-dont-know-people-in-puerto-ricoans-are-fellow-citizens.html.

Hansen, Claire. 2017. "Poll Finds Americans Don't Know Puerto Ricans Are Citizens." *National News* (blog), *US News and World Report*. September 26, 2017. https://www.usnews.com/news/national-news/articles/2017-09-26/almost-half-of-americans-dont-know-puerto-ricans-are-us-citizens-poll.

Hartley-Parkinson, Richard. 2017. "More than 1,000,000 Left without Power as Hurricane Irma Batters Caribbean." *News* (blog), *Metro*. September 7, 2017. https://metro.co.uk/2017/09/07/military-video-shows-scale-of-devastation-in-st-martin-after-hurricane-irma-6909387/.

Kantrow-Vázquez, Michelle. 2017. "Sir Richard Branson: P.R., Rosselló Have Been 'Fantastic.'" *Tourism & Transportation* (blog), *NimB*. September 12, 2017. https://newsismybusiness.com/richard-Rossello-fantastic/.

Kardashian, Kim. 2017. "This picture breaks my heart! I will be donating to Puerto Rico and help them get the food & water they desperately need. Please donate!" Twitter. September 26, 2017, 1:01 a.m. https://twitter.com/KimKardashian/status/912542705850429440?lang=es.

Levin, Jonathan. 2019. "President Trump Keeps Quoting a Misleading $91 Billion Figure for Puerto Rico Aid. Here Are the Facts." *Politics* (blog), *Time*. May 6, 2019. https://time.com/5584116/president-trump-puerto-rico-aid/.

Masters, Jeff. 2019. "Climate Change Made Hurricane Maria's Heavy Rains Nearly 5 Times More Likely to Occur." *Weather Underground News and Blogs* (blog), *Weather Underground*. April 16, 2019. https://www.wunderground.com/cat6/Climate-Change-Made-Hurricane-Marias-Heavy-Rains-Nearly-5-Times-More-Likely-Occur.

Milken Institute School of Public Health. 2018. *Ascertainment of the Estimated Excess Mortality from Hurricane Maria in Puerto Rico*. Washington, DC: Milken Institute School of Public Health, The George Washington University.

National Environmental Satellite, Data, and Information Service. 2017. "Hurricane Maria Lashes Puerto Rico." *NOAA*. September 20, 2017. https://www.nesdis.noaa.gov/news/hurricane-maria-lashes-puerto-rico.

NWS San Juan. 2017. "215PM FLASH FLOOD EMERGENCY for A Dam Failure in Isabela Municipality y Quebradillas Municipality in Puerto Rico… #prwx." Twitter. September 22, 2017, 2:20 p.m. https://twitter.com/NWSSanJuan/status/911294241460105218.

Rosselló, Ricardo. 2018. "Primeras 100 HORAS DE MARIA—El Documental Sub. Inglés." Ricardo Rosselló. September 24, 2018. 22:50. https://youtu.be/D-0BafLQ5fY.

Talmazan, Yuliya, and Phil Helsel. 2017. "Puerto Rico's Failing Guajataca Dam Endangers Thousands." *Weather* (blog), *NBC News*. September 23, 2017. https://www.nbcnews.com/news/weather/puerto-rico-s-failing-guajataca-dam-endangers-thousands-n804096.

Wilson, Christopher. 2018. "Study on Hurricane Casualties Fuels Talk of Statehood for Puerto Rico." *Yahoo! News* (blog), *Yahoo*. May 30, 2018. https://www.yahoo.com/news/study-hurricane-casualties-fuels-talk-statehood-puerto-rico-211055727.html.

CHAPTER 3

Bayon, Miguel. 2017. "De Los Tuits." *El Nuevo Dia*. October 24, 2017.

Bomey, Nathan. 2017. "Trump: Puerto Rico's Massive Debts Should Be Wiped Out." *Money* (blog), *USA Today*. October 4, 2017. https://www.usatoday.com/story/money/2017/10/04/donald-trump-puerto-rico-debts/730744001/.

Cillizza, Chris. 2017. "Trump's Puerto Rico Event Was Way Worse Than His Tweets." *CNN Politics* (blog), *CNN*. October 4, 2017. https://edition.cnn.com/2017/10/03/politics/trump-puerto-rico/index.html.

El Nuevo Dia. 2019. "Un Puño en la Boca." Editorial y Opinión (blog), *El Nuevo Dia*. March 31, 2019. https://gda.com/detalle-de-la-noticia/?article=3916375.

FEMA. 2023. "How a Disaster Gets Declared." FEMA. April 25, 2023. https://www.fema.gov/disaster/how-declared.

Government Accountability Office. 2019. *Medicaid: Territories' Financing Provisions and Challenges They Face Accessing Medicaid*. Washington, DC: US Government Accountability Office. https://www.gao.gov/assets/700/700197.pdf.

GW Today. 2018. "GW Researchers: 2,975 Excess Deaths Linked to Hurricane Maria." *Home* (blog), *GW Today*. August 29, 2018. https://gwtoday.gwu.edu/gw-researchers-2975-excess-deaths-linked-hurricane-maria.

Levy, Gabrielle. 2017. "Trump Compares Puerto Rico Response to Katrina." *Politics* (blog), *US News and World Report*. October 3, 2017. https://www.usnews.com/news/politics/articles/2017-10-03/trump-compares-puerto-rico-response-to-katrina.

Manji, Irshad. 2020. "How to Cancel 'Cancel Culture' and Revive Dialogue in a Polarized Time." Filmed November 2020. Video, 38 mins. https://ypo.ivy.com/learning-modules/how-to-cancel-cancel-culture-revive-dialogue-in-a-polarized-time-with-irshad-manji.

Milken Institute School of Public Health. 2018. *Ascertainment of the Estimated Excess Mortality from Hurricane Maria in Puerto Rico*. Washington, DC: Milken Institute School of Public Health.

Miller, Zeke, and Alexandra Jaffe. 2020. "Trump Says Former Chief of Staff Gen. John Kelly 'Was Unable to Handle the Pressure of this Job.'" *Boston Globe* (blog), *Boston Globe*. September 4, 2020. https://www.bostonglobe.com/2020/09/04/nation/disgrace-joe-biden-slams-president-trump-over-alleged-comments-mocking-us-war-dead/.

Mukunda, Gautam. 2023. "Picking Presidents: How to Make the Most Consequential Decision in the World." Filmed November 2023. Video, 1 hour. https://ypo.ivy.com/learning-modules/how-to-pick-a-president-with-gautam-mukunda.

Nakamura, David, and Ashley Parker. 2018. "'It Totally Belittled the Moment;' Many Look Back in Dismay at Trump's Tossing of Paper Towels in Puerto Rico." *Politics* (blog), *The Washington Post*. September 18, 2018. https://www.washingtonpost.com/politics/it-totally-belittled-the-moment-many-look-back-in-anger-at-trumps-tossing-of-paper-towels-in-puerto-rico/2018/09/13/8a3647d2-b77e-11e8-a2c5-3187f427e253_story.html.

NotiUno (@NotiUno 630). 2017. "President Trump to Governor Rosselló: "You are a hard working Governor. So much has been to rebuilt. We've done a great job in Puerto Rico." Facebook, October 19, 2017, 12:50 p.m. https://www.facebook.com/watch/?v=1532481200178576.

Rainie, Lee, Scott Keeter, and Andrew Perrin. 2019. "Trust and Distrust in America." *Research Topics* (blog), *Pew Research Center*. July 22, 2019. https://www.pewresearch.org/politics/2019/07/22/trust-and-distrust-in-america/.

Rapfogel, Nicole. 2022. "Without Congressional Action, Puerto Rico Faces Severe Medicaid Funding Cuts." *Cap 20* (blog), *American Progress*. November 3, 2022. https://www.americanprogress.org/article/without-congressional-action-puerto-rico-faces-severe-medicaid-funding-cuts/.

Reuters. 2019. "Trump Slams Puerto Rico Leaders, Says Governor Is 'Terrible.'" *World* (blog), *Reuters*. July 22, 2019. https://www.reuters.com/article/idUSKCN1UH21P/.

Ross, Janell. 2017. "In Puerto Rico, Trump's Paper-towel Toss Reveals where his Empathy Lies." National (blog). Washington Post. October 6, 2017. https://www.washingtonpost.com/news/post-nation/wp/2017/10/06/in-puerto-rico-trumps-paper-towel-toss-reveals-where-his-empathy-lies/.

CHAPTER 4

Agencia EFE. 2019. "Tasa de Desempleo en Puerto Rico Registra su Cifra más Baja en Cuatro Décadas (8.1%, EFE)." *Yahoo! Finanzas* (blog), *Yahoo!* August 16, 2019. https://es-us.finanzas.yahoo.com/noticias/tasa-desempleo-puerto-rico-registra-170624781.html.

Bayon, Miguel (@miguelbayonart). 2019. "Ya No Hay de Otra… #rickyrenuncia #puertorico #governador #renuncia." Instagram. July 24, 2019.

Bradford, Hazel. 2019. "First Puerto Rico Restructuring Debt Deal Approved." *Economy* (blog), *Pensions & Investments*. February 5, 2019. https://www.pionline.com/article/20190205/ONLINE/190209905/first-puerto-rico-debt-restructuring-deal-approved-for-cofina.

CNN. 2008. "Puerto Rican Governor Charged in Campaign Finance Probe." *Politics* (blog), *CNN*. March 27, 2008. http://edition.cnn.com/2008/POLITICS/03/27/puerto.rico.governor/index.html.

Cortes Chico, Ricardo. 2018. "Ricardo Rosselló Destaca que la Nomina del Gobierno se Redujo en un 10%." *Locales* (blog), *El Nuevo Dia*. December 19, 2018. https://www.elnuevodia.com/noticias/locales/notas/ricardo-rossello-destaca-que-la-nomina-del-gobierno-se-redujo-en-un-107/.

Coto, Danica. 2019. "Puerto Rico Gov Apologizes for Private Chat that Drew Ire." *News* (blog), *Insider*. July 11, 2019. https://www.insider.com/puerto-rico-gov-apologizes-for-private-chat-that-drew-ire-2019-7.

El Nuevo Dia. 2019. "Rosselló Tiene Poca Competencia Electoral." *El Nuevo Dia*. May 3, 2019.

Figueroa, Barbara. 2019. "Ricardo Rosselló: 'No Voy a Renunciar.'" *Gobierno y Politica* (blog), *Primera Hora*. July 12, 2019. https://www.primerahora.com/noticias/gobierno-politica/notas/ricardo-rossello-no-voy-a-renunciar/.

Kumneger Media. 2023. "Federal Prosecutor's Office Requests to Dismiss the Charges against the Former Director of ASES Angela Avila." *Kumneger Media* (blog), *Kumneger*. November 8, 2023. https://kumnegermedia.com/federal-prosecutors-office-requests-to-dismiss-the-charges-against-the-former-director-of-ases-angela-avila/.

Nag, Anwesha. 2021. "'Everybody Has a Plan until They Get Punched in the Mouth.'—How Did the Famous Mike Tyson Quote Originate?" *MMA* (blog), *Sportskedia*. January 5, 2021. https://www.sportskeeda.com/mma/news-everybody-plan-get-punched-mouth-how-famous-mike-tyson-quote-originate.

Navia, Patricio. 2021. "Latin America's Anti-Incumbent Wave Will End in Tears." *Elections* (blog), *Americas Quarterly*. August 16, 2021. https://www.americasquarterly.org/article/latin-americas-anti-incumbent-wave-will-end-in-tears/.

Panel Sobre el Fiscal Especial Independiente. 2020. "In Re: Ricardo Rosselló Nevares, et al. 2020. DI-FEI-2020-0005." November 23, 2020. http://panelfei.com/wp-content/uploads/2020/11/Resoluci%C3%B3n-del-Panel-In-Re-Ricardo-Rossell%C3%B3-Nevares-et-al.pdf.

PR News Wire. 2020. "Declaración del Exgobernador de Puerto Rico con Respecto a Su Exoneración por Parte de Fiscal Independiente." *PR News Wire*. November 25, 2020. https://www.prnewswire.com/news-releases/declaracion-del-exgobernador-de-puerto-rico-con-respecto-a-su-exoneracion-por-parte-de-fiscal-independiente-809282531.html.

Primera Hora. 2019. "Otra Amenaza de Muerte Contra Rosselló." *Policia y Tribunales* (blog), *Primera Hora*. July 22, 2019. https://www.primerahora.com/noticias/policia-tribunales/notas/otra-amenaza-de-muerte-contra-rossello/.

Primera Hora. 2020. "Cronologia Historica." *Primera Hora*. July 20, 2020.

CHAPTER 5

Anthony, Luis. 2018. "Ricardo Rosselló Governor of Puerto Rico at the 109th Annual NAACP Convention." LuisAnthony40HD. July 17, 2018. 15:37. https://www.youtube.com/watch?v=tl6BUHbQM1k&t=4s.

Bayon, Miguel. 2017. "Para la Estadidad." *El Nuevo Dia*. June 3, 2017.

Bernal, Rafael. 2021. "Puerto Rico's Former Governor Stages a Comeback." *Latino* (blog), *Politico*. June 15, 2021. https://thehill.com/latino/558587-puerto-ricos-former-governor-stages-a-comeback/.

Berke, Richard. 1991. "Washington Talk; Behind-the-Scenes Role For a 'Shadow Senator.'" *The New York Times*. March 27, 1991. https://www.nytimes.com/1991/03/27/us/washington-talk-behind-the-scenes-role-for-a-shadow-senator.html.

Caputo, Marc. 2017. "Rubio, Puerto Rico Governor Spar over Tax Reform." *Politico* (blog), *Politico*. December 19, 2017. https://www.politico.com/story/2017/12/19/rubio-puerto-rico-governor-tax-fight-305996.

Congressional Research Service. 2022. *Political Status of Puerto Rico: Brief Background and Recent Developments for Congress*. Washington, DC: Congressional Research Service.

Daugherty, Alex. 2017. "Rubio: Congress Isn't Doing Enough to Help Puerto Rico." *Politics and Government* (blog), *Miami Herald*. October 8, 2017. https://www.miamiherald.com/news/politics-government/article179722371.html.

Editorial Board. 2017. "Congress Should Help Puerto Rico—Not Hurt It." *Opinions* (blog), *The Washington Post*. December 14, 2017. https://www.washingtonpost.com/opinions/congress-should-help-puerto-rico--not-hurt-it/2017/12/14/f03226ee-e0f8-11e7-8679-a9728984779c_story.html.

El Vocero. 2021. "Rosselló El Mas Votado." *El Vocero*.

Failla, Zak. 2021. "New Poll Reveals Percentages of Americans Who Want to Secede by Region." *Politics* (blog), *White Plains*. August 1, 2021. https://dailyvoice.com/new-york/whiteplains/politics/new-poll-reveals-percentages-of-americans-who-want-to-secede-by-region/812724/.

Harris, Kamala (@kamalaharris). 2022. "We must protect voting rights." Instagram, January 10, 2022.

Hatzipanagos, Rachel. 2018. "The 'Decolonization' of the American Museum." *National* (blog), *The Washington Post*. October 11, 2018. https://www.washingtonpost.com/nation/2018/10/12/decolonization-american-museum/.

King, Ledyard. 2017. "Rubio Presses White House to Ramp Up Rescue of Puerto Rico." *Florida* (blog), *TCPalm*. September 26, 2017. https://www.tcpalm.com/story/news/local/florida/2017/09/26/rubio-presses-white-house-ramp-up-rescue-puerto-rico/706637001/.

McElwee, Sean, and John Ray. 2020. "Voters Have Moved in Favor of DC and Puerto Rico Statehood." *Data for Progress* (blog). September 8, 2020. https://www.dataforprogress.org/blog/2020/9/8/voters-favor-dc-and-puerto-rico-statehood.

NotiCel. 2021. "Ricardo Rosselló Envia Carta al Congreso Sobre el Estatus Para Ver 'Si el Gas Pela.'" *Ahora* (blog), *NotiCel*. November 22, 2021. https://www.noticel.com/ahora/top-stories/20211122/ricardo-rossello-envia-carta-al-congreso-sobre-el-estatus-para-ver-si-el-gas-pela/.

NotiUno. 2021. "EXCLUSIVA: Ricardo Rosselló Aceptaría ser Delegado Congresional si el Pueblo lo Elige Vía Write In." *Gobierno y Politica* (blog), *NotiUno*. May 13, 2021. https://www.notiuno.com/noticias/gobierno-y-politica/ricardo-rossell-aceptar-a-ser-delegado-congresional-si-el-pueblo-vota-por-l-write-in/article_b01de6e6-b328-11eb-bf8f-6fdcf16ea8c3.html.

Padro Ocasio, Bianca. 2018. "Puerto Rico Governor Calls for Political Organization." *Orlando Sentinel*. January 13, 2018.

Perez Pintado, Amanda. 2023. "Ricardo Rosselló Nevares Participa Virtualmente en la Convencion del PNP." *Politica* (blog), *El Nuevo Dia*. August 26, 2023. https://www.elnuevodia.com/noticias/politica/notas/ricardo-rossello-nevares-participa-virtualmente-en-la-convencion-del-pnp/.

Rosselló, Ricardo. 2012. *Un Mejor Puerto Rico es Posible, Vol. I*. Puerto Rico: Editorial de la Universidad de Puerto Rico.

Sesin, Carmen. 2022. "Why Florida Latinos Turned Out in Favor of Republicans." *Latino* (blog), *NBC News*. November 15, 2022. https://www.nbcnews.com/news/latino/florida-latinos-turned-favor-republicans-rcna57167.

Stacom, Don. 2018. "Murphy, Blumenthal to Tour Puerto Rico's Storm Damage." *News* (blog), *Hartford Courant*. January 1, 2018. https://www.courant.com/2018/01/01/murphy-blumenthal-to-tour-puerto-ricos-storm-damage/.

Thompson, Sonia. 2021. "The US Has the Second-Largest Population of Spanish Speakers—How to Equip Your Brand to Serve Them." *Leadership* (blog), *Forbes*. May 27, 2021. https://www.forbes.com/sites/soniathompson/2021/05/27/the-us-has-the-second-largest-population-of-spanish-speakers-how-to-equip-your-brand-to-serve-them/.

UK Parliament. 2023. "Shadow Cabinet." *Glossary* (blog), *UK Parliament*. Accessed January 20, 2023. https://www.parliament.uk/site-information/glossary/shadow-cabinet/.

Van Dam, Andrew. 2022. "People Are Fleeing Puerto Rico, Guam, and Every Other US Territory. What Gives?" *The Washington Post*, September 23, 2022. https://www.washingtonpost.com/business/2022/09/23/american-territories-population-loss/.

World Population Review. 2023. "District of Columbia Population." *States* (blog), *World Population Review*. Accessed July 23, 2023. https://worldpopulationreview.com/states/district-of-columbia-population.

CHAPTER 6

Bayon, Miguel. 2017. "La Reforma Laboral." *El Nuevo Dia*. January 21, 2017.

Beck, Rebecca. 2020. "Investigation into Former Missouri Governor Who Resigned Finds 'No Evidence of Any Wrongdoing.'" *CNN Politics* (blog), *CNN*. February 13, 2020. https://www.cnn.com/2020/02/13/politics/eric-greitens-no-wrongdoing-investigation-missouri/index.html.

Brown, Nick. 2016. "Puerto Rico's Other Crisis: Impoverished Pensions." *Reuters Investigates* (blog), *Reuters*. April 7, 2016. https://www.reuters.com/investigates/special-report/usa-puertorico-pensions/.

Cherney, Mike. 2013. "Borrowing Maneuver Catches Flak." *Articles* (blog), *The Wall Street Journal*. December 2, 2013. https://www.wsj.com/articles/SB10001424052702304579404579234441072889918.

Cortes Chico, Ricardo. 2013. "Introspeccion un Año Despues." *El Nuevo Dia*. November 3, 2013.

El Nuevo Dia. 2010. "Admite Fracaso de la Ley de Comunidades Especiales." *Locales* (blog), *El Nuevo Dia*. October 15, 2010. https://www.elnuevodia.com/noticias/locales/notas/admite-fracaso-de-la-ley-de-comunidades-especiales/.

El Tiempo. 1998. "Puerto Rico. Gorbachov Ataca AEU." *Archivo* (blog), *El Tiempo*. June 14, 1998. https://www.eltiempo.com/archivo/documento/MAM-770838.

El Vocero. 2019. "Enfasis en Salud y Educacion." *El Vocero*. April 25, 2019.

Gorbachev, Mikhail. 2007. *Mikhail Gorbachev: Memoirs*. New York: Doubleday.

Internews Service. 2013. "Vuelven a Educación Conserjes Despedidos Bajo Ley 7." *Noticias* (blog), *Metro*. August 7, 2013. https://www.metro.pr/pr/noticias/2013/08/07/vuelven-educacion-conserjes-despedidos-ley-7.html.

Mandela, Nelson. 2013. *Long Walk to Freedom*. Boston: Little, Brown.

Marino, John. 2008. "Puerto Rican Governor Charged in Campaign Scam." *US News* (blog), *Reuters*. March 27, 2008.

https://www.reuters.com/article/us-puertorico-governor-indictment-idUSN3R37784920080327.

Meyer, Jeff. 2014. "Puerto Rico Gets Credit Rating Downgrade." *Latest News* (blog), *Borgen Project*. February 19, 2014. https://borgenproject.org/puerto-rico-gets-credit-rating-downgrade/.

NotiUno (@notiuno). 2016. "Un día como hoy hace 10 años (2006) administración Aníbal Acevedo Vilá comenzó a cobrar el IVU de 7% (hoy 11.5%) avalado por Legislatura PNP." Twitter, November 15, 2016, 5:16 a.m. https://twitter.com/notiuno/status/798469785063489536.

NotiUno. 2019. "Tildan de 'Cínico' al Gobernador y Velan Contratos que se Cocinan para 'Educación Gratuita.'" *NotiUno* (blog), *NotiUno*. April 26, 2019. https://www.notiuno.com/noticias/gobierno-y-politica/tildan-de-c-nico-al-gobernador-y-velan-contratos-que-se-cocinan-para-educaci-n/article_dbed0216-67d0-11e9-a43e-f76ee50bcbfc.html.

Pierson, Paul. 2004. *Politics in Time: History, Institution, and Social Analysis*. New Jersey: Princeton Press.

Primera Hora. 2013. "A García Padilla 'Le Vale' Lo Que Piensen de él Las Agencias Crediticias." *Gobierno y Politica* (blog), *Primera Hora*. April 2, 2013. https://www.primerahora.com/noticias/gobierno-politica/notas/a-garcia-padilla-le-vale-lo-que-piensen-de-el-las-agencias-crediticias-video/.

Rivera, Ivan. 2021. "El Fenomeno Rosselló." *Opinion* (blog), *El Vocero*. July 6, 2021. https://www.elvocero.com/opinion/el-fen-meno-rossell/article_efee3fde-c717-11eb-b0bc-eb6334ae24d8.html.

Rosselló, Pedro. 2018. *A Mi Manera Vol. 2*. Puerto Rico: Biblioteca Pedro Rosselló.

CHAPTER 7

Agencia EFE. 2019. "Crean Plataforma Digital de Registro de Cabilderos del Gobierno de P.Rico." *Yahoo! Noticias* (blog), *Yahoo!* July 2, 2019. https://es-us.noticias.yahoo.com/crean-plataforma-digital-registro-cabilderos-180429531.html.

Bayon, Miguel (@miguelbayonart). 2018. "*#caricaturas #caricatura #ricardorosello @ricardoRosselló @beatrizisabelRosselló @badbunnypr #concierto #badbunny #tamosbien #puertorico*." Instagram, October 15, 2018. https://www.instagram.com/p/Bo-e3CEADQy.

Bayon, Miguel. 2017. "Oneil." *El Nuevo Dia*. March 8, 2017.

Caro Gonzalez, Leysa. 2017. "Mujeres Asumen el Liderato del Pais." *Politica* (blog), *El Nuevo Dia*. January 28, 2017. https://www.elnuevodia.com/noticias/politica/notas/mujeres-asumen-el-liderato-del-pais/.

Concilio de Mujeres. 2019. *Informe de Labores y Logros*. Puerto Rico: Gobierno de Puerto Rico. https://laobradeRosselló.com/3311-2/.

Consejo Asesor del Gobernador en Asuntos LGBTT. 2019. *Informe de Labores y Logros*. Puerto Rico: Gobierno de Puerto Rico. https://laobradeRosselló.com/3100-2/.

Delgado, Alex. 2019. "Escandalos sin Control." *NotiUno* (blog), *NotiUno*. July 8, 2018. https://www.notiuno.com/noticias/gobierno-y-politica/esc-ndalos-sin-control/article_8c0b1034-9733-11e9-bd36-8710c3fd85f4.html.

Dicklitch-Nelson, Susan, Indira Rahman, Scottie Thompson Buckland, Berwood Yost, and Cuong Nguyen. 2021. *F&M Global Barometers: LGBT Human Rights in 203 Countries and Regions, 2011–2018*. Lancaster, PA: Franklin & Marshall College.

F&M Global Barometers. n.d. "F&M Global Baromers." F&M Global Barometers. Accessed May 10, 2023. https://www.fandmglobalbarometers.org/.

Finkel, Eli, Christopher A. Bail, Mina Cikara, Peter H. Ditto, Shanto Iyengar, Samara Klar, Lilliana Mason, Mary C. McGrath, Brendan Nyhan, and James N. Druckman. 2020. "Political Sectarianism in America." *Science* 370, no. 6516 (October). DOI: 10.1126/science.abe171.

GayCities. 2018. "Destination of the Year." GayCities. Accessed June 3, 2023. https://www.gaycities.com/best-of-2018/destination-of-the-year.

Hacienda. 2019. "Hacienda Informa Cierre de Año Fiscal 2018–2019 con Cifra Récord de Recaudos que Ascienden a $11,376 Millones." Accessed July 10, 2023. http://hacienda.pr.gov/sobre-hacienda/sala-de-prensa-virtual/comunicados-de-prensa/hacienda-informa-cierre-de-ano-fiscal-2018-19-con-cifra-record-de-recaudos-que-ascienden-11376-millones.

Hernandez, Luis. 2018. "Rosselló Convierte en Ley Proyecto para Búsqueda del Inspector General." *NotiUno* (blog), *NotiUno*. January 3, 2018. https://www.notiuno.com/rossell-convierte-en-ley-proyecto-para-b-squeda-del-inspector-general/article_70707397-2b6f-5ea5-b1f7-32d9dc803bd3.html.

Human Rights Campaign. 2019. "Puerto Rico's Governor Issues Historic Executive Order Protecting Youth from Dangerous 'Conversion Therapy.'" *News* (blog), *Human Rights Campaign*. March 27, 2019. https://www.hrc.org/news/puerto-ricos-governor-issues-order-protecting-youth-from-conversion-therapy.

Ibarra Vázquez, Genesis. 2017. "Héctor O'Neill se Declara Culpable en Caso por Violencia de Género y Hostigamiento Sexual." *Noticias* (blog), *El Nuevo Dia*. November 24, 2021. https://www.elnuevodia.com/noticias/tribunales/notas/hector-oneill-se-declara-culpable-en-caso-por-violencia-de-genero-y-hostigamiento-sexual/.

Manji, Irshad. 2020. "How to Cancel 'Cancel Culture' and Revive Dialogue in a Polarized Time." Filmed November 2020. Video, 38 mins. https://ypo.ivy.com/learning-modules/how-to-cancel-cancel-culture-revive-dialogue-in-a-polarized-time-with-irshad-manji.

Metro. 2018. "Puerto Rico Recibe el Premio Destino del Ano LGBTQ+." *Metro*. December 17, 2018.

Meyer, Herbert. 1993. *Hard Thinking: The Fusion of Politics & Science*. Washington: Storm King Press.

Panel Sobre el Fiscal Especial Independiente. 2020. "In Re: Ricardo Rosselló Nevares, et al. 2020. DI-FEI-2020-0005." November 23, 2020. http://panelfei.com/wp-content/uploads/2020/11/Resoluci%C3%B3n-del-Panel-In-Re-Ricardo-Rossell%C3%B3-Nevares-et-al.pdf.

Rivera, Maricarmen. 2018. "Rosselló se Proclama Feminista." *Contenido Destacado* (blog), *El Vocero*. November 26, 2018. https://www.elvocero.com/gobierno/rossell-se-proclama-feminista/article_9e98512e-f1a4-11e8-84f3-5fb1b546205a.html.

Ruiz Kuilan, Gloria. 2018. "El Gobernador Convierte en Ley el Código Anticorrupción." Accessed July 3, 2023. https://www.ocpr.gov.pr/articulos/el-gobernador-convierte-en-ley-el-codigo-anticorrupcion/.

Serrano, Oscar. 2019a. "Misogyny, Corruption and Leaked Messages: The Story of the Demise of Puerto Rico's Governor." *Voices* (blog), *Independent*. July 27, 2019. https://www.independent.co.uk/voices/puerto-rico-ricardo-rossello-governor-resigns-leaked-messages-telegram-a9023306.html.

Serrano, Pedro. 2019b. "Denuncia Indulto de Ricardo Rosselló a Pastor Homofóbico." *PedroJulioSerrano* (blog), *pedrojulioserrano.com*. August 14, 2019. https://pedrojulioserrano.com/2019/08/14/denuncia-indulto-de-ricardo-rossello-a-pastor-homofobico/.

SinComillas. 2017. "Gobernador Firma Ley de Igualdad Salarial." *Economia* (blog), *SinComillas*. March 8, 2017. https://sincomillas.com/gobernador-firma-ley-de-igualdad-salarial/.

Soto, Fernando. 2020. "Rosello: 'Este Lamentable Incidente Fue Utilizado por Mis Opositores Políticos.'" *Nacionales* (blog), *Pasa La Voz*. November 25, 2020. https://pasalavoznoticias.com/rosello-este-lamentable-incidente-fue-utilizado-por-mis-opositores-politicos/.

Stetler, Brian. 2019. "These Journalists Exposed the Corruption That Led to Puerto Rico's Mass Protests." *CNN Business* (blog), *CNN*. July 24, 2019. https://www.cnn.com/2019/07/22/media/investigative-journalism-ricardo-rossell/index.html.

Thompson, Nigel. 2019. "From #RickyLeaks to #RickyRenuncia: The Political Hurricane That Swept Puerto Rico." *Politcs* (blog), *Al Dia News*. August 21, 2019. https://aldianews.com/en/politics/policy/political-hurricane.

Univision. 2019. "Aumenta la Presión Contra Rosselló: Hallan 5 Delitos en el Chat y Avanza el Proceso para Su Destitución." *Politica* (blog), *Univision*. July 24, 2019. https://www.univision.com/noticias/politica/aumenta-la-presion-contra-rossello-hallan-5-delitos-en-el-chat-y-avanza-el-proceso-para-su-destitucion.

CHAPTER 8

Anthony, Luis. 2016. "Ricardo Rosselló Educa a David Bernier." LuisAnthony40HD. September 15, 2016. 1:39. https://www.youtube.com/watch?v=GkgFGP39LEA.

Associated Press. 2020. "Puerto Rico's Federally Created Financial Oversight Board Upheld by Supreme Court." *Latino* (blog), *NBC News*. June 1, 2020. https://www.nbcnews.com/news/latino/puerto-rico-s-federally-created-financial-oversight-board-upheld-supreme-n1221046.

Bayon, Miguel. 2017. "Todo Bajo Control." *El Nuevo Dia*. February 6, 2017.

Brown, Nick. 2017. "In Puerto Rico Bankruptcy, Mutual Funds Compete with Themselves." *Business News* (blog), *Reuters*. July 28, 2017. https://www.reuters.com/article/us-puertorico-debt-funds-idINKBN1AD0GP.

Caribbean Business. 2016. "10 Asuntos que Debes Saber Sobre el Plan para Puerto Rico." *Puerto Rico* (blog), *Caribbean Business*. August 7, 2016. https://cb.pr/10-asuntos-que-debes-saber-sobre-el-plan-para-puerto-rico/.

Childs, Mary. 2018. "Puerto Rico Reaches Agreement on Cofina Debt." *FocusFund* (blog), *Barrons*. August 10, 2018. https://www.barrons.com/articles/puerto-rico-reaches-agreement-on-cofina-debt-1533920320.

Denis, Nelson. 2015. "Due to Crisis, More Puerto Ricans Now Live in the US Than on the island" *Politics* (blog), *The Atlantic*. July 6, 2015. https://www.theatlantic.com/politics/archive/2015/07/due-to-crisis-more-puerto-ricans-now-live-in-the-us-than-on-the-island/432246/.

El Nuevo Dia. 2018. "Mea Culpa." *El Nuevo Dia*. March 6, 2018.

El Nuevo Dia. 2019. "Admite Errores." *El Nuevo Dia*. April 25, 2019.

Fonseca, Jay (@jayfonsecapr). 2016. "Una buena exposición de Rosselló de lo q es el empleador unico. Si eso se implementa bien es bueno. El ejemplo de DACO de Rosselló fue bueno." Twitter, October 16, 2016, 8:03 p.m.

Giel, Dawn. 2017. "Puerto Rico Starts $70 Billion Bankruptcy Proceedings, Biggest Ever for Municipal Bond Market." *Municipal Bonds* (blog), *CNBC*. May 3, 2017. https://www.cnbc.com/2017/05/03/puerto-rico-officially-triggers-bankruptcy-protection-proceedings-.html.

Giel, Dawn. 2018. "Sens. Warren and Sanders Introduce Bill That Would Slash Puerto Rico's Debt." *Politics* (blog), *CNBC*. July 25, 2018. https://www.cnbc.com/2018/07/25/senators-warren--sanders-introduce-bill-that-would-slash-puerto-rico.html.

Heath, Thomas, and Tory Newmyer. 2017. "Puerto Rico, with $73 billion in Debt, Forced Toward Bankruptcy." *Business* (blog), *The Washington Post*. May 3, 2017.

https://www.washingtonpost.com/business/economy/puerto-rico-with-73-billion-in-debt-forced-toward-bankruptcy/2017/05/03/92e39d76-3020-11e7-9534-00e4656c22aa_story.html.

Heritage Foundation. 2017. "Moving Puerto Rico Forward: A Conversation with Governor Ricardo Rosselló of Puerto Rico." *Budget And Spending* (blog), *Heritage Foundation*. April 26, 2017. https://www.heritage.org/budget-and-spending/event/moving-puerto-rico-forward-conversation-governor-ricardo-rossello-puerto.

Jones, Jeffrey. 2010. "President's Support Usually Unaffected by State of Union." *Politics* (blog), *Gallup*. January 26, 2010. https://news.gallup.com/poll/125396/president-support-usually-unaffected-state-union.aspx.

Medwar, Peter. 1977. *My Life in Science*. New York: Harper Collins.

Meyer, Herbert. 1993. *Hard Thinking: The Fusion of Politics and Science.* Washington: Storm King Press.

Reuters Staff. 2015. "Hatch: Puerto Rico Bill Only Immediate Option to Help Territory." *Bond News* (blog), *Reuters*. December 15, 2015. https://www.reuters.com/article/usa-congress-puerto-rico-idUSL1N1441TW20151215.

Rosselló, Ricardo. 2012. *Un Mejor Puerto Rico es Possible, Vol. I.* Puerto Rico: Editorial de la Universidad de Puerto Rico.

Senate Finance. 2016. "Hatch: Puerto Rico Bill Only Immediate Option to Help Territory." *Chairman's News* (blog), *United States Senate Committee on Finance.* June 29, 2016. https://www.finance.senate.gov/chairmans-news/hatch-puerto-rico-bill-only-immediate-option-to-help-territory.

Stojanovic, Lorae, and David Wessel. 2022. "Puerto Rico's Bankruptcy: Where Do Things Stand Today?" *Commentary* (blog), *Brookings.* August 17, 2022. https://www.brookings.edu/articles/puerto-ricos-bankruptcy-where-do-things-stand-today/.

Sullivan, Laura. 2018. "How Puerto Rico's Debt Created a Perfect Storm before the Storm." *Special Series* (blog), *NPR.* May 2, 2018. https://www.npr.org/2018/05/02/607032585/how-puerto-ricos-debt-created-a-perfect-storm-before-the-storm.

World Bank. 2023. *GDP Growth (Annual %)—Puerto Rico.* Washington, DC: The World Bank Group. https://data.worldbank.org/indicator/NY.GDP.MKTP.KD.ZG?locations=PR.

CHAPTER 9

Celeste, Anniesmell (@Anniesmell_Bori). 2019. "Está si me dio vergüenza y tristeza, lo bajo q llegan con tal de hacer daño, está brutal miren esto. Miren quién post eso tan denigrante y a quién defiende La Colectividad Feminista Internacional." Twitter. Jul 12, 2019. 1:13 p.m.

Cruz, Adria. 2012. "Einstein para Gobernador?" *Primera Hora.* August 30, 2012.

De Llano, Pablo. 2017. "La Primera Dama de Puerto Rico Dice que Paulo Coelho Escribió 'Cien Años de Soledad.'" *Libros* (blog), *El Pais.* November 4, 2017. https://verne.elpais.com/verne/2017/11/04/mexico/1509828141_450483.html.

Frei, Frances. 2022. "How to Boost Your Bottom Line by Building Trust." *YPO Edge* (blog), *YPO.* November 8, 2022. https://www.ypo.org/2022/11/boost-your-bottom-line-by-building-trust/.

Guy, Clarissa. 2021. "The Other: The Harmful Legacy of Human Zoos." *Rocky Mountain PBS* (blog), *PBS.* April 15, 2021. https://www.rmpbs.org/blogs/rocky-mountain-pbs/the-harmful-legacy-of-human-zoos/.

Hall, Andrew. 2019. "Want to Reduce Polarization in Congress? Make Moderates a Better Job Offer." *Institute for Economic Policy Research* (blog), *Stanford University.* June 2019. https://siepr.stanford.edu/publications/policy-brief/want-reduce-polarization-congress-make-moderates-better-job-offer.

Luttrell, Andy. 2021. "The Psychology of Dehumanization." AndyLuttrellPsych. February 4, 2021. 11:38. https://www.youtube.com/watch?v=QuNbNNqtMvs.

MacArthur, Robert Stuart. 1906. "Man and Monkey Show Disapproved by Clergy." *The New York Times.* September 10, 1906.

Manji, Irshad. 2020. "How to Cancel 'Cancel Culture' and Revive Dialogue in a Polarized Time." Filmed November 2020. Video, 38 mins. https://ypo.ivy.com/learning-modules/how-to-cancel-cancel-culture-revive-dialogue-in-a-polarized-time-with-irshad-manji.

Metro Puerto Rico. 2017. "Ricardo Rosselló se Vacila su Plan." *Noticias* (blog), *Metro*. February 10, 2017. https://www.metro.pr/pr/noticias/2017/02/10/ricardo-rossello-se-vacila-plan.html.

Meyer, Herbert. 1993. *Hard Thinking: The Fusion of Politics & Science*. Washington: Storm King Press.

Padgett, Jeremy, Johanna L Dunaway, and Joshua P Darr. 2019. "As Seen on TV? How Gatekeeping Makes the US House Seem More Extreme." *Journal of Communication* 69, no. 6 (December). https://doi.org/10.1093/joc/jqz039.

Petsko, Christopher, Ryan F Lei, Jonas R Kunst, Emile Bruneau, and Nour Kteily. 2020. "Blatant Dehumanization in the Mind's Eye: Prevalent Even among Those Who Explicitly Reject It?" *Journal of Experimental Psychology: General* 150, no. 6 (June). DOI: 10.1037/xge0000961. 29.

Pew Research Center. 2021. *Beyond Red vs. Blue: The Political Typology*. Washington, DC: Pew Research Center. https://www.pewresearch.org/politics/2021/11/09/beyond-red-vs-blue-the-political-typology-2/.

Pew Research Center. 2023. "Public Trust in Government: 1958–2023." *Research Topics* (blog), *Pew Research Center*. September 19, 2023. https://www.pewresearch.org/politics/2022/06/06/public-trust-in-government-1958-2022/.

Residente, iLe, Bad Bunny. 2019. "Afilando los Cuchillos." *Genius* (blog). *Genius*. July 17, 2019. https://genius.com/Residente-ile-and-bad-bunny-afilando-los-cuchillos-lyrics.

CHAPTER 10

Acosta, Jim, and Kevin Liptak. 2019. "Exclusive: Puerto Rico Governor Warns White House: 'If the Bully Gets Close, I'll Punch the Bully in the Mouth.'" *CNN Politics* (blog), *CNN*. March 28, 2019. https://www.cnn.com/2019/03/28/politics/ricardo-rossell-donald-trump-puerto-rico-funding/index.html.

Baldassari, Delia, and Andrew Gelman. 2008. "Partisans without Constraint: Political Polarization and Trends in American Public Opinion." *American Journal of Sociology*, 114, no. 2 (2008). DOI: 10.1086/590649.

Bloomberg Daybreak. 2019. "Puerto Rico Unvails $35 Billion Restructuring Plan to Exit Bankruptcy." *News* (blog). *Bloomberg*. June 17, 2019. https://www.bloomberg.com/news/videos/2019-06-17/puerto-rico-unveils-35-billion-restructuring-plan-to-exit-bankruptcy-video.

Bayon, Miguel. 2017. "En el Zapato de Trump." *El Nuevo Dia*. May 3, 2017.

Caribbean Business. 2019. "Asociacion de Maestros Aclara Acuerdo de Negociacion con la Junta Fiscal." *Caribbean Business* (blog), *Caribbean Business*. June 6, 2019. https://cb.pr/asociacion-de-maestros-aclara-acuerdo-de-negociacion-con-la-junta-fiscal/.

Colon Santiago, Leyrian. 2018. "Productor de Hamilton Destaca a Ricardo Rosselló Como el que Motivara el Traslado de Hamilton al CBA." *Cultura* (blog), *Pulso Estudiantil*. December 24, 2018. https://pulsoestudiantil.com/productor-de-hamilton-destaca-a-ricardo-rossello-como-el-que-motivara-el-traslado-de-hamilton-al-cba/.

Dandekar, Pranav, Ashish Goel, and David Lee. 2013. "Biased Assimilation, Homophily, and the Dynamics of Polarization." *Proceedings of the National Academy of Sciences of the United States of America* 110, no. 15 (March). https://doi.org/10.1073/pnas.1217220110.

DellaPosta, Daniel. 2020. "Pluralistic Collapse: The 'Oil Spill' Model of Mass Opinion Polarization." *American Sociological Review* 85, no. 3 (June). doi.org/10.1177/0003122420922989.

Dialogo. 2018. "Chocan Nuevamente la Administracion Universitaria y la Heend." *Noticias* (blog), *Dialogo*. November 30, 2018. https://dialogo.upr.edu/chocan-nuevamente-la-administracion-universitaria-y-la-heend/.

Discover Puerto Rico. 2019. "The History-Making Engagement of Hamilton in Puerto Rico." Accessed August 20, 2022. https://www.discoverpuertorico.com/article/history-making-engagement-hamilton-puerto-rico.

Druckman, James, and Matthew Levendusky. 2019. "What Do We Measure When We Measure Affective Polarization?" *Public Opinion Quarterly* 83, no. 1 (Spring): 114–122. https://doi.org/10.1093/poq/nfz003.

Druckman, James, Samara Klar, Yanna Krupnikov, Matthew Levendusky, and John Ryan. 2020. "Affective Polarization, Local Contexts and Public Opinion in America." *Nature Human Behaviour* 5, no. 1 (November): 20–38. https://doi.org/10.1038/s41562-020-01012-5.

El Nuevo Dia. 2019. "Majestuosa Visita en La Fortaleza." *El Nuevo Dia*.

Farley, Robert. 2019. "Trump Misleads on Aid to Puerto Rico." *Factcheck Posts* (blog), *FactCheck.org*. April 2, 2019. https://www.factcheck.org/2019/04/trump-misleads-on-aid-to-puerto-rico.

Finkel, Eli, Christopher A. Bail, Mina Cikara, Peter H. Ditto, Shanto Iyengar, Samara Klar, Lilliana Mason, Mary C. McGrath, Brendan Nyhan, and James N. Druckman. 2020. "Political Sectarianism in America." *Science* 370, no. 6516 (October). DOI: 10.1126/science.abe171.

Galioto, Katie. 2019. "Trump Boasts He's Taken Better Care of Puerto Rico Than 'Any Living Human Being.'" *White House* (blog), *Politico*. March 28, 2019. https://www.politico.com/story/2019/03/28/trump-boats-hes-taken-better-care-of-puerto-rico-than-any-living-human-being-1243077.

Hamilton Survey. 2000. "Political Attitudes of Young Americans." *Polls* (blog). *Hamilton*. October 16, 2000. https://www.hamilton.edu/news/polls/political-attitudes-of-young-americans.

Hare, Christopher, and Keith Poole. 2014. "The Polarization of Contemporary American Politics." *Polity* 46, no. 3 (July): 411–29. DOI: 10.1057/pol.2014.10.

Kreps Daniel. 2019. "Lin-Manuel Miranda Returns to 'Hamilton' Role as Puerto Rico Residency Begins." *Sub-culture* (blog). *RollingStone*. January 12, 2019. https://www.rollingstone.com/culture/culture-news/lin-manuel-miranda-hamilton-puerto-rico-778304/.

Manji, Irshad. 2020. "How to Cancel 'Cancel Culture' and Revive Dialogue in a Polarized Time." Filmed November 2020. Video, 38 mins. https://ypo.ivy.com/learning-modules/how-to-cancel-cancel-culture-revive-dialogue-in-a-polarized-time-with-irshad-manji.

Marcial Ocasio, Jennifer. 2018. "Problemas de Seguridad Obligan a Mover a Hamilton en Puerto Rico al Centro Bellas Artes." *News* (blog). *Orlando Sentinel.* December 18, 2018. https://www.orlandosentinel. com/2018/12/22/problemas-de-seguridad-obligan-a-mover-hamilon-en-puerto-rico-de-la-upr-al-centro-de-bellas-artes/.

Marks, Peter. 2019. "An Emotional Opening for *Hamilton* in Puerto Rico—Not Just for Lin-Manuel Miranda but an Island Still Reeling from a Storm." *Theatre & Dance* (blog), *The Washington Post.* January 12, 2019.

https://www.washingtonpost.com/entertainment/theater_dance/an-emotional-opening-for-hamilton-in-puerto-rico--not-just-for-lin-manuel-miranda-but-an-island-still-reeling-from-a-storm/2019/01/12/22da5900-15-40-11e9-b6ad-9cfd62dbb0a8_story.html.

Miranda, Luis (@vegalteno). "@HamiltonMusical Puerto Rico is moving to @CBASanturce leaving behind a renovated first class @UPRRP Theatre, keeping our promise @Lin_Manuel to Puerto Rico & addressing security concerns." Twitter, December 21, 2018, 8:13 p.m.

Murphy Marcos, Coral. 2021. "Trump Delayed $20bn in Aid to Puerto Rico after Hurricane Maria, Report Finds." *US Politics* (blog), *The Guardian.* April 22, 2021. https://www.theguardian.com/world/2021/apr/22/hurricane-maria-puerto-rico-trump-delayed-aid.

Pew Research Center. 2023. *Americans' Dismal Views of the Nation's Politics.* Washington, DC: Pew Research. https://www.pewresearch.org/politics/2023/09/19/americans-dismal-views-of-the-nations-politics/.

San Juan Daily Star. 2019. "Rosselló Says Cutting Pensions Is an 'Ideological Obsession.'" *San Juan Daily Star.* May 17, 2019.

Sen, Amartya. 2007. *Identity and Violence.* New York: W. W. Norton & Company.

Telemundo PR. 2018. "Cancelan Presentaciones en Bellas Artes para dar Paso a Hamilton." *Tendencias* (blog), *Telemundo PR.* December 27, 2018. https://www.telemundopr.com/noticias/puerto-rico/cancelan-presentaciones-en-bellas-artes-para-dar-paso-a-hamilton/115703/.

Zhu, Qiaoquiao. 2021. "Investing in Polarized America: Real Economic Effects of Political Polarization." *Social Science Research Network* (January). http://dx.doi.org/10.2139/ssrn.3820979.

CHAPTER 11

Agencia EFE. 2018. "La Cámara de Representantes de Puerto Rico Aprueba una Medida para Derogar la Ley 80." *Centroamerica y Caribe* (blog), *Que Pasa Media.* June 14, 2018. https://quepasamedia.com/noticias/mundo/centroamerica-y-caribe/la-camara-de-representantes-de-puerto-rico-aprueba-una-medida/.

Avila-Claudio, Ronald. 2018. "Cámara de Representantes no Tiene los Votos para Derogar Ley 80." *Locales* (blog), *Metro.* June 11, 2018. https://www.metro.pr/pr/noticias/2018/06/11/camara-representantes-no-los-votos-derogar-ley-80.html.

Bauza, Nydia. 2018. "Rivera Schatz Invita al Gobernador a Hablar de la Ley 80." *Gobierno y Politica* (blog), *Primera Hora.* June 19, 2018. https://www.primerahora.com/noticias/gobierno-politica/notas/rivera-schatz-invita-al-gobernador-a-hablar-de-la-ley-80/.

Bayon, Miguel. 2017. "En Manos de Taylor Swain." *El Nuevo Dia*. April 22, 2017.

Caribbean Business. 2018. "Resumen del Proyecto de la Reforma Laboral de Rosselló." *Caribbean Business* (blog), *Caribbean Business*. May 12, 2018. https://cb.pr/resumen-del-proyecto-de-la-reforma-laboral-de-rossello/.

Caro Gonzalez, Leysa, and Alex Figueroa Cancel. 2018. "El Senado Derrota Otra Vez el Plan de Rosselló." *El Nuevo Dia*. July 4, 2018.

El Nuevo Dia. 2020. "La Economia Crecio Antes de la Salida de Rosselló." *El Nuevo Dia*. May 16, 2020.

El Nuevo Dia. 2018. "El Senado Derrota Otra Vez El Plan de Rosselló." *El Nuevo Dia*. July 4, 2018.

Gonzalez, Juan. 2017. "Puerto Rico's $123 Billion Bankruptcy Is the Cost of US Colonialism." *Politics* (blog), *The Intercept*. May 9, 2017. https://theintercept.com/2017/05/09/puerto-ricos-123-billion-bankruptcy-is-the-cost-of-u-s-colonialism/.

Kingdon, J. W. 1984. *Agendas, Alternatives, and Public Policies*. New York: Pearson.

Kołodko, Grzegorz W. 2021. "Economics and Politics of the Great Change: Mikhail Gorbachev Versus Deng Xiaoping." *Kwartalnik Nauk o Przedsiębiorstwie* 58, no. 1 (April): 5–15. DOI: 10.15407/etet2021.01.005.

Rivera Clemente, Yaritza. 2018. "A Salvo el Bono, Pero Se Va La Ley 80." *Contenido Relevante* (blog), *El Vocero*. May 21, 2018. https://www.elvocero.com/gobierno/a-salvo-el-bono-pero-se-va-la-ley-80/article_3cd010f8-5ca8-11e8-8440-83e3cfa3b4c9.html.

Suarez Torres, Limarys. 2015. "Rosselló Promete Eliminar Cerca de 40 Agencias." *El Nuevo Dia*. November 11, 2015.

Zubok, Vladislav. 2017. "The Soviet Union and China in the 1980s: Reconciliation and Divorce. Cold War History." *Cold War History* 17, no. 2 (April): 1–21. DOI: 10.1080/14682745.2017.1315923.

CHAPTER 12

Agencia EFE. 2018. "Rosselló Aumenta el Salario Mínimo a los Empleados de Construcción." *Economia* (blog), *El Nuevo Dia*. June 18, 2018. https://www.elnuevodia.com/negocios/economia/notas/rossello-aumenta-el-salario-minimo-a-los-empleados-de-construccion/.

Agencia EFE. 2019. "Celebran en el Foro de Saop Paulo la Anunciada Dimision de Rossello." *Noticias* (blog). *Yahoo*. July 26, 2019. https://es-us.noticias.yahoo.com/comienza-caracas-xxv-encuentro-foro-172133425.html.

Anthony, Luis. 2019. "Ricardo Rosselló Puerto Rico Envía Ayuda Humanitaria a Venezuela." LuisAnthony40HD. February 21, 2019. 5:15. https://www.youtube.com/watch?v=775600WrsOo.

Cybernews. 2019. "Admiten que Ayuda de Puerto Rico No Ha Llegado a Venezuela." *Tendencias* (blog), *Telemundo PR*. February 8, 2019. https://www.telemundopr.com/noticias/puerto-rico/secretario-de-estado-admite-que-ayuda-no-ha-llegado-a-venezuela-2/614/.

El Colombiano. 2019. "Puerto Rico Logró Entrar Ayuda Humanitaria a Venezuela." *Mundo* (blog), *El Colombiano*. February 7, 2019. https://www.elcolombiano.com/internacional/puerto-rico-logro-entrar-ayuda-humanitaria-a-venezuela-HH10175673.

El Nuevo Herald. 2018. "Gobernador de Puerto Rico le Sale al Paso a Comentario de Maduro." *Noticias* (blog), *El Nuevo Herald*. May 20, 2018. https://www.elnuevoherald.com/noticias/florida/sur-de-la-florida/article211551169.html#storylink=cpyhttps://www.elnuevoherald.com/noticias/florida/sur-de-la-florida/article211551169.html.

El Sentinel. 2018. "Gobernador de Puerto Rico Anuncia Privatizacion del Sistema Energetico de la Isla." *News* (blog), *Orlando Sentinel*. January 22, 2018. https://www.orlandosentinel.com/elsentinel/os-es-gobernador-puerto-rico-privatizacion-autoridad-energia-electrica-20180122-story.html.

Energy Sage. 2023. "Cost of Electricity in Florida." *FL Data Explorer* (blog), *EnergySage*. October 22, 2023. https://www.energysage.com/local-data/electricity-cost/fl/.

Fernandez, Raquel, and Dani Rodrik. 1991. "Resistance to Reform: Status Quo Bias in the Presence of Individual-Specific Uncertainty." *The American Economic Review* 81, no. 5 (December): 1146–55. http://www.jstor.org/stable/2006910.

Hogan, William. 1991. "Economic Reforms in the Sovereign States of the Former Soviet Union." *Brookings Papers on Economic Activity* 1991, no. 2 (January): 303–19. https://doi.org/10.2307/2534595.

Massol-Deya, Arturo, Jennie Stephens, and Jorge Colon. 2018. "Renewable Energy for Puerto Rico." *Science* 362, no. 6410 (2018): 7. DOI: 10.1126/science.aav5576.

MetroPR. 2019a. "Abogado Edwin Prado Asesoró Legalmente a Rosselló." *Noticias* (blog), *Metro.PR*. August 13, 2019. https://www.metro.pr/pr/noticias/2019/08/13/abogado-edwin-prado-asesoro-legalmente-a-rossello.html.

MetroPR. 2019b. "Frente Comun en Defensa de las Alcaldias." *Metro.PR*. March 25, 2019. https://issuu.com/servicios_pr/docs/20190315_sanjuan.

Quintero, Laura. 2018. "Maestras Llevan Luto a Fortaleza." *El Vocero*. March 8, 2019.

Rosselló, Ricardo. 2012. *Un Mejor Puerto Rico es Posible, Vol. I*. Puerto Rico: Editorial de la Universidad de Puerto Rico.

CHAPTER 13

Brown, Nick, Robin Respaut, and Jessica Resnick-Ault. 2017. "Special Report: The Bankrupt Utility behind Puerto Rico's Power Crisis." *US. News* (blog), *Reuters*. October 4, 2017. https://www.thestar.com.my/news/world/2017/10/05/special-report-the-bankrupt-utility-behind-puerto-ricos-power-crisis.

Cusick, Daniel. 2018. "Puerto Rico Pledges to Go All-Renewable by 2050." *Environment* (blog), *Scientific America*. November 21, 2018. https://www.scientificamerican.com/article/puerto-rico-pledges-to-go-all-renewable-by-2050/.

El Sentinel. 2018. "Gobernador de Puerto Rico Anuncia Privatizacion del Sistema Energetico de la Isla." *News* (blog), *Orlando Sentinel*. January 22, 2018. https://www.orlandosentinel.com/elsentinel/os-es-gobernador-puerto-rico-privatizacion-autoridad-energia-electrica-20180122-story.html.

MetroPR. 2018. "Le Ponen Se Vende." Metro.PR. January 23, 2018.

Rosselló, Ricardo. 2004. *8 Anos de Grandes Obras para el Pueblo.* Self-published.

Telemundo PR. 2019. "Rosselló Propone Establecer Condados en Puerto Rico." *Tendencias* (blog), *Telemundo PR.* March 26, 2019. https://www.telemundopr.com/noticias/puerto-rico/exponen-concepto-de-nuevo-modelo-organizacional-para-municipios/102843/.

Volpe, Michael. 2019. "The Complicated Evolution of PREPA." *Culture* (blog), *Al Dia.* April 15, 2019. https://aldianews.com/en/culture/heritage-and-history/complicated-evolution.

CHAPTER 14

Bayon, Miguel. 2017. "De Ricardo Rosselló." *El Nuevo Dia.* July 18, 2017.

Caribbean Business. 2019. "Gobierno Defiende Reduccion de Salarios de Jefes de Agencia." *Caribbean Business* (blog), *Caribbean Business.* https://cb.pr/gobierno-defiende-reduccion-de-12-5-en-salarios-de-jefes-de-agencia/.

Delgado, Alex. 2021. "Estadidad: Jennifer vs. Ricky." *Opinion* (blog), *NotiUno.* May 14, 2021. https://www.notiuno.com/noticias/gobierno-y-politica/columna-estadidad-jenniffer-vs-ricky/article_9f3a8ab4-b4d1-11eb-b081-9f7656b1412b.html.

Figueroa, Barbara. 2016. "Rosselló Dice que Tiene Plancha'o su Gabinete." *Gobierno y Politica* (blog), *Primera Hora.* November 4, 2016. https://www.primerahora.com/noticias/gobierno-politica/notas/rossello-dice-que-tiene-planchao-su-gabinete/.

Hall, Andrew. 2019. "Want to Reduce Polarization in Congress? Make Moderates a Better Job Offer." *Institute for Economic Policy Research* (blog), *Stanford University.* June 2019. https://siepr.stanford.edu/publications/policy-brief/want-reduce-polarization-congress-make-moderates-better-job-offer.

Hernández, Luis. 2017. "Miles Participan de Iniciativa de Primera Dama." *NotiUno* (blog), *NotiUno.* October 31, 2017. https://www.notiuno.com/miles-participan-de-iniciativa-de-primera-dama/article_38995f8c-3cc1-5b5b-9c90-95f0f3fee3cd.html.

Hernández, Zaida. 2015. *Pasión de Guerrera.* Puerto Rico: Divinas Letras.

Hoyos, Josue. 2018. "US Army's Top Engineer 'Not Satisfied' with Puerto Rico's Post-Maria Recovery." *ABC y News* (blog), *ABC News.* February 18, 2018. https://abc7news.com/news/us-armys-top-engineer-not-satisfied-with-puerto-ricos-post-maria-recovery/3123220/.

Metro. 2019. "Exigen al Gobernador Dejar sin Efecto Altos Salarios de Parte de Su Gabinete." *Noticias* (blog), *Metro.* February 11, 2019. https://www.metro.pr/pr/noticias/2019/02/11/exigen-al-gobernador-dejar-sin-efecto-altos-salarios-parte-gabinete.html.

Micro Juris. 2018. "Nueva Aplicación Móvil CESCO Digital." *Noticias* (blog). *Microjuris.* June 25, 2018. https://aldia.microjuris.com/2018/06/25/nueva-aplicacion-movil-cesco-digital/.

NotiCel. 2016. "Nombramientos de Rosselló, Pugna Entre el Padre y la Mano Derecha." *Gobierno* (blog), *NotiCel*. November 27, 2016. https://www.noticel.com/gobierno/ahora/politica/20161127/nombramientos-de-rossello-pugna-entre-el-padre-y-la-mano-derecha/.

Pew Research. 2023. "Public Trust in Government: 1958–2023." *Research Topics* (blog), *Research Center*. September 19, 2023. https://www.pewresearch.org/politics/2022/06/06/public-trust-in-government-1958-2022/.

Smart, Geoff, and Randy Street. 2008. *Who*. New York: Ballantine Books.

Vázquez, Aixa. 2019. "Se Acaban las Filas Largas en el Cesco con Nuevo Sistema de Citas." *NotiCentro* (blog), *Wapa TV*. June 18, 2019. https://www.wapa.tv/noticias/locales/se-acaban-las-filas-largas-en-el-cesco-con-nuevo-sistema-de-citas_20131122454732.html.

CHAPTER 15

Bayon, Miguel. 2017. "Ojo Publico." *El Nuevo Dia*. January 8, 2016.

Caribbean Business. 2017. "Rosselló Envia Carta a la Junta de Control Fiscal." *Caribbean Business* (blog), *Caribbean Business*. January 19, 2017. https://cb.pr/documento-rossello-envia-carta-a-la-junta-de-control-fiscal/.

El Nuevo Dia. 2017a. "100 Dias." *El Nuevo Dia*. April 10, 2017.

El Nuevo Dia. 2017b. "La Juramentación de Ricardo Rosselló que el Pueblo No Vio." *Noticias* (blog), *El Nuevo Dia*. January 1, 2017. https://www.elnuevodia.com/noticias/politica/fotogalerias/la-juramentacion-de-ricardo-rossello-que-el-pueblo-no-vio/.

El Sentinel. 2018. "Gobernador de Puerto Rico Anuncia Privatizacion del Sistema Energetico de la Isla." *News* (blog), *Orlando Sentinel*. January 22, 2018. https://www.orlandosentinel.com/elsentinel/os-es-gobernador-puerto-rico-privatizacion-autoridad-energia-electrica-20180122-story.html.

El Vocero. 2017. "Este es Nuestro Gran Momento." *El Vocero*. January 3, 2017.

Micro Juris. 2017. "Ricardo Rosselló Nevares Firma las Primeras 6 Ordenes Ejecutivas de su Gestión." *Al Dia* (blog), *Microjuris*. January 3, 2017. https://aldia.microjuris.com/2017/01/03/ricardo-rossello-nevares-firma-las-primeras-6-ordenes-ejecutivas-de-su-gestion/.

NotiCel. 2016. "Encuesta Gira a Favor de la Privatización de la AEE." *Gobierno* (blog), *NotiCel*. September 24, 2016. https://www.noticel.com/gobierno/ahora/20160924/encuesta-gira-a-favor-de-la-privatizacion-de-la-aee/.

Primera Hora. 2018. "Reaccionan al Mensaje del Gobernador Sobre Privatización de la AEE." *Gobierno y Politica* (blog), *Primera Hora*. January 22, 2018. https://www.primerahora.com/noticias/gobierno-politica/notas/reaccionan-al-mensaje-del-gobernador-sobre-privatizacion-de-la-aee/.

Steinmetz, Katy. 2018. "Governor Ricardo Rosselló: Puerto Rico Is a 'Geopolitical Black Hole.'" *Politics* (blog), *Time*. May 9, 2018. https://time.com/5271767/puerto-rico-governor-donald-trump-statehood-hurricane-maria/.

Vendryes, Thomas. 2010. "Land Rights in Rural China since 1978." *China Perspectives* 4, (2010): 87–99. DOI: 10.4000/chinaperspectives.5345.

CHAPTER 16

Agencia EFE. 2019. "Rosselló Espera Que la Economía de Puerto Rico Crezca Tras Prolongada Crisis." *Mercado Global* (blog), *El Diner*. June 12, 2019. https://eldinero.com.do/84919/rossello-espera-que-la-economia-de-puerto-rico-crezca-tras-prolongada-crisis/.

Bayon, Miguel. 2017. "Ricardo Rosselló como Director de Escuela." *Opinion* (blog), *El Nuevo Dia*. May 5, 2017. https://www.elnuevodia.com/opinion/isla-en-su-tinta/ricardo-rossello-como-director-de-escuela/.

Cartwright, Hannah. 2017. "Puerto Rico Governor Gives Territorial Budget Address." *Headlines* (blog), *Pasquines*. June 8, 2017. https://pasquines.us/2017/06/08/puerto-rico-governor-gives-territorial-budget-address/.

Collins, Jim. 2001. *Good to Great: Why Some Companies Make the Leap and Others Don't*. New York: Harper Business.

Duckworth, Angela. 2016. *Grit: The Power of Passion and Perseverance*. New York: Scribner.

Evan, Aimee. 2023. *Student Centered School Improvement*. Potomac, MD: New Degree Press.

Jacobsen, Scott. 2021. "Conversation with Dr. Ricardo Rosselló Nevares on Family History, Catholic Schooling, Being Alone, Mathematics, Bioengineering, and Gifted Identification: Former Governor, Puerto Rico." *In-Sight: Independent Interview-Based Journal* 26.A (February). https://in-sightpublishing.com/2021/02/22/rossello-1/.

Jover Tovar, Alejandra. 2016. "Denuncian que Rosselló Impondrá la Segunda Parte de la Ley 7." *Gobierno y Politica* (blog), *Primera Hora*. September 12, 2016. https://www.primerahora.com/noticias/gobierno-politica/notas/denuncian-que-rossello-impondra-la-segunda-parte-de-la-ley-7/.

NotiUno. 2019. "*Estás* Son las Cuatro Agencias que Rosselló Busca Consolidar Bajo el DTOP." *NotiUno* (blog), *NotiUno*. January 29, 2019. https://www.notiuno.com/noticias/estas-son-las-cuatro-agencias-que-rossell-busca-consolidar-bajo-el-dtop/article_37f46f84-2327-11e9-b01a-bfa50a6609b2.html.

Rosselló, Ricardo. 2012. *Un Mejor Puerto Rico es Posible, Vol. I*. Puerto Rico: Editorial de la Universidad de Puerto Rico.

Rosselló, Ricardo. 2019. *Fiscal Accountability: Two Years of Results*. Puerto Rico: Government of Puerto Rico. https://laobraderossello.com/wp-content/uploads/2020/07/Rendicion_cuentas_EN.pdf.

Stojanovic, Lorae, and David Wessel. 2022. "Puerto Rico's Bankruptcy: Where Do Things Stand Today?" *Commentary* (blog), *Brookings*. August 17, 2022. https://www.brookings.edu/articles/puerto-ricos-bankruptcy-where-do-things-stand-today/.

Telemundo PR. 2021. "Junta de Control Fiscal Accede a No Recortar las Pensiones." *Junta de Supervision Fiscal* (blog), *Telemundo PR*. October 14, 2021. https://www.telemundopr.com/noticias/puerto-rico/junta-accede-a-no-2-recortar-las-pensiones-a-un-8-5/2268913/.

Telemundo Houston. 2018. "Rosselló Presenta el Nuevo Modelo del Plan de Salud Vital." *Noticias* (blog), *Telemundo Houston*. September 25, 2018. https://www.telemundohouston.com/noticias/puerto-rico/gobernador-rechazo-de-trump_tlmd-puerto-rico/2004398/.

US Department of Education. 2019. *The Nation's Report Card: 2019 Mathematics State Snapshot Report: Puerto Rico*. Washington, DC: US Department of Education. https://nces.ed.gov/nationsreportcard/subject/publications/stt2019/pdf/2020013PR8.pdf.

CHAPTER 17

ABC News. 2018. "Puerto Rican Governor Wants 'Equal Treatment.'" Filmed June 21, 2018, in the White House. Facebook Video, 1:18. https://www.facebook.com/ABCNews/videos/puerto-rican-governor-wants-equal-treatment-asks-pres-trump-for-statehood/10157374410243812/.

Banucci, Rebecca. 2016. "Compromisos Para Comunidades LGBTT y Organizaciones Religiosas por Igual." *Politica* (blog), *El Nuevo Dia*. September 10, 2016. https://www.elnuevodia.com/noticias/politica/notas/compromisos-para-comunidades-lgbtt-y-organizaciones-religiosas-por-igual/.

Bayon, Miguel (@miguelbayonart). 2017. "Quiero dedicar esta ilustración a esos héroes anónimos y conocidos, que extendieron y extienden sus manos a lo alto de la montaña, Sin recibir nada a cambio, sólo por el hecho gratificante de saber que hacen bien." Instagram, October 20, 2017. https://www.instagram.com/p/Baerxq4HAl8/.

Bresnahan, John, Jennifer Scholtes, and Heather Caygle. 2018. "Shutdown Ends after Trump Signs Budget Deal." *Congress* (blog), *Politico*. February 9, 2018. https://www.politico.com/story/2018/02/08/congress-massive-budget-deal-2018-398189.

Fox, Lauren, Phil Mattingly, and Ted Barrett. 2018. "Senate Leaders Announce Two-Year Budget Deal." *CNN Politics* (blog), *CNN*. February 8, 2018. https://www.cnn.com/2018/02/07/politics/senate-announces-deal-budget-caps-agreement/index.html.

HUD. 2018. "HUD Awards Record $18.5 Billion for Puerto Rico Hurricane Recovery." April 10, 2018. https://archives.hud.gov/local/pr-vi/news/pr2018-04-10.cfm.

Mazzei, Patricia. 2018. "What Puerto Rico Is, and Isn't, Getting in Disaster Relief." *US* (blog), *The New York Times*. February 8, 2018. https://www.nytimes.com/2018/02/08/us/puerto-rico-disaster-relief.html.

NotiUno. 2020. "Gutiérrez y Velázquez Votan Contra Proyecto que Beneficia a Puerto Rico." *NotiUno* (blog), *NotiUno*. August 27, 2020. https://www.notiuno.com/gutierrez-y-vel-zquez-votan-contra-proyecto-que-beneficia-a-puerto-rico/article_69d658a7-6a21-5a39-8342-6713451120a6.html.

Rosselló, Ricardo. 2017. *Build Back Better: A Request for Federal Assistance for Disaster Recovery*. New York: Ford Foundation, 100 Resilient Cities, Government of Puerto Rico, and State Government of New York.

CHAPTER 18

ABC News. 2018. "Puerto Rican Governor Wants 'Equal Treatment.'" Filmed June 21, 2018, in the White House. Facebook Video, 1:18. https://www.facebook.com/ABCNews/videos/puerto-rican-governor-wants-equal-treatment-asks-pres-trump-for-statehood/10157374410243812/.

Bayon, Miguel. 2017. "Todo Esta Bien." *El Nuevo Dia*. August 2, 2017.

Blake, Aaron. 2017. "Trump Gave Himself a '10' on Puerto Rico. Then He Tried to Get Its Governor to Do the Same." *The Fix* (blog), *The Washington Post*. October 19, 2017. https://www.washingtonpost.com/news/the-fix/wp/2017/10/19/trump-gave-himself-a-10-on-puerto-rico-then-he-tried-to-get-its-governor-to-do-the-same/.

Brown, Jack. 2017. "Body Language Analysis №4098: President Trump and Puerto Rico's Governor Ricardo Rosselló—A Candid Moment in the Oval Office—Nonverbal and Emotional Intelligence." *Dr Jack Brown* (blog), *Medium*. October 21, 2017. https://medium.com/@DrGJackBrown/body-language-analysis-4098-president-trump-and-puerto-ricos-governor-ricardo-rossell%C3%B3-a-bbaf070cd9cd.

Delgado, Jose. 2018. "Rosselló Advocated for Statehood." *News* (blog), *El Nuevo Dia*. June 21, 2018. https://www.elnuevodia.com/english/news/story/rossello-advocated-for-statehood/.

Delkic, Melina. 2017. "Trump Tells Puerto Rico Governor: 'Did We Do a Great Job?'" *US* (blog), *NewsWeek*. October 19, 2018. https://www.newsweek.com/trump-tells-puerto-rico-governor-did-we-do-great-job-688783.

Edelman, Adam. 2018. "Trump Says 3,000 Did Not Die in Puerto Rico Hurricane, Claims Democrats Manipulated Numbers." *Trump Effect* (blog), *NBC News*. September 13, 2018. https://www.nbcnews.com/politics/donald-trump/trump-claims-3-000-did-not-die-puerto-rico-hurricane-n909221.

Klein, Betsy, and Maegan Vazquez. 2018. "Trump Falsely Claims Nearly 3,000 Americans in Puerto Rico 'Did Not Die.'" *CNN Politics* (blog), *CNN*. September 14, 2018. https://www.cnn.com/2018/09/13/politics/trump-puerto-rico-death-toll/index.html.

NowThis News. 2020. "Nobody Knows More Than Trump about Anything: A Supercut." NowThis News. January 23, 2020. 2:16. https://www.youtube.com/watch?v=sR3f95BGIiA.

Olorunnipa, Toluse, and Jonathan Levin. 2018. "Trump Says Puerto Rico Governor Blamed Power Plant Flaw on Storm; Rosselló Asked Trump to Push for Statehood for the Territory." *Politics* (blog), *Bloomberg*. June 21, 2018. https://www.bloomberg.com/politics/articles/2018-06-21/trump-says-puerto-rico-governor-blamed-power-plant-flaw-on-storm#xj4y7vzkg.

PBS NewsHour. 2017. "WATCH: President Trump and Puerto Rico Governor Rosselló Speak in the Oval Office." PBS NewsHour. October 19, 2017. 35:48. https://www.youtube.com/watch?v=KjTspG9_hrc.

Perez, Evan, and Katelyn Polantz. 2018. "Paul Manafort and Special Counsel Close to Deal for Guilty Plea." *CNN Politics* (blog), *CNN*. September 13, 2018. https://www.cnn.com/2018/09/13/politics/manafort-plea/index.html.

Polantz, Katelyn. 2018. "Paul Manafort Pleads Guilty and Agrees to Cooperate with Muller Investigation." *CNN Politics* (blog), *CNN*. September 14, 2018. https://www.cnn.com/2018/09/14/politics/paul-manafort-guilty-plea/index.html.

Scott, Rick (@ScottforFlorida). 2018. "I disagree with POTUS– an independent study said thousands were lost and Gov. Rosselló agreed. I've been to Puerto Rico 7 times & saw devastation firsthand. The loss of any life is tragic; the extent of lives lost as a result of Maria is heart wrenching. I'll continue to help PR" Twitter, September 13, 2018, 11:45 a.m. https://twitter.com/ScottforFlorida/status/1040265322270474242.

Torres Gotay, Benjamin. 2018. "La Vida Mas Alla del Cuarto." *Las Cosas por su Nombre* (blog), *El Nuevo Dia*. July 1, 2018. https://www.elnuevodia.com/opinion/las-cosas-por-su-nombre/la-vida-mas-alla-del-cuarto/.

CHAPTER 19

Bayon, Miguel. 2017. "De Rosselló a Trump." *El Nuevo Dia*. August 11, 2017.

Bernal, Rafael. 2018. "Puerto Rico Governor: DOJ Marijuana Decision Shows 'Lack of Knowledge.'" *Latino* (blog), *The Hill*. January 4, 2018. https://thehill.com/latino/367524-puerto-rico-governor-slams-doj-marijuana-announcement/.

Caribbean Business. 2017. "Resumen del Proyecto de la Reforma de Permisos." *Caribbean Business* (blog), *Caribbean Business*. February 7, 2018. https://cb.pr/resumen-del-proyecto-de-la-reforma..

EFE. 2017. "Cámara Representantes de Puerto Rico Aprueba el Proyecto de Reforma Laboral." *Mundo* (blog), *The San Diego Union-Tribune*. January 23, 2017. https://www.sandiegouniontribune.com/en-espanol/noticias/mundo/efe-3157480-12526028-20170123-story.html?expandComments=true.

EFE. 2019. "Tasa de Desempleo en Puerto Rico Registra Su Cifra Mas Baja en Cuatro Décadas." *Economia* (blog), *El Economista America*. August 16, 2019. https://www.eleconomistaamerica.com/economia-eAm/amp/10043145/Tasa-de-desempleo-en-Puerto-Rico-registra-su-cifra-mas-baja-en-cuatro-decadas.

El Nuevo Dia. 2017. "Presenta su Reforma Laboral." *El Nuevo Dia*. January 10, 2017.

El Nuevo Dia. 2020. "La Economia Crecio Antes de la Salida de Rosselló." *El Nuevo Dia*. May 16, 2020.

Hacienda. 2019a. "Hacienda Informa Cierre de Año Fiscal 2018–2019 con Cifra Récord de Recaudos que Ascienden a $11,376 millones." August 6, 2019. http://hacienda.pr.gov/sobre-hacienda/sala-de-prensa-virtual/comunicados-de-prensa/hacienda-informa-cierre-de-ano-fiscal-2018-19-con-cifra-record-de-recaudos-que-ascienden-11376-millones.

Hacienda. 2019b. "Gobernador Rosselló Nevares Convierte en Ley el Nuevo Modelo Contributivo." December 10, 2018. https://hacienda.pr.gov/sobre-hacienda/sala-de-prensa-virtual/comunicados-de-prensa/gobernador-rossello-nevares-convierte-en-ley-el-nuevo-modelo-contributivo.

Hernandez, Jose Rafael. 2019. "Legisladores del PPD Califican Como 'Un Fracaso' la Reforma Laboral de Rosselló Nevares." *Gobierno y Politica* (blog), *Presencia PR*. April 30, 2019. https://www.presenciapr.com/legisladores-del-ppd-califican-como-un-fracaso-la-reforma-laboral-de-rossello-nevares/.

Herb. 2017. "Puerto Rico Becomes Latest County to Legalize Medical Cannabis." *Legalization* (blog), *Herb*. July 22, 2017. https://herb.co/news/legalization/puerto-rico-legalizes-medical-cannabis/.

MBA@Syracuse. 2021. "With Viewership and Revenue Booming, Esports Set to Compete with Traditional Sports." *Blog* (blog), *Syracuse University*. June 2021. https://onlinegrad.syracuse.edu/blog/esports-to-with-traditional-sports/.

Metro. 2019. *Permisos de Construccion*. Puerto Rico: Metro.

Metro. 2019. "Rosselló Firma Legislación para Autorizar Apuestas en Deportes y Juegos Electrónicos." *Noticias* (blog). *Metro*. July 29, 2019. https://www.metro.pr/pr/noticias/2019/07/29/rossello-firma-legislacion-para-autorizar-apuestas-en-deportes-y-juegos-electronicos.html.

Munoz, Nicolás. 2017. "La Reforma Laboral del Gobernador Ricardo Rosselló Entre el Flexitime y la Ley de Cierre." *Blog* (blog), *Nicolás Munoz PR*. January 16, 2017. https://nicolasmunozpr.com/2017/01/16/la-reforma-laboral-del-gobernador-ricardo-rossello-entre-el-flexitime-y-la-ley-de-cierre/.

NotiCel. 2013. "Gobernador da Primer 'Home Run' con 10,000 Empleos." *Politica* (blog), *NotiCel*. January 16, 2023. https://www.noticel.com/politica/ahora/economia/20130116/gobernador-da-primer-home-run-con-10000-empleos/.

Ojeda, German. 2022. "La Facilidad Para Hacer Negocios En Puerto Rico: Un Reto Continuo." *Economia* (blog). *Sin Comillas*. March 1, 2022. https://sincomillas.com/la-facilidad-para-hacer-negocios-en-puerto-rico-un-reto-continuo/.

Picker, Leslie, and Dawn Giel. 2018. "Puerto Rico's Governor Is Bullish on Blockchain as Part of Island's Comeback." *Bitcoin* (blog), *CNBC*. February 16, 2018. https://www.cnbc.com/2018/02/16/puerto-ricos-governor-is-bullish-on-blockchain-as-part-of-islands-comeback.html.

PwC. 2023. "Puerto Rico: Individual—Taxes on Personal Income." PWC Worldwide Tax Summaries. March 3, 2023. https://taxsummaries.pwc.com/puerto-rico/individual/taxes-on-personal-income.

Rodriguez-Castro, Francisco. 2018. "Rosselló 20 Months On: Even with Obstacles, Improvements Are Present." *Caribbean Business*. November 15, 2018.

World Bank. 2023. *GDP Growth (Annual %)—Puerto Rico*. Washington, DC: The World Bank Group. https://data.worldbank.org/indicator/NY.GDP.MKTP.KD.ZG?locations=PR.

CHAPTER 20

Bayon, Miguel. 2016. "Formula Estadidad Al Rescate." *Primera Hora*. November 6, 2016.

Galston, William, and Elaine Kamarck. 2022. "Is Democracy Failing and Putting Our Economic System at Risk?" *Research* (blog), *Brookings*. January 4, 2022. https://www.brookings.edu/articles/is-democracy-failing-and-putting-our-economic-system-at-risk/.

CHAPTER 21

Bayon, Miguel. 2016. "Idea." *El Nuevo Dia*. December 1, 2016.

Burgos, Cindy. 2014. "Ricky Rosselló Perdona a Fortuño por Llamar Cáncer a Su Padre." *Noticias* (blog), *Metro*. September 28, 2014. https://www.metro.pr/pr/noticias/2014/09/29/ricky-rossello-perdona-a-fortuno-por-llamar-cancer-a-su-padre.html.

Davis, Tom. 2011. "Time to Tear Down Ideological Walls." *Story* (blog), *Politico*. September 11, 2011. https://www.politico.com/story/2011/09/time-to-tear-down-ideological-walls-063206.

El Nuevo Dia. 2012. "Primera Consulta Plebiscitaria." *El Nuevo Dia*. March 10, 2012.

Hall, Andrew. 2019. "Want to Reduce Polarization in Congress? Make Moderates a Better Job Offer." *Institute for Economic Policy Research* (blog), Stanford University. June 2019. https://siepr.stanford.edu/publications/policy-brief/want-reduce-polarization-congress-make-moderates-better-job-offer.

Manji, Irshad. 2020. "How to Cancel 'Cancel Culture' and Revive Dialogue in a Polarized Time." Filmed November 2020. Video, 38 mins. https://ypo.ivy.com/learning-modules/how-to-cancel-cancel-culture-revive-dialogue-in-a-polarized-time-with-irshad-manji.

Munoz, Angel. 2021. "José Elías: Una Voz del Oeste En el Sur." *Inicio* (blog), *Periodico El Sol*. August 20, 2021. https://periodicoelsolpr.com/2021/08/20/jose-elias-una-voz-del-oeste-en-el-sur/.

Padgett, Jeremy, Johanna L Dunaway, and Joshua P Darr. 2019. "As Seen on TV? How Gatekeeping Makes the US House Seem More Extreme." *Journal of Communication* 69, no. 6 (December): 696–719. https://doi.org/10.1093/joc/jqz039.

Pew Research Center. 2021. "Beyond Red vs. Blue: The Political Typology." *Politics & Policy* (blog), *Pew Research Center*. November 9, 2021. https://www.pewresearch.org/politics/2021/11/09/beyond-red-vs-blue-the-political-typology-2/.

Robbins, Tony. 2023. "Abundance 360." Filmed March 2023 in Los Angeles. Video, 1 hr. https://www.abundance360.com/summit.

Torres, José Elias. 2006. *Filiberto Ojeda Rios: Su Prouesta, Su Vision*. Puerto Rico: Ediciones Callejon inc. https://libros787.com/products/filiberto-ojeda-rios.

Theriault, Sean. 2008. *Party Polarization in Congress*. United Kingdom: Cambridge University Press.

CHAPTER 22

Bayon, Miguel (@miguelbayonart). 2019. "Ya no hay de otra... #rickyrenuncia #puertorico #governador #renuncia." Instagram, July 24, 2019. https://www.instagram.com/p/B0TdZbrBte9/.

BBC. 2018. "South Africa: Cape Town Slashes Water Use Amid Drought." *News* (blog). *BBC*. January 18, 2018. https://www.bbc.com/news/world-africa-42731084.

Bradford, Hazel. 2019. "First Puerto Rico Debt Restructuring Deal Approved for COFINA." *Economy* (blog), *Pensions & Investments*. February 5, 2019.

https://www.pionline.com/article/20190205/ONLINE/190209905/first-puerto-rico-debt-restructuring-deal-approved-for-cofina.

Cortes Chico, Ricardo. 2019. "Crece la Cifra de Puertorriqueños que Deciden Volver." *El Nuevo Dia*. April 28, 2019.

2018. "Ricardo Rosselló Destaca que la Nomina del Gobierno se Redujo en un 10%." *Locales* (blog), *El Nuevo Dia*. December 19, 2018. https://www.elnuevodia.com/noticias/locales/notas/ricardo-rossello-destaca-que-la-nomina-del-gobierno-se-redujo-en-un-107/.

Dalio, Ray. 2022. "How to See the World." Filmed November 2022 in New York. Video, 24:57. https://ypo.vhx.tv/ypo-edge-1/videos/how-to-see-the-world-ray-dalio-1080p.

Ellsmoor, James. 2019. "Puerto Rico Has Just Passed Its Own Green New Deal." *Under 30* (blog), *Forbes*. March 25, 2019. https://www.forbes.com/sites/jamesellsmoor/2019/03/25/puerto-rico-has-just-passed-its-own-green-new-deal/.

Estadisticas PR. 2018. "Delitos Tipo I." Estadisticas.PR. Accessed Month February 2, 2023. https://estadisticas.pr/index.php/en/inventario-de-estadisticas/delitos_tipo_i.

Hacienda. 2019. "Hacienda Informa Cierre de Año Fiscal 2018–2019 con Cifra Récord de Recaudos que Ascienden a $11,376 millones." August 6, 2019. http://hacienda.pr.gov/sobre-hacienda/sala-de-prensa-virtual/comunicados-de-prensa/hacienda-informa-cierre-de-ano-fiscal-2018-19-con-cifra-record-de-recaudos-que-ascienden-11376-millones.

Hernández Pérez, Maribel. 2019. "Otorgan Permanencia a 2,558 Maestros Transitorios." *Gobierno y Politica* (blog), *Primera Hora*. June 10, 2019. https://www.primerahora.com/noticias/gobierno-politica/notas/otorgan-permanencia-a-2558-maestros-transitorios/.

Jeffery, Lyn. 2022. "Foresight." Virtual YPO Event. April 11, 2022.

McGregor, Jena. 2017. "The Most Memorable Passage in George W. Bush's Speech Rebuking Trumpism." News (blog). Washington Post. October 20, 2017. https://www.washingtonpost.com/news/on-leadership/wp/2017/10/20/the-most-memorable-passage-in-george-w-bushs-speech-rebuking-trumpism/.

Obama, Barack. 2008. "Transcript of Obama Speech." *Story* (blog). *Politico*. March 18, 2008. https://www.politico.com/story/2008/03/transcript-of-obama-speech-009100.

Policia de Puerto Rico. 2019. "Incidencia Criminal Delito Tipo 1." Accessed March 3, 2022. https://policia.pr.gov/division-estadisticas-de-la-criminalidad/.

PRFAA. 2018. "Puerto Rico Governor Rosselló Nevares Announces Lowest Unemployment Rate in Almost 50 Years amidst Increased Employment Opportunities." July 25, 2018. https://www.prnewswire.com/news-releases/puerto-rico-governor-rosselló-nevares-announces-lowest-unemployment-rate-in-almost-50-years-amidst-increased-employment-opportunities-300686709.html.

Redaccion SinComillas. 2020. "Disminuye la Tasa de Pobreza." *Economia* (blog), *SinComillas*. January 22, 2020. https://sincomillas.com/disminuye-la-tasa-de-pobreza/.

Reuters Staff. 2019. "New Sales Tax Bond Issued under Latest Puerto Rico Debt Restructuring." *Bankruptcy News* (blog), *Reuters*. February 12, 2019. https://www.reuters.com/article/usa-puertorico-bonds/new-sales-tax-bonds-issued-under-latest-puerto-rico-debt-restructuring-idUSL1N2071K8.

CHAPTER 23

Bayon, Miguel. 2017. "Para Reconstruir." *El Nuevo Dia*. October 1, 2017.

Baldassarri, Delia, and Andrew Gelman. 2008. "Partisans without Constraint: Political Polarization and Trends in American Public Opinion." *American Journal of Sociology* 114, no. 2 (2008): 408–46. DOI: 10.2139/ssrn.1010098.

Collins, Jim. 2001. *Good to Great: Why Some Companies Make the Leap and Others Don't*. New York: Harper Business.

Dimock, Michael and Richard Wike. 2020. "America is Exceptional in the Nature of its Political Divide." *Policy & Politics* (blog), *Pew Research Center*. November 13, 2020. https://www.pewresearch.org/short-reads/2020/11/13/america-is-exceptional-in-the-nature-of-its-political-divide/.

McCoy, Jennifer, and Murat Somer. 2018. "Toward a Theory of Pernicious Polarization and How It Harms Democracies: Comparative Evidence and Possible Remedies." *The ANNALS of the American Academy of Political and Social Science* 681, no. 1 (December): 234–71. https://doi.org/10.1177/0002716218818782.

Mitchell, Amy, Jeffrey Gottfried, Jocelyn Kiley, and Katerina Eva Matsa. 2014. "Political Polarization & Media Habits." *Research Topics* (blog), *Pew Research Center*. October 21, 2014. https://www.pewresearch.org/journalism/2014/10/21/political-polarization-media-habits/.

Perez Pintado, Amanda. 2023. "Ricardo Rosselló Nevares Participa Virtualmente en la Convención del PNP." *Política* (blog), *El Nuevo Dia*. August 26, 2023. https://www.elnuevodia.com/noticias/politica/notas/ricardo-rossello-nevares-participa-virtualmente-en-la-convencion-del-pnp/.

PR News Wire. 2020. "Declaración del Exgobernador de Puerto Rico con Respecto a Su Exoneración por Parte de Fiscal Independiente." PR News Wire. November 25, 2020. https://www.prnewswire.com/news-releases/declaracion-del-exgobernador-de-puerto-rico-con-respecto-a-su-exoneracion-por-parte-de-fiscal-independiente-809282531.html.

Rosselló Ricardo. 2021. *First Quarterly Report Congressional Delegation*. Washington, DC: Delegates US.

Zhu, Qiaoqiao. 2021. "Investing in Polarized America: Real Economic Effects of Political Polarization." *Social Science Research Network* (January). http://dx.doi.org/10.2139/ssrn.3820979.

CHAPTER 24

Acevedo, Sebastian, Nicole LaFramboise, and Joyce Wong. 2017. *Caribbean Tourism in the Global Marketplace: Trends, Drivers, and Challenges*. IMF eLibrary. https://www.elibrary.imf.org/display/book/9781484315194/ch03.xml.

Avritzer, Leonardo. 2010. "Living Under a Democracy: Participation and Its Impact on the Living Conditions of the Poor." *Latin American Research Review* 45 (2010): 166–85. http://www.jstor.org/stable/27919218.

Besley, Timothy, and Marta Reynal-Querol. 2014. "The Legacy of Historical Conflict: Evidence from Africa." *American Political Science Review* 4, no. 2 (May): 319–36. https://doi.org/10.1017/S0003055414000161.

Borders, Max. 2019. "The Evolution of Governance in 9 Stages." *Politics* (blog), *FEE Stories*. September 21, 2019. https://fee.org/articles/the-evolution-of-governance-in-9-stages/.

Discover Puerto Rico. 2021. "LiveBoricua." Discoverpuertorico.com. Accessed June 22, 2023. https://www.discoverpuertorico.com/live-boricua.

El Nuevo Dia. 2019. "Rosselló Propone Reformar el Proceso Presupuestario." *El Nuevo Dia*. March 11, 2019.

Finkel, Eli, Christopher A. Bail, Mina Cikara, Peter H. Ditto, Shanto Iyengar, Samara Klar, Lilliana Mason, Mary C. McGrath, Brendan Nyhan, and James N. Druckman. 2020. "Political Sectarianism in America." *Science* 370, no. 6516 (October). DOI: 10.1126/science.abe1171.

Gomez, Renzo. 2022. "Peru's President Pedro Castillo Arrested after Attempting to Dissolve Congress." *Peru* (blog), *El Pais*. December 7, 2022. https://english.elpais.com/international/2022-12-07/perus-president-pedro-castillo-dissolves-congress-and-declares-emergency-government.html.

Gonzalez, Joanisabel. 2019. "Rosselló Propone Reformar el Proceso Presupuestario." *El Nuevo Dia*. March 11, 2019.

Government of Puerto Rico. 2019. *FY20 Budget Explanatory Memorandum: Building a Citizen Centered Government*. Puerto Rico: Government of Puerto Rico.

Harari, Yuval. 2015. Sapiens: *A Brief History of Humankind*. New York: Harper Publishing.

Hauenstein Center. 2011. "Gleaves Whitney: 'The Untold Story of the Constitutional Convention.'" Hauenstein Center. July 29, 2011. 50:06. https://www.youtube.com/watch?v=Ktsf7cMHM8c.

Henderson, David. 2020. "10% Less Democracy." *Regulation* (blog), *Cato Institute*. Summer 2020. https://www.cato.org/regulation/summer-2020/10-less-democracy.

Instituto de Estadisticas. 2018. "Asociación Americana de Estadísticas exige a Rosselló que

no desmantele el Instituto de Estadísticas de Puerto Rico." *Comunicados de Prensa* (blog). *Estadisticas.PR*. January 25, 2018. https://estadisticas.pr/en/comunicados-de-prensa/asociacion-americana-de-estadisticas-exige-rossello-que-no-desmantele-el-instituto-de-estadisticas.

International IDEA. 2022. "Global Democracy Weakens in 2022." *News* (blog), *IDEA*. November 30, 2022. https://www.idea.int/news-media/news/global-democracy-weakens-2022.

Javier, Gary. 2017. "El Cuatrienio de Rosselló ha Terminado." *Opinion* (blog), *El Nuevo Dia*. February 17, 2017. https://www.elnuevodia.com/opinion/isla-en-su-tinta/el-cuatrienio-de-rossello-ha-terminado/.

Jones, Garret. 2020. *10% Less Democracy: Why You Should Trust Elites a Little More and the Masses a Little Less*. Palo Alto, CA: Stanford University Press.

Kantrow-Vázquez, Michelle. 2017. "Rosselló Signs Law Creating DMO for P.R." *Tourism & Transportation* (blog), *NimB*. March 31, 2017. https://newsismybusiness.com/Rossello-signs-creating/.

Kelso, Sterling. 2023. "The 10 Most Innovative Travel and Hospitality Companies of 2023." *Most Innovative Companies* (blog), *Fast Company*. March 2, 2023. https://www.fastcompany.com/90849146/most-innovative-companies-travel-hospitality-2023.

McGonigal, Jane. 2022a. *Imaginable: How to See the Future Coming and Feel Ready for Anything—Even Things That Seem Impossible Today*. New York: Spiegel & Grau.

McGonigal, Jane. 2022b. "Urgent Optimism for a Changing World: Jane McGonigal." Filmed November 2022 in New York. Video, 14:00. https://ypo.vhx.tv/ypo-edge-1/videos/jane-mconigal.

Metro. 2018. "Investigan por Corrupción a Designado al DMO." *Noticias* (blog), *Metro*. March 15, 2018. https://www.metro.pr/pr/noticias/2018/03/15/investigan-corrupcion-designado-al-dmo.html.

National Constitution Center. n.d. "Preamble: We the People." *The Constitution* (blog), *National Constitution Center*. Accessed June 20, 2023. https://constitutioncenter.org/the-constitution/preamble.

Navia, Patricio. 2021. "Latin America's Anti-Incumbent Wave Will End in Tears." *Elections* (blog), *Americas Quarterly*. August 16, 2021. https://www.americasquarterly.org/article/latin-americas-anti-incumbent-wave-will-end-in-tears/.

Nayak, Venkatesh. 2022. "Data Bill: Is it Meant to Protect our Data or Hide Government's Secrets?" *Opinion* (blog). *Deccan* Herald. December 3, 2022. https://www.deccanherald.com/opinion/data-bill-is-it-meant-to-protect-our-data-or-hide-government-s-secrets-1168207.html.

NotiCel. 2018. "Rosselló Refuerza Control Sobre el Instituto de Estadisticas." *Gobierno* (blog), *NotiCel*. November 28, 2018. https://www.noticel.com/gobierno/ahora/top-stories/20181128/rossello-refuerza-control-sobre-el-instituto-de-estadisticas/.

Pew Research Center. 2021. "Democrats Mostly View Voting as a 'Fundamental Right'; Republicans More Likely to Say It's a 'Privilege.'" *Research Topics* (blog), *Pew Research Center*. July 21, 2021. https://www.pewresearch.org/fact-tank/2021/07/22/wide-partisan-divide-on-whether-voting-is-a-fundamental-right-or-a-privilege-with-responsibilities/ft_2021-07-22_votingattitudes_01a/.

Pew Research Center. 2023. *Americans' Dismal Views of the Nation's Politics*. Washington, DC: Pew Research. https://www.pewresearch.org/politics/2023/09/19/americans-dismal-views-of-the-nations-politics/.

Primera Hora. 2018. "Exsecretaria de Prensa de Rosselló ya Tiene Trabajo en el DMO." *Noticias* (blog), *Primera Hora*. August 3, 2018. https://www.primerahora.com/noticias/puerto-rico/notas/exsecretaria-de-prensa-de-rossello-ya-tiene-trabajo-en-el-dmo/.

Rosselló, Ricardo. 2012. *Un Mejor Puerto Rico es Posible, Vol. I.* Puerto Rico: Editorial de la Universidad de Puerto Rico.

Rosselló, Ricardo. 2016. "Plan para Puerto Rico." *Biblioteca Virtual OGP* (blog), *PR.gov*. June 7, 2016. https://bvirtualogp.pr.gov/ogp/Bvirtual/reogGubernamental/PDF/Programas/PPPR.pdf.

Swee Keat, Heng. 2014. "Reflections of Our Singapore Conversation." Docs (blog). Reach. January, 2014. https://www.reach.gov.sg/docs/default-source/reach/reach-files/read/oursingaporeconversationreflection.pdf.

Univision Radio. 2019. "Acusan a Ricardo Rosselló de Violar las Leyes del Instituto de Estadistica." Filmed January 2019 in Puerto Rico. Video, 3:20. https://www.univision.com/radio/puerto-rico-wkaq-am/acusan-a-ricardo-rossello-de-violar-las-leyes-del-instituto-de-estadistica.

Velez, Gustavo. 2023. "El Milagro Turistico Puertorriqueno." *El Nuevo Dia*. November 8, 2023.

Victoria840. 2016. "Ricardo Rosselló Propone Crear Instituto Pro-Activo Para Capitalizar Retos Futuros." *Victoria840* (blog), *Victoria840*. February 24, 2016. https://www.victoria840.com/ricardo-rossello-propone-crear-instituto-pro-activo-para-capitalizar-retos-futuros/.

Wike, Richard, Janell Fetterolf, Shannon Schumacher, and J.J. Moncus. 2021. *Citizens in Advanced Economies Want Significant Changes to Their Political Systems*. Washington, DC: Pew Research Center. https://www.pewresearch.org/global/2021/10/21/citizens-in-advanced-economies-want-significant-changes-to-their-political-systems/.

CHAPTER 25

Allen, Jonathan. 2023. "Biden vs. Trump 2024 Would Be the Rematch Nobody Wants." *2024 Elections* (blog), *NBC News*. April 25, 2023. https://www.nbcnews.com/politics/2024-election/biden-vs-trump-2024-rematch-nobody-wants-rcna80933.

Axelrod, Tal. 2023. "Biden Has Enormous Polling Lead in Democratic Primary, despite Challenge from RFK Jr." *Politics* (blog), *ABC News*. July 27, 2023. https://abcnews.go.com/Politics/biden-despite-challenge-rfk-jr-enormous-polling-lead/story?id=101666471.

Bayon, Miguel. 2017. "Trump Vendra para Conocer Impacto de Irma." *Primera Hora*. September 15, 2017.

Blanton, Dana. 2023. "Fox News Poll: Support for Haley Doubles in GOP Primary, She Tops Biden by Four." *Elections* (blog), *Fox News*. October 11, 2023. https://www.foxnews.com/official-polls/fox-news-poll-haley-doubles-gop-primary-biden.

Doherty, Erin. 2023. "Poll: Most Americans Don't Want Biden or Trump to Run." *Politics & Policy* (blog), *Axios*. April 25, 2023. https://www.axios.com/2023/04/25/2024-trump-biden-presidential-rematch.

Galston, William, and Elaine Kamarck. 2022. "Is Democracy Failing and Putting Our Economic System at Risk?" *Research* (blog), *Brookings*. January 4, 2022. https://www.brookings.edu/articles/is-democracy-failing-and-putting-our-economic-system-at-risk/.

Garcia, Gilbert. 2023. "Biden vs Trump: The Inevitable Rematch Nobody Wants." *Columnist* (blog), *San Antonio Express News*. April 26, 2023. https://www.expressnews.com/columnist/gilbert-garcia/article/biden-vs-trump-inevitable-rematch-nobody-wants-17917534.php.

Manji, Irshad. 2020. "How to Cancel 'Cancel Culture' and Revive Dialogue in a Polarized Time." Filmed November 2020. Video, 38 mins. https://ypo.ivy.com/learning-modules/how-to-cancel-cancel-culture-revive-dialogue-in-a-polarized-time-with-irshad-manji.

Meyer, Herbert. 1993. *Hard Thinking: The Fusion of Politics & Science*. Washington: Storm King Press.

Murray, Mark. 2023. "NBC News Poll: Nearly 70% of GOP Voters Stand behind Trump amid Indictment and Investigations." *2024 Elections* (blog), *NBC News*. April 23, 2023. https://www.nbcnews.com/politics/2024-election/nbc-news-poll-nearly-70-gop-voters-stand-trump-indictment-investigatio-rcna80917.

Musk, Elon (@elonmusk). 2022. "The far left hates everyone, themselves included!" Twitter, April 29, 2022, 8:28 a.m. https://twitter.com/elonmusk/status/1520017094007476224.

NDI. n.d. "Changing the Face of Politics." NDI. Accessed April 24, 2023. https://www.ndi.org/changing-face-politics.

Pew Research Center. 2021. *Beyond Red vs. Blue: The Political Typology*. Washington, DC: Pew Research Center. https://www.pewresearch.org/politics/2021/11/09/beyond-red-vs-blue-the-political-typology-2/.

Quintero, Laura. 2017. "Asume el Reto y la Responsabilidad." *Politica* (blog), *El Vocero*. October 4, 2017. https://www.elvocero.com/gobierno/politica/asume-el-reto-y-la-responsabilidad/article_a1a4227f-9d61-5314-b917-3c7802ef762b.html.

Wike, Richard, Janell Fetterolf, Shannon Schumacher, and J.J. Moncus. 2021. *Citizens in Advanced Economies Want Significant Changes to Their Political Systems*. Washington, DC: Pew Research Center. https://www.pewresearch.org/global/2021/10/21/citizens-in-advanced-economies-want-significant-changes-to-their-political-systems/.

ACKNOWLEDGEMENTS

Bayon, Miguel. 2017. "Ojo Publico" *El Nuevo Dia*. January,8 2017.

Made in the USA
Columbia, SC
27 June 2024

37641219R00226